ALI SHARIATI
AND THE FUTURE OF SOCIAL THEORY

Studies in Critical Social Sciences Book Series

Haymarket Books is proud to be working with Brill Academic Publishers (www.brill.nl) to republish the *Studies in Critical Social Sciences* book series in paperback editions. This peer-reviewed book series offers insights into our current reality by exploring the content and consequences of power relationships under capitalism, and by considering the spaces of opposition and resistance to these changes that have been defining our new age. Our full catalog of *SCSS* volumes can be viewed at https://www.haymarketbooks .org/series_collections/4-studies-in-critical-social-sciences.

ALI SHARIATI AND THE FUTURE OF SOCIAL THEORY

Religion, Revolution, and the Role of the Intellectual

EDITED BY
DUSTIN J. BYRD
SEYED JAVAD MIRI

Haymarket Books
Chicago, IL

First published in 2017 by Brill Academic Publishers, The Netherlands.
© 2017 Koninklijke Brill NV, Leiden, The Netherlands

Published in paperback in 2018 by
Haymarket Books
P.O. Box 180165
Chicago, IL 60618
773-583-7884
www.haymarketbooks.org

ISBN: 978-1-60846-113-4

Trade distribution:
In the U.S. through Consortium Book Sales, www.cbsd.com
In the UK, Turnaround Publisher Services, www.turnaround-uk.com
In Canada, Publishers Group Canada, www.pgcbooks.ca
All other countries, Ingram Publisher Services International, ips_intlsales@
ingramcontent.com

Cover design by Jamie Kerry and Ragina Johnson.

This book was published with the generous support of Lannan Foundation
and the Wallace Action Fund.

Printed in United States.

10 9 8 7 6 5 4 3 2 1

Library of Congress Cataloging-in-Publication Data is available.

Contents

Acknowledgements

First, we would like to acknowledge the contributors to this edited volume. Without their meticulous and important work on Ali Shariati, we would be impoverished in terms of our knowledge of his revolutionary intellect and his lasting legacy. Although Shariati is the original repertoire of wisdom from which we draw, it is with these scholars, from all parts of the world, that Shariati's work is preserved, elevated and expanded upon for generations to come. We would also like to thank Jamie Groendyk who helped prepare the manuscript, as well as the editorial and production staff at Brill, who make academic publishing an enjoyable experience. Last but not least, we would like to thank the Institute of Humanities and Cultural Studies in Tehran, Iran, which funded the First International Seminar on Shariati and the Future of Human Sciences in December 2015. It, and the insightful discourses we engaged in at the conference, inspired us to pull our resources together and write this book.

About the Contributors

Mahdi Ahouie

is Assistant Professor of politics in the department of "Iranian Studies," Faculty of World Studies, University of Tehran (Iran). He received his Ph.D. in international relations from the Graduate Institute of International and Development Studies, University of Geneva (Switzerland). Dr. Ahouie was a visiting scholar at the German Institute of Global and Area Studies (GIGA) in 2013, and a postdoctoral fellow at the Geneva Foundation for interreligious and intercultural Research and Dialogue through 2009–2010.

Bader Mousa Al-Saif

M.A., M.T.S., Ed.M., is a Ph.D. candidate in History at Georgetown University with a focus on the history of the Middle East and North Africa, the history of Islam, Islamic thought, and religious renewal. His article, "Neither Fulul nor Ikhwan: Abdulrahman Yusuf and the Rise of an Alternative Current in Post-Morsi Egypt," was published in Mathal. His co-authored chapter, "Higher Education and Contestation in Kuwait After the Arab Spring: Identity Construction and Ideologies of Domination in the American University of Kuwait," appeared in an edited volume on Education & the Arab Spring. Al-Saif's two encyclopedia entries on Islamic renewal and Kuwait and war have appeared in ABC-Clio's Islam and The Sage Encyclopedia of War. Al-Saif holds a Master of Education and a Master of Theology, both with honors from Harvard University, and a Master of Law with distinction from the School of Oriental and African Studies, University of London. Al-Saif graduated summa cum laude from Boston College with a double major in political science and history.

Sophia Rose Arjana

is a scholar of religion whose areas of research include Islam, pilgrimage, liberation theology, and popular culture. She has taught at Iliff School of Theology, University of Denver, and University of Colorado. Her published work includes book chapters and articles on Shi'i pilgrimage architecture, liberation theology, Islamophobia, and Muslims in popular culture. Her first monograph *Muslims in the Western Imagination* (Oxford, 2015) was a CHOICE Outstanding Academic Title of 2015. In 2017, she will publish two books, *Pilgrimage in Islam: Traditional and Modern Practices* (Oneworld) and *Veiled Superheroes: Islam, Feminism, and Popular Culture* (Lexington Press).

M. Kürşad Atalar

is a graduate of the Public Administration & Political Science department of the Middle East Technical University (METU) (1990). He received his bachelor of science degree in 1994, and his doctorate in 2002 from the same University. The title of his master thesis is "Definitions of Politics and Their Reflections in the Minds of Turkish Voters," and that of doctoral thesis "Radical Islamism in Turkey: The Cases of Gradualism of Ercümend Özkan and Militanism of Hizbollah." He has been working as a governmental officer in General Directorate of Meteorology since 1984. He has written several books, *Düşüncede Devrim* (Revolution in Mind), *On Tez* (Ten Thesis), *Düşüncenin Okullaşması* (Systematization of Thought), *Düşüncenin Siyaseti* (The Politics of Thought), *Sembol Şahsiyetler* (Symbolic Figures of Islamic Revivalism). He also translated Mark A. Kishlansky's *The Sources of the West*, Albert Hourani's *Islam in the European Thought*, Immanuel Wallerstein's *The Modern World-System* and H.A.R. Gibbs' *Modern Trends in Islam* into Turkish.

Dustin J. Byrd

is Associate Professor of Religion, Philosophy and Arabic at Olivet College in Michigan, USA, where he specializes in the Critical Theory of the Frankfurt School as well as Contemporary Islamic thought. Along with publishing numerous articles, he is also the author of the recent book *Islam in a Post-Secular Society: Religion, Secularity and the Antagonism of Recalcitrant Faith* (Brill, 2016), and is the co-editor of the book *Malcolm X: From Political Eschatology to Religious Revolutionary* (Brill, 2016). His latest book, *Unfashionable Objections to Islamophobic Cartoons: L'affaire Charlie Hebdo*, will be released in 2017 (Cambridge Scholars Press). Currently, He is researching the various forms of neo-fascism that have arisen in the West in reaction to political Islam.

Eric Goodfield

is Assistant Professor with the American University of Beirut's Civilization Studies Program and the Department of Political Studies and Public Administration. He is author of Hegel and the Metaphysical Frontiers of Political Theory, as well as a variety of writings on non-Western/comparative political thought and modern and contemporary political philosophy. A former Fulbright Fellow, Eric has previously lived and worked in Korea, Thailand, Armenia, Kyrgyzstan, Egypt and Germany.

Teo Lee Ken

is a PhD candidate in the Department of Malay Studies, National University of Singapore (NUS). In 2015 he was a departmental visitor in the Department of Pacific and Asian History in the School of Culture, History and Language at the Australian National University (ANU). His research interests include Malaysian intellectual history, focusing on the history of justice and political history, and the comparative history of Malaysian, Iranian and Indonesian political thought. In 2014, his paper Challenging Authoritarian Nationalism: Social Ethics and the Intellectual Minority in Malaysia was awarded the Research Paper Prize for best paper at the Third Annual Conference on the Muslim World 2014 in Marmara University, Istanbul.

Georg Leube

is Assistent (Adjunct Lecturer) at the Chair of Islamic Studies, Bayreuth University, Germany, working on the iconography of authority in 15th century Eastern Anatolia / Western Iran under the so-called Turkmen Dynasties of the Ak- and Karakoyunlu. As a Post-Doc researcher, he was employed from 2015 to 2016 in the ANR-DFG funded project DYNTRAN, Dynamics of Transmission, at Marburg University, Germany. He received his PhD on Early Islamic History and Historiography at Bayreuth University, Germany, in 2014, and his Magister Artium at Freiburg University, Germany, in 2011 with the edition, translation and commentary of an Arabic Alchemistic manuscript. He has taught a wide variety of courses on the history and society of the pre-modern and modern Islamic World and is especially interested in the contexts of transcultural transmission and reception.

Seyed Javad Miri

is a professor of sociology and history of religions at the Institute of Humanities and Cultural Studies in Tehran, Iran. He is a Swedish/Iranian social theorist from Hammarstrand and has written over 50 books and 100 articles in English, Persian, and Swedish on various issues in the fields of Philosophy, Religion and Social Theory. His recent book, *Reimagining Malcolm X: Street Thinker Versus Homo Academicus*, was published by University Press of America in 2016. His upcoming book, *Dialectics of Being: Ali Shariati's View on Human Being*, is due to be published by Naghde Farhang House in 2017.

Carimo Mohomed

was born in 1973, in the former Portuguese colony of Mozambique. He holds a Ph.D. in Political Theory and Analysis. Based in Lisbon (Portugal), his research interests are the History of Political Ideas in the Islamic world, particularly in

South Asia, and the relations between Religion and Politics in different cultural and civilizational contexts, including Political Theology. He serves as an Executive Member of the International Political Science Association Research Committee "Religion and Politics" (RC 43); he is a Member of the British Society for Middle Eastern Studies' "Faith, Politics, and Society" Research Network; and he serves on the Editorial Board of the International Journal of Islamic Thought, published jointly by the International Society of Muslim Philosophers and Theologians (ISOMPT) and the Department of Theology and Philosophy, National University of Malaysia.

Chandra Muzaffar

is the President of the International Movement for a Just World (JUST), an international NGO based in Malaysia, which seeks to critique global injustice and to develop an alternative vision of a just and compassionate civilization guided by universal spiritual and moral values. Chandra is also the Chairman of the Board of Trustees of the 1Malaysia Foundation. He has published extensively on civilizational dialogue, international politics, religion, human rights and Malaysian society. The author and editor of 31 books in English and Malay, among his most recent are A World in Crisis: Is There a Cure? and Critical Concerns from East to West. Chandra was Professor and Director of the Centre for Civilizational Dialogue, University of Malaya (1997–1999) and Professor of Global Studies at Universiti Sains Malaysia (2007–2012) Chandra travels abroad frequently, giving lectures and speaking at seminars and conferences. He is also a regular speaker at meetings at home in Malaysia. Chandra is the recipient of a number of international awards related to his scholarship and social activism.

Khosrow Bagheri Noaparast

is currently a Professor of Philosophy of Education at the University of Tehran. He has contributed to a wide range of topics in philosophy of education, religion, and personal construct psychology, from different viewpoints, such as constructive realism, neo-pragmatism, action theory, deconstruction, Hermeneutics, and Islamic philosophy of education. In 2011, he was awarded a First Order Medal of Research (The Distinguished Researcher) by the University of Tehran. Among the important works are, "Toward a More Realistic Constructivism" in Advances in Personal Construct Psychology (Jai Press, 1995), "Celebrating moderate dualism in the philosophy of education: A reflection on the Hirst-Carr Debate" Journal of Philosophy of Education: The Journal of the Philosophy of Education Society of Great Britain, 2013, 47 (4), "Richard Rorty's conception of philosophy of education revisited" Educational Theory 2014, 64 (1).

Fatemeh Shayan

is an assistant professor at Isfahan University, Iran and a post-doctoral scholar at University of Tampere (UTA), Finland. She completed her doctoral study, along with many academic publications in international journals, in the Faculty of Management at UTA and defended her dissertation in December 2014. She was also a researcher at UTA during 2013–2014. Her latest book, *Security in the Persian Gulf Region*, was published by Palgrave MacMillan. Her research areas include energy policy, natural gas, European Union energy issues, Russia, Iran and Qatar energy issues, and Persian Gulf security complex.

Esmaeil Zeiny

is Research Fellow at the Institute of Malaysian and International Studies (IKMAS), National University of Malaysia (UKM). Currently, he is a visiting Research Fellow at the Department of Creative Arts and English, La Trobe University, Australia. He has received his PhD in Postcolonial Literature in English from the National University of Malaysia. His research interests lie at the intersection of literary studies, political theory, and cultural studies. His work addresses questions about identity, representation, colonialism and postcolonialism.

CHAPTER 1

Introduction

Dustin J. Byrd and Seyed Javad Miri

Part One (*Dustin J. Byrd*)

Only rarely do revolutionary and prophetic voices arise precisely when history needs them. Being both religious and secular, the examples of Malcolm x, John Brown, Karl Marx, Che Guevara, Patrice Lumumba, Dr. Martin Luther King Jr., Nelson Mandela, Stephen Bantu Biko, Subcomandante Marcos (Rafael Sebastián Guillén Vicente), Mahatma Gandhi, Herbert Marcuse, Rudi Dutschke, Fred Hampton, Huey Newton, Eldridge Cleaver, Fidel Castro, Emir 'Abd al-Qādir ibn Muḥyiddīn al-Jazā'rī and Muhammad 'Allama Iqbal, all come immediately to mind as being prophetic individuals who successfully married both revolutionary theory and praxis in their struggles against injustice, exploitation and the commodification, functionalization and degradation of human life. However, it is not the case that they arise because their own free will, or simply from their own volition, but rather they appear due to the confluences of history that mold their prophetic critique and their revolutionary praxis. In other words, the brutality of history impels them to set aside the comforts of life, and to courageously challenge the prevailing political, economic and cultural conditions of their time. In the long course of history, these voices are the instruments by which a more just an equal world reveals itself, not only as being *desirable*, but also as being *possible*. These prophetic voices, which disturb not only the confidence of the powerful ruling elites, but also the somnambulant stupor of the powerless masses, often meet their deaths in cruel and premature ways. Whether it is the prophets of the Hebrew Scriptures, Jesus of Nazareth, 'Alī bin Abī Ṭālib and his son Ḥussein, or the many other voices of dissent that have pushed history against the grain, their fierce opposition to entrenched and unaccountable power engenders tyrannical and barbaric reactions. The ruling elites in any given society are history's martyr-makers, and they thrive on the submission of the same people whom the prophetic voices wish to awaken from the long hibernation forced upon them. But we today, who stand in the shadows of such towering martyrs, many of whom were intellectuals, philosophers and sociologists, stand firm in solidarity with them precisely because they represent what Karl Marx still remembered in his early writings: the "divine spark" that refuses to submit to irrational and oppressive authority; the "divine spark" that seeks a better and more reconciled peaceful future; the "divine spark" that refuses to be extinguished under the jackboot of tyranny; the divine spark that loudly declares "No!"

Some of these martyrs are purely religious figures, while others are purely secular. Others bridge the seemingly insurmountable gap between the religious and the secular, bringing these two antagonistic ways of being-in-the-world into a powerful and critical alliance. It is clear that only few scholars and activists throughout history have been able to accomplish this great work of reconciliation, and only fewer still have been able to deploy that work into the ongoing global struggle for human emancipation. Shining brightly among these was Ali Shariati, the Iranian sociologist, radical author, humanitarian, scholar of religion and revolutionary Shi'i Muslim, who uncompromisingly fought for the liberation of the Iranian people against the tyranny of Muhammad Reza Shah Pahlavi, the American imposed Shah of Iran. Educated both in the ancient depth of the Shi'a religious traditions and the contemporary secular social sciences of the West, Ali Shariati found the shared geography of both the Islamic tradition and the Western Enlightenment, both of which, when true to their core values, bend history towards justice in the name of the innocent victims; they oppose history as the perpetuation of Golgotha and Karbalā.' Within a time where Islam and the western Enlightenment are often declared incompatible, and inherently hostile, he found an organic way to saturate the Enlightenment with Islamic social and moral sensitivities, as well as impregnate Islam with a sense of Marxian class-consciousness, by which the class antagonisms within Iranian society were sharpened within the consciousness of its population. In this sense, Islam regained and reloaded its original uneasiness (*unbehagen*) with the corrupt world and the unjust status quo it perpetuates, and the Enlightenment was able to crawl out of the cold instrumental-rationality it had imprisoned itself within by the *dialectic of Enlightenment* and the positivist sciences, which cared very little for the unnecessary suffering of the finite human. In Shariati, Karl Marx and Abū Dharr al-Ghifārī, the first Muslim "socialist," became a unified force. In other words, through his "Red Shi'ism" (Shi'ism saturated with class consciousness), Islam and the best of the Western Enlightenment became radical comrades in an active struggle against human oppression, suppression, and geo-political tyranny. Through this revolutionary marriage, history revealed the important role of the *prophetic* within an age of social apathy; within an age of sterile thought; within an age of contentless religious formalism and spirit-destroying religious fundamentalism, and within an age of cowardly quietism, Shariati revealed the power of the intellectual to challenge recalcitrant power.

Ali Shariati was an unlikely revolutionary. Intellectuals, schoolteachers, and professors are not generally regarded for their political courage under fire. Although many have been jailed for their dissenting rhetoric and opposition to dictatorial state policies, few have been able to frame the entire discourse, the entire argument, and the entire vocabulary by which an enchained people emancipate themselves, as Shariati did during the revolution in Iran. This non-capitulating rejuvenation of Shi'a Islam, by which the average believer nourished themselves on the steadfast courage of the martyr Ḥussein ibn ʿAlī, can be summed up in his most famous phrase: "Every day is ʿĀshūrā'; every day is Karbalā.'"

Through his combination of Shi'a Islam and the radical Third World Philosophy of Frantz Fanon, Patrice Lumumba, Che Guevara, Malcolm x, Louis Massignon, Jacque Berque and even the existentialist philosopher Jean Paul Sartre, Shariati spoke to two different worlds, making the case for an alternative to the binary Cold War options: a submission to American neo-liberal colonialism or Soviet style forced integration and submission to Moscow's political hegemony. Shariati instead championed an enlightened and thus reinvigorated Islam that could govern itself, wherein Islam was the *guide* of the people and not their *manager*. This of course "radicalized" Islam, but not in the same way that is discussed when speaking of al-Qa'eda, ISIS (DAESH) and other terrorist groups – the false prophets of Islamism. Shariati radicalized Islam by a future-oriented-return to its most radical roots, best exemplified by the *sunnah* (way) of Muhammad and his family, reacquainting the Muslim ummah with its original *zeitgeist:* a theologically oriented demand and revolt for social justice. In this way, Islam represented the *universal* longing for human emancipation, human flourishing and human solidarity, and rejected the *particularity* of the interests of the ruling elites, a given dynasty and/or a given Shah. Wherein the "radicality" of Islam fell into a long slumber post-assassination of Ḥussein, as it was "championed" (functionalized) by the ruling class of each competing dynasty and empire, Shariati's class-conscious-induced work rededicated Islam to whom it first appealed to in Mecca and Medina: the poor, the excluded, the down-trodden, the widows, the orphans, the oppressed, as well as those individuals of strength who were willing to fight for the cause of the unjust society's victims. This *zeitgeist* was powerfully resurrected in Shariati's work and was translated into his political praxis and subsequently into those he inspired to rebel against the unjust conditions of the modern neo-liberal world order, all in the name of a better, more reconciled, just and peaceful future society.

Ali Shariati is of course primarily associated with the Iranian Revolution – the greatest emancipatory accomplishment within the Muslim community in the second half of the 20th century. However, his legacy is pertinent outside of Iran, outside of the Shi'a tradition, and outside of the mere telling of history. He is most important to the present moment, wherein the non-conforming voice of resistance – one that does not lose track of the humanity of the enemy – is sorely absent. Terrorism, counter-terrorism, attack and reprisal, mockery and retaliation for mockery, war on old men, women, children, ethnic and religious minorities, the abandonment of the compassionate and merciful *Sunnah* of the Prophet Muhammad, and the betrayal of the once liberating western articulations of egalitarianism and communitarianism, are all hallmarks of today's so-called "clash of civilization." Ali Shariati's radicalism should not be confused with such immorality. His was a morally principled revolutionary system of thought and praxis, one that does not retreat into barbarity and the inhumanity of today's mechanistic *totalen krieg* (total war). Without a doubt, Ali Shariati would weep for the innocent victims of terrorism perpetrated in the streets of Paris, Nice, Brussels, San Bernardino, Orlando, New York, and London, just as much as he would weep for the Muslim victims of terrorism perpetrated in the streets of Istanbul, Baghdad, Dhaka, Damascus, Mogadishu, al-Raqqa, Sana'a and in his own beloved country of Iran. As he wrote in his book *Religion vs. Religion,* "when I look at all of humanity, as a unified genus, I look at it with one value because it has been created by one hand [of God] ..."[1] Thus was his dedication to the *ecumenical* model of the Prophet Muhammad.

Amidst the contemporary degeneration to a new *Age of Jāhilīyah* (ignorance) and a new height of intellectual lethargy, both in the Islamic world and in the West, we, intellectuals today, have a lot to learn from the bold life and work of Dr. Ali Shariati. Despite his corpus, we have become equally illiterate in religious matters and ignorant of the benefits of secular modernity. We have lost sight of our moral compass while simultaneously we have become experts in the most efficient means of capital accumulation, mass distraction, mass murder and aggressive warfare. In such an age, we have forgotten how to see our faces, and the faces of our children, in the tired and abused faces of those who do not look like us – the recent war on refugees both in Europe and in the United States of America attests to our increasing slide into human-inhumanity. As such, we have forgotten how to step into the shoes of the "other" as we have grown coldly narcissistic – unable to see past our own perceived self-interest. Then there is the proverbial "value-gap," wherein some lives are seemingly worth more than others due to their race, gender and/or religious identity. In this sense, Ali Shariati is not just a "historical example" of

---

1   Ali Shariati, *Religion vs. Religion.* Trans. Laleh Bakhtiar. (Chicago: ABC International Group, 2003), 27.

a prophetic voice, but rather is an intellectual/activist *source of emulation* – a modern theo-philosophical *"marja-i taqlīd"* (source of emulation) to use a Shi'a term, as he fought against all forms of inequality, oppression and systematic exploitation of humanity. However, we must not simply *emulate* the courage and philosophical depth of Shariati's example, but must develop his thought and praxis even further. As intellectuals, we must not retreat into the existentially diminished ghettos of our academic institutions, but rather live our convictions as Shariati did, and be willing to pay the price.

Anything less would be a betrayal of his memory and legacy.

Part Two (*Seyed Javad Miri*)

I think one of the most important questions regarding Shariati is how to understand his legacy. For instance, there are thinkers and scholars who have tried to locate his discourse within the parameters of Marxism or Socialism; but there are again other scholars who have rejected this approach and instead focused on other aspects of Shariati's thought by arguing that he presents a modernist Islam; but again there are other researchers who dispute all these categorizations by arguing that Shariati is an anarchist; and even there are scholars and thinkers who have argued that Shariati could not be classified as a Muslim thinker but a disguised Catholic thinker, and apart from all these labels that target his overall ideological positions, we have had scholars who argue that he cannot be considered even as a sociologist or scholar of social sciences because of his lack of coherent positions in his various academic approaches. To all these labeling industries I can only state that they have not studied Shariati's text in a systematic fashion.

Let me introduce two important concepts, which are useful in terms of interpretative approaches. I think we need to distinguish between "reading a text" and "interpreting a text." I take the word "reading" in the sense that one reads a newschapter or an advertisement in everyday mode rather than sitting and analyzing the context of the news while one reads a newschapter over breakfast or on the way to the office. This is what I call "reading a text." Of course, I am aware that the word "reading" could even mean analyzing or even appraising, but I want to reformulate this word so I can make a technical distinction between reading a text and interpreting a text. When I use the concept of "interpreting a text," I do not only refer to interpretative forms of analyzing and comprehending a text, but I would like to highlight another aspect of these interpretative activities that are as important as other acts of interpretation, and, in my view, they seem to be absent when reading a text as opposed to interpreting it. In other words, when we read a text, we do not see the context or the intellectual tradition, which a text arises from, rather we see that in a separate form as though this piece of news has fallen down upon us in a spontaneous moment of ecstasy or accident. However, when interpreting a text, one needs to locate the text within a tradition, and through that tradition approach the text in such a way that we can slowly build up the necessary building blocks for comprehension. Otherwise, we fall prey to the same labeling games that have been ongoing for some time, at least as far as Shariati is concerned. To put it differently, if we assume that it is possible to make a distinction between the concept of "reading" and "interpreting" a text, then we could establish a hermeneutic principle that by the latter we do not refer to the text in a glancing form but rather we contextualize the text within an intellectual tradition, which gives referential points of departure to the overall act of cognition. If these observations are legitimate, then I would like to pose another question: What is the locus of Shariati's position. In other words, where does he come from? What is his main concern? Can we reduce his intellectual activities into his Muslimness? In other words, when we talk about Immanuel Kant or G.W.F. Hegel, do we categorize their intellectual or philosophical positions in reference to their respective confessional perspective? When thinking about the intellectual significance of Hegel, very few people make a correlation between his philosophizing and his confessional inclination, as there is a tacit assumption that Hegel is working on universal questions which a human being qua human being is faced by, and there is no need to ask about Hegel's religious position as this had no impact, whatsoever, on his universal reflections. But when talking about Shariati as a non-western scholar, the dominant position has been to reduce him into a faith-bound context and confine the significance of his discourse within Islamicate questions and concerns, thus ruling out any universality in his work. In other words, Hegel speaks to humanity at large but Shariati speaks only to a faith-bound community in a peripheral context that does not have any universal significance. Upon reflection, I think this position is based on grand assumptions which could be considered as part of what we term as "Eurocentrism." In other words, when we assume that western form of reasoning corresponds to humanity at large but an Iranian form of rationality corresponds merely to Muslim or a faith-bound community, we are, in fact reproducing Eurocentric bias in an intellectual and so-called academic fashion. Thus, I think the distinction between "reading" and "interpreting" is a crucial hermeneutic act, which could assist us in establishing Shariati's position beyond the labeling industry, which have deprived us from seeing Shariati's intellectual position in an integral fashion.

In my view, Shariati is best understood within the context of post-colonial intellectual tradition, where the concept of the human person has been divided into two broad forms of "Human Being" and "The Native." In Shariati's view, the world has been divided by the "subject," which is the Eurocentric form of human person, and the "object," which corresponds to the humanity at large, which lies outside the West. "The Native" is an *object*, or what Malcolm X conceptualizes as "House Negro," and the "Human Being" is what Malcolm X terms the "Master." Shariati tries to see in what fashion one could emancipate the relationship between the "House Negro" and the "Master." The entire discourse of Shariati is based within strategies to revive a form of awareness that may exist within the soul of what Malcolm X terms as the "Field Negro," as the latter seems to have a sense of subjectivity which defies the hegemonic strategies of the "Master." Here the "Master" should not be understood in an anthropomorphic sense. For instance, the master could be understood as the "master narrative" in world politics, or even westernization as the master narrative form of modernity, which has mesmerized natives for centuries and has deprived them from seeing the world from different perspectives. When Shariati talks about religion, mysticism, literature, philosophy, art, ideologies and all forms of cognitions, he is conceptualizing all these forms in relation to emancipative power, which could set the natives free; but this is not only about natives. Why? The relationship that has been established between natives and western forms of being human has not only been detrimental to natives, it has deprived the Eurocentric form of humanity from a sane state of being human itself. In other words, as Frantz Fanon says, the colonizer has become colonized too, but in another fashion. This is to argue that the discourse Shariati develops does not only have confessional significance, but rather has global appeal and even universal importance in his intellectual paradigm.

Apart from these remarks, we should also add that the sociological and social-theoretical importance of Shariati has not been conceptualized properly at the academic level globally. For instance, when Anthony Giddens wrote his *Introduction to Sociology*, there was no reference to Shariati as a social theorist or sociologist. How should we understand this form of constructing the narratives of sociology in the mainstream historiographical position on the discipline? There are many critiques against these constructions, but the most pervasive one is the Eurocentric vision of the discipline, which does not allow Giddens to consider the various forms of sociology, nor the multiple ways in which social theories are constructed.

Shariati's position in the discipline of sociology is another issue that should be further explored. However, in this volume, we have attempted to examine

one particular sociological engagement that we find important, that of Shariati and Durkheim. In other words, how to understand the classics of social
theory has been one of Shariati's major concerns. In reading his body of work,
we can see that he demonstrated his non-Eurocentric understanding of the
classics by critically engaging with the works of Emile Durkheim, Max Weber,
Karl Marx and others. Many scholars, who have not engaged with Shariati in
an interpretive form of dialogue, have hastily concluded that Shariati had an
ideological conception of the West. These conclusions were based on the writings of Hamid Algar, who poorly translated aspects of Shariati's work under
the title *Marxism and Other Western Fallacies: An Islamic Critique*. Additionally,
these translations appeared within a revolutionary context, where the world
was witnessing the last revolution of the 20th century. In the context of the
Cold War, these scholars misjudged Shariati's concept of the West. Their work
misrepresents Shariati by construing him as an ideologue of Islamic Revolution who considered the West and all its traditions as fallacies based on a theological position or confessional form of understanding the "other." To put it
differently, we have needed for some time to deconstruct the misconceptions
that dictate our understanding of Shariati and his work. Today we are faced
with many forms of Shariati, which is mainly the result of reading Shariati
without interpreting him within the intellectual tradition from which he came.
This book is an attempt to take a step toward that goal.

CHAPTER 2

Shariati, Enlightenment and the Return of the Universal for Comparative Political Thinking

Eric Goodfield

Both the Enlightenment thought of the 17th and 19th centuries, as well as the post-colonial thinking of the 20th century, which arose in its wake and defined itself against it, are commonly seen as incompatible and irreconcilable. However, there is a basic unity that presides over both: the revolt against the universal. In this chapter I argue that, in either the case of contemporary cultural pluralism inspired by the European Enlightenment, or in the case of the hermetics of a "return to self" (*Bāzgasht be khishtan*) that is inspired by the anti-colonialisms of Iranian author Ali Shariati, there is a fundamental misunderstanding or blind spot in their dealings with the universal. Rather than imagining that identity, origins and foundations are jeopardized – either by the cosmopolitan guest or for the particular host – in theoretical border-crossings that seek universality through dialogue, I argue that no such absolute risk exists. Rather, historical foundations and privileged notions of individual and collective identity are inalienable and beyond absolute loss. Despite our formulaic categorizations of self and other, what is dialectically exposed or eclipsed, received or rejected, nonetheless impresses its universalizing influence: the absent other was and is always already present. Given this relational dialectic, I close arguing for comparative political thinking and that such cross-cultural, trans-historical or international exchange is always an embedded relationship that resists methodological inoculation and systematization.

I start by developing a critical approach to the theoretical legacy of Enlightenment thought as it relates to the question of universality. This trend in contemporary thought takes its roots in the emergence of modernity as a revolutionary moment. This sort of approach is neither novel nor rare, and we have the likes of Rousseau, Hegel, Marx and the Frankfurt School to thank for that. In particular, I organize my thoughts around the way the individual subject is deployed in what I consider to be a fairly general and pronounced, though perhaps often unconscious, dimension of contemporary theoretical culture. Having developed this context, I take up a line of comparative political thought that offers a turn on the dilemma of the subject as I introduce it in the context of the European Enlightenment. Here I consider Shariati's critique of European Enlightenment and post-Enlightenment theory and experience. I engage Shariati for several reasons. First, he is a non-western thinker who possessed a deep intellectual relationship with the West. Secondly, he attempted to fuse western notions of freedom with a form of Shia Islam that continues to be deeply troubling for contemporary clerical Shi'ism. That is, my interest in Shariati lies in his bursting two bubbles, one western and one that he conceives of as eastern. I argue that the shortcomings of Shariati's radical avenue of departure on modern thought are present in western and contemporary theoretical approaches to cultural pluralism as well. This critique opens both pluralist as well as post-colonial thought up to a confession of the deeply universalist conditions which predicate their projects' emancipatory potentials.

Shariati and Counter-Enlightenment

I think that it is safe to say that contemporary social and political thought sets its sights on diminishing the Enlightenment's legacy of "foundationalist" metaphysical claims. This legacy, as it is widely held, assumes autonomy from language, history and culture, and reproduces injustice, inequality and colonial relations of power. The problematics that foundationalist "metanarratives" imply have been recognized by thinkers as diverse as Michel Foucault, Jürgen Habermas, Jacques Derrida and John Rawls. In essence, this central tenet of critique has become a cornerstone of the culture of contemporary political thought. Yet, as Cornelius Castoriadis has brought out, there remains a deep "crisis of identification" in contemporary society and its theoretical outputs, one that is wracked with what he terms the disintegration of "social imaginary significations" and a crisis of cohesive social meanings and purposes.[1] As he illuminates, this has lead to the "collage conformism"[2] of postmodernist theory and contemporary social reality, one which thwarts the possibility for a substantive identity development towards autonomy, and, as such, the richness of social relations upon which it is premised: lacking a system of values or meaning, Castoriadis suggests that we are reduced to mimicry and appropriation in order to fulfill basic social needs.

---

1   C. Castoriadis, "The Crisis of Identification," *Thesis Eleven,* 49, 1997 and his *The Imaginary Institution of Society,* 1998.

2   Ibid., 94. Collage conformism is a state where, lacking a core of meaningful social identity, individuals opportunistically appropriate elements of identity, one from the other, in order to "posit society" as a means to survival. He witnesses this process as a "monstrous illusion" which has led to "desocialization" in the face of the continuity of social needs and the normative relevance of society.

This dynamic is not one to be merely understood along the partitioning line of the modernist-postmodernist divide. Rather the ongoing deflation and dismissal of modernity's universalist claims has led to a contemporary fragmentation of both social and linguistic meaning for the elaboration of new normative possibilities to replace the troubled ethical legacy of the Enlightenment. In reaction to the universal "grand narratives" of Enlightenment modernity, contemporary claims call for the annulment of all such universals; be they postmodernist or liberal claims to negative liberty. In so doing they carry on with the project of normative cancellation, which Hegel witnessed in the *Phenomenology of Spirit* as the core thrust of the Enlightenment's assault upon traditional belief and custom.[3] The success of this period's political and epistemological revolt against its foundations in the pre-modern world cast a normative shadow, which has significantly occluded subsequent discourse in its legitimate theoretical range of ethical and political possibilities. In this way, the Enlightenment attack upon its own traditional basis in feudalism and Christianity is recast as the universal critique of all religious, traditional and customary life in the postmodernist counter-revolt. In this context, a severe problem arises: what becomes of Islamic, Christian, Buddhist, Hindu, Confucian, Taoist or other foundationalist[4] ideals and traditions in compliance with such an ethic of metaphysical leveling? Roxanne Euben poses the question from another angle: "How do we ... make sense of the increasingly foundationalist turn of political practice within a theoretical discourse that no longer sees any place for metaphysics in political life?"[5]

Here, there is a line of influence that runs from social and political life into theorization and back to historical experience again. By this I want to suggest that both theory and the theorist participate in the social world and consciousness that grounds political discourse and identity. I believe that modern freedom and the ramifications of the revolt that brought it about pose stark challenges that run to the heart of notions of identity, which have become sacrosanct in many theoretical quarters. The questions arise: what is problematical about discourses that dismiss foundationalist tradition and instead emerge from and prioritize the autonomous subject, and what do they obscure? What has this doctrinal emphasis and the abstract prioritization of the subject meant for theory and practice? Furthermore, how may theorists operating within the

---

3 G.W.F. Hegel, *The Phenomenology of Spirit*, trans. A.V. Miller (London: Oxford U. Press, 1977), §540.

4 As extant, if not alloyed, forms of religious, ethical and customary tradition.

5 Roxanne Euben, "Comparative Political Theory: An Islamic Fundamentalist Critique of Rationalism," *Political Theory*, Vol 59.

frameworks of western discourses attempt to come to grips with a privileged and often unconscious predisposition to certain forms of agency, which may well follow in the train of the Enlightenment's intellectual legacy and project of metaphysical leveling?

In order to begin to come to grips with some of these questions and the issue of Castoriadis' socially dispossessed subject, I would like to turn to the thought of Ali Shariati. Shariati himself was most active in late 1960s' and 70s' Iran, although his earlier years of study in Paris also saw him actively involved in translation and writing. He is best known for sewing together Jean-Paul Sartre's notions of freedom and Fanon's doctrine of anti-colonial autonomy and self-emancipation in the context of the Shia revolution that swept aside the Shah in 1978–1979. Beyond this, I would offer that Shariati represents a unique perspective on, as he would call it, East-West relations. On the one hand, Shariati is working with deeply western conceptions of freedom and liberty that tap into notions of authenticity, recognition and autonomy. On the other hand, he conceives of Enlightenment in mystical terms and Islam in particular as an opportunity to move beyond the limited perspectives of the three great forms of humanism, which restrain progress: liberalism, Marxism and existentialism. In essence, he puts before us the thesis that an essential aspect of our moral and ethical selves was eclipsed in the revolt that initiated the modern world in and against much of what had been so foundational before.

Shariati is keenly aware of the progress which modernity has brought and is not longing after a romantic return to origins. Rather he wants to unburden the colonized from their current captivities so as to release them to their deeper spiritual *vocations*: I want to emphasize the plural here because he believes that there is more than one viable path through this terrain. In short, western political conceptions of positive freedom are conjoined to the mystical endeavoring after meaning and purpose that comes not through reverence to catechistic doctrine, but through subjective reflection and exploration. With this short introduction to his intellectual persona aside, let us now turn to consider how he stands as a self-styled, non-western critic of western modernity.

In his abundant reflections on the West, Shariati echoes the crisis of modernity I earlier introduced. His reading of a West bounded by modern values takes root in an understanding of the revolutionary aspect of the Enlightenment. He writes:

> The bourgeois outlook and culture, which was comprised of materialism, hedonism, and individualism, replaced the culture and the outlook of *the* past, which were dependent upon collective religion and virtues. Consequently, utility replaced value and rationality replaced theosophic

feeling (intuition), power-seeking in all aspects, particularly in science, replaced principles of the search for truth, and "living for" replaced "for living."[6]

Here Shariati's understanding recalls the young Hegel's, and we understand that the process suggests more than a simple progression. Shariati suggests that while we as moderns generally praise the core ideals of modernity, perhaps set aside from those of modernization, we are at the same moment culpable for the spiritual resources, which he considers lost under the rubble of the Middle Ages. While modernity does a great service in overturning the tyrannies of the past and seeking to finally liberate the potentiality of the many encumbered by the collective demands of the one, the unintended consequences remain the loss of what he considers the essence of man's nature: love, idealism, and existential significance. The alienation of man's spiritual potentials to the bourgeois impulse of the mastery of nature and society here relegates humanity to forms of absurdity, futility and alienation, which are well inscribed in the history of western thought, one that has proved a troubling dimension to theorists of robust negative and positive liberty alike. Shariati's concern with what he refers to as the "vile and fossilizing life of consumption" offers us a form exogenous critique of freedom.[7] It is this vantage, at once intimate and at the same time alien to the West and its theoretical fixations, that I find so engaging in his thought.

Out of this analysis, Shariati proposed a turning inward towards the moral heritage of a culture and its experience. In his struggles with European colonialism in general and post-colonial Pahlavi Iran in particular, he was caught up with what he considered to be the material and spiritual impoverishment of the East. He held that these two dimensions – the material and the spiritual – run in tandem, and accompany one another. There is no prior. The loss of one resource invites the loss of the other and the confidence of the possession of one invites the acquisition of the other as well. The expropriation of the wealth of the East here is not understood to be limited to the material; colonialism leaves the colonized with a depletion of spiritual resources as well. In line with his roots in Fanon, it is the duty of the oppressed to regain possession of home and heritage. This inward reaching, he conceives of as a utilization of the cultural and intellectual heritage of a people: "a return to self." Shariati's anti-universalism is in key ways on a par with contemporary trends here. The goal is the tearing down of an exploitative value hierarchy

---

6   Ali Shariati, *Man and Islam*, (New Jersey: Islamic Publications International, 2006), 24.
7   Ibid., 30.

that converts material and political ascendancy into moral and cultural subjection. Shariati's anti-universalism however, with its radical roots in the struggles of the anti-colonial movements and alignments of the Cold War era may not speak well to us today in our attempts to overcome the spiritual and social impoverishment that negative liberty and agency have implied for social and political consciousness. The current crisis seems to be one of the fragile universal, and this current has inspired a small countermovement of thinkers to seek its preservation as a mode of resistance against the dominant forms of difference proliferated and legitimated by global capitalism.[8]

To contest Shariati's anti-universalist notion of autonomy and liberty, I propose that it is not only the privileged and possessed past of a nation alone that ought to dictate the bearing of its current moral compass. Rather the dialogue across horizons and historical barriers offers illumination as well. Where the colonial and Cold War scenarios made these invidious sources for self-discovery, I believe that today they are all the more necessary in dealing with the forms of universalist leveling and de-differentiation that has accompanied globalization. Where contemporary thought now seeks ethical recourse to the anti-universalist camp, it privileges the voices of the formerly oppressed and eclipsed subjectivities of the subalterns as the most valued sources of legitimacy and expression. While the accomplishment of these trends are certainly not to be overlooked, it has nonetheless also given safe harbor to essentializing, culturalist and ethno-nationalist sentiments as well as the hypertrophic subjectivism that upends liberal tolerance itself in the labyrinth of identity politics. That is, the explosion of liberalism's ideals of tolerance and pluralism has resulted in a widespread turning away from universalist discourse altogether and with no recourse to reflection.

Thus, where we take seriously the distinction between the universal and the universalizing, I recognize the capacity for transformative forms of dialogue coming not through a one way transfixed gaze into either primordial forms of ethno-national identity or hypertrophic forms of individual identity, but rather a discourse between *interiors* and *exteriors*: one which transgresses the boundaries of privileged notions of self and identity. This transgression works in recognition of the differences and perhaps the seeming impermeability of varying forms of identity – social, cultural or historical – which nonetheless may work to relate their forms of the absolute, of meaning, to and through one another in a spiritual striving for the other, who, as Hegel so energetically informed us, is in fact also part and parcel of the self.

---

8   In particular, contemporary French thinkers such as Jean Luc Nancy, Gilles Deleuze, Allain Badiou, Antonio Negri, Philippe Lacoue-Labarthe and select others.

As with many others within the putative western tradition, Shariati wishes to overcome the depredations of negative liberty upon the alienated modern individual – be it a person or a people – by empowering them with a positive liberty excavated out of a common collective past conceived of as a national, cultural and historical legacy.[9] This past he seems to hold is a safe refuge and resource for the slave consciousness that, in line with Fanon, must rise up to historical awareness and take action to secure its right and recognition. The act alone is understood as an end in itself where human dignity demands the attempt. Yet his revolutionary preoccupation with the subaltern and the violence required to liberate leaves a blind spot in his thought. The return to origins and self is not the only source of self-esteem and consciousness that speaks to a person or people. The unknown self speaks as well – the one that lies beyond the boundaries of known values and experiences – and this horizon of dialogue promises progress on the limits of understanding, internalized preoccupations and wasted potentialities of national and individual forms of identity politics. The turn inwards legitimized in the anti-universalist thrusts of the postmodern revolt against foundationalist metanarratives, the explosion of liberalism into the multiplicities of identity and recognition politics or Shariati's anti-colonial slave revolt against western lordship, all result in an occlusion of universalist axes of discourse and all, to one degree or another, privilege the closure of positive forms of liberty at the level of discourse which embrace the other. The emphasis here is on the preservation of a specialized and endangered subject who must close the horizons of human universality and so universalize itself in order to achieve historical agency and esteem.

Comparativity and the Question of Method

The youthful project of comparative political thinking presents us with the possibility of a venture that represents a real alternative to the anti-universalist positions of contemporary liberal, postmodern or postcolonial approaches. As my study of Shariati's thought highlights, rather than imagining that identity, origins and foundations are jeopardized in theoretical dialogues across national, linguistic or cultural borders, no such absolute jeopardy exists. Indeed, historical foundations and privileged notions of individual and collective identity are inalienable and beyond absolute loss. What is dialectically exposed and even eclipsed, nonetheless impresses its influence on that which has succeeded and ascended.

---

9   Shariati carries out explicit work on this subject in his chapter on the "Extraction and Refinement of Cultural Resources" in his *Man and Islam.*

The traditional field of political theory has largely sought to protect the status of its western canon of political thought – Socrates to John Rawls – and has been partial to maintaining a myth of an enclosed tradition. In this, it has been culpable of the fallacious assumption that exposing the tradition and its boundaries may mean a fundamental transformation or loss of its content and import. I argue that this has always and is already the case. The excluded other of political theory has always been present and expressed though not always identified. The opening up of these borders may in fact be far more promising than the conservative view imagines; the emancipation of contemporary theory from the privileging of both author and its concept as subject may be overwhelmed in the moment of engaging the alien other. That is, many of the dilemmas that beset the culture of contemporary theory may in fact be the result of this repressed alterity and excluded otherness. Redeeming a so-called western legacy of political thought may in fact require risking its own peculiar and privileged form of subjectivity amongst a larger community of theoretical traditions. Following Shariati's lead, theoretical integration into this larger political landscape offers itself as a radical extension of the individual will to self-understanding. In this, I imagine a turn on the nature of engagement with meaning and value beyond a self-enclosed and occluded narrative of modernity.

The ongoing preservation of a closed canon in the field of political theory has a rich story behind it. For much of its modern history, political theory operated within the boundaries defined for it by political science. The latter, a development that emerges in the context of early 20th century Anglo-American positivism, had little interest in taking either the history of western or non-western political ideas seriously. Instead, from the 1920's through the 1960's, political science pressed political theorists to adapt to an agenda that would see it advance the interests of empirical research. In the wake of this legacy, many political theorists and philosophers have struggled to recover and take the history of political thought seriously, as it has been received as a contiguous intellectual tradition. This has meant that there has been a great deal of attention to the great thinkers – Plato, Aristotle, Augustine, Hegel, Marx and others – right up and until today. While this victory for political thought has meant an inclusivist and expanding approach to the history of western ideas, it has not been until extremely recently that western political theorists began to explore and cross the boundaries – historical and geographic – that have divided the western tradition from its various "others." Crucially, this divide has affected not only its understanding of its fellows, but of itself and its own plural origins and formation as well.

Against this history, a countermovement from within western political theory itself arose in the late 1990's, which sought to reconnect political theoretic inquiry with the larger, embodied global horizon it found itself in. This movement has come to be known as comparative political theory (CPT) and has such figures as Fred Dallmayr, Roxanne Euben, Cary Nederman and Anthony Parel as its founders. There are varieties of concerns that animate the budding field of CPT. First and foremost, it seeks to bring attention to the issue of the glaring absence of the non-European, non-Judeo-Christian and non-Greco Roman elements in the canon of political theory. As Dallmayr brought out in the late 1980's, the discipline of political theory has for most of its contemporary existence been a "Plato to NATO" enterprise, essentially a rehearsal of the canon beyond which little or nothing relevant was considered to exist. The problem becomes glaring in the latter half of the 20th century, as global exchange becomes the norm rather than the exception, along with intertwining cultures, nations, identities, languages and histories as never before. The triumphalism of western political thought had become an impediment to its own continued relevance and progress in this context.

Beyond a general agreement regarding the timeliness and perhaps inevitability of a more cosmopolitan vision, two primary debates have arisen amongst practitioners of CPT. First is the issue of comparativity. Looming against the background of orientalist appropriations of non-western traditions in the 17th, 18th and 19th centuries, CPT theorists have struggled to reconsider how traditions of political thought peripheral and external to the western tradition can be tapped without reasserting the very hegemonic and ethnocentric trend, which so insulated and limited political thought to begin with. That is how CPT work can be done without reproducing the insular paradigms of traditional western political thought on which they had been trained in their attempts to genuinely cross beyond the threshold of western experience and prejudice. In addition, how can these journeys avoid or overcome incommensurate concepts, worldviews and practices? If there are raw differences that cannot be rationally understood, how can real dialogue and exchange be more than an exercise in diplomatic formality between cultures? Anthropological, postcolonial, linguistic and hermeneutic perspectives have all been considered and to a certain extent, they are all now part and parcel of what it means to do CPT, though not in an unproblematic way as the field continues to find its feet. While thus trying to respect the immanent and embodied knowledge these traditions present in and of themselves, and what they conceal in terms of internal diversity, these theorists have had to struggle with maintaining an equally important and countervailing interest in the outsider's methodological and analytic rigor in the context of their disciplinary commitments as well. As Farah Godrej has framed the situation, comparative political theorists:

> On the one hand, ... are called upon to be part anthropologists or eth-
> nographers, developing an existential connection with the communities
> within which the text is read, and immersing themselves in the lived ex-
> perience of the text. On the other hand, they are called upon to revert to
> the stance of external observer and commentator, constructing cultural
> accounts in order to represent the experience of the text, and articulating
> how these insights may be used to illumine our political life.[10]

My studies of Enlightenment-inspired pluralism, as well Shariati's anti-colonial "return to self," bear implications for both debates. On the first issue, it recog-nizes that comparativity requires both an insider's understanding of the intel-lectual, linguistic and historical nuances of the traditions being compared on the one hand, as well as a rigorous deployment of the categories and concerns of political theory on the other.

Despite these opportunities, as Megan Thomas pointed out, the emphasis upon the textual authority of great books remains an orientalist enterprise that will likely reproduce an orientalist worldview.[11] That is, textual tradition falsely suggests a monolithic unity between traditions that likely never existed and certainly never existed in practice, and eliminates non-textual forms from our comparative view. Such forms could include oral, artistic, social or linguis-tic modes. Given the conflicting imperatives of textual interpretation and exe-gesis on the one hand, and that of existential understanding and embodiment on the other, we seem to be presented with difficult choices. For some there is reliance on Gadamer's hermeneutic notion of the fusion of horizons through dialogue. For Gadamer through dialogue and contextual self-reflection, we are able to transcend our own standpoints. This permits him to call for the inher-ent unity of both our own as well as others' viewpoints such that we are never fully captive to our histories and environments, and the introduction of hori-zons beyond our own allow us to revise our own prejudices.

For others, such as those of the Cambridge school and Quentin Skinner, dia-logue itself is not enough, requiring rigorous attention to synchronic embed-ment of texts in the specificity of historical contexts. The historicizing of political theory diminishes the possible benefits of dialogue and instead locates the rel-evant dialogue in a specific time and place. This point of view may be said to seal off the present from the past, and our contexts from those of others. In the

---

10   Farah Godrej, "Towards a Cosmopolitan Political Thought: The Hermeneutics of Inter-
      preting the Other," Polity, 41(2), (2009): 135–165.

11   Megan Thomas, "Orientalism and Comparative Political Theory" The Review of Politics,
      72 (4), (2010): 653–677.

face of these two extreme methodological concerns for CPT, I would emphasize that the two orientations of fact gathering and analysis on the one hand,
and personal, lived and desiring insight on the other, can work hand-in-hand
to make comparative efforts successful in achieving what the field of CPT has
had in mind since its inception. Despite positivist intentions to the contrary,
both knowledge and understanding have always been an integral part of western political thought, as we have known it. As Roxanne Euben has brought
out, the origins of our use of theory in the Greek notion of theoria suggests
travel to new peoples and institutions in order to learn about the other and,
by extension, as a means of rediscovering the self. In this context, she puts the
methodological urge into perspective. She writes:

> ... the motivations for travel as well as its consequences are contingent
> and unpredictable, a complex and mercurial interaction of the personal,
> political, historical, and institutional at once suggestive of loose patterns
> and resistant to any attempt to "model" which journeys and conditions
> will produce or predict a critically reflective or tolerant "attitude."[12]

With Euben, CPT or any other such cross-cultural, trans-historical or
international exchange is always an embedded relationship that resists
methodological inoculation. Overcoming past violence to the other, textual,
historical, cultural, will only open up the way for new and better-informed
forms of misunderstanding. However, these misunderstandings are not merely
reflections of the self's relationship with the other, but also with the self. The
dilemma of transparency applies not only to our engagement with the other
but to the self as well, and this is all too easily missed. Both implacable conflict as well as deepened mutualism are possible outcomes, and will ultimately
reflect the needs and underlying prejudices of both parties. While CPT practitioners come out of a pluralist program of inclusive dialogue, they will also
inevitably confront non-plural foundationalisms that reject the possibility of
dialogue. Thus, CPT must also be ready to make valorizing choices that may
require the rejection of forms of dialogue that require adherence, conversion
or self-abnegation. Of course, these relationships may overturn our perspectiv-
ism and lead us to totalizing forms of self-understanding that undo CPT's own
ethical foundations rooted in a pluralist ontology: such are the risks of real
difference and travel.

---

12   Roxanne Euben, *Journeys to the Other Shore: Muslim and Western Travelers in Search of
      Knowledge*, (Princeton: Princeton University Press, 2006), 13.

Conclusion

To conclude, global modernity means cultural essentialisms setup in the spirit of anti and post-colonial efforts to ditch hegemonic discourses can often result in a failure to reflect the inherent universalities of contemporary reality; today, sometimes East is West and vice versa, especially where traditions and actors continue to speak to each other through the medium of various globalized institutions and experiences. While we may not want to ethically and politically represent the other, we are always already speaking to and engaged with them in today's world. Thus, what the practice of CPT does promise, and as my study of Shariati's work in connection to the Enlightenment has sought to provide, is a universal horizon of theoretical relationality that opens the opportunity for greater self-reflection. In the face of the problems of cultural commensurability and discursive asymmetries of power, it brings uncharted critical insight to a variety of Eurocentric preconceptions and paradigms – liberalism, positivism, logocentrism, pluralism, rationalism and post-colonialism amongst them – which continue to ground political theory. It promises to bring political theory out of a state of provinciality which only holds it back from a more global maturity and the deepening of its canonical insights and convictions on matters of the good life and the concept of the political.

Bibliography

Castoriadis, Cornelius. "The Crisis of Identification," *Thesis Eleven* 49, (May, 1997): 85–98.

Castoriadis, Cornelius. *The Imaginary Institution of Society*. Cambridge, MA: The MIT Press, 1998.

Euben, Roxanne. "Comparative Political Theory: An Islamic Fundamentalist Critique of Rationalism," The Journal of Politics, Vol 59, No. 1 (Feb., 1997): 28–55.

Euben, Roxanne. *Journeys to the Other Shore: Muslim and Western Travelers in Search of Knowledge*. Princeton: Princeton University Press, 2006.

Godrej, Farah. "Towards a Cosmopolitan Political Thought: The Hermeneutics of Interpreting the Other," Polity, 41(2), (2009).

Hegel, G.W.F. *The Phenomenology of Spirit*. Translated by A.V. Miller. London: Oxford University Press, 1977.

Shari'ati, Ali. *Man and Islam*. New Jersey: Islamic Publications International, 2006.

Thomas, Megan. "Orientalism and Comparative Political Theory" The Review of Politics, 72 (4), (2010): 653–667.

CHAPTER 3

Ideology by Any Other Name: Social Sciences and the Humanities as Western Catechism

Carimo Mohomed

Come, friends, let us abandon Europe; let us cease this nauseating, apish imitation of Europe. Let us leave behind this Europe that always speaks of humanity, but destroys human beings wherever it finds them.

⁘

1

In 1976, the year before Ali Shariati's death, Edward Said (1935–2003), in an interview given to *Diacritics*, while referring to Middle East studies, observed that most Middle East experts were social scientists whose expertise was based on a handful of clichés about Arab society, Islam and the like, handed down like tatters from the 19th century Orientalists, and that a whole new vocabulary of terms was bandied about: modernization, elites, development, stability were talked about as possessing some sort of universal validity, but that in fact they formed a rhetorical smokescreen hiding ignorance on the subject. For him, the new Orientalist jargon, i.e., of the 20th century, was hermetic discourse, which could not prepare one for what was happening in Lebanon for example, or in the Israeli-occupied Arab territories, or in the everyday lives of the Middle Eastern peoples.[1]

Two years later, in 1978, and the year after Ali Shariati's death, Said would develop these and other themes in his seminal book *Orientalism.*[2] Nevertheless,

---

1   Edward W. Said, *Power, Politics and Culture: interviews with Edward W. Said* (London: Bloomsbury, 2005), 34.

2   Besides being the title of his book, *Orientalism* was the generic term that Edward Said employed to describe the western view on the Orient (the Middle East and/or Islamic world), and also the discipline by which that region and/or concept was, and still is sometimes, approached systematically, as a topic of learning, discovery, and practice.

and despite the reactions it produced, this book was not the first to mount criticism of western scholarship; the critique of western knowledge of the Orient is at least as old as modern Orientalism itself and has been recurrent.[3] For example, Abd-al-Rahman al-Jabarti (1753–1825), the Egyptian chronicler and a witness to Napoleon's invasion of Egypt in 1798, had no doubt that the expedition was as much an epistemological as a military conquest.[4]

In Iran, Jalal al-i-Ahmad (1923–1969), with his *Gharbzadegi* (*Occidentosis/ Westoxication*),[5] had explored the subordination to the West in all areas, and much of what he described and analyzed was not unique to Iran and could be encountered almost anywhere, imperialism having imposed itself on Asia and Africa.[6] Parts of *Gharbzadegi* are reminiscent of other works of cultural self-analysis by the victims of imperialism: the writings of Frantz Fanon (1925–1961) and an important book in Turkish, Mehmet Doğan's *Batililasma Ihaneti* (*The treachery that is Westernization*), which has gone through five

---

3   Just to cite here some examples, one can refer Norman Daniel's *Islam and the West: the making of an Image* (Edinburgh: The University Press, 1960) and *Islam, Europe and Empire* (Edinburgh: Edinburgh University Publications, 1966); and in French, Alain Grosrichard's *Structure du sérail: la fiction du despotisme asiatique dans l'Occident classique* (Paris: Seuil, 1979), which was translated into English as *The Sultan's Court: European Fantasies of the East* (London: Verso, 1998). Published in France only a year after Said's book, Alain Grosrichard's *The Sultan's Court* is a fascinating and careful deconstruction of Western accounts of "Oriental despotism" in the seventeenth and eighteenth centuries, focusing particularly on portrayals of the Ottoman Empire and the supposedly enigmatic and opaque structure of the despot's power and his court of viziers, janissaries, mutes, dwarfs, eunuchs and countless wives. Drawing on the writings of travelers and philosophers such as Montesquieu, Rousseau and Voltaire, Grosrichard goes further than merely cataloguing their intense fascination with the vortex of capriciousness, violence, cruelty, lust, sexual perversion and slavery which they perceived in the seraglio. Deftly and subtly using a Lacanian psychoanalytic framework, he describes the process as one in which these leading Enlightenment figures were constructing a fantasmatic Other to counterpose to their project of a rationally based society. *The Sultan's Court* sought not to refute the misconceptions but rather to expose the nature of the fantasy and what it can reveal about modern political thought and power relations more generally.

4   For further details on Said's book impact, please refer to Gyan Prakash's "Orientalism Now" in *History and Theory*, Vol. 34, No. 3 (Oct., 1995), 199–212, and Mohammad R. Salama's *Islam, Orientalism and Intellectual History* (London: I.B. Tauris, 2011), who develops further some of Said's theses and explores others; for al-Jabarti's chronicle, please refer to *Napoleon in Egypt: Al-Jabarti's Chronicle of the French Occupation, 1798*. Introduction by Robert L. Tignor and Translation by Shmuel Moreh (Princeton: Markus Wiener Publishers, 1993), and Mohammad R. Salama, 153–162.

5   Jalal al-i Ahmad, *Occidentosis: a plague from the West*. Translated by Robert Campbell. Annotations and Introduction by Hamid Algar (Berkeley: Mizan Press, 1984).

6   One can even argue that the process of westernisation/modernisation was also imposed on the West itself, a kind of Westernisation of the West.

editions since its first publication in 1975 but remains unknown outside Turkey. Some of the theses of *Gharbzadegi* also anticipate with remarkable precision points made by Edward Said: the generally invisible but significant links between orientalist scholarship and imperialist politics; the meaningless claim of orientalism to constitute a specialization in itself, without further definition; and the orientalist's assumption that the Muslim East is at bottom static and passive material for analysis by superior minds. Common to *Gharbzadegi* and *Orientalism* is even a denunciation of the *Encyclopaedia of Islam*.[7]

Al-i Ahmad spoke of "occidentosis" as of tuberculosis, and as an infestation of weevils, attacking from the inside.[8] For him, Occidentosis had two poles or extremes – two ends of one continuum. One pole was the Occident, by which

---

7   As these lines are being written, the Centre for Islamic Studies of the Turkish Religious Foundation is publishing its own *TDV Encyclopedia of Islam*, because it considers the *Encyclopedia of Islam*, published by Brill, as inadequate, with ommisions, mistakes and containing unsubstantiated claims and erroneous evaluations. I am referring to this fact to illustrate that some areas of "scholarship" are not neutral.

8   Cemil Aydin's *The Politics of Anti-Westernism in Asia: Visions of World Order in Pan-Islamic and Pan-Asian thought* (New York: Columbia University Press, 2007), by using a comparative approach, gathers new insights on how the unfolding global dominance of the West was received, conceived and contested in different parts of the world. This criticism and critique of the West was nothing exclusively Iranian, or Islamic: it was global, including in the West. For example, Carl Gustav Jung (1875–1961), on a trip to the United States, went to visit the Indians of New Mexico and after talking with one of them he fell into a long meditation: "For the first time in my life, so it seemed to me, someone had drawn for me a picture of the real white man. It was as though until now I had seen nothing but sentimental, prettified colour prints. This Indian had struck our vulnerable spot, unveiled a truth to which we are blind. I felt rising within me like a shapeless mist something unknown and yet deeply familiar. And out of this mist, image upon image detached itself: first Roman legions smashing into the cities of Gaul, and the keenly incised features of Julius Caesar, Scipio Africanus, and Pompey. I saw the Roman Eagle on the North Sea and on the banks of the White Nile. Then I saw St. Augustine transmitting the Christian creed to the Britons on the tips of Roman lances and Charlemagne's most glorious forced conversions of the heathen; then the pillaging and murdering hands of the Crusading armies. With a secret stab I realised the hollowness of that old romanticism about the Crusades. Then followed Columbus, Cortes, and the other conquistadors who, with fire, sword, torture, and Christianity came down upon even these remote Pueblos dreaming peacefully in the Sun, their Father. I saw, too, the peoples of the Pacific islands decimated by firewater, syphilis, and scarlet fever carried in the clothes the missionaries forced on them. It was enough. What we from our point of view call colonisation, missions to the heathen, spread of civilisation, etc., has no other face – the face of a bird of prey seeking with cruel intentness for distant quarry – a face worthy of a race of pirates and highwaymen. All the eagles and other predatory creatures that adorn our coats of arms seem to me apt psychological representatives of our true nature." In Carl Gustav Jung's *Memories, dreams, reflections* (London: Fontana Press, 1995), 276–277.

he meant all of Europe, Soviet Russia, North America, and South Africa, the developed and industrialized nations that could use machines to turn raw materials (not only iron ore and oil, or gut, cotton, and gum tragacanth; but also myths, dogmas, music, and the higher worlds) into more complex forms that could be marketed as goods.

The other pole was Asia and Africa, or the backward, developing or nonindustrial nations that had been made into consumers of western goods. However, the raw materials for those goods came from the developing nations: oil from the shores of the Gulf, hemp and spices from India, jazz from Africa, silk and opium from China, anthropology from Oceania, and sociology from Africa. Here, Al-i Ahmad is careful to explain that westerners imported anthropology from Oceania and sociology from Africa in the sense that the empirical data on which they founded their theories were gathered in those continents and, as Mohammad R. Salama clearly asserts, anthropology was a famous academic discipline involved in that particular field of colonial cultural production, which was perhaps the most productive rubric under which the native "Other" was imported and exported from Europe.[9] From the real differences of non-European peoples, nineteenth-century anthropologists constructed another being of a different nature; differential cultural and physical traits were constructed as the essence of the African, the Arab, the Aboriginal, and so forth. When colonial expansion was at its peak, while the European powers were engaged in a scramble for Africa, anthropology and the study of non-European peoples became not only a scholarly endeavor but also a broad field of public instruction. The so-called "Other" was imported to Europe – in natural history museums, public exhibitions of primitive peoples, in sociological and archeological research – and thus made increasingly available for the popular imagination. Nineteenth-century anthropology presented the Islamic world, as well as many non-European peoples and cultures, as underdeveloped versions of Europeans and their civilizations, namely, as signs of primitiveness that represented stages on a very long road of European civilizations. The anthropological presentation of non-European others within the evolutionary theory of civilizations served to confirm and validate the eminent position of Europeans and thereby legitimate the colonialist project as a whole.[10]

---

9   Mohammad R. Salama, *Islam, Orientalism and Intellectual History* (London: I.B. Tauris, 2011), 240, footnote 65.

10   For further details, please refer to Gérard Leclerc. *Anthropologie et colonialisme: essai sur l'histoire de l'africanisme* (Paris: Fayard, 1972); Talal Asad (ed.). *Anthropology and the Colonial Encounter* (London: Ithaca Press, 1973); Nicholaus Thomas. *Colonialism's Culture: Anthropology, Travel, and Government* (Princeton, N.J.: Princeton UP, 1994); Michel de

In Chapter 7 of his book, *Asses in Lions' Skins, or Lions on the Flag*, Al-i Ahmad says that an occidentotic has severed his ties with the depths of society, culture, and tradition, having no link between antiquity and modernity, nor even a dividing line between old and new. All his preoccupations and Western products are more essential to him than any school, mosque, hospital, or factory. The occidental hangs on the words and handouts of the West. He has nothing to do with what goes on in the East. The occidental seeks to learn only what some orientalists have said and have written about within his field. Even when he wants to learn about the East, he resorts to western sources. It is for this reason that orientalism ('almost certainly a parasite growing on the root of imperialism') dominates thought and opinion in the occidental nations.

On the subject of Islamic philosophy, the customs of Yogis in India, the prevalence of superstitions in Indonesia, the national character of the Arabs, or any other eastern subject, the occidental regards only western writings as proper sources and criteria. This is how he comes to know even himself in terms of the language of the orientalist. With his own hands, he has reduced himself to the status of an object to be scrutinized under the microscope of the orientalist. Then he relies on the orientalist's observations, not on what he himself feels, sees, and experiences. For Al-i Ahmad, this was the ugliest symptom of *occidentosis*: to regard yourself as nothing, not to think at all, to give up all reliance on your own self, your own eyes and ears, to give over the authority of your own senses to any pen held by any wretch who has said or written a word as an orientalist.

From an epistemological point of view, Al-i Ahmad says that he has not the foggiest notion when orientalism became a "science." If one says that some westerner is a linguist, dialectologist, or musicologist specializing in eastern questions, this is defensible. Or, if we say he is an anthropologist or sociologist, this again is arguable to an extent. But what does it mean to be an orientalist without further definition? Does it mean to know all the secrets of the eastern world? That was why he spoke of a parasite growing on the root of imperialism. This orientalism attached to UNESCO had its own organizations in turn, its biennial or quadrennial congress, its member bodies, its comings and goings.

Some scholars still consider the existence of the Middle East and/or Islamic world as a coherent, single object of reality that can be grasped, and continue to analyse it through their framework and try to fit external reality into it. To use Said's words,

---

Certeau. *The Writing of History* (New York: Columbia University Press, 1992); and Michael Hardt and Antonio Negri. *Empire* (Cambridge, Mass.: Harvard UP, 2000).

the object of such knowledge is inherently vulnerable to scrutiny; this object is a "fact" which, if it develops, changes, or otherwise transforms itself in the way that civilizations frequently do, nevertheless is fundamentally, even ontologically stable. To have such knowledge of such a thing is to dominate it, to have authority over it. And authority here means for "us" [the West] to deny autonomy to "it" [the Middle East and/or the Islamic world] since we know it and it exists, in a sense, *as* we know it.[11]

For a social scientist to be an expert in "Islamic Studies" is to study "Islam" as an object of social science and to know "Islam" as a fact. For him or her, 'there are still such things as *an* Islamic society, *an* Arab mind, *an* Oriental psyche. Even the ones whose specialty is the modern Islamic world anachronistically use texts like the *Qur'an* to read into every facet of contemporary Egyptian or Algerian society. Islam, or a seventh-century ideal of it, constituted by the Orientalist, is assumed to possess the unity that eludes the more recent and important influences of colonialism, imperialism, and even ordinary politics.'[12]

As Al-i Ahmad acknowledged, Ahmad Fardid (1909–1994) coined the word *Gharbzadegi* and it would probably have lapsed into obscurity were it not for this book. But beyond the word there are also a number of themes first evoked by Al-i Ahmad that recurred with increasing insistence in later years, and all point to a reevaluation both of history and of national identity. In all of these respects, as well as several others, Al-i Ahmad appears as the precursor of Ali Shariati. The two men are known to have met at least twice, in 1968, and themes such as cultural authenticity, the role of the socially committed intellectual, the problems posed by the presence of the machine in a traditional society, discussed cursorily, even impressionistically, by Al-i Ahmad, were taken up in much greater detail by Shariati and made the subject of a series of lectures and books.

This essay, by using mainly some of Shariati's works, argues that the Social Sciences and the Humanities were, and still are in some quarters of the academic world, a catechism. Usually, a catechism is a summary or exposition of doctrine and serves as a learning introduction to the sacraments traditionally used in catechesis, or Christian religious teaching of children and adult converts. Catechisms are doctrinal manuals – often in the form of questions followed by answers to be memorised – a format that has been used in non-religious or secular contexts as well. Early catecheticals emerged from Graeco-Roman mystery religions, especially the late cult of Mithras, meant

---

11   Said, *Orientalism*, 32.

12   Ibid., 301.

to educate their members into the secretive teachings, which competed with the Christian Church as an underground religion in the 1st to 4th centuries CE, and allegedly shared its many ritual practices. Today, they are characteristic of Western Christianity but are also present in Eastern Christianity. The choice of this word is not accidental: the Social Sciences and the Humanities, if we consider Anthropology, History, and other fields, emerged with the aim to emancipate scholars from normative thinking, i.e., with the aim to arrive at knowledge of human society and human beings free from value judgements or value prescriptions. Consequently, the relationship between religion, which was relegated to the realm of "irrationality," and social sciences was from its inception a precarious one. However, Social Sciences and the Humanities are just like any other religious discourse, but more insidious, pernicious and de-humanising, considering the various attempts by "science" to use "objective" evidence to disprove the *reality* of any human being's subjective experience, and because they are under the guise of "scientific" and, hence "objective and neutral, representing reality accurately" when in fact they are nothing more than an ideology, i.e., a collection of beliefs held by an individual, group or society, and a comprehensive normative vision that is considered the correct way, in this case the way of the religion called "West."

2

In *Extraction and Refinement of Cultural Resources* and *Reflections of Humanity*, Ali Shariati dwells precisely on this and other themes.[13] For him, as a nation and a society possessed economic resources, rich in energy, but worthless when raw, it also possessed vast cultural and spiritual resources that had been accumulated throughout history. An inept and incompetent nation would sit upon such rich treasures that were capable of making people comfortable, in the process keeping its people ignorant, stagnant and deprived. At the time that he was addressing such issues, he knew of large nations in Asia and Africa that owned vast and rich cultural resources, but who were stereotyped as backward, ignorant and spiritually and morally bankrupt. There was a correspondence between the cultural and economic resources of a nation. In short, a generation looking for a way to solve its economic and cultural spiritual problems and to transform its society into a progressive and creative one, had to possess

---

13   Available at http://www.shariati.com/english/culture.html, http://www.shariati.com /english/machine.html, and http://www.iranchamber.com/personalities/ashariati/works /reflections_of_humanity.php.

a historical and cultural awareness as well as technical scientific expertise. This did not mean it should merely emulate another progressive society. Rather, it had to posses an independent experience, as well as original principles and virtues, with a new mission moving towards its goals.

In those years, the enlightened generations of Asia and Africa had come into direct contact with the philosophical, cultural and spiritual schools of Europe. In the past (e.g. in the 19th century), when an educated Asian returned from Europe, he would merely recount his memories, and whatever he said people would accept. This was the only type of connection between Asians and Europeans. In the days of Shariati, however, Asian and African freethinkers were well acquainted with Europe due to several reasons. Those handful of eastern free-thinkers were conscious of themselves as well as their cultural and spiritual values, that they had realized despite the fact that they possessed great and rich cultures brimming with spirituality, philosophy, and knowledge of life, they were so "culturally" poverty stricken (due to alienation from their roots) that they had their mouths open for any European cultural morsels.[14]

Having studied existentialism, Shariati gave an example of that 'opening the mouth for any European cultural morsels.' Anxiety, which had been the most basic spirit of existentialism in the past one hundred years (man's estrangement with the material world – his anxiety due to his inability to find direction and the right way), made up the bulk of the most fundamental problems of existentialism. He saw that such problems were as easy as "learning the alphabet" in eastern theosophy. They had existed in Lao-tse, Buddhism and Islamic theosophy long ago, and there were rich experiences in such areas. However, he noticed that an Iranian freethinker went to Europe without knowing anything about Islam and his own history other than those things he learned at home and in his high school books. He studied literature, philosophy and art, and when he returned home, he offered elementary concepts that were taught in Iranian high schools and religious seminars. For example, after

---

14   Li Chen's *Chinese Law in Imperial Eyes: Sovereignty, Justice, and Transcultural Politics* (New York: Columbia University Press, 2015), an extensively researched book, helps us to understand how there was a shift in Britain's legal cultural perceptions of Qing China in light of both the changes within Great Britain and the growing importance of China in the economics of its empire, as tensions mounted to a showdown over the opium trade. Chen documents this process, showing how British views of Chinese law and its administration evolved from seeing them as not too different from Western practices to considering them the punitive acts of "Oriental despots," labelled as bloodthirsty, punitive, and barbaric, a view that Chen reminds us prevails even today in Western literature and which was even taken up by Chinese themselves in the late nineteenth century, as reformers critiqued their own culture in efforts to modernize.

going to Europe and learning that Jean-Paul Sartre (1905–1980) talked about "Choisir" – meaning *determinism* and *free-will* in Persian – that same free-thinker, returning to Iran, thought that he was offering something new, ignoring that determination and free-will had always been in circulation and usage in his own culture, especially in the philosophical, spiritual, and theosophical writings of the Islamic culture.

Ali Shariati noticed that there was an exact correspondence between the economic and the spiritual fate of the East. As he mentioned before, a nation that is incapable of utilizing its own material resources remains hungry, no matter how rich it is. Similarly, if a nation cannot know its own cultural and spiritual resources and is incapable of extracting, refining, and turning them into energy, it will remain ignorant and backward while sitting in piles of spiritual and cultural resources. The same type of correspondence existed between the role of cultural and material resources in the fate of a society. That is, those who were incapable of utilizing their resources had to extend their hands for rations from foreigners.

Shariati saw that the conscious Europe, which knew easterners better than themselves, utilized the cultural and spiritual resources of others and built new schools of thought and ideas. Since the eastern were not worthy of a conscious utilization of their own spiritual resources, their freethinkers had to beg them, and it never dawned on them that what they were receiving were their own raw materials. Since they were not able to utilize their own resources, they were accused of savagery, ignorance, spiritual, moral, and material poverty.

It was impossible to achieve economic independence without having achieved spiritual independence, and vice versa. These two were interdependent as well as complimentary conditions. In order to have an independent character in the material, social, and economic sphere, an independent consciousness before the West, and vice versa, had to be developed, as well as the consciousness of how the West had deprived them of their cultural and spiritual resources, and consequently trained a generation of easterners who had lost the capability of utilizing the rich treasures of their own thought, ethics, spirit, and culture. In reality they had become estranged from their own resources.[15]

---

15   Michael Greenhalgh's *The Military and Colonial Destruction of the Roman Landscape of North Africa, 1830–1900* (Leiden: Brill, 2014) shows how, after the French invaded Algeria in 1830 and found a landscape rich in Roman remains, they proceeded to re-use to support the constructions such as fortresses, barracks and hospitals needed to fight the natives (who continued to object to their presence), and to house the various colonisation projects with which they intended to solidify their hold on the country, and to make it both modern and profitable. Arabs and Berbers had occasionally made use of the ruins, but it was still a Roman and Early Christian landscape when the French arrived. In the space of

What had the West done to the East that the latter had become alienated and become unworthy of its own material resources? It was obvious for Shariati: quoting Omar Mawloud, an African thinker, he considered that in order to turn a man into a subservient, obedient, and trusting creature, his personality had to be stripped away, because as long as he had character he could not be a servant. And in order to get a good ride from a nation, human feelings had to be taken away from them, or at least weakened. As long as the Easterner felt he was independent, noble, and worthy, he would never fawn and wag his tail for a western morsel to be thrown to him. As was noticed, there was a dialectic relationship between the East and the West: superior vs. inferior, western vs. eastern and white vs. black.[16]

---

two generations, this was destroyed, just as were many ancient remains in France, in part because "real" architecture was Greek, not Roman.

16   For anyone having doubts, Shariati tells his own personal experience at the Sorbonne in Paris: "In the 20th century an M.D. writes his dissertation on the subject of the cells of the blacks vs. whites. And a group of world famous professors offer him his degree since he has proven that brain cells of the black man's cortex are inferior to white's or that the curvature of the tail in a black's cell is less than that of the white's." Despite the fact of what happened in Europe in the first half of the 20th century, despite Nazism, Fascism, Colonialism, or Apartheid, despite the Holocaust and colonial atrocities against "inhumans" and "savages," with their casual massacres of civilians and organized slaughter, regardless of two World Wars, with their massive aerial bombardments of civilians and the rounding up of millions into concentration camps, regardless the use of napalm against civilians, Guantánamo, extraordinary renditions, extrajudicial killings and drone warfare against "unlawful" combatants, with collateral damage, or the current debates on immigration and refugees in Europe, regardless of all of this or the fact that the majority of the world's largest arms exporters are western, there are still "scholarly" books being written and published on *The uniqueness of Western Civilization* (Leiden: Brill, 2011). One cannot imagine how it would be if "they" were not "civilized." As Carl Gustav Jung asserted, 'quite apart from the barbarities and blood baths perpetrated by the Christian nations among themselves throughout European history, the European has also to answer for all the crimes he has commited against the dark-skinned peoples during the process of colonization. In this respect the white man carries a very heavy burden indeed. It shows us a picture of the common human shadow that could hardly be painted in blacker colors. The evil that comes to light in man and that undoubtedly dwells within him is of gigantic proportions [...] Since it is universally believed that man *is* merely what his consciousness knows of itself, he regards himself as harmless and so adds stupidity to iniquity. He does not deny that terrible things have happened and still go on happening, but it is always 'the others' who do them. And when such deeds belong to the recent or remote past, they quickly and conveniently sink into the sea of forgetfulness, and that state of chronic woolly-mindeness returns which we describe as "normality" [...] It is in the nature of political bodies always to see the evil in the opposite group, just as the individual has an

Shariati then adds other examples, such as the way history was, and still is, taught at (western) schools: "From the second and third grades on, children are indoctrinated with the myth that westerners are superior to easterners. Even university professors and thinkers in all areas of the universities cherish the feeling of racial superiority."[17]

Talking about culture, Shariati says that it is the spiritual, mental, moral, and historical accumulations of a nation, similar to natural resources and, just like the natural resources were formed throughout centuries of animals and plants being pressurized within layers in the depth of the earth, culture too was formed throughout history, due to the appearance and demise of successive generations, becoming accumulated and forming the spiritual assets of a nation. The personality of a generation depended upon the constant flow of past accumulations of spiritual, mental, ethical, artistic, and theosophical nurturing, to the extent that a generation could digest his past savings, he could receive nourishment from the makings of its own century. And like the tree which had grown roots deeper in the soil could utilize the sun, air, and nitrogen best, an individual who fed on his own history possessed a personality that was capable of choosing and shaping his tomorrow. It was impossible for an individual who had no past to have a future. Whoever had no past had to begin from zero, and whoever was not familiar with its own culture was primitive.

For Shariati, the exploitative sociology of Europe had realized that in order to be able to rob the East, to ride on her back, and to deceive her, it was imperative to strip her from her personality. Once this was accomplished, the East

---

ineradicable tendency to get rid of everything he does not know and does not want to know about himself by foisting it off on somebody else. Nothing has a more divisive and alienating effect upon society than this moral complacency and lack of responsibility, and nothing promotes understanding and *rapprochement* more than the mutual withdrawal of projections. This necessary corrective requires self-criticism, for one cannot just tell the other person to withdraw them. He does not recognize them for what they are, any more than one does oneself. We can recognize our prejudices and illusions only when, from a broader psychological knowledge of ourselves and others, we are prepared to doubt the absolute rightness of our assumptions and compare them carefully and conscientiously with the objective facts.' In Carl Gustav Jung's *The Undiscovered Self* (New York: Signet, 2006), 94–95, 99–100.

17   Ali Shariati refers explicitly the French sociologist André Siegfried (1875–1959) and his ideas on racial superiority expressed in *L'Âme des peuples* (Paris: Hachette, 1950). In what refers to what should be taught, and why, there was a controversy, not long ago, in the United States about the newest version of the Advanced Placement (AP) U.S. History course. For further details, please refer to Elizabeth Yale's *AP Course Controversy: When Do We Say "We" in History?* available at http://religionandpolitics.org/2015/03/10/ap-course -controversy-when-do-we-say-we-in-history/.

would proudly follow the West and, with unspeakable lunacy and thirst, would consume western goods. The exploiter, in this case the West, wanted to see his machines work all of the time. Furthermore, it wanted to see all originality, religion, tastes, and various talents destroyed, so that all races could be changed to become consumers of his products. In order to achieve this purpose, the exploiter searched for ways to deprive a nation of its personality, which was defined as the unique aspects of a culture that differentiates it from another. Therefore, a generation, like a tree, had to be severed from its roots so that it could be used and manipulated any way the exploiter wished.

Depriving a nation of its history and cutting it off from its culture with subsequent alienation of the present generation from its cultural resources, had reached a point that the cultures which possessed the proudest religions, most progressive philosophical thinking, the most delicate arts, created the grandest civilization and contributed the most experience to human history, had become, in Shariati's times, so alienated with their past possessions that they had been transformed into a sort of human being that had to re-learn how to dress, eat, read, and write.

For Shariati, during the Crusades, the Islamization of Christianity created Protestantism, and Christianity, which throughout centuries was the cause of retardation, was transformed into a builder and energizer of Europe. The transformation of Christian Europe from Catholic to Protestant meant changing a corrupt religious spirit to a social religious spirit, building a grand civilization upon centuries of western retardation and inertia, and that was the reason why those societies were living in poverty and ignorance while the West and its thinkers, by looting such cultures, were trying to enrich their own cultures.

3

One of Said's worries, regarding Orientalism, was the danger and temptation of employing its formidable structure of cultural domination by formerly colonised peoples upon themselves or upon others.[18] Ali Shariati was not immune to it. His views on Protestantism, elaborated in *Where shall we begin?* and in the interview *Mission of a Free Thinker*, echoes an argument which was developed precisely by social "scientists" and Orientalists from the 19th century, not surprisingly Protestant ones.[19] Answering the question of what must be

---

18   Said, *Orientalism*, 25.

19   Ali Shariati, *Mission of a free thinker*. Available at http://www.shariati.com/english/begin/
      begin1.html,   http://www.iranchamber.com/personalities/ashariati/works/where_shall_
      we_begin.php, and http://www.shariati.com/english/mission/mission1.html.

the relationship between the freethinkers and society, Shariati considered, patronisingly, that one should be aware of the fact that they, the easterners, were living in the thirteenth century, while Europe was in the 20th. So, 'we must first discover in what century we live, and then understand our own ideas and teach them. To use 19th century ideas on a 13th century society not only leaves us hanging in the air, but it is also useless when we are unable to find any listener the same things that our freethinkers are faced with now. Our free-thinkers are living in the 13th century but their words, thoughts, and ideas are borrowed from the Western European intellectuals of the 19th and 20th centuries.'[20]

Basically, Shariati is accepting, without any criticism, the Western conception of History and Time, which is something odd, because Shariati was aware that, for example, Iran was much older than (historical) Islam or that there had been other civilizations and cultures before Christ. Shariati even considered that there were nations in the world, which were living in a pre-historic stage, namely, they had not entered the historic period yet. Therefore, to be in the 20th century was different from living in it. Accordingly, Shariati considered that it was necessary to first discover 'our own century, and then learn from identical freethinkers of Europe who are sympathetic to our ideas of our centuries. We are now living in the 13th or 14th centuries (the end of the Middle Ages, or the onset of the modern age).'[21]

Surprisingly, and although he is aware of the predatory and exploitative nature of western Capitalism, Shariati even accepts implicitly that the goal is an industrial capitalist society. For him, the Middle Ages, in Europe, was the period of transition from feudalism and traditional religion to a bourgeois society which signified an open world-vision, revolutionary bourgeoisie, and protest against religion, and, at the time he was speaking, 'we have all these conditions in our society. However, we have to find out what Europe did in the 13th and 14th centuries. And what were the reasons that European free-thinkers played their role so well that they changed the frozen and the stagnant Middle Ages to a new Europe?'[22]

By using Max Weber (1864–1920) and other sociologists, Shariati gives the answer: the basic factors that helped to bring about the new civilization in Europe were economical and intellectual in nature. Economically feudalism changed to bourgeoisie. In place of the reactionary and lowly aristocrats, the bourgeoisie emerged. This was due to East–west relations, the Crusaders, the discovery of America and Australia, mercantilism, and the exploitation of Africa, Asia, Latin America, and even North America. Intellectually, the change

---

20   Ibid.
21   Ibid.
22   Ibid.

was from Catholicism to Protestantism. The 14th century freethinker did not negate religion, he transformed his inclination from the hereafter to this world; from tendency towards spirit, nature, ethics, and ascetism to work and effort; from sufism to objection and from self-centeredness to society-centeredness. In short, the same powerful cultural and religious resources, which lay dormant in the heart of Europe were changed to moving, emerging, creative, and constructive forces by the free-thinkers. Therefore, Shariati considered that 'we must depend upon this fact, rather than what Sartre, Marx, and Rousseau say. What these people say has to do with our next two centuries. We must work for the society in which we live now rather than for our own sole mental and physical satisfaction. What is important to us now are Luther's and Calvin's works, since they transformed the Catholic ethics (which had imprisoned Europe in tradition from centuries) to a moving and creative force.'[23] He also noticed that those countries which had changed the Catholic religion from its reactionary form to a creative and protesting force had made headway (America, England or Germany). On the other hand, those countries which had kept Catholicism (for example, Spain and Italy) had remained in the condition of the Middle Ages.[24]

One can say, without being rude, that Ali Shariati here had his mouth open for any European cultural morsels.

It is a truism to consider that the failure of Islam to modernise was due to the fact it has had no Reformation. The Reformation, it is said, loosened the intellectual shackles of medieval Christendom and led to the development of capitalism and the emergence of the rational individual as the basic constituent of society. The development of Protestantism is also seen as instrumental in the secularisation of European society. Together, these developments crystallised into political institutions that were constitutional and democratic. Max Weber and Benjamin Kidd's theories on Protestantism, capitalism, and forms of government, developing Karl Marx's theory of modes of production and Montesquieu's stereotypes on eastern despotism, were elaborated in the late 19th and early 20th century, a period of economic, social, political, military, institutional, scientific and cultural strength of some European countries, especially the "Protestant" ones, like Great Britain and Germany, or the French Third Republic, which was under Positivism's momentum in addition to its application of

---

23   Ibid.

24   It is curious to notice that during the financial crisis in the European Union, a crisis which has not ended, it was common to hear and read "experts," social "scientists" and even politicians in Portugal and Spain use these same arguments to explain why the Portuguese and the Spanish did not have a work ethic.

laïcité. With their theories, Weber and Kidd (who was openly racist), justifyed the landscape of their own times with something they thought had happened with the Reformation, and projected on the past their historical situation, and explained the backwardness of Roman Catholic countries. It should be noted that the creation of a territorial German Nation-State in the 19th century, under Otto von Bismarck (1815–1898) went hand-in-hand with a struggle against the Roman Catholic Church, a struggle known as the *Kulturkampf.* In the process of German unification, the social "scientists" (sociologists, political scientists, etc.) were very important in legitimizing "scientifically," for example by using history, the wishes of the political powers.

The Reformation, which was a historical process of Western European Christianity, did not mean the loosening of the intellectual shackles of medieval Christendom. That movement aimed at the abuses of the Catholic Church in Rome, and it produced a period of great political and religious violence, which only ended in 1648, with the Peace of Westphalia, putting an end to the Thirty Years' War, and even after that religious hostilities continued with the revocation of the Edict of Nantes in 1685. In many Reformed countries it was unthinkable to be a subject of the Crown or a Prince without adhering to the religion of the ruler (*cujus regio, ejus religio*), and many Protestant countries still have State religions today.[25] Suddenly, a process which was a particular feature of a particular region of Europe, became a universal law which had to be replicated everywhere, like the laws of physics or mathematics.

On the other hand, it is ironic to note that many of the so-called fundamentalist, extremist, or Islamist movements claim that the individual has the right, and duty, to read and interpret the *Qur'an* without any intermediation; it seems that DAESH (a.k.a. ISIS, ISIL etc.) is putting forward the Reformation of Islam, and with great success, considering all the political and religious violence which it is producing ...

Although Shariati considered erroneous the opinion of most contemporary enlightened individuals who thought that religion (i.e., Islam) played a negative role in the society by causing the masses to neglect their actual and material lives, and although he asserted that the anti-religious experience of Christianity in the Middle Ages could not be extended to the Islamic world, whether its past or its present, the fact is that Shariati ends up

---

25   It is ironic that Jean-Jacques Rousseu (1712–1778), in book 4, Chapter 8 of his *Du Contrat Social ou Principes du droit politique*, published in 1762, praises the prophet Muhammad for having established a political system which united the spiritual and the temporal, thus preventing the constant conflict which existed in Europe between the kings and the Catholic Church.

using a grill of analysis which is similar to the arguments of the absence of Reformation.[26]

Returning to Ali Shariati's thought, he considered that easterners had been civilization builders and humanity's teachers throughout man's history, so much so that they owned a collection of vast and deep cultural, mental, and social experiences of humanity. It was time to mend and fill the gap in order to be able to think independently and know "ourselves." The strength had to be found to choose, and turn into a creative force, the past's historical, religious, theosophical, and literary factors, which had transformed into superstition and opiate, thus causing inertia and corruption in our societies. 'The westerners, unlike what they did to Africans, did not negate our past, they metamorphosised it. And when we look at our own new portrait we hated it. Consequently, we began to run towards our "metamorphosized" past and religion, as well as towards European schools and culture.'[27]

4

Another important subject that Shariati approaches is the debate on culture and barbarism, or the question of who is civilized and who is modern. He discusses it in the light of Islamic doctrine, and stresses that this point had to be kept in mind, particularly as a matter of concern for individuals within the educated classes of Islamic societies upon who laid the burden of responsibility and leadership of the *ummah*.

Modernity was one of the most delicate and vital issues confronting the people of non-European countries and Islamic societies. A more important issue was the relationship between an imposed modernization and genuine civilization. One had to discover if modernity – as was claimed – was a synonym for being civilized, or if it was an altogether different issue and social phenomenon having no relation to civilization at all. Unfortunately, modernity had been imposed on non-European nations under the guise of civilization. For the past one hundred and fifty years, the West had undertaken the task of modernizing men with missionary zeal. All non-European nations were put in

---

26   In 1965, in a review to Erwin I.J. Rosenthal's *Islam in the Modern National-State*, in *The Journal of Religion*, Vol. 47, No. 3, (Jul., 1967), 259–260, Isma'il R. Al-Faruqi (1921–1986) had already lambasted the author for his incapability of putting aside his own cultural predilections and prejudices.

27   Ali Shariati, *Extraction and Refinement of Cultural Resources.* http://www.shariati.com /english/culture.html, two last paragraphs.

close contact with the West and western civilization and were to be changed to "modern" nations. Under the guise of civilizing nations, acquainting them with culture, they presented the non-European and third world nations with that modernity, which they persisted in calling "ideal civilization." The intellectuals should have understood years ago and made people realize the difference between civilization and modernity, but they failed to do so. Before proceeding to any further discussion, Shariati defined certain terms on which he intended to concentrate, which, if left ambiguous, would render the discussion vague:

Intellectual: An intellectual is one who is conscious of his own "humanistic status" in a specific social and historical time and place. His self-awareness lays upon him the burden of responsibility. He responsibly, and self-consciously, leads his people in scientific, social and revolutionary action.

Assimilation: This was at the root of all the troubles and constraints facing the non-western and Muslim countries, applying to the conduct of an individual who, intentionally or unintentionally, starts imitating the mannerisms of someone else. A person exhibiting this weakness forgets his own background, national character and culture, or, if he remembered them at all, recalled them with contempt. Obsessively, and with no reservation, he denied himself in order to transform his identity. Hoping to attain the distinctions and the grandeur, which he saw in another, the assimilator attempted to rid himself of perceived shameful associations with his original society and culture.

Alienation: The process of forgetting or becoming unfamiliar with or indifferent to one's self, i.e., one loses the self and directs their perceptions from within another person or thing. This grave social and spiritual illness manifested itself in many different shapes and forms depending on various factors. One factor that contributed to the alienation of the human being were the tools with which someone worked. It is seen as another kind of "control by jinns," which possessed humanity and alienated individual or even an entire class from itself. Yet, that which was more real, more frightening, and more damaging, was the omnipresent form of alienation; such alienation thoroughly affected the Iranians, the Muslims, the Asians, and the Africans: that is, "cultural alienation."

Culture is a collection of intellectual, non-material artistic, historical, literary, religious and emotional expressions (in the form of signs, traditions, customs, relics, mores) of a nation which have accumulated in the course of its history and acquired unique form, signifying the pains, desires, temperaments, social characteristics, life patterns, social relations and economics structure of a nation. When one feels his own religion, literature, emotion, needs and pains through his own culture, one feels his own self, the very social and historical self (not the individual self), the source from which this culture has originated.

Therefore, culture was the expression and super-structure of the real being of one's society; actually the whole history of one's society. But certain artificial factors, probably of a dubious nature, crept into a society which once had well defined social conditions or social relations, developed through a specific historical framework, and aquainted it with pains, sufferings, emotions and sentiments which had an alien spirit and were a product of a different past, a different society (different both socially and economically).

These artificial factors wiped out any real culture and in the process substituted a false culture suitable for different conditions and an altogether different historical stage, a different economy, and a different political and social setup. Then, when one wished to feel his own real self, one found himself conceiving another society's culture instead of his own and bemoaning troubles not his at all.

> The dark skinned man of Africa, the Berber of North Africa, the Persian and Indian in Asia, each has a particular past and unique present. However, they feel inside particular pain and concern which they regard as their own, but which are actually offshoots of problems of periods following the Middle Ages, the 16th century renaissance, 17th century liberalism, the scientific progress of the 18th century, and the ideologies of the 19th century and the capitalist societies that came into being after World Wars I and II. And because they associated with people they thought more intelligent, polished, respectable and wealthy than myself. My conceptions of myself are not as I actually am in reality, but as "they" are; that is, I am alienated.[28]

In this way non-European societies became alienated by European societies; their intellectuals no longer felt eastern, groaned like an eastern person or aspired to be eastern people. The intellectual did not suffer because of his own social problems, rather he conceived of the pain, sufferings, feelings and needs of a European in the final stage of capitalistic and materialistic success and enjoyment.

> Thus, today the most painful disorder possible sweeps non-European countries, the psychological disorder of non-Europeans who possess a unique character and yet deny it. They hold in mind something alien. They conceive of someone else and imitate him blindly. These non-European

---

28   Ali Shariati, *Reflections of Humanity.* http://www.iranchamber.com/personalities/ashariati/works/reflections_of_humanity.php.

countries in the past were real and genuine. If you had visited these countries, say two hundred years ago, they would have lacked today's western
civilization, but each and every one of them had its own authentic and
solid civilization. They were unique: their desires, their delicacies, their
forms of worship and all their good and bad behaviour; their action, their
beauties, their philosophy, their religion – everything belongs to them.[29]

For instance, if someone had gone to a country like India or any African country, he would know that they had their own unique tastes and buildings. They
composed their own unique poetry, pertinent to their culture, and relevant
to their lives. They had their own unique social manner. They had their own
unique colors, maladies, desires and religions. All they had was their own. In
spite of the fact that they were far below the level of present day civilization
and material enjoyment, still, what they had, however trifling, was their own.
They were not sick, poor they were, but poverty is something different from
sickness.

But today, western societies have been able to impose their philosophy, their way of thinking, their desires, their ideas, their tastes and
their manners upon non-Europeans countries to the same extent that
they have been able to force their symbols of civilization (technological
innovations) into these countries which consume new products and gad-
gets; countries which can never adjust themselves to European manners,
longing, tastes and ways of thinking.[30]

The problem concerned making people in Asia and Africa consumers of
European products. Their societies had to be structured so they would
buy European products. That meant changing a nation literally. They had to
change the nation, and they had to transform the man in order to change his
clothing, his consumption pattern, his adornment, his abode and his city. What
part of him needed to be changed first? His morale and his thinking. Who could
change the spirit of a society, the morale of a society and the way of thinking of
a nation? In this respect, the European capitalist, engineer or producer could
do little. Rather, it was the business of the enlightened European intellectuals
to plan a special method of perverting the mind, the taste and lifestyle of the
non-European, not in a way that he himself chooses – since the change he desires might not necessitate the consumption of European products – rather his

---

29   Ibid.
30   Ibid.

desires, his choices, his suffering, his sorrow, his tastes, his ideals, his sense of
beauty, his tradition, his social relations, his amusements, all had to be changed
so that he could be coerced into becoming a consumer of European industrial
products. Thus, the big producers and big European capitalists of the 18th and
19th centuries let the intellectuals handle this project. This was the project: all
the people of the world had to become uniform. They had to live alike and they
had to think alike. However, it was practically impossible for all the nations to
think in the same way. What structural elements go into the personality and
spirit of a man and nation? Religion, history, culture, past civilization, education and tradition – all of these are the structural elements of a man's personality and spirit and, in its general term, of a nation. Clearly, these elements
differed from one society to another. They resulted in a Europe form, while
another developed in Asia and in Africa. Yet, according to European capitalist,
they all had to become the same. The differences in spirits, as well as intellectual traditions, of the nations of the world had to be destroyed in order for men
to become uniform. They had to conform, wherever they were, to a single pattern, a pattern provided by Europe: it showed all Easterners, Asians, Africans,
how to think, how to dress, how to desire, how to grieve, how to build their
houses, how to establish their social relations, how to consume, how to express
their view, and finally how to like and what to like. Soon it was realized that
a new culture called "modernization" was presented to the whole world. Modernity was the best method of diverting the non-European world from their
own molds, thoughts and personalities. It became the sole task of Europeans
to place the temptation of "modernization" before the non-European societies
of any complexion. The Europeans realized that by tempting the inhabitants
of the East with a compulsive desire for "modernization" he would cooperate with them to deny his own past and desecrate and destroy – with his own
hands – the constituents of his own unique culture, religion and personality.
Therefore, the temptation and longing for "modernization" prevailed all across
the Far East, Middle East, Near East and in Islamic and Black countries – and to
become "modern" was synonymous with becoming like the Europeans.

For Shariati, strictly speaking, "modernized" meant modernized in the
realm of consumption. One who became modernized was one whose tastes
desired "modern" items to satisfy his wants. In other words, he imported from
Europe new forms of living as well as modern products, and he refused to use
new types of products and lifestyles developed from his own national past.
Westerners, however, could not just tell others they were going to reshape their
intellect, mind and personality for fear of awakening resistance. Therefore, the
Europeans had to make non-Europeans equate "modernization" with "civilization" to impose the new consumption pattern upon them, capitalizing on the
universal desire for civilization. "Modernization" was defined as "civilization,"

and thus people cooperated with the European plans to modernize. Even more than the bourgeois and capitalist, the non-European intellectual labored mightily to change consumption patterns and lifestyles in their societies. Since the non-Europeans could not produce the new products, they became automatically dependant upon the technology, which produced for them and were expected to purchase.

Modernization changed traditions, mode of consumption and material life from old to new. People made the old ways; machines produce the new.[31] To make all the non-Europeans modernized, they first had to overcome the influence of religion, since religion caused any given society to feel a distinctive individuality. Religion postulated an exalted intellectuality to which everyone related intellectually. If this intellect was crushed and humiliated, the one who identified himself with it felt also crushed and humiliated. Therefore, native intellectuals began a movement against "fanaticism." As Frantz Fanon said: 'Europe intended to captivate the non-European by the machine. Can a human or society be enslaved by a machine or certain European product without taking away or depriving him of his personality?'[32] No, it could not. The personality had to be wiped out first. Since religion, history, culture, as a totality of intellect, thought, amassed art and literature gave personality to a society, they all had to be destroyed, too.

> In the 19th century I [Shariati] would feel as an Iranian that I was attached to a great civilization of the 4th, 5th, 6th, 7th, and 8th centuries of Islam which was unparalleled in the world and had the whole world under its influence. I would feel that I was attached to a culture, more than two thousand years old, which in various forms and shapes, had created new intellectualism, new art and literature in the world of humanity. I would feel that I was attached to the Islam that was the newest, the most sublime and the most universal religion, creating all those intellectualities and dissolving all those different civilizations in itself to create a greater civilization. I would feel attached to the Islam which created the most beautiful spirit and the most sublime face of humanity, and I could also feel, as a human, that I had a unique personality in the eyes of the world and every person in it. So how could they convert such an "I" into a gadget whose only function is to consume new products?[33]

---

31   It should be stressed that, including in Europe, there were many who were very critical of the machine, for example the aforementioned Carl Gustav Jung, Carl Schmitt (1888–1985), or Martin Heidegger (1889–1976), the later being very influential on Ahmad Fardid.

32   As quoted by Shariati in *Reflections of Humanity*.

33   Ibid.

They would deprive him of his personality. He had to be dispossessed of all the "I's" he felt within. He had to be forced to believe himself related to a humbler civilization, a humbler social order, and accept that European civilization, western civilization and the European race were superior. Africa had to believe that an African was a savage, so that he was tempted to become "civilized" and put himself readily into the hands of the Europeans who would determine his fate. The poor man did not realize that he was being modernized instead of being civilized. That was why one could see that suddenly in the 18th and 19th centuries the Africans were described as savages and cannibals. Those Africans who had dealt with the Islamic civilisation for centuries were never known as cannibals. Suddenly the Black African became a cannibal, had a special smell, had a special race.[34]

> The grey part of his brain does not work, and the forepart of his brain, like the Asian's, is shorter compared to the Westerner's! Even their doctors and biologists have "proven" (!) that the Westerner's brain has an extra gray peel, which Easterners and Blacks lack!! They also have 'proven' that the Westerner's brain has an additional length to the genes in the brain cells which allows him to think better than a non-Westerner! Then we see that a new culture was built on a basis of "Western superiority" and "the superiority of its civilization and its people." They made us and the world believe that the European was exceptionally talented mentally and technically, whereas the Easterner had strange emotional and gnostic talents[35] and the Negro was only good for dancing, singing, painting and sculpture. Consequently, the world was divided into three distinct races: one which can think, that is, the European (!) (right from the days of ancient Greece up to now!) and the one which can only feel or make poetry, the Easterner, who has only mystical and gnostic feelings, and the Black, who can dance, sing and play good jazz. Then this very way of thinking, which was introduced to the world to justify the need for

---

34   It is always useful to recall the way Africans were treated in the United States in the 19th and 20th centuries, and still are now. Tameka B. Hobbs. *Democracy Abroad, Lynching at Home: Racial Violence in Florida* (Gainseville: University Press of Florida, 2015); Julie Buckner Armstrong. *Mary Turner and the Memory of Lynching* (Athens: University of Georgia Press, 2011); and Amy Kate Bailey, Stewart E. Tolnay. *Lynched: The Victims of Southern Mob Violence* (Chapel Hill: University of North Carolina Press, 2015) are all a very good starting point.

35   For further details on this, please refer to David T. Schmit's "The Mesmerists inquire about 'Oriental Mind Powers': West meets East in the search for the Universal Trance." *Journal of the History of the Behavioral Sciences*, Vol. 46, 1 (Winter 2010), 1–26.

modernizing the non-European nations, became the basis of thought for the non-European elites as well.[36]

One could see how a conflict between the "modernized" and the "old-fashioned" in non-European societies was created for one hundred years; a conflict which was, and still is, the most senseless fight one has ever seen: 'Modernization in what? In consumption, not in mind. Old fashioned in what? In the form of consumption. It was natural that the fight ended in favor of modernization, and even if it had ended otherwise, it would not have been to the benefit of the masses.'[37]

In this fight, the fight between the modernized and civilized, the European was the leader. In the name of civilization, the campaign for modernization was carried on, and then for one hundred years, for more than one hundred years, the non-European societies themselves strove to become modernized under the leadership of their sophisticated intellectuals.

As Jean-Paul Sartre in the preface to Fanon's *The Wretched of the Earth* pointed out,

> We would bring a group of African or Asian youth to Amsterdam, Paris, London ... for a few months, take them around, change their clothes and adornments, teach them etiquette and social manners as well as some fragment of language. In short, we would empty them of their own cultural values and then send them back to their own countries. They would no longer be the kind of person to speak their own mind; rather they would be our mouthpieces. We would cry the slogans of humanity and equality and then they would echo our voice in Africa and Asia.[38]

These were the persons who convinced people to lay aside their orthodoxy, discard their religion, get rid of native culture (as these had kept them behind the modern European societies) and become westernized from the tip of the toe to the top of the head. However, it was not so simple to civilize a nation or a society. Civilization and culture were not European-made products whose ownership made anyone civilized. Nevertheless, they had to make believe that all modernization nonsense was a manifestation of civilization,

---

36   Ali Shariati, *Reflections of Humanity*.

37   Ibid.

38   As quoted by Shariati in *Reflections of Humanity*. First published in French in 1961, Frantz Fanon's *Les Damnés de la Terre* had a preface by Jean-Paul Sartre, and has been translated into many languages, including Persian by Ali Shariati.

and we eagerly threw away everything we had, even our social prestige, morality and intellect, to become thirsty suckers of what Europe was eager to trickle into our mouths. This is what modernity really means. Thus a being was created devoid of any background, alienated from his history and religion, and a stranger to whatever his race, his history and his forefathers had built in this world; alienated from his own human characteristics, a second-hand personality whose mode of consumption had been changed, whose mind has been changed, who had lost his old precious thoughts, his glorious past and intellectual qualities and has now become empty within.[39]

As Jean Paul Sartre put it: 'In these societies an "assimilate" – meaning a quasi-thinker and quasi-educated person – was created, not a real thinker or intellectual.'

5

For Shariati, a *real* intellectual was one who knew his society, was aware of its problems, could determine its fate, was knowledgeable about its past and who could decide for himself. However, those quasi-intellectuals in non-European societies succeeded in influencing the people by being intermediaries between those who had the products and those who had to consume it. Aquainted both with the Europeans and with his own people, the mediator eased the way of colonization and exploitation, and that was why they created native intellectuals who did not dare to choose for themselves, who did not have the courage to maintain their own opinions and who could not decide for themselves. As Fanon said,

in order for Eastern countries to be the followers of Europe and imitate her like a monkey, they should have proven to the non-Europeans that they do not possess the same quality of human values as the Europeans do. They should have belittled their history, literature, religion and art to make them alienated from all of it. We can see that the Europeans did just that.[40]

---

39   Ibid.
40   As quoted by Shariati in *Reflections of Humanity*.
         In his *The Theft of History* (Cambridge: Cambridge University Press, 2006), Jack Goody, building on his own previous work, extends further his highly influential critique of what

They had created a people who did not know their own culture, but still were ready to despise it. They knew nothing about Islam but said bad things about it. They could not understand a simple poem but criticized it with poorly chosen words. They did not understand their history but were ready to condemn it. On the other hand, without reservation they admired all that was imported from Europe. Consequently, a being was created who, first became alienated from his religion, culture, history and background, and then came to despise them. He was convinced he was inferior to the European, and when such a belief took root in him, he tried to refute himself, to sever his connections with all the objects attached to him, and consequently tried to make himself into a European, who was not despised and looked down upon. He was then able to say, 'Thank God I am not an Easterner since I modernized myself sufficiently to reach the level of a European.'

In addition, while the non-European was happy with the idea that he had been modernized, the European capitalist and bourgeois laugh at their success in converting him into a consumer of their surplus production.

In *Where shall we begin?*, Ali Shariati wanted to draw attention to where one should strategically proceed in a particular society, in a given period of time, in order to achieve the shared objectives and to protect the values which were at the time subject to cultural, intellectual and social onslaughts. The gravest tragedy in traditional societies in general, and in the Muslim societies in particular, was that there was a lack of communication and a difference of outlook between the masses and the educated class. Due to the broad influence of mass media, literacy, and education in the industrial countries of the West, the masses and the intellectuals understood each other rather well and shared a relatively similar outlook. In Europe, a university professor could easily communicate with the "uneducated" masses. According to Shariati, the western professor did not perceive himself to be of higher stature than the masses, neither did the masses treat him as an untouchable person wrapped in a piece

---

he sees as the pervasive Eurocentric or occidentalist biases of so much western historical writing, and the consequent 'theft' by the West of the achievements of other cultures in the invention of (notably) democracy, capitalism, individualism and love. Nevertheless, and as Tonio Andrade draws our attention to, Jack Goody persists in using the 1492 Schema. For further details, please refer to Tonio Andrade. "Beyond Guns, Germs, and Steel: European Expansion and Maritime Asia, 1400–1750." *Journal of Early Modern History* 14 (2010), 165–186. Also illuminating are E.H. Dance's *History the Betrayer: a study in bias* (London: Hutchinson, 1960) and more recently Catherine Coquery Vidrovitch's *Enjeux politiques de l'histoire colonial* (Marseille: Agone, 2009) a book in which she defends that French "national" history should include the history of slavery and colonialism.

of cellophane.[41] Unfortunately, under the modern culture and educational system, the young people of non-western countries were being educated and trained inside invincible and fortified fortresses. Once they reentered the society, they were placed in certain occupational and social positions completely isolated from the masses. In effect, the new intelligentsia lived and moved alongside the people, but in a closed "golden cage" of exclusive circles. As a result, on the one hand, the intelligentsia pursued life in an ivory tower without having any understanding of their own society, and on the other hand, the uneducated masses were deprived of the wisdom and knowledge of the very same intellectuals whom the masses had sponsored (albeit indirectly) and whose flourishing they had provided for.

The greatest responsibility of those who wished to rebuild their society and bring together the unintegrated, and at times, antagonistic elements of the society into a harmonious whole was to bridge the gap between those two poles – the pole of theory and the pole of practice – and to fill that great abyss of alienation between the masses and the intellectuals. For any responsible enlightened soul who wanted to achieve something, regardless of his ideological conviction, it was a duty to build a bridge between the beautiful, valuable, and the mysterious (in the mind of the masses) island of the intellectuals and the land of the masses; a bridge across which both the intellectuals and the masses could interact. Regardless of any answer to the question 'Where shall we begin,' and regardless of the agreement with Shariati's answer, one could not help but accept and agree with that fundamental principle: the first step was to build such a bridge.

Implicit in the question 'Where shall we begin?' there was an understanding on the part of the audience, and the person who posed such a question, that two prior questions namely, 'Who should begin?' and 'For what purpose?' had already been answered. Obviously, the question of where to begin was asked by those who had a sense of responsibility with regard to their time and society and wished to do something about it. Undoubtedly, they were the enlightened souls, for only such individuals felt a social responsibility and had a sense of social mission. One who was not enlightened was not responsible either.

Shariati notes that he stresses "enlightened souls" and not those who had obtained degrees. "Enlightened" did not mean "intellectual," a word which had incorrectly been translated into Persian as "enlightened" (roshan fekr), and which referd to a person who did mental (as opposed to manual) work. Such an individual may or may not be an enlightened soul. Conversely, a person may

---

41   The French sociologist Pierre Bourdieu (1930–2002) would certainly disagree with Shariati on this rather naïve vision of Western academia.

not be an intellectual if he worked in a factory for example – but he may nevertheless be an enlightened soul. The relation between the two was not that of
two interrelated concepts. Not every intellectual was enlightened and vice versa. The enlightened soul was a person who was self-conscious of his "human
condition" in his time and historical and social setting, and whose awareness
inevitably and necessarily gave him a sense of social responsibility. In addition, if he happened to be educated he may be more effective. If not, perhaps
less so. Nevertheless, this was not a general rule, for sometimes an uneducated
individual may play a much more important role.

A study of the societies that have leaped forward from the oppressive colonial state to a very progressive, aware and dynamic state, demonstrated that
their leaders, and those who assumed leadership in the revolution and the scientific and social movements, had often been unintellectual. The social movements in Africa, Latin America and Asia easily proved this principle, which
had very few exceptions. One could safely conclude that revolutionary leaders
had rarely belonged to the educated classes.

In the modern time, when man had reached a dead end within his evolv-
ing society, and when the underdeveloped countries were struggling with numerous difficulties and shortcomings, an enlightened soul was one who could
generate responsibility and awareness and give intellectual and social direction to the masses. Accordingly, an enlightened person was not necessarily one
who had inherited and continued the works of Galileo, Copernicus, Socrates,
Aristotle, and Ibn-Sīnā (Avicenna). Modern scientists such as Einstein and
Von Braun complemented and continued their achievements. In principle,
the responsibility and the rule of contemporary enlightened souls of the
world resembled that of the prophets and the founders of the great religions –
revolutionary leaders who promoted fundamental structural changes in the
past. Prophets were not in the same category as philosophers, scientists, technicians or artists. The prophets often emerged from among the masses and
were able to communicate with the masses, introducing new mottos, pro-
jecting new visions, starting new movements, and begeting new energies in
the conscience of the peoples of their particular time and places. The great
revolutionary *uprooting* – and yet *constructive* – movements of the prophets
caused frozen, static and stagnant societies to change their directions, lifestyles, outlooks, cultures and destinies. Those prophets were therefore neither
in the category of the past scientists or philosophers, nor were they in the category of unaware common people. Rather, they belonged to a category of their
own. They neither belonged to the commoners, who were usually the products
and captives of ancient traditions and social structures, nor did they belong
to the community of the scientists, philosophers, artists, mystics, monks or

clergymen, who were captives of abstract concepts and often overwhelmed with their own scientific or inner explorations and discoveries.

Similar to the prophets, the enlightened souls also belonged neither to the community of scientists, nor to the camp of the unaware and stagnant masses. They were aware and responsible individuals whose most important objective and responsibility was to bestow the great God-given gift of "self-awareness" (*khod agahi*) to the general public. Only self-awareness transformed the static and corrupt masses into a dynamic and creative cantor, which fostered genius and gave rise to great leaps, which in turn became the springboard for the emergence of civilization, culture and great heroes.

Clearly then, it was the enlightened soul who should begin preaching the call for awareness, freedom and salvation, to the deaf and unhearing ears of the people; it is the enlightened souls who should inflame the fire of a new faith in the hearts of the masses, and show them a new social direction in their stagnant society. This was not a job for the scientists, because they had a clear-cut responsibility: understanding the status quo as well as discovering and employing the forces of nature and of man for the betterment of the material life of the people. Scientists, technicians and artists provided scientific assistance to their nations, or to the human race, in order to help them to improve their lot and be better at what they are. Enlightened souls, on the other hand, taught their society how to "change" and provided the orientation of that change. They fostered a mission of "becoming" and paved the way by providing an answer to the question, 'What should we become?'

A scientist justifies, explains, and creates the conditions for producing as affluent, comfortable, strong, and leisurely life as possible. At most, he discovers the "facts," whereas an enlightened person identifies the "truth." A scientist produces light, which may be utilized either for right or wrong objectives; an enlightened person, analogous to a "tribal guide" (*ra'id*), is the vanguard of the caravan of humanity, showing society the right path; he invites us to initiate a journey, and leads us to our final destination. Since science is power and enlightenment light, from time to time, the scientist serves the interests of oppression and ignorance, but the enlightened person, of necessity and by definition, opposes tyranny and darkness.

Shariati then explores the word *hekmat* (wisdom), which is often used in the Qur'ān and within the Islamic cultural milieu. It conveyed the same meaning he had attributed to enlightenment. Even when there was a discussion of knowledge (*'elm*), it did not refer to technical, scientific or philosophical learnings. It meant neither "religious knowledge" (those disciplines which a religious student studied, i.e., jurisprudence, tradition, life of the Prophet, the Qur'ānic interpretation, ethics, theology etc.) nor "temporal knowledge" (those disciplines which were pursued by social and/or natural science students, i.e., physics, medicine, sociology, literature, psychology, history, etc.). These were collections of specialized information and cultural knowledge, which were taught particularly as courses in a specific educational system. While religious and secular knowledge could be helpful for enlightened awareness (*agahi-e-roshanfekri*), and may serve as valuable tools at the disposal of the enlightened individuals, they were not in-and-of-themselves the desired "light" or awareness. That kind of knowledge (*'elm*), which was emphasized in Islam, was an awareness unique to man, a divine light and a source of consciousness of the social conscience. As the famous tradition put it, 'Knowledge is a light which God shines in the heart of whomever He desires.' It was this awakening, illuminating, guiding and responsibility-generating knowledge which Shariati called the "divine light," not the teachings of physics, chemistry, literature jurisprudence, etc. The former beget faith and responsibility of the kind the uneducated Abū Dhar al-Ghifari al-Kinani possessed but Ibn-Sīnā (Avicenna) and Molla Sadrā did not. That was why sometimes an uneducated person emerged and energized life in a static society and lead it towards a clear objective, while numerous scientists did not even take the first step towards generating changes, self-awareness, formations of a common ideal, or a new faith in the conscience of their society. On the contrary, by utilizing their scientific power, the scientists may act as forces hindering the progress of their own national societies as well as that of humanity. Therefore, the goal of the enlightened soul was to bestow upon their contemporaries a common and dynamic faith, as well as to help them acquire self-awareness and formulate their ideals.

The greatest responsibility of the enlightened soul was to identify the real causes of the backwardness of his society and discover the real cause of the stagnation and degeneration of his people. Moreover, he should educate his slumbering and ignorant society as to the basic reasons for its ominous historical and social destiny. Then, based on the resources, responsibilities, needs and suffering of his society, he should identify the rational solutions, which would enable his people to emancipate themselves from the status quo. Based on appropriate utilization of the resources of his society and an accurate diagnoses of its suffering, an enlightened person should try to find out the true causal relationships between misery, social illness and abnormalities, and the various internal and external factors. Finally, an enlightened person would transfer this understanding beyond the limited group of his colleagues to the society as a whole.

Contemporary "intellectuals" generally believe that dialectical contradictions at work in any society, of necessity move the society forward toward freedom and revolution, and gave birth to a new state of being. According to this logic, mere "poverty" or "class diferences," which symbolized the existence of social conflicts, inevitably lead to a dialectical contradiction, which in turn created motion in the society. In reality, however, this was no more than a big illusion. No society would be mobilized to obtain its freedom merely because of the existence of class difference or tragic disparity between rich and poor. Poverty and class conflict may exist in a society for thousands of years without causing any structural transformation. Dialectics had no *intrinsic* motion. Considering that motion in any given society was the product of transformation of the social conflict from within the society into the conscience of its members, the responsibility of the enlightened person was obvious. Briefly, it was 'to transfer the shortcomings and abnormalities of his society into the mind and conscience of the members of that society.' Then, the society would take it from there. Another definition of the enlightened person was that he was one who was aware of the existing social conflicts and their real causes, who knew the needs of his age and his generation, who accepted responsibility for providing solutions as to how his society could be emancipated, who helped his society to shape and define its collective goals and objectives and, finally, who took part in mobilizing and educating his static ignorant society. In a word, a contemporary enlightened person should continue in the path of the prophets. His mission is to "guide" and work for justice, his language is compatible with his time, and his proposed solutions conform to cultural values of his specificity.

Summarizing the points raised, Shariati says that given the culture and specific definition of the "enlightened," as a person with a prophetic mission, the objectives and responsibilities of such a person were to transform the existing social conflicts from the context of the society into the feelings and self-consciousness of its members. An enlightened person should obtain the raw materials from his contemporary society and social life. There existed no universal type of enlightened person, with common values and characteristics everywhere. Shariati writes, 'our own history and experience have demonstrated that whenever an enlightened person turns his back on religion, which is the dominant spirit of the society, the society turns its back on him.'[42] Opposition to religion by the enlightened person deprived society of the possibility of becoming aware of the benefits of its young and enlightened generation. Due to their unique worldviews and awareness, enlightened individuals can play the most effective and long-lasting role in educating and mobilizing the masses of

---

42   Ali Shariati, *Where shall we begin?* http://www.shariati.com/english/begin/begin7.html, first paragraph.

their society. With great intensity, the society expected its enlightened persons to educate it concerning various elements of danger, reactionism, corruption, anachronism and confusion. To emancipate and guide the people, to give birth to a new love, faith, and dynamism, and to shed light on people's hearts and minds and make them aware of various elements of ignorance, superstition, cruelty and degeneration in contemporary Islamic societies, an enlightened person should start with "religion." By that Shariati meant 'our peculiar religious culture and not the one predominant today.'[43] Such a movement would unleash energies that would enable the enlightened Muslim to:

(1) Extract and refine the enormous resources of the society and convert the degenerating agents into energy and movement;

(2) Transform the existing social and class conflicts into conscious awareness of social responsibility, by using artistic, literary and speaking abilities, as well as other possibilities at hand;

(3) Bridge the ever-widening gap between the 'island of the enlightened person' and the 'shore of the masses' by establishing kinship links, fostering understanding between them, thus putting the religion, which came about to revive and generate movement, at the service of the people;

(4) Make the weapon of religion inaccessible to those who had undeservedly armed themselves with it and whose purpose was to use religion for personal reasons, thereby acquiring the necessary energy to motivate people;

(5) Launch a religious renaissance through which, by returning to the religion of life and motion, power and justice, would on the one hand incapacitate the reactionary agents of the society and, on the other hand, save the people from those elements that were used to narcotize them. By launching such a renaissance, these hitherto narcotizing elements would be used to revitalize society, give awareness and fight superstition. Furthermore, returning to and relying on the authentic culture of the society would allow the revival and rebirth of cultural independence in the face of western cultural onslaught;

(6) And finally, eliminate the spirit of imitation and obedience, which was the hallmark of the popular religion, and replace it with a critical revolutionary, aggressive spirit of independent reasoning (*ijtihād*). All of these may be accomplished through a religious reformist movement, which would extract and refine the enormous accumulation of energy in the society, enlighten the era, and awaken the present generation. It was for

---

43   Ibid.

the above reasons that Shariati, 'as a conscientious teacher who has risen from the depth of pains and experience of his people and history, hope that the enlightened person will reach a progressive self-awareness. For whereas our masses need self-awareness, our enlightened intellectuals are in need of "faith.""[44]

In the interview *Mission of a Free Thinker*, replying to the question of 'who must make us, ourselves or someone else,' Shariati responded that no one but ourselves could make us, similar to the way African freethinkers did. An African used to be denounced in France, thrown out of restaurants in the United States, and was not heeded as a human being in England. However, he had gained self-consciousness, even though some still did not know how to write. Once Shariati had come across a vendor in France. He was Muslim, and the verses of the Qur'ān he had memorized were the ones that were beneficial to his social struggle. The same thing was true about the personalities he knew and the history he had read. All these were giving him self-consciousness. He was so familiar with each country and was analyzing the world's problems to such a degree that he was stunned. Who had trained this man? Had he been trained by a UNESCO expert, a prophet, Sorbonne leftist professors, or himself?

The blackman of Shariati's time was the same man who was being despised in the 17th and 18th centuries in Paris. In the 15th and 16th centuries, they were stowed away in ships destined for America. They were bought at insignificant prices and sold at much higher prices in the United States and Australia. At the time, these slaves did not realize that they were despised, but they do now. However, the nature of the contempt, and the existence of contradiction by themselves, were not responsible factors for gaining consciousness. As long as man's volition has not discovered the contradiction, it will remain within a societal context for a thousand years. A blackman must feel the contempt in order to become a factor in awakening others.

> I must recognize and feel my enemy. But as long as I have not felt him, I go to him blindfolded, and even take pride in going close to him so he would not be my enemy anymore. The Iranian man who is proud of working under a European (who has destroyed his country and history), no longer has an enemy but a boss. And the boss does not create consciousness in the servant. An enemy is anti-thesis who can create consciousness but only if it is "realized" that such a contradiction exists. The free-thinker's and artist's functions are to remove the contradictions and discrepancies

---

44   Ibid.

that exist in the heart of a society and enter them into the feeling and consciousness of the society. As long as such contradictions exist in objectivity they will not cause any movement. In the twentieth century we still witness societies that live in feudalism; something that belongs to the second and third epochs of man's history. Or, there are still societies which have not entered the historical period; that is, they possess no clothing and no handwriting. Therefore, contradiction must enter subjectivity in order to cause movement. This is why poverty does not cause movement, it is the feeling of poverty that does.[45]

6

I conclude this essay attempting to answer the following question: despite some of the criticisms made of Shariati's thought, what can we learn from him? With this in mind, I make mine Dawud Reznik's words.[46]

Epistemologically, one must be aware of Shariati's critique of Cartesian dualism. He describes the Islamic worldview as fundamentally anti-dualist, since it is impossible for humans to access the unmediated realm of absolute Knowledge, which is only God's to behold. For Shariati, attempts at achieving epistemological objectivity, contingency-less truth, and factual purity are misguided and idolatrous. In particular, Shariati criticizes the western project of positivism as falsely proclaiming its ability to separate knowledge from its human context. He describes this deceit as a sinful skirting of social responsibility; science has been separated from the fabric of society, and as such, it has lost touch with people's thoughts. Not being able to criticize the present situation, it no longer helps solve life's problems. It no longer concerns itself with the fate of society and its ability to control its own destiny and achieve its ideals.

Shariati chastises the *mala,* or intellectuals, for aligning themselves with the *mutrif,* or exploiting classes, arguing that all science should actively affirm its human interests, rather than pretending to rise above them. Human knowledge should thus always be recognized as having been produced through human social relations. What separates Shariati's epistemological perspective from other critiques of Cartesian dualism made by the *Geisteswissenschaften* schools of pragmatism, phenomenology, and postmodernism, is his emphasis

---

45   Ali Shariati, *Mission of a free thinker.*
46   Robert Heck and Dawud Reznick, "The Islamic Thought of Ali Shariati and Sayyid Qutb," available at https://pt.scribd.com/document/28702122/The-Islamic-Thought-of-Ali-Shariati-and-Sayyid-Qutb.

on the inherent axiological quality of knowledge. He sees the inextricable link between subject and object as judgment. In this regard, he believes that humanity's defining feature is its ability to approach the world in terms of value, which consists of the link that exists between man and any phenomenon, behavior, act, or condition where a motive higher than that of utility is at issue; it might be called a sacred tie, as it is bound up with reverence and worship to the extent that people feel it justifiable to devote or sacrifice their very lives to this tie. What grants man, a non-material being, an *independence* from – as well as a *superiority* over – all other natural beings, is his high regard for value.

Shariati has thus introduced a new co-founding principle to the standard existentialist doctrine: it is an *ethical* existence that precedes essence. All human knowledge, including basic self-awareness, emerges from a fundamental position relative the universal values of Good and Evil, or as Shariati calls them the "infinitely exalted plus" and "infinitely vile minus."[47]

Using this epistemological framework, Shariati argues that all developments in knowledge, even the supposedly secular rationalism of the Enlightenment, represent a form of religion as an ethical proposition of faith: history knows no era or society, which lacks religion. That is, there is no historical precedence of a non-religious society. There has been no non-religious human being in any race, in any era, in any phase of social change on any part of the earth.

Since all human knowledge is intrinsically tied to the human knower, and all humans are religious, all knowledge is thereby necessarily religious. In short, Shariati views the history of thought as a struggle of religious concerns. Specifically, epistemological conflict through the ages has symbolized the struggle between the religion of legitimation (*shirk*/polytheism) and the religion of revolution (*tawḥīd*/monotheism). Multitheism is characterized by idolatry, beliefs in various forms of determinism and predetermination, and reactionary attempts to conserve the conditions of dualism and inequality that have pervaded human societies throughout history. Monotheism reflects the prophetic attempt to destroy all idols, abolish all social hierarchy, and thus construct the Kingdom of God on earth. Within this context, Shariati distinguishes between Good and Evil using "the transcendental dimension of human existence" as his defining criteria. The evil multitheists worship the idols of either the measurably physical (materialism) or the manifestly thinkable (idealism), without recognizing that neither is as virtuous as the supernatural and supra-logical spirit of God that can never be fully begotten; man's propensity for what actually

---

47   Ali Shariati, *On the Sociology of Islam*. Translated from the Persian by Hamid Algar. Berkeley: Mizan Press, 1979, 88–97.

exists degrades him. By pursuing values that do not exist in nature, he is lifted above nature, and the spiritual and essential development of the species is secured. In other words, Good knowledge emerges from love of existence as a dynamic movement oriented towards the future, rather than servitude to the idols of the present-past.[48]

To summarize, Shariati's epistemology posits that all knowledge is inherently value-laden relative to the universal ethics of Good and Evil which join existence in preceding essence. All knowledge must therefore be situated within the historical struggle between the religions of legitimation and revolution. Shariati thus advances an axiological epistemology that collapses Cartesian dualism without affirming a subjectivist, "anything-goes" ethical relativism.

Methodologically, and consistent with the axiological anti-dualism of his epistemology, Shariati prescribes a methodology of critical hermeneutics. Because only God has universal knowledge of cause and effect, any attempts at unearthing an absolute semiotics is futile and impossible. Instead, Shariati argues that the only appropriate model for advancing human knowledge is the continuous interpretation of facts relative to their social construction and religious politics. Broken down into its constituent parts, Shariati's hermeneutical method involves 'objection, criticism, and the inner choice or selection of the individual.'[49]

This process of negative dialectics emerges from the idol-destroying tradition in Islamic monotheism; one must seek out and supersede the fundamental contradictions of human thought, since only God's thought is complete, infinite, and limitless. The first part of Shariati's method calls for objecting to any human knowledge that claims to be universal and free from interpretation: 'the necessity of the religion of monotheism is rebellion, denial, and saying 'no' before any other power.'[50]

The point here is that Godly knowledge cannot be humanly beholden, and so any human attempts to build Godly knowledge must be resolutely rejected as the construction of a temple of idolatry. In Shariati's words, 'How disgraceful ... are all fixed standards. Who can ever fix a standard?'[51]

---

48 For further details on Shariati's conception of monotheism and multitheism, please refer to his "The World-View of Tauhid" in *On the Sociology of Islam* (Berkeley: Mizan Press, 1979), 82–87, and particularly to his lectures which were published in *Religion vs. Religion*. Translated from the Persian by Laleh Bakhtiar and foreword by Andrew Burgess. Albuquerque: Abjad, [1988], 47.

49 Ali Shariati, *Religion vs. Religion*, 52.

50 Ibid., 39.

51 Ali Shariati, *On the Sociology of Islam*, 94.

Following the objection to supposedly pure knowledge, human agency must be recognized as the basis for the production of all human knowledge. Hence, Shariati advocates a line of interpretive criticism that traces the construction of knowledge back to the human presence and power relations. He calls on all monotheists to recognize that 'the course ... [a multitheist] has chosen for our humiliation is the best guide for us to choose as the way to our glory: Returning from the same way that he has led us.'[52]

The negation of God, which the multitheist has promoted through an idolatrous claim to value-freedom, must thus be itself negated. Criticism can only be accomplished by discovering the contradictions and limits of the knowledge in question, particularly with reference to its axiological quality; fixed and motionless forms that have become crystallized into ineffective "sacred" institutions should be transformed into moving and active elements, with a clearly defined role in the existential movement of society.

This process, of recognizing the qualitative aspects of knowledge, allows for a nuanced understanding of the history of any knowledge. In particular, Shariati urges the situating of knowledge relative to the political struggle between multitheists and monotheists. These combined efforts of both objection and criticism ultimately result in a religiously vital democratization of knowledge, as persons can only begin to make informed decisions about faith when idols have been destroyed. Citing the example of the Prophet and his companions, Shariati encourages all to become conscious self-aware *mujahideen*.

Shariati asserts true belief in God can only be actualized through this process, which comes as a result of critically interpreting all knowledge: Correct thought is the prelude to correct knowledge, and correct knowledge is the prelude to belief. These three taken together are the necessary attributes of an aware conscience and of any movement that strives in practice and theory for the attainment of perfection. When knowledge has been negated, critiqued, and situated relative its axiological-religious roots, the enlightened individual can perform his/her prophetic-like duty of shining the light of revelation on others so they too can begin to 'discern things as they really are.'[53]

In short, Shariati's negative dialectical method of critical hermeneutics flips the mainstream scientific methodology of positive knowledge creation on its head. Instead of converting human experience into empirical data in order to abstract supposedly objective facts, critical interpretation grounds all knowledge into its existential constitution: the historical politics of personal ethics, value, and religion. Representing a truly democratic understanding of religious

---

52   Ali Shariati, *Hajj: Reflections on its Rituals*. (Chicago: Kazi Publications, 1992), 34.

53   Shariati, *Religion vs. Religion*, 12.

faith, Shariati's method calls for criticism of all knowledge in order to attain consciousness of its limitations and ethical implications. Only then can the individual make the 'dutiful and aggressive passage'[54] to monotheistic faith.

Finally, in what refers to social ontology, Shariati's imagery for social order is perhaps the most important element of his liberation theology. Much of his writings are dedicated to detailing the subtle nuances of *tawḥīd*, or the Islamic concept for the absolute unity of God, as a social ontology. This metaphor allows for the indivisibility of humanity without the imposition of abstract structural mechanisms or systemic metaphors, since all humans are understood to be God's creation. As with his discussions of epistemology and methodology, Shariati describes *tawḥīd* first by contrasting it from its opposite, *shirk*, or the legitimation of social inequality based on multitheistic beliefs and idolatry. *Shirk* rears its ugly head in both realism and nominalism, the traditional social ontologies of western mainstream thought. Realists conceive of society as a structural whole requiring the assimilation and integration of its individual parts according to an abstract, mechanistic logic that is supposedly divorced from human agency.

This imagery of society, as an autonomous system *sui generis,* has historically been used by social theorists as a way to control what they perceive to be the innate chaos and disorder of individuals if left to their "human nature." Employing his critical hermeneutical method, Shariati rebukes realist social imagery. He points out the political interests of multitheism as the axiological underpinnings of realist ontologies that legitimate an assimilatory social order; it is multitheism which continuously denies social power, social control, the responsibility of human beings in their fate, their expectations and the physical, spiritual, and instinctive needs of individuals, all to the advantage of the coercive and wealthy forces.

Hence, Shariati highlights the power interests involved in the western realist tradition, including the neo-liberal ideal of the capitalist market as a supposedly neutral arbiter of social life. Nominalism, on the other hand, posits that only the individual is existentially real, and thus social ties are simply utilitarian means for achieving self-centered, egocentric ends. This social Darwinist image of society legitimates a survival of the fittest scenario, whereby individuals compete for a scarce quantity of resources to survive. Shariati shrewdly points out that the same multitheist interests involved in realism are at play in promoting nominalism. In his eyes, individualistic social imagery is used as a means to divide-and-conquer the masses and reinforce the inequalities in society produced by *shirk*; it is also multitheism which opens

---

54   Shariati, *Hajj: Reflections on its Rituals*, 207.

separate metaphysical accounts for each of its members so that, through this means, the assembling of people would be transformed into dispersion and isolation.

His point here is that a religion of revolution is thoroughly undermined when the masses are viewed as self-interested monads competing for individual salvation. Shariati also identifies the undemocratic nature of realist conceptions of history, which are supposedly driven spontaneously or by elites. This contradicts the model set forth in the Qur'ān, which posits that al-nas, or "the masses," are actually the ones behind historical change. Thus, according to Shariati, the religion of legitimation offers two contradictory images of social order to keep persons from recognizing their inherent equality as common creations from God: society as a structural whole constraining its individual parts and society as an aggregation of autonomous, sovereign atoms. Both of these social ontologies are used by those who profit from an alienated, fragmented, and unequal society to keep the masses from recognizing their common existential ancestry in God and consequently effecting revolution. In opposition to the realist and nominalist metaphors of shirk, Shariati defines tawḥīd as simply 'the unity of nature with metanature, of man with nature, of man with man, of God with the world and with man.'[55]

Shariati describes the personage of society as the "Household of God," a metaphor that asserts the existential equality of all humanity as the common product of the divine realm of creation. Tawḥīd also mandates the liberating framework of praxis, or the unity and simultaneity of thought and action. Shariati again cites the example of the Prophet and his companions, who did not 'divide up life into two sections, the first consisting exclusively of talk and the second, exclusively of action.'[56]

With tawḥīd, social order is presupposed between persons without having to resort to the assimilatory ideals, contractual obligations, or other structural props of realist social imagery. In other words, humans need not belittle or deny themselves to fit into an autonomous social totality. Instead, as Shariati points out, the relation of God and man is one of reciprocity, where self-knowledge and knowledge of God come to be synonymous, or, alternatively, where the former functions as a preliminary to the latter. Hence, in tawḥīd, true actualization of one's individuality reinforces the inherent sociality of human existence and the essential unity-in-diversity of God's creation. At the

---

55   For further details on Shariati's conception of the masses (al-nas), please refer to his "The Philosophy of History: Cain and Abel," and, especially, "The Dialectic of Sociology" in On the Sociology of Islam (Berkeley: Mizan Press, 1979).

56   Ibid., 41.

same time, however, Shariati describes the individual in *tawḥīd* as fundamentally different from the nominalist notion of atomistic, zero-sum sovereignty.
In *tawḥīd*, the individual can only recognize his/her uniqueness relative to
another, which means having to always view oneself in reference to the totality of God's creation. In this manner, Shariati argues that to the extent that the
man of *tawḥīd* perceives his poverty, he perceives his wealth; to the extent that
he feels humility, he feels a pride, a glory, within himself; to the extent that
he has surrendered to the service of God, he rises against whatever powers,
systems, and relations exist.[57]

The point here is that by resisting the zero-sum logic preached by a society
of *shirk*, an individual remains true to the virtues of God's creation and realizes
tawḥīd. Shariati lays out a social ontology that manages to collapse dualism
while reaffirming individuality. He refutes the idolatry of worshipping abstract
schemes like realist assimilation or nominalist individualism. Instead, persons
in society are essentially tied together through their common creator and can
therefore feel secure in actualizing their uniqueness and individuality as a
mutual recognition of *tawḥīd*.

For Shariati, a hyper-emphasis on the purity of practice in Islam mirrors
the problems of the secular movement of western positivist science in its
standardization, formalism, and technical rigor. Relating this attitude to the
"five pillars" of Islam, Shariati offers a fundamental break with tradition. For
instance, although he does not critique the rituals that accompany *ṣalāt*,
Shariati expands and re-conceptualizes it; since worship, when conscious and
heartfelt, becomes a manifestation of all absolute sacred values, the worship-
per nourishes these values in a relative human mode in his own being. The
practice of prayer thus becomes less a matter of technique and more an issue
of the destruction of idols through one's actions. In this manner, prayer can
be as varied in its formal manifestations as the historical circumstances and
multitheistic idols that Muslims face, since 'whether you consider yourself
responsible to the people or to God, in practice, our work is the same, our responsibility, the same.'[58]

Shariati recognizes that *zakāt*, the outlawing of *ribā*, and other traditional
forms of wealth redistribution in Islam, no matter how efficient or progressive, will not be able to resolve the systemic inequalities and class hegemony
produced by capitalist modes of economic relations. Thus Shariati actively

---

57   Ali Shariati, "Mysticism, Equality, and Freedom" in *Marxism and other Western Fal-
      lacies: an Islamic Critique*. Translated by R. Campbell. N.p.: Islamic Foundation Press,
      n.d., 76.

58   Shariati, *Hajj: Reflections on its Rituals*, 34.

promotes the abolishment of private property as a necessary part of Islamic faith, proclaiming that 'true Islam is true socialism.'[59]

He refutes the notions of "God's property" that is currently used to legitimate an Islamic variant of capitalism: "wealth belongs to God" and God has given it (in trust) to the people ... [Property] is not the property of special individuals. Rather, it is property that belongs to the people. God is the owner of property, that is, the owner of the property is the people because the people and God are in one front as 'people are of the family of God.'[60] It is clear that the guardian of the family is in the same front as his own family.[61] Here Shariati invalidates arguments for a narrowly defined Islamic economic system that perpetuates private property relations given his belief in the *tawḥīd* of Allah that should manifest in the indivisibility of humanity and its economic resources.

Through making a sort of "post-modern turn," Shariati does not have to reject principles of social justice for fear of not conforming to the mandates of history. Indeed, for Shariati, the struggle between *shirk* and *tawḥīd* is a historical one, and therefore he seeks the dialectical "way out" of the contemporary situation of sin. Without rejecting or undermining Islamic identity and/or practice, Shariati asserts a new type of Islam that is centered on the obligation not to worship idols. As he so brilliantly illustrates, true monotheism is always already a paradoxical solution to the ever-worsening existential crisis of humanity, since only through the complete surrendering to the irrational and unknown can humanity hope to transcend the labyrinth of multitheism in which it has lost itself. For Shariati, the moment of pure *tawḥīd* in Islam is yet to be found, for it has no precedent in the past or manifestation in the present; it can only therefore be realized in the future.

As Shariati argued in *Mission of a Free Thinker*, one should not think of a particular source which gives us awareness. For instance, an untrue story about the seventh century would provide him with awareness since he would look for the context, the persons, and the purpose for which the story was written. The point is when one has a methodology at hand, a lie will help him to recognize specific periods in the past. In order to accomplish this, one must have a specific outlook, and look for particular things in history as well as look at history from a specific angle. We can, then, use a piece of information to find the necessary ingredients for building our present cultural foundations and awareness, as well as familiarize ourselves with the conditions of our today as well as our tomorrow. Those individuals who have been successful in Africa

---

59   Shariati, *Religion vs. Religion*, 6.
60   Ibid., 47.
61   Ibid.

and Asia have been the ones that have been able to teach European philosophies *and forget them*. They were able to get to know their societies, find and propose new solutions, based upon their existing cultural, historical, and social resources, and create a new foundation.

The Europeans/westerners used to believe in their own superiority, and had created a type of thinking atmosphere, called "egocentrism," which was self-centeredness. An egocentric individual does not count others as human beings. Even humanists, anthropologists, and socialists were caught in the snare of egocentrism. Human relations to them were limited to the relations among their own classes. They did not discuss universal relations. Shariati could never forget that in the 19th century the great socialists, humanists, and upholders of democracy and equality talked about everything (they even meticulously analyzed the minute relationships between the worker and the employer), but never mentioned exploitation.

In human and social problems, we must not apply strict scientific methodology. For instance, when dealing with a scientific issue, we concentrate upon its validity or invalidity. However, in social problems we must not pay attention to the logic of the statement, rather, we must focus on the *geography* of the issue. The easterners were the victims of the same talks that bestowed life upon the West. Thus, it is obvious that apart from the truth, falsity, logicality, and illogicality of a social issue, one must take into consideration the geography of an issue. We must not concentrate on mere "talks and words," rather, we must evaluate the "talker" first.

Bibliography

Ahmad, Jalal al-i. *Occidentosis: A Plague from the West*. Translated by Robert Campbell. Annotations and Introduction by Hamid Algar. Berkeley: Mizan Press, 1984.

Andrade, Tonio. "Beyond Guns, Germs, and Steel: European Expansion and Maritime Asia, 1400–1750" *Journal of Early Modern History* 14 (2010), pp. 165–186.

Armstrong, Julie Buckner. *Mary Turner and the Memory of Lynching*. Athens: University of Georgia Press, 2011.

Asad, Talal (Ed.). *Anthropology and the Colonial Encounter*. London: Ithaca Press, 1973.

Aydin, Cemil. *The Politics of Anti-Westernism in Asia: Visions of World Order in Pan-Islamic and Pan-Asian thought* (New York: Columbia University Press, 2007).

Bailey, Amy Kate and Stewart E. Tolnay. *Lynched: The Victims of Southern Mob Violence*. Chapel Hill: University of North Carolina Press, 2015.

Chen, Li. *Chinese Law in Imperial Eyes: Sovereignty, Justice, and Transcultural Politics*. New York: Columbia University Press, 2015.

de Certeau, Michel. *The Writing of History*. New York: Columbia University Press, 1992.

Dance, E.H. *History the Betrayer: a Study in Bias*. London: Hutchinson, 1960.

Daniel, Norman. *Islam and the West: The Making of an Image*. Edinburgh: The University Press, 1960.

Daniel, Norman. *Islam, Europe and Empire*. Edinburgh: Edinburgh University Publications, 1966.

Fanon, Frantz. *Les Damnés de la Terre*. Paris: François Maspéro, 1961.

Goody, Jack. *The Theft of History*. Cambridge: Cambridge University Press, 2006.

Greenhalgh, Michael. *The Military and Colonial Destruction of the Roman Landscape of North Africa, 1830–1900*. Leiden: Brill, 2014.

Grosrichard, Alain. *Structure du sérail: la fiction du despotisme asiatique dans l'Occident classique*. Paris: Seuil, 1979.

Hardt, Michael and Antonio Negri. *Empire*. Cambridge, MA: Harvard University Press, 2000.

Heck, Robert and Dawud Reznick. "The Islamic Thought of Ali Shariati and Sayyid Qutb," available at https://pt.scribd.com/document/28702122/The-Islamic-Thought-of-Ali -Shariati-and-Sayyid-Qutb.

Hobbs, Tameka B. *Democracy Abroad, Lynching at Home: Racial Violence in Florida*. Gainseville: University Press of Florida, 2015.

Jung, Carl Gustav. *Memories, Dreams, Reflections*. London: Fontana Press, 1995.

Jung, Carl Gustav. *The Undiscovered Self*. New York: Signet, 2006.

Leclerc, Gérard. *Anthropologie et colonialisme: essai sur l'histoire de l'africanisme*. Paris: Fayard, 1972.

Moreh, Shmuel (Trans.). *Napoleon in Egypt: Al-Jabarti's Chronicle of the French Occupation, 1798*. Princeton: Markus Wiener Publishers, 1993.

Prakash, Gyan. "Orientalism Now," *History and Theory*, Vol. 34, No. 3 (Oct., 1995), pp. 199–212.

Said, Edward W. *Orientalism*. New York: Vinatge, 1979.

Said, Edward W. *Power, Politics and Culture: Interviews with Edward W. Said* London: Bloomsbury, 2005.

Salama, Mohammad R. *Islam, Orientalism and Intellectual History*. London: I.B. Tauris, 2011.

Shariati, Ali. *Hajj. Reflections on its Rituals*. Chicago: Kazi Publications, 1992.

Shariati, Ali. *Marxism and other Western Fallacies: an Islamic Critique*. Translated by R. Campbell. N.p.: Islamic Foundation Press, n.d.

Shariati, Ali. *On the Sociology of Islam*. Translated by Hamid Algar Berkeley: Mizan Press, 1979.

Shariati, Ali. *Religion vs. Religion*. Translated by Laleh Bakhtiar Albuquerque: Abjad, [1988?].

Shariati, Ali. *Extraction and Refinement of Cultural Resources.* Available at http://www
.shariati.com/english/culture.html.

Shariati, Ali. *Mission of a free thinker.* Available at http://www.shariati.com/english
/mission/mission1.html.

Shariati, Ali. *Reflections of Humanity.* Available at http://www.iranchamber.com
/personalities/ashariati/works/reflections_of_humanity.php.

Shariati, Ali. *Where shall we begin?* Available at http://www.shariati.com/english
/begin/begin7.html.

Schmit, David T. "The Mesmerists inquire about 'Oriental Mind Powers': West meets
East in the search for the Universal Trance," *Journal of the History of the Behavioral
Sciences,* Vol. 46, 1 (Winter 2010), pp. 1–26.

Thomas, Nicholaus. *Colonialism's Culture: Anthropology, Travel, and Government*
Princeton, NJ: Princeton University Press, 1994.

Vidrovitch, Catherine Coquery. *Enjeux politiques de l'histoire colonial.* Marseille: Agone,
2009.

Yale, Elizabeth. *AP Course Controversy: When Do We Say "We" in History?* available at
http://religionandpolitics.org/2015/03/10/ap-course-controversy-when-do-we-say
-we-in-history/.

CHAPTER 4

Spokesmen of Intellectual Decolonization: Shariati in Dialogue with Alatas

Esmaeil Zeiny

... colonialism is not simply content to impose its rule upon the present and the future of a dominated country. Colonialism is not satisfied merely with holding a people in its grip and emptying the native's brain of all form and content. By a kind of perverse logic, it turns to the past of the oppressed people, and distorts it, disfigures and destroys it.[1]

∴

Introduction

As one of the momentous historical events of the 20th century, the decolonization of Africa and Asia altered the world entirely. In the immediate decades following World War II, between 1945 and 1965, more than three dozen states gained autonomy and independence in both Asia and Africa. However, the process of decolonization was dissimilar in different regions; in some areas, decolonization took place peacefully and orderly, whereas in some other areas it was achieved after a protracted revolution and war between the natives and the colonizers. For instance, in 1946, France retreated from Syria and Lebanon after several ruinous encounters with the locals. In the Southern part of Asia, India gained its autonomy in 1947 after a series of social movements led by Mahatma Gandhi. In fact, Britain's decision to grant independence to India arose primarily out of essentiality, not to mention that Gandhi's successful method of non-violent resistance, such as civil disobedience, had also played an important role in changing the perceptions of colonial powers. In West Asia, the British pulled back from Palestine in 1948 but left behind the new state of Israel with a larger portion of Palestine. Within two decades after World War II, almost all European colonies in Africa became thoroughly independent. In countries

---

1 Fanon, Franz. *The Wretched of the Earth.* (Harmondsworth, Middlesex, England: Penguin Books Ltd., 1974), 170.

such as Nigeria, with only a few white residents, decolonization was carried out in a way similar to India. Reforms were made in the constitution and the Nigerians were given seats in the administration, and then the parliamentary election followed suit, resulting in an independent Nigeria in 1960. In other countries like Kenya, with more white settlers, decolonization did not occur rapidly, as the colonizers and the colonized had engaged in confrontation that ultimately led to the independence in 1963.

Without a doubt, the aftermath of World War II had a dramatic impact upon the formation and strengthening of nationalist movements in both Asia and Africa. Moreover, it solidified a worldwide sentiment against colonialism that coerced the imperial powers to begin to look for proper exit strategies. Melvin Goldberg confirms this sentiment and argues that it was 'only after the war did the powers begin to take decolonization seriously, and even then the speed at which it proceeded was neither anticipated nor welcomed in many quarters.'[2] Therefore, it goes without saying that what helped decolonization to gain momentum was the nationalist and the global disposition, but has decolonization been really complete? The former empires of Europe seemingly disintegrated in 1950's and 1960's but still maintained their presence in some of their old colonies, joined now by the United States, for the purpose of controlling the production of oil and other interests. For instance, in Iraq, the Anglo-American companies had an exclusive monopoly on the oil sectors until nationalization in 1972. Even then, decolonization was not complete and has been still in process. The colonizers ostensibly left their colonies, but have made a sad comeback with the soft weapons of neo-colonialism manifested through cultural control. Out of cultural control emerged the discourse of "modernity," which was taken as the extreme opposite of "tradition" by some intellectuals of the colonized nations. The dramatic impact of 'cultural colonization' translated itself through the belief amongst the elites that the colonized would not survive if they did not adopt modernity in their societies. At the other end of the spectrum, traditionalism emerged and encouraged returning to tradition to discard the West. On the complexity of interaction between "tradition" and "modernity" in the colonized nations in West Asia, historian Albert Hourani writes,

It would be better ... to see the history of this period as that of a complex interaction: of the will of ancient and stable societies to reconstitute themselves, preserving what they had of their own while making the necessary changes in order to survive in the modern world increasingly

---

2   M. Goldberg, "Decolonization and political socialization with reference to West Africa." *The Journal of Modern African Studies*, 24 (4) (1986): 666–667.

organized on other principles, and where the centers of world power have lain for long, and still lie, outside the Middle East.[3]

Decolonization, indeed, has been a very complex process. What raised many eyebrows about Westernism applies *mutatis mutandis* to traditionalism. In both of these groups, there was a conspicuous dearth of creativity and originality. Quite obviously, the dichotomy between "tradition" and "modernity" was overstated as old and new, or "tradition" and "modernity" were not always antithetical and certainly cultures never remain static. As opposed to the two ends of an intellectual pole, this chapter explores a "third way" in the process of decolonization by drawing upon two Muslim intellectuals, termed here as "spokesmen of intellectual decolonization": Ali Shariati from Iran and Syed Hussein Alatas from Malaysia. Before delving into the "third way" of decolonization, this chapter first reviews the issue of modernity and the intellectuals' take on it in the context of Iran. Unlike many developing countries, Iran has never been colonized but was briefly occupied by the Russians and the British before and during World War I. Despite this, it maintained its autonomy throughout history. However, like many other non-Western states, the Iranian culture has experienced close contact with western civilization. Both Shariati and Alatas are against consuming the intellectual packages imported from the West wholeheartedly, and they suggest an intellectual abandonment of western modernity through their concepts of "homeless intellectual" and "captive mind." Utilizing Shariati's take in returning to one's authentic roots and Alatas' anti-captive-mind standpoint, I argue that these two concepts work in tandem to achieve an ideal intellectual decolonization. Anchored within such discourse, this chapter examines how successful these thoughts were in challenging the naturalized assumptions of the western self-fashioned narrative of "modernity."

Modernity and Its Discontent

Before explaining the process of modernity in Iran, a definition of "modernization" is in order. As a value-neutral and a multi-dimensional concept, modernization, inherently, is neither "good" nor "bad," but change is a *sine qua non* of the modernization process, which brings with it constructive and/or destructive effects.[4] In this fashion, modernization is not a unitary, static and

---

3 Albert Hourani, Phillip Khoury, and Mary Wilson, *The Modern Middle East.* (New York: I.B. Tauris, 2004), 4.

4 D.A. Chekki, *Modernization and Kin Network.*

homogeneous concept, and as a result does not have the same impact wherever it occurs. In other words, it is almost next to impossible for modernization to take place in the same way twice, as timing, sequence and cultural milieus differ strikingly. The changes in Africa, as the result of the modernization process, could be of an essentially dissimilar character and have very different results from those changes that occurred in Asia. It is noteworthy to mention that there is a delicate distinction between "modernization" and "modernity." 'Many attributes of modernization, like widespread literacy or modern medicine, have appeared, or have been adopted, in isolation from other attributes of a modern society. Hence, modernization in some spheres of life may occur without resulting in "modernity."'[5] Moreover, modernity is a state of mind – expectation of progress, inclination to growth, willingness to accustom oneself to change.[6] Modernization here refers to a kind of social change that emanated in the industrial revolution of England between the years 1760–1830, and the French political revolution in 1789–1794. A distinction ought to be made between individual and societal modernization as well. Individual modernity and societal modernity are two different social phenomena; the former does not necessarily correspond with the latter, and conversely, the latter does not correlate with the former. A modern individual is not indicative of a modern society and a modern society does not necessarily mean that all the individuals living in the society are modern.[7] Modernization in the present study refers to societal modernization in the context of Iran, although in some occasions reforms were implemented to modernize individuals.

Iran's encounter with modern ideas and institutions dates back to the mid-nineteenth century but its early ties with modern Europe can be traced back to the sixteenth century, at the time of Shah Abbas, when Persia entered the community of nations. Yet Iran's lettered strata were not affected by the European intellectual revolution between 1600 and 1800. Boroujerdi argues that the West was considered 'less as a philosophical threat and more as an exotic cultural edifice worthy of voyeuristic gaze' for the elite sect of Persia during the seventeenth- and eighteenth-century.[8] However, this sentiment

---

5 Reinhard Bendix, "Tradition and Modernity Reconsidered," in *Essays in Comparative Social Stratification*, ed. Leonard Plotnicov and Arthur Tuden. (Pittsburgh: University of Pittsburgh, 1970), 311.

6 Daniel Lerner, *The Passing of Traditional Society: Modernizing the Middle East.* (New York: Free Press of Glencoe, 1964) iix.

7 Chekki, *Modernization.*

8 Mehrzad Boroujerdi, "The Ambivalent Modernity of Iranian Intellectuals," in *Intellectual Trends in Twentieth-Century Iran: A Critical Survey*, ed. Negin Nabavai. (Gainesville, FL, University Press of Florida: 2003), 12.

changed in the early nineteenth century with the interventions of Russia and Britain on the one hand, and western interference and exploits on the other. At that point, the West was no longer a vague entity, but rather turned into a real political foe; it became a cultural adversary and ideological threat for Persians, to the extent that even the king of Qajar, Nāṣer al-Dīn Shāh, expressed his disapproval of European presence in Persia, saying, 'I wish that never a European had set foot on my country's soil; for then we would have been spared all these tribulations' he continued, 'but since the foreigners have unfortunately penetrated into our country, we shall at least make the best possible use of them'[9] Later in the Pahlavi's era, the state-sponsored modernization during the 1960's and 1970's impacted the economic relations, social institutions and cultural patterns of the country.

Modernization programs, such as land reform, modified the existing structure of rural Iran and left the peasants with no choice but to migrate to urban areas and seek their fortunes in the cities as the hope to take their land back was crushed when the government seized the ownership of the land.[10] As the result, a major exodus of the rural populace to the urban centers occurred. The urban way of life was also profoundly transfigured by the reforms of those years and the traditional social structures had experienced serious tension as an aftereffect of the Pahlavi's modernization programs.[11] The reforms were enacted to transmute Iran from a poor traditional society and a decentralized state system into a centralized and industrialized country.[12] The motivation to industrialize Iran so rapidly after the Second World War arose in part due to Reza Shah's foreign policy objectives. The Shah desired to turn Iran into a world power by preventing the foreign powers from occupying Iran militarily (as it had happened during the two world wars), and by inserting some modifications in the everyday life structures and modernizing the country in a western manner. To expedite his aims, the Shah opted to institutionalize massive and dramatic industrialization projects in lieu of more practical ones that would help the traditional people. Western techniques and practices were so hurriedly accepted that the scarcity in skilled and semi-skilled laborers was overlooked. However, these reforms were not introduced in the political power structure and they, in fact, somehow helped the state have a more structured autocratic powerful government.

---

9   Quoted in Haas, William S, *Iran*. (New York: AMS Press, 1966), 35.
10   Robert E. Looney, *Economic Origins of the Iranian Revolution*. (Toronto: Pergamon Press, 1982), 47–48.
11   Ali Mirsepassi, *Intellectual Discourse and politics of modernization: Negotiating Modernity in Iran*. New York: Cambridge University Press, 2004.
12   Amin Saikal, *The Rise and Fall of the Shah*. Princeton, Princeton University Press, 1980.

The country owed its rapid industrializations to the oil production revenue that was a source of income for the Shah and made him independent of popular taxation. Consequently, the grass roots were excluded from influencing development, and they were denied any meaningful political status. The economic, social and cultural relations of the country were rapidly changing without participation of the people troubled by these transformations. It was not only the ordinary people who could not have a say, but the oppositional intellectuals were strictly controlled, they could not be allowed to exert influence over the direction of the modernization process; thus, people were largely alienated from the process. The concept of modernization as used in this study is synonymous with the concept of 'westernization' because the sources for change came from western countries. Following the westernization programs, the Pahlavi state made a great effort in breaching the society from tradition while failing to offer the people any institutions to voice their grievances. Therefore, modernization in this respect "occurred without resulting in 'modernity'"; this can challenge the assumption that modernization has systemic qualities.[13] Contrary to this view, the different components in the modernization process are historically distinct and therefore a progress along one line does not necessarily suggest a progress along another. While applying those reforms, the Pahlavi regime neglected to accommodate those social and economic changes in the context of Iranian cultural and historical experiences. The fast modernization policies established by the Pahlavi dynasty in Iran caused dissatisfaction amongst the popular and traditional forces. This progress, and the displacement associated with it, along with the lack of institutions and organizations for public interest articulation, led to a mentality of resistance and even enmity towards modernization and/or westernization.

Iranian Intellectuals at the Crossroad

The intellectual activity in Iran over the past two centuries deserves a pause for reflection. The 19th–20th century in Iran witnessed a tormented intellectual life. Indeed, this tormented intellectual life came from the clash between two sources of influence for intellectuals: The West and Islam. The older generation of intellectuals had mostly a clerical background and frequented the religious centers in both Iran and Iraq to study Islam. Later, during the modernization period, the trend had changed and many traveled to Europe to further their studies. These two groups of intellectuals gave birth to two different stands. For some, the West became the paragon of virtue and progress, whereas for others

---

13   Bendix, "Tradition and Modernity Reconsidered," 311.

it was a symbol of colonialism/imperialism, remaining highly critical of the West. Boroujerdi (1996) argues these intellectuals were not just observers of changes within the society; rather they were participants in the cultural transformation of the country as well. Undoubtedly, the intellectuals had served as 'crucial intermediaries and interpreters between their own culture and that of the West'[14] Their active and dynamic contribution in the evolution of Iranian identity cannot not be neglected, as their interpretation of the Iranian past and present, and that of the West, have greatly shaped and impacted the Iranians' attitude towards issues such as 'nationalism' and 'modernity.'

Before going any further with the intellectual activity in Iran, the question raised here is who is an intellectual? Sreberny and Khiabany (2008) argue that the growing number of individuals ranging from feminists to leftists, who are involved in recreating a public space of debate, can be considered intellectuals. This definition conjures up what Lerner (1964) observed as the overproduction of intellectuals in Iran during the 1950's. In a lecture entitled "Representation of Intellectual," Edward Said believes the intellectual is an,

> individual endowed with a faculty for representing, embodying, articu
> lating a message, a view, an attitude, philosophy or opinion to, as well as
> for, a public. And this role has an edge to it, and cannot be played without
> a sense of being someone whose place it is publicly to raise embarrass
> ing questions, to confront orthodoxy and dogma (rather than to produce
> them), to be someone who cannot easily be co-opted by governments or
> corporations and whose raison d'être is to represent all those people and
> issues that are routinely forgotten or swept under the rug.[15]

The task of intellectuals is therefore to recognize the vital position that they can adopt as a public awakening force in a society against the outsider plundering forces. As it has been mentioned earlier, societies' mentality towards modernity (westernization) and nationalism were hugely influenced by the intellectuals. As Shils states, 'the gestation, birth, and continuing life of the new states of Asia and Africa, through all their vicissitudes, are in large measure the work of intellectuals'[16] To articulate it simply, it is not feasible to study and analyze the trajectory of modernization, nationalism, and secularization

---

14   Mehrzad Boroujerdi, "Contesting Nationalist Constructions of Iranian Identity," *Critical studies of the Middle East*, 26 (12) (1998): 21.

15   Edward Said, *Representations of the Intellectual.* (New York: Pantheon Books, 1994), 11.

16   Edward Shils, "The intellectuals in the political development of the New States" in *Political Change in Underdeveloped Countries: Nationalism and Communism,* ed. John Kautsky. (New York: John Wiley and Sons, 1963), 195.

in under-developed countries such as Iran without considering the social importance of the intelligentsia. As bearers of such concepts as historical consciousness, modernism, nationalism, and culture, these intellectuals should
have bridged the gap created by the process of modernization/westernization
and diminished the concomitant alienation. As instigators of ideas, they were
expected to negotiate with the effective modernity while concurrently "holding the West at bay" in a political sense of the term. Instead, those intellectuals who embraced modernity and adopted its extensive vocabulary believed
that the wholesale adoption of the Western civilization was the only single
way to progress. On the other hand, the oppositional intellectuals had every
reason to oppose the Pahlavi regime, as in an age of 'republicanism, radicalism and nationalism, the Pahlavis appeared in the eyes of the intelligentsia to
favor monarchism, conservatism, and Western imperialism.'[17] This period of
"nothingness," "fatigue," "loneliness," and "darkness" compelled the progressive
intellectuals to develop a critical attitude towards modernity; they resorted
to nativism or local answers to decolonize the country completely. This par-
adigm-shift to native culture had manifested itself differently; some had embraced the pre-Islamic Iranian heritage like Mehdi Akhavan Sales, and many
others romanticized the rural life to express their disapproval of the discourse
of modernity.[18] Blindingly following the tradition or imitating the West made
intellectuals like Shariati and Alatas think of a "third way" in decolonizing the
Muslim societies.

Intellectual Decolonization

That many scholars have studied the discourse about modernity in Islamic
societies is suggestive of the significance of the question in Iran and other
Muslim countries. In fact, since the 19th century encounter with European colonialism, the question of modernity has been the most significant issue in
many Islamic countries, both at the theoretical and practical level. All through
the 19th and 20th centuries, and even today, the tension between modernity and the Islamic tradition has been one of the key features of the primary
social, political, philosophical, and cultural debates in the Muslim societies.
Modernists often highlight the lack of progress in Islamic countries, attribute
it to the absence of modernity and are in favor of extreme changes in accordance with current western self-fashioned narratives of modernity. This group
of western-oriented and western-educated elites called for the modernization

---

17   Ervand Abrahamian, *Radical Islam: The Iranian Mojahedin*. (London: I.B. Tauris, 1989), 17.

18   Mirsepassi, *Intellectual Discourse*.

of their country through westernization and top-down secularization. Contrarily, traditionalists often regarded the servility of Muslim societies to western colonialism and imperialism as a repercussion of neglecting the Islamic heritage and traditional culture, and called for circumventing modernity and embracing Islam's cultural and religious traditions. Aiming for an alternative to both extremes of modernism and traditionalism, another group of intellectual came up with a new perspective of transformation for Muslim nations through an amalgamation of local religious/cultural traditions and western norms and institutions. Hegemonic modernism and essentialist culturalism have been severely criticized by this group and consequently they have negotiated a third way between the total acceptance and the total rejection of modernity.

As opposed to the dichotomous forces of modernism and traditionalism, these intellectuals have been seeking to develop a concurrent critique of modernity and local/traditional culture and have been trying to elevate strategies for successfully being-in-the-(modern)-world and preserving the tradition as well. Shariati and Alatas are two of the intellectuals who opted for a third way. They could be considered the earliest postcolonial thinkers who paid a great deal of attention to cultural and academic issues in the confrontation between the imperial West and the responses from the East. The concern of these two intellectuals, in light of which their works as a whole can be understood, is liberation from a condition of cultural, economic, political and academic oppression. Although Shariati's primary frame of reference is Iran and Alatas' is Malaysia, both of them develop ideas within the tradition of Islamic thought, and since both of them situate their countries in a broader spectrum in the context of the Islamic and the Third World, the relevance of their works goes beyond the Iranian and Malaysian society. For Shariati, the tragedy of modernism began when the intelligentsia accepted the colonialists' ideas wholeheartedly. That the wholesale adoption of western civilization as the only road to progress, in Shariati's view, is the Trojan Horse of western imperialism. He criticized reform-minded intellectuals such as Mirza Malkum Khan, the founder of the modern Iranian "enlightenment," who proposed the idea of 'Western civilization without the Iranian identity,' and figures such as Seyyed Hassan Taqizadeh, the first Iranian to suggest that 'we must become westernized body and soul'[19]

However, I would like to depart from Shariati's thought here and argue that even those intelligentsias who favored modernization were also reluctant to let go of traditional thinking and culture abruptly. A glimpse at the historical

---

[19]   Ali Shariati, "The Pyramid in Cultural Sociology," in *Man and Islam*, trans. Fatollah Marjani. (North Haledon, NJ: Islamic Publications International), 1981a.

pedigree of westernization discloses that these intellectuals did pay attention to tradition but for them modernity was more important than tradition because it offered them a better standard of living. This point has not skipped the attention of the historian Mangol Bayat (1982), who argues that although the reform-minded intellectuals, such as Mirza Fath Ali Akhundzadeh (1812–1878), Mirza Taqi Khan Amir Kabir (1807–1852), and Mirza Malkum Khan (1833–1908), were persuaded that the rationale behind the European power and prosperity lies in the western scientific knowledge, they were not ready to forego the full panoply of their tradition. She writes, 'the so-called modernist thought of the turn of the century, despite its loud call for westernization, was in spirit and form, if not in content, deeply rooted in tradition.' She continues that this modernity was 'bearing as much the mark of the Irano-Islamic heritage outwardly rejected by some of its spokesmen, as of the European system it strongly wished to emulate.'[20] However, Shariati is right to take umbrage with the fact that some of these intellectuals could not recognize the difference, and even contradiction, between modernity and civilization. What was imported into the country was not civilization, but rather modernity, as for Shariati civilization refers to a capacity for intellectual and material production, and 'a high level in society's cultural and spiritual growth and an elevated state of human spirit and outlook.'[21] Considering this definition, civilization suggests alert actions of self-generation, volition and an innovative adoption that could neither be imitated nor imposed.

Shariati is of the idea that civilization only occurs if its foundation is based on the society's own past and present cultural achievements.[22] Thus, what some intelligentsia accepted was by no means civilization but a process of modernization, which made a cleavage between the peoples of a society and their history and culture. Modernity, Shariati argues, is not a pseudo-morphosis of western civilization in the East, but rather it is a product of western imperialism, consciously devised to stymie the progress of culture and civilization in the East. Shariati perceives the danger of losing faith in one's own ability to produce the cultural and material values if non-western nations turn into mere consumers of the West, which is how the myth of perfect western culture and civilization makes sense. Shariati continues that the West became interested in the history, culture and religion of the East only to reshape, reconstruct and

20   Mangol Bayat, *Mysticism and Dissent: Socioreligious Thought in Qajar Iran*. (Syracuse, N.Y.: Syracuse University Press, 1982), 173–174.

21   Ali Shariati, "Bazgasht beh khish" ("Return to the Self"), C.W. 4. The Complete Collection of Works [CD ROM]. Tehran: Shariati Cultural Foundation, 1350/1971b), 140.

22   Navabi, *Reform and Revolution*.

represent them in a way that disgusts the native intellectuals. This is the cultural colonialism that he refers to, which aims to generate a de-cultured individual without roots in their society; such a process aims to hollow out all historical and cultural contents that creates longing to be replaced with meaning and substance by the West.[23] This modernity was neither authentically western nor Iranian; it would not recreate and reconstruct the Irano-Islamic values and would not reproduce the western values as well. Therefore, it lacked certain creativity and furthermore depersonalized an individual from history, culture and religion.[24] Modernity had created a deep schism between the majority who still treasured past, culture and tradition, and the minority who liked to see themselves and their society modernized.

The tension between modernity and tradition was too deep-seated for Shariati to be pacified by criticism. He diagnosed two major characteristics in every aspect of Iranian intellectual and artistic life, (1) 'alienation, or even in some instances "hatred" from "self," from their own religion, culture, worldview, and character; and (2) a deep, obsessive, or even boastful pretension to attachment to the West, and rootless and vulgar modernism.'[25] To do away with the tension, he thinks the 'responsible intellectual' should be awakened. Shariati categorizes the modernized populations into three groups, (1) "the consumptionist assimile," who are mindlessly imitating the West and are unable to judge or think independently and have no sense of social responsibility; (2) the "pseudo-intellectuals," who were the right men for imperialism since they were trained to work with the administrative system of a modern society.[26] However, it is the third group whose ideas of westernization, Shariati considers the most serious, as he writes, 'the great tragedy is the assimilation of the intellectuals, namely thinkers who have responsibility for directing social ideas and for guiding society's spirit, culture, and faith.'[27] He continues, 'our basic problem is not the illiteracy of the common people but the half-illiteracy of our intellectuals.'[28] The problem of the intellectual who favored modernism was a 'misconception of social time,' as these intellectuals resided in a society

23   Ali Shariati, Ali. CW, Vol. 25: *Man without Self*. The Complete Collection of Works [CD ROM]. Tehran: Shariati Cultural Foundation, 1982.

24   Ibid.

25   Ali Shariati, "Cheh bayad kard?" ("What is to be done?"), C.W. 20. The Complete Collection of Works [CD ROM]. (Tehran: Shariati Cultural Foundation, 1350/1971a), 35.

26   Ali Shariati, "Iqbal mosleh-e gharn-e akhir" (Iqbal the Reformer of the Present Time), C.W. 5. The Complete Collection of Works [CD ROM]. (Tehran: Shariati Cultural Foundation, 1349/1970), 146.

27   Ibid., 268–269.

28   Ali Shariati, "Cheh bayad kard?" ("What is to be done?"), 41.

that was like the 14th–15th century but took their ideas and notions from the 19th–20th century Europe.[29] They practically and theoretically have a colonial approach in the name of a scientific approach. They discuss democracy and sciences where modern sciences have not fallen into place yet. They exercise their free thoughts, not against the rulers of the country, but against the traditional institutions.[30] They thought of problems that never existed in their own society but nevertheless, proposed solutions to those problems. They were living in a country of centuries of stagnation but articulated the philosophical cynicism of the Europeans of postwar generation and represented that cynicism in their literature, arts and ideology. The most conspicuous consequence of the intellectuals' misreading of social time was the misplaced anti-religiosity that troubled the grassroots.[31]

Shariati is of the idea that both the culture of tradition and modernity had caused social decay and spiritual poverty. While criticizing 'the infatuated modernists and the retarded traditionalists,' he calls the two groups passive imitators, and instead he chose a third way, describing his position as being "a homeless intellectual" (this is what I call intellectual decolonization on his behalf), who is neither satisfied with the tradition nor is happy with the modernism, but at the same time does not discard them. In Shariati's view, the cultures of tradition and modernity are the distorted representations of two higher forms of culture and civilization, neither of which could be thrown away. Despite his attack on the culture of both tradition and modernity, in his view, tradition has the ability to produce a culture conducive to progress. Yet on the other hand, he does not repudiate the idea of "western modernity" as a whole, as he believes that a Muslim could learn a great deal from the West, especially if they understand the foundation of progress in the history of the West. As a homeless intellectual, the third way for him is to take what is most useful, significant and relevant from both the West and the tradition. Concurrent with his disdain for those who condemn the West and its sciences without knowing it, Shariati despises the traditional notion that independence and national resistance implies jettisoning the West in its totality. The West should not be rejected as a whole because they do not represent a monolithic doctrine. For Shariati, the only legitimate condemnation of westernization occurs when one has comprehensive knowledge of western culture and civilization along with a

---

29   Navabi, *Reform and Revolution*, 25.

30   Jalal Al-e Ahmad, *Occidentosis: A Plague from the West*, trans. R. Campbell. Berkeley: Mizan Press, 1984.

31   Ali Shariati, "Bazgasht beh khish" ("Return to the Self"), 97.

deep understanding of their own society, history, culture and religion.[32] He is not only interested in reading the major European authors but also uses them to achieve his goals.

Shariati utilizes both Marx and Weber to teach his students about the economic base and superstructure. Yet he criticizes both of them for understanding 'half of the social reality,' as Marx emphasizes the primacy of the base that is one half of a society, and Weber highlights the significance of the latter which makes the other half.[33] A close reading of Shariati's writings corroborates that his primary frame of reference, his notions of class, state apparatus, society, history, economy and culture are all highly influenced by Marxism. With regard to tradition, he concludes that to decolonize a country, a domestic and indigenous conception had to be formulated. Thus, he continues, Al-e Ahmad's critique of the secular political culture of the time, which neglected the Islamic culture of Iran, proposed a 'returning to one's root.' Shariati's ideas on religion and Islamic culture become clear in his correspondence with Franz Fanon. In his letter, Shariati expresses his disapproval and disagreement with Fanon over the essentiality of leaving religion in order for a nation to progress and conquer imperialism. He, instead, believes that a society must retain and regain its cultural and religious heritage as they can achieve the same ends. To him, religion, or more specifically the Islamic tradition, is the most powerful element for uniting the peoples and guiding them towards progressive objectives.[34] Shariati cogently argues for the essentiality of a rediscovery of the national psyche before fighting the West. It is only with a domestic and an inherent ideology rooted in its own political culture that Iran can gain its respect by resisting imperialism. Within such a discourse, religion finds its ties with the idea of "roots," and 'roots are a conceptualized public ontology ... [which] becomes a theory of authenticity.'[35] Authenticity here can be a modern prescription for accepting modernity while maintaining the cultural and political independency. Shariati's concern here is to adopt modernity according to the needs of our society and history without allowing it to master the society. In discussing the issue of "roots" in relation to Islam, he states,

> When we say, "return to one's roots," we are really saying one's cultural roots ... some of you may conclude that we Iranians must return to our

---

32   Ali Shariati, "Cheh bayad kard?" ("What is to be done?").

33   Ali Shariati, Ali. *Islamshenasi*. 3 vols. Collected Works Nos. 16, 17, and 18. The Complete Collection of Works [CD ROM]. (Tehran: Shariati Cultural Foundation, 1360/1981), 126.

34   Mirsepassi, *Intellectual Discourse*.

35   Ibid., 122.

racial roots [Aryan]. I categorically reject this conclusion. I oppose racism, fascism, and reactionary returns ... [our people] do not find their
roots in [pre-Islamic] civilizations ... for us to return to our roots [means
rediscovery of] our Islamic roots.[36]

The above passage demonstrates Shariati's belief that only tradition, and in
this sense religion, can mobilize masses to create a new society free from the
ills of the West. While discarding some traditional doctrines of the religion,
in this case, Shi'ism, he manages to draw some ideologies from it and gives it
a progressive aura to secure the faithfulness of the young revolutionary intelligentsia. However, this progressive aura had to be cautiously orchestrated to
be accordant with the anti-colonial and anti-western attitude. Homeless intellectuals like Shariati would not, therefore, blindingly follow the legacy of their
ancestors and would not become a mere consumer of the imported intellectual packages from the West. He admits once that, 'in the existing powerful bi-
polar intellectual context, the third way intellectuals like me, will constantly be
misunderstood and their message will not be comprehended correctly.'[37] That
is why the traditionalists oftentimes refer to him as an anti-western intellectual
and draw upon his critique of the West in a one-sided manner, thus reducing him to an ideologue supporting a totalitarian traditionalism.[38] His idea of
"originalism" and "returning to one's roots," have been turned into *nativism*.

While Shariati tries to resist the cultural colonization through his notions
of "returning to one's roots" and "homeless intellectual," Syed Hussein Alatas,
another spokesperson of intellectual decolonization, introduces ways to resist
"intellectual imperialism" in an era when knowledge of the rest of the world
is highly impacted by the sheer power of western culture. Intellectual imperialism is, in fact, the 'domination of one people by another in their world of
thinking.'[39] Back in the colonial period, intellectual imperialism was imposed
by colonial domination through setting up schools, educating people and raising up elites who could help control the colonized. Indoctrination through
the colonial education system played a momentous role in this intellectual

---

36   Shariati, quoted in Abrahamian, *Radical Islam*, 116.
37   Shariati, quoted in Mohammad Amin Ghaneirad, "Critical Review of the Iranian Attempts
      towards the Development of Alternative Sociologies." *International Journal of Social Sci-
      ences*, 1 (2) (2011), 39.
38   Ibid.
39   Syed Hussein Alatas, quoted in Syed Farid Alatas, "Social Theory as Alternative Discourse,"
      in *Decolonising the University: The Emerging Quest for Non-Eurocentric Paradigms*, eds.
      Claude Alvares and Shad Saleem Faruqi. (Pulau Pinang, Malaysia: Penerbit Universiti
      Sains Malaysia, 2012), 209.

imperialism. However, intellectual imperialism today, argues Syed Hussein Alatas (2006), is a form of hegemony that is 'not imposed by the West through colonial domination, but accepted, willingly with confident enthusiasm, by scholars and planners of the former colonial territories and even in the few countries that remained independent during that period.'[40] Encountering modernity in terms of academia, he brings our attention to the less-noticed fact that while other forms of western dominance, such as political and economic dominance, are usually resisted, *we welcome intellectual domination*. We are ready to accept anything that originates in the West so much so that we become hesitant in trying to validate ourselves.[41] We are nonchalant to our own tradition, seek western education, go by their standards and never question them, and boast of receiving a degree at the proximity of the rulers. This total capitulation is a sort of self-perpetuating academic imperialism. The predominance of the West through the power structure existing in the production and distribution of knowledge resources has led the non-western scholars to think less of themselves and turn into passive recipients of knowledge. Hence, they develop what Syed Hussein Alatas (1972) calls a "captive mind" that arises from the 'overdependence on the western intellectual contribution in the various fields of knowledge.'[42] His "captive mind" captures our attention about the production of scholarship described as colonial knowledge and its fundamental consequences on the "natives."[43]

Colonial knowledge and the captive mind are the twin concepts that inform each other.[44] Alatas believes that the captive mind is a victim of Orientalism and Eurocentrism – hence the mode of knowing has been termed colonial knowledge. The captive mind is defined as an 'uncritical and imitative mind dominated by an external source, whose thinking is deflected from an independent perspective.'[45] It is an "uncritical imitation" that spread through

---

40   Syed Hussein Alatas, "The Autonomous, the Universal and the Future of Sociology." *Current Sociology*, 54 (1) (2006): 7–8.

41   Claude Alvares, "A Critique of Eurocentric Social Science and the Question of Alternatives," in *Decolonising the University: The Emerging Quest for Non-Eurocentric Paradigms*, eds. Claude Alvares and Shad Saleem Faruqi. Pulau Pinang, Malaysia: Penerbit Universiti Sains Malaysia, 2012.

42   Syed Hussein Alatas, *The Autonomous*, 8.

43   Syed Hussein Alatas, "The Captive Mind in Development Studies." *International Social Science Journal*, xxiv (1) (1972): 9–25.

44   Shanta Nair-Venugopal, *The Gaze of the West and Framings of the East*. Basingstoke, UK: Palgrave Macmillan, 2012.

45   Syed Hussein Alatas, "The Captive Mind and Creative development." *International Social Science Journal*, 36 (1974): 692.

'almost the whole of scientific intellectual activity' including 'problem-setting, analysis, abstraction, generalization, conceptualization, description, explanation, and interpretation.'[46] Alatas first expounded the concept in 1972, that, in fact, led to the current nature of scholarship in the non-western world, especially its dominance in the social sciences and humanities. However, the problem of mental captivity was first put forth in the 1950's when he referred to the 'wholesale importation of ideas from the western world to eastern societies,' ignoring their socio-historical context as a primary problem of colonialism.[47] Some of the characteristics of a captive mind includes the non-creativity and incapability of 'raising original problems,' incapability of conceiving 'analytical method independent of current stereotypes'; incapability of 'separating the particular from the universal in science and thereby properly adapting the universally valid corpus of scientific knowledge to the particular local situation'; a captive mind is also 'fragmented in outlook,' it is 'alienated from the major issues of society' and 'its own national tradition, if it exists, in the field of intellectual pursuit'; it is unaware of 'its own captivity and the conditioning factors making it what it is,' and it 'is a result of Western dominance over the rest of the world.'[48]

What Syed Hussein Alatas said of the mental captivity of intellectuals more than four decades ago still holds true, as the captive mind is real and pervasive in our society today. Trained almost entirely in the western sciences, the captive mind enjoys reading the western authors, and is educated primarily by western teachers, either in the West or through their available works in local institutions of education.[49] Many of our intellectuals and university/college teachers read the works of western authors and teach them, yet they are not aware of this academic dependency, and those who are conscious of it do not bother to make an effort to change it. Our teachers use textbooks that are developed in countries very different than ours. They appear to have been total victims of the captive mind. Thus, Alatas' concept of captive mind resonates perfectly with the notions of mimicry and repetition that have been considered as one of the most effective strategies of colonial power and knowledge.[50] However, it

---

46   Alatas, *The Captive Mind in Development Studies*, 11–12.

47   Syed Hussein Alatas, 1956, quoted in Seyd Farid Alatas, 2004. "The Meaning of Alternative Discourses: Illustrations from Southeast Asia," in *Asia in Europe, Europe in Asia*, eds. Srilata Ravi, Mario Rutten, Goh Beng Lan. (Leiden: Institute of Southeast Asian Studies, 2004), 60.

48   Alatas, *The Captive Mind and Creative Development*, 691.

49   Syed Farid Alatas, "Intellectual and Structural Challenges to Academic Dependency." *International Sociological Association, E-Bulletin*, 2008.

50   Nair-Venugopal, 2012.

should be noted that he is not against a "constructive imitation" which may lead to emulation. He argues that, 'no society can develop by inventing everything on its own. When something is found effective and useful, it is desirable that it should be adopted and assimilated, whether it be an artifact or an attitude of mind.'[51] He believes that the dominance of western science has both positive and negative effects. While the former should be maintained and used, the latter should be avoided. He criticizes those who reject the West wholeheartedly as he believes 'ignoring a valuable contribution from the West is as negative as uncritically accepting whatever is served on the academic platter.'[52] He is cognizant of the urgency not to reject the western social science in total, but rather he selectively adapts it to local needs with caution.

The selectively adapted knowledge from the West is not based on the premises of originality but on a criteria of relevance, which is formed by virtue of 'consciousness of the problems of academic imperialism, mental captivity and uncritical imitation.'[53] He aptly understands that this academic imperialism is a soft power of the West and can be a more powerful base for imperialism than its hard power. To diffuse this academic imperialism, he proposes an autonomous Asian social science tradition be generated. The important element to include in forming a particular tradition is, (1) 'The raising and treatment of definite problems,' (2) 'the application of definite methodologies,' (3) 'the recognition of definite phenomena,' (4) 'the creation of definite concepts,' and (5) 'the relation with other branches of knowledge.'[54] The very first prerequisite in forming an autonomous tradition is a group of creative and independent intellectuals. The autonomy of tradition leans on studies of historical phenomena believed to be unique to a particular area or society. As Syed Farid Alatas argues, autonomous traditions need to be 'informed by local/regional historical experiences and cultural practices' as well as by alternative philosophies, epistemologies, histories, and the arts. By proposing an autonomous Asian social science tradition, Syed Hussein Alatas has no intention of separating Asian social science from that of the West or the rest of the World. Rather he opines that a greater deal of attention should be paid to the development of knowledge elsewhere, especially in the West, but the problem is to identify the significant from the trivial.

---

51   Alatas, *The Captive Mind and Creative Development,* 692.

52   Syed Hussein Alatas, "The Development of an Autonomous Social Science Tradition in Asia: Problems and Prospects." *Asian Journal of Social Science,* 30 (1) (2002): 150.

53   Syed Farid Alatas, "Indigenization: Features and Problems," in *Asian Anthropology,* eds. Jan van Bremen, Eyal Ben-Ari, and Syed Farid Alatas. (New York: Routledge, 2005), 240.

54   Syed Hussein Alatas, *The Development of an Autonomous Social Science in Asia,* 151.

Alatas classifies knowledge into four categories that an autonomous social science should develop: (1) Foundational knowledge, which refers to 'knowledge of the foundation of Asian societies, their culture, religion and other crucial aspects of societal life,' (2) consolidative knowledge, which means 'knowledge that consolidates and strengthen the foundation,' (3) reactive knowledge, which refers to 'knowledge that is required to react to ideas that tend to strengthen or corrode the basis of social life,' and (4) developmental knowledge, which is 'knowledge required to attain peace, justice, welfare and insight into human living.'[55] All the above-mentioned types of knowledge are pertinent to making an autonomous social science tradition. By proposing an autonomous Asian social science tradition, Alatas strives for eradicating the dominance of the western knowledge in Asian societies where almost all of the institutions of higher education follow the same path and have the same educational structure. The dominance of western knowledge structure leaves little room for our people to get to know indigenous knowledge. For example, in sociology, the likes of Max Weber and Emile Durkheim are more known than non-European social thinkers. The West, too, does not acknowledge the contributions made by non-Europeans in different fields, and this, argues Syed Farid Alatas, is the 'new orientalism' of today, which is 'the neglect and silencing of non-Western voices.'[56]

Conclusion

When the former European colonial power left their colonies, neo-colonialism began as its replacement. This neo-colonialism aims to colonize the culture of the Third World countries, through the guise of modernity. A great number of intellectuals from the non-western world embraced it and argued that it is the only path to progress. At the other spectrum, oppositional intellectual turned to tradition to reject the West and its ideologies. Homeless intellectuals such as Shariati and Alatas approached modernity from a "third way." While both of them are against being mere consumers of the imported packages from the West, they admit that the desirable and useful Western ideas should not be discarded. Both of them document how the rise of Western dominance can impoverish non-westerners, and as a result, suggest utilizing one's own cultural and religious tradition to resist it. Shariati's "homeless intellectual" position and his ideas of "returning to one's roots," and Alatas' anti-captive

---

55   Ibid., 154.
56   Alatas, *Social Theory as Alternative Discourse*, 199.

mind stance stand along with his proposal on "an autonomous Asian social science tradition," works wonders in intellectually decolonizing a nation. Unlike decolonization, which is a process of confrontation, the relationship between intellectual decolonization and colonialism/imperialism is a dialogical process in which the voices of both the colonized and the colonizers carry equal weight. Shariati and Alatas, as two spokespersons of intellectual decolonization, choose the dialogue over confrontation with the West. But now the questions to be asked here is whether post-1979 Iran is the society Shariati envisioned for his country? Whether Shariati and Alatas have been successful in challenging the western discourse of modernity both in the fields of culture and academia? Their success has to be measured in terms of a growing audience during and after their active career. Scrutinizing the current condition of our society and its academia will also allow us to answer the question. Efforts at decolonizing the captive mind and resisting the West intellectually remains an unfinished project and needs attentive and creative intellectuals to follow their path.

Bibliography

Abrahamian, Ervand. *Radical Islam: The Iranian Mojahedin*. London: I.B. Tauris, 1989.

Alatas, Syed Farid. 2004. "The Meaning of Alternative Discourses: Illustrations from Southeast Asia," in Ravi, S., Rutten, M., Beng Lan, G. (eds) *Asia in Europe, Europe in Asia*. Institute of Southeast Asian Studies, 2004.

Alatas, Syed Farid "Indigenization: Features and Problems," In *Asian Anthropology*, edited by Jan van Bremen, Eyal Ben-Ari and Syed Farid Alatas. Routledge: New York, 2005.

Alatas, Syed Farid "Intellectual and Structural Challenges to Academic Dependency." *International Sociological Association, E-Bulletin*, 2008.

Alatas, Syed Farid "Social Theory as Alternative Discourse." In *Decolonizing the University: The Emerging Quest for Non-Eurocentric Paradigms*, edited by Claude Alvares and Shad Saleem Faruqui. Pulau Pinang, Malaysia: Penerbit Universiti Sains Malaysia, 2012.

Alatas, Syed Hussein. "The Captive Mind in Development Studies." *International Social Science Journal*, xxiv(1) (1972): 9–25.

Alatas, Syed Hussein. "The Captive Mind and Creative Development." *International Social Science Journal*, 36 (1974): 691–699.

Alatas, Syed Hussein. "The Development of an Autonomous Social Science Tradition in Asia: Problems and Prospects." *Asian Journal of Social Science*, 30(1) (2002): 150–157.

Alatas, Syed Hussein. "The Autonomous, the Universal and the Future of Sociology." *Current Sociology*, 54(1) (2006): 7–23.

Al-e Ahmad, J. 1984. *Occidentosis: A Plague from the West*, (R. Campbell, Trans.). Berkeley: Mizan Press.

Alvares, Claude. "A Critique of Eurocentric Social Science and the Question of Alternatives." In *Decolonizing the University: The Emerging Quest for Non-Eurocentric Paradigms*, edoted by Claude Alvares and Shad Saleem Faruqi. Pulau Pinang, Malaysia: Penerbit Universiti Sains Malaysia, 2012.

Bayat, Mangol. *Mysticism and Dissent: Socioreligious Thought in Qajar Iran*. Syracuse, N.Y.: Syracuse University Press, 1982.

Bendix, Richard. "Tradition and Modernity Reconsidered." In *Essays in Comparative Social Stratification*, edited by Leonard Plotnicov and Arthur Tuden. Pittsburgh, PA: University of Pittsburgh, 1970.

Boroujerdi, Mehrzad. *Iranian Intellectuals and the West: The Tormented Triumph*. New York: Syracuse University Press, 1996.

Boroujerdi, Mehrzad. Contesting Nationalist Constructions of Iranian Identity. *Critical Studies of the Middle East*, 26 (12) (1998).

Chekki, D.A. *Modernization and Kin Network*. Brill, 1974.

Fanon, Franz. *The Wretched of the Earth*. Harmondsworth, Middlesex, England: Penguin Books Ltd., 1974.

Ghaneirad, Mohammad Amin. "Critical Review of the Iranian Attempts towards the Development of Alternative Sociologies." *International Journal of Social Sciences*, 1(2) (2011): 125–144.

Goldberg, M. "Decolonization and political socialization with reference to West Africa." *The Journal of Modern African Studies*, 24(4) (1986).

Haas, William S. *Iran*. New York: AMS Press, 1996.

Hourani, Albert H., Phillip Khoury and Mary Wilson. *The Modern Middle East*. New York: I.B. Tauris, 2004.

Lerner, Daniel. *The Passing of Traditional Society: Modernizing the Middle East*. New York: Free Press of Glencoe, 1964.

Looney, Robert. E. *Economic Origins of the Iranian Revolution*. Toronto: Pergamon Press, 1982.

Mirsepassi, Ali. *Intellectual Discourse and Politics of Modernization: Negotiating Modernity in Iran*. New York: Cambridge University Press, 2004.

Nair-Venugopal, Shanta. *The Gaze of the West and Framings of the East*. Basingstoke, UK: Palgrave Macmillan, 2012.

Navabi, Abbas. *Reform and Revolution in Shi'i Islam: The Thought of Ali Shariati*. Dissertation. Indiana University, 1988.

Said, Edward. *Representations of the Intellectual*. New York: Pantheon Books, 1994.

Saikal, Amin. *The Rise and Fall of the Shah*. Princeton, Princeton University Press, 1980.

Shariati, Ali. "Iqbal mosleh-e gharn-e akhir" (Iqbal the Reformer of the Present Time), C.W. 5. The Complete Collection of Works [CD ROM]. Tehran: Shariati Cultural Foundation, 1349/1970.

Shariati, Ali. "Cheh bayad kard?" ("What is to be done?"), C.W. 20. The Complete Collection of Works [CD ROM]. Tehran: Shariati Cultural Foundation, 1350/1971a.

Shariati, Ali. "Bazgasht beh khish" ("Return to the Self"), C.W. 4. The Complete Collection of Works [CD ROM]. Tehran: Shariati Cultural Foundation, 1350/1971b.

Shariati, Ali. "The Pyramid in Cultural Sociology," in *Man and Islam*. Translated by Fatollah Marjani. North Haledon, NJ: Islamic Publications International, 1981a.

Shariati, Ali. "Islamshenasi." 3 vols. C.W. 16, 17, and 18. The Complete Collection of Works [CD ROM]. Tehran: Shariati Cultural Foundation, 1360/1981.

Shariati, Ali. "Man without Self." C.W. 25: The Complete Collection of Works [CD ROM]. Tehran: Shariati Cultural Foundation, 1982.

Shils, Edward. "The Intellectuals in the Political Development of the New States." In *Political Change in Underdeveloped Countries: Nationalism and Communism*, edited by John Kautsky. New York: John Wiley and Sons, 1963.

Sreberny, Annabelle and Gholam Khiabany. "Becoming Intellectual: The Blogestan and Public Political Space in the Islamic Republic." In *Iranian Intellectuals: 1997–2007*, edited by Lloyd Ridgeon. New York: Routledge, 2008.

CHAPTER 5

Ali Shariati's Critique of Durkheim's Sociology of Religion

Seyed Javad Miri

Introduction

In this chapter, the author has attempted to inquire about the relevance of Ali Shariati's critique of Durkheim's sociology of religion. There are innumerable studies on Durkheim and the Durkheimian sociology of religion but we have almost no comprehensive research on the Shariatian reading of the Durkheimian sociology of religion. Here, the author has worked on the notion of the elementary form of religion as understood by Durkheim within the Shariatian frame of reference. Shariati argues that Durkheim has misunderstood the question of elementariness by equating the "collective soul" and "religious emotion" as in Shariati's view these two are fundamentally different in kind and substance. In other words, here the author is attempting to legitimize the Shariatian frame of reference while engaging the Durkheim's sociology of religion.

Relocating Durkheimian Sociology of Religion

The question of religion occupies a pivotal position within Shariati's frame of reference is due to the fact that he was trying to find a lucid framework for what he termed as "post-scientific religion" vis-à-vis a "pre-scientific religion," deeming the latter to be passé while encouraging non-western intellectuals to participate in the founding of the fundamentals for a future post-scientific *logos*.[1] In *Revisiting the History of Religions*, Shariati argues that Durkheim 'is the most important sociologists who has been able to craft the most sophisticated thesis against religion within the frame of sociology of religion which

---

1 Seyed Javad Miri, *Reflecting upon Theoretical Poverty of Human Sciences in Iran*. Tehran: Publishing House of Sociologists, 2015.

made other old critiques of religion redundant.'[2] Furthermore, Shariati argues that,

> the most renowned religion which Durkheim relies on – and all sociologists, directly or indirectly, have been influenced by – is totemism. Of course, it should be noted that he has not invented this field of research, but rather scholars such as Spencer or Langton have come up with this notion, but the credit goes to Durkheim who has conceptualized totemism as a modern sociological thesis against religion, and as a matter of fact it should be considered as the most sophisticated anti-religious thesis in the contemporary era.[3]

Surely, different sociologists within the field of sociology and anthropology of religion have construed totemism differently, but few are familiar with Shariati's reading of this question. I would like to narrate his understanding of totemism in detail, as this is his point of departure when criticizing Durkheim, and by extension, it is classical sociology's stance on religion, which in Shariati's view, should also be the platform for humanity's future search for a novel frame of meaning. I will expand on this point later on in this debate.

Through Shariati's reading of classical accounts of totemism, one can understand totemism as pertaining to,

> aboriginal clans – and native tribes which exist today in Africa, North America and Australia – [who] worship a thing or an animal. In other words, members of a clan worship a particular animal or a bird and if you ask them why, for instance, do you worship a parrot, they would answer you by saying that we are parrots. If you ask them how could you be a parrot, the answer is that our ancestor – from whom we all have originated – was a parrot. In other words, after the physical annihilation the great ancestor was transformed into a white parrot and now the parrot is the soul of the clan, and protects us and also prays for our well-being and brings for us blessings. This is to argue that the parrot stands for the clan's ancestor who has been transformed into this new shape, and due to the fact that the parrot as a species will exist forever – but a particular parrot will die, the species is eternal and everlasting – thus the clan's ancestor

---

2   Ali Shariati, *Collected Works*, 14. *Tarikh ve Shenakht Adyan* (Revisiting the History of Religions). (Tehran: Sahami Enteshar Publication, 1399/2009), 60.

3   Ibid., 64.

would live in the form of a parrot forever. In other words, when members of a particular clan worship a parrot this is, indeed, another form of worshipping their own ancestor, and when they worship their own ancestor, they are actually worshipping the common soul of their own society, which exists in every and each of the members of this particular clan. The clan forbids, for instance, the consumption of a meat which belongs to its own totem but the same does not apply for members of other clans. Therefore, we can assume that if the meat of a cow is forbidden among Hindus in India, then the reason has to do with the conception of Aryans who considered the cow as their totem. In other words, in the totem the members of a clan can see the manifestation of their own ancestor, and this correspondence endowed upon that animal a kind of sacredness and veneration.[4]

Shariati argues that Durkheim attempts, based on his reading of totemism, to discover the roots of religion. One could ask whether by worshipping the totem,

members of the clan are not actually sanctifying their own deity, their own ultimate source of being, i.e. the eternal truth which is the awe-inspiring endorser of the clan – namely their common grand ancestor? This is a very pivotal question which should be taken seriously as one needs to know the reason behind their devotion and worship. In other words, why is there any need for devotion? Because the common ancestor is the only dimension which is shared by all individuals and different members of various families of the same tribe who have been scattered around ... but thanks to the aura of the common ancestor shall find solidarity with each other. Thus, members of a totemic tribe when worshipping their own totem are actually worshipping their common ancestor, and when they are worshipping their common ancestor, as a matter of fact, they are celebrating their sole dimension, which is shared by everyone in the same tribe, and when they worship their sole shared aspect of different individuals in their society, this means that they celebrate/worship their own collective soul and the spirit of their collectivity. This is to state that totemism (or worshipping of a totem) is transformed into collectivism (or worshipping of society).[5]

---

4   Ibid., 65.
5   Ibid., 66.

In Shariati's view, this is the essence of what Durkheim had been trying to argue in his entire sociological discourse. In other words, Shariati argues that this is what the Durkheimian thesis on religion is all about. To put it differently,

> individuals who stand under one flag and sanctify the flag, their act of flag-veneration should be understood as the worshipping of the common denominator of all members of the same society. The same logic works among members of an aboriginal tribe who do not know each other and have no direct relationship to one another. By worshipping the totem, they are, as a matter of fact, celebrating the collective conscience of their own community, which is shared by everyone. This is to argue that the sanctification of a totem is based on the logic that individuals assume a kind of sacredness for their own society, as tribal members considered a kind of sanctity for their grand ancestor, as they believed he supported them, and the same logic works for the members of a human society today, i.e. the soul of collectivity is alive and is the eternal endorser of individuals. In other words, individuals die but society lives on, and this means society is not equal to generations and individuals. But in individuals there is an essence which remains and lives forever, and that core is a collective soul, the very nature of this soul is collective order.[6]

Repositioning Theology in Durkheimian Sociology

The questions of sacredness in totemism is an important question Shariati attempts to engage. He argues that sacredness,

> which totemists assign to their totem and the kind of relationship which they feel towards their own totem, is a kind of relationship which exists between an individual and a society, because the individual is born by society. That's why all individuals consider themselves as procreated of the totem. Thus, the totem is the eternal emblem of society; individuals come and perish, but the collective, as well as the collective soul, remains, and the sanctity, which is attached to the totem (or even society), is due to its eternality.[7]

---

6   Ibid., 66–67.

7   Ibid., 67.

In my view, Shariati is not much interested in Durkheimian sociology as it is understood within the social sciences. To the contrary, I think he takes on Durkheim from within a theological perspective. In other words, Shariati discerns a theological thread in Durkheim's sociology, which has generated little debate within sociological circles in general, and in the Iranian sociological context in particular. For instance, in *Revisiting the History of Religions*, there is a footnote where Shariati refers to atheistic theories and anti-religious perspectives that are discussed by Iranian scholars, such as,

> fear as the source of religion, ownership as the source of religion, and other outdated theories which belong to 16th and 17th centuries in Europe. If we are serious about countering atheistic theories in the modern world we should engage with advanced theories that critique religion, and one of the most complex theories of this kind belongs to Emile Durkheim, who talks about the primacy of society or collectivism.[8]

Reconsidering the Question of "Origins of Religion"

In Shariati's view, Durkheim's main theses regarding the origins of religion are often discussed by sociologists and are popular among atheists. This is an interesting aspect in his approach to Durkheim which has not been discussed in detail, either by Iranian sociologists or scholars in the global context. However, it seems that Shariati does not share the Durkheimian view on the origins of religion, particularly in terms of totemism. But what are his reasons in refuting Durkheim? It seems Shariati finds a contradiction in Durkheim's own argument as far as elementary forms of religious life are concerned, and that is a question which Shariati thinks is worth reflecting on. Because, if Shariati could prove the inapplicability of Durkheim's atheistic theory of religion, then by extension he could establish his thesis on post-scientific meaning-system which should be created by all intellectuals who are heirs to the great spiritual tradition of Islam.

In a passage in *Revisiting the History of Religions*, Shariati tells us that he was searching in various books for answers to Durkheim's thoughts on religion, but later on realized that Durkheim had made certain pronouncements in his *The Elementary Forms of Religious Life* that were in complete contradiction to

---

8 Ibid., 68.

his sociological theories of religion.[9] What are the contradictions that Shariati referred to in the Durkheim's discourse? In particular, Shariati argues that in accordance to Durkheim's own arguments,

> the main principle is that religious worship consists of tribal devotion and social worship, and the reason for diversity of deities is due to the fact that each clan or tribe is in need simultaneously of a manifestation of its collective soul and each clan is in need of distinction and independence from other tribes, and the totem fulfills both of these functions. Thus, in general, religion is the manifestation of a society in the minds of its individuals. God is the manifestation of the collective soul in the individual soul. The relationship between the devotee and the devoted is ... the relationship of the individual with the soul of the collective, i.e. in relation to its tribe. Also, religion in the form of a totem is the manifestation of a particular independence of a particular society vis-à-vis other societies. Consequently, as a totem or God, or even the relationship between individuals and a totem – which is the relation between an individual with his/her society – is the manifestation of a society's soul. One of the salient aspects of totemic religion is endowing distinction, differentiation, and creating independence for a society vis-à-vis other societies. By demonstrating that this society is related to a dog, its totem therefore is a dog, and the other society's totem is a parrot, and the other one is a bear or pig.[10]

We should ask, what then is Shariati's point when rereading Durkheim's thesis on totemism? He seems to have discovered a contradiction in Durkheim's sociology of religion, which underlies his critique and other atheistic theories of religion. Shariati states that it is in this context that Durkheim argues,

> some sociologists imagine that the transmission of religion from a society or a clan to another society or tribe, is particular to highly developed human civilization and complex religions. On the contrary, to this assumption, scholars like Muller, Spencer and Taylor – both in Australia and North America – have demonstrated how religion and religious belief-systems [move] from one tribe to another, and have shown how people of one clan come to accept the religious ideas and beliefs of others, thanks to cultural exchanges and encounters.[11]

---

9   Ibid.
10   Ibid.
11   Ibid., 68–69.

Here, Shariati argues that Durkheim has simply contradicted himself by accepting transmission of religion from one tribe to another. Why is this so? What are the arguments Shariati advances when he states that Durkheim contradicted himself? Surely, Shariati has based his arguments on sound evidence which we should review, especially considering that such evidence is rarely considered by sociologists worldwide. In other words, within the mainstream sociological currents, we are accustomed to hearing arguments constructed by "core-sociologists" rather than "periphery-sociologists," such as Shariati. Furthermore, it seems to me that Shariati has an important point, and this point, in my estimation, is worth dwelling upon, as far as classical social theory is concerned. Shariati writes,

> I agree that the totem is a tribal and social manifestation, but if feeling towards and belief in the totem is similar to a specific religious emotion, and it is not other than that, and if all other religions are the evolved forms of totemism, and if religion from its primitive form – up to its most developed system – has had the role in creating distinction for a particular collective soul, and by doing so it could give a specific characteristic to a particular society vis-à-vis other societies, then how could one assume that other societies would accept the collective soul of this particular society? Because religion – in its form of religious beliefs – has a separating function which distinguishes a particular society from other societies – in accordance to Durkheim's view – and at the same time, it accepts the beliefs of other societies – Durkheim's next view – this view looks like as though we [Iranians], through our flag – which itself is a kind of totem – feel as Iranians, and in this fashion we are separated from others, as other societies through their flags do the same. Therefore, the flag is the reason which we separate from others and by which we earn our independence. In other words, others recognize us through our flag and we recognize them by their respective flags, but imagine, in the middle of these mechanisms, French people, for instance, by seeing our flag, start to like the color of our flag and hence choose our flag, and we, on the other hand, by seeing the flag of France, and due to its beautiful colors renounce our own flag, and instead choose their flag. The crucial question here is that the flag fulfils a function, and that is the function of distinctionality, i.e. to distinguish us from them and them from us. If a particular society is not dissolved in us and we are not dissolved in them, the acceptance of others' flag is not possible.[12]

---

12   Ibid., 69.

Contraditions in Durkheim's Position on Religion

It seems Shariati is engaged in a very serious debate with the French tradition of social theory represented by towering sociologists such as Emile Durkheim and Felicien Challaye.[13] He holds that Durkheim and Felicien Challaye confirm that,

> in Melanesia, out of five different tribes and clans, i.e. five distinct societies there must be five different totems as manifestations of five distinct collective souls which could demonstrate their differences both among individuals and their respective tribes and clans. But in reality, what we witness among these primitive societies demonstrates a different scenario, namely we can see that clan A has a distinct totem, and clan B has accepted many beliefs, rules and religious rituals of clan A, and people in clan B have accepted the belief-system of clan A, then perform the same ceremonies as though they belong to their own. Here we need to reflect upon this issue, namely if the religious emotion, i.e. devotion (worship) is the manifestation of an individual's relationship with its own society, then this person in his own society cannot imitate and feel the relationship of another person in another society. Such a thing is impossible unless we assume that totemism is the manifestation of an individual's relationship with its own society, but, religious emotion is of a totally different kind which may have mixed together in primitive societies. As we see, while I adore my own flag and through my own flag I worship the eternal soul of my nation and my own society, and also through my own flag I distinguish between my society and other societies, and in this fashion I sense the distinctivity of my own society, at the same time I have fallen in love with another religion, which has come from another society, I may even convert. Although in primitive societies, and even in Greek mythology, religious manifestations or deities could be the same as national manifestations – and function as endorsers of the city-state of Athena or Sparta – even there could be instances where these two forms of semblances are distinguishable from each other, i.e. national manifestations stay stable while religious symbols transform. This distinction is doubtless an indication that these two emotive aspects are not of similar origin.[14]

---

13   Miri, 2015a.
14   Shariati, *Collected Works,* 70.

Shariati is attempting to demonstrate that Durkheim misreads the question of "religious emotion," due to the fact that there is contravening historical evidence that is based on the very foundations upon which Durkheim has established his sociology of religion. In other words, by arguing that totemism could, at best, explain the characteristics of the "collective soul," Shariati is trying to pull the rug from under Durkheim's sociology of religion, which, in his opinion, is the main point of atheistic tendencies at a global stage. However, it is important to understand the foundational premises of what Shariati distinguishes as two kinds of emotions, i.e. religious emotion and collective soul. In *Revisiting the History of Religions*, Shariati attempts to outline his reasons by arguing that these two feelings are different because,

> it is impossible to assume that a person who belongs to a society and his religion [based on the Durkheimian argument] would be the manifestation of his society's soul without changing his society [and] his religion. It is evident that an individual from society A, who takes the religion of society B, has not taken the manifestation of collective soul from society B. Surely he has taken a kind of emotion which is fundamentally different than the collective soul of the same society.[15]

Shariati dwells upon this problem by giving illustrations which are instructive when conceptualizing the distinctions between these two forms of emotions, i.e. social soul and religious feeling. He argues that the distinction between these two dimensions is crucial and demonstrable through various examples. For instance, Shariati takes the question of "nationality" (the sense of belonging to a society, clan or tribe) and the concept of "emblem" (the sense of adoring a totem) as two distinct but interrelated instances which could function as points of entries when critiquing Durkheim. In other words,

> for me as an Iranian there is no possibility to adopt the French flag but I could take the French technology or literature and philosophy due to the fact that technology, literature or even philosophy are not expressions of the French collective soul. On the contrary, they are products of human reflections which allow me as an Iranian to imitate them, as French people are also able to learn and take our poetry and mysticism for the same reason that poetry is not a manifestation of the Iranian collective soul.[16]

---

15   Ibid.
16   Ibid.

This is the first critique Shariati levels at Durkheim, but there is a second critique which Shariati develops in regard to the question of distinctionality. As Durkheim argues,

> when individuals in a given society worship their own totem, as a matter of fact they are worshipping their own collective soul, which means that people who are from the same tribe have, indeed, a common soul, which they have to worship. But the question is that there are many cases which have been observed among aboriginal tribes where in the same society that has a religion, a minority among this given society convert to another religion, this means that socially and genetically they consider themselves as offspring of their own totem and also worship the totem of the majority but from a religious point of departure, they have accepted the religion from another clan [... this is an issue which needs to be reflected upon as this distinction may change the makeup of sociological problematizations of religion in a fundamental fashion].[17]

In other words, this demonstrates a very crucial distinction between "religious emotion" and "collective soul." In Shariati's view, this shows that,

> the kind of religious sensibility is different than the type of collective soul. There are many instances where the collective soul has manifested itself in a given religion such as Judaism, or religious soul has manifested itself in a given race or society – and we can give as an example the social religion which existed in Greece, where religion was the manifestation of the Greek soul and her collective soul. But even in these two cases, history demonstrates that when the Roman Empire was founded, they adopted Greek religions and Greek religious symbols, while at the same time they dissolved the Greek society. While having their own collective soul, the Jewish religion was popular during the age of Dhu Nuwas among Arabs in general, and Yemeni tribes in particular. This means that they were Jewish in terms of religion without being the offspring of Israel. There is no doubt that these two types of souls are distinguishable and their distinctionality is clearly demonstrable in history.[18]

One may wonder whether Shariati is attempting to justify the supernaturality of religious belief as the reason why he postulates different arguments against

---

17   Ibid.
18   Ibid., 71.

Durkheim's theory of totemism, or are there other issues which operate within the Shariatian frame of reference? I think this is a very poignant question which needs to be reflected upon as Shariati's approach is theological in nature. In *Revisiting the History of Religions* he clearly rules out this assumption by stating that,

> Here, I do not want to put forward arguments in favor of supernatural origins of religion; on the contrary, I want to state that in clear contradiction to Durkheim's position, the worship of a religious deity is not similar in terms of its kind or substance to the worship of a social symbol. In other words, worshipping the relationship between man and his religious deity (or the object of worship) is not of the same nature as the relationship between an individual and the collective soul of his society. An individual's relationship with his own forebear may be a kind of worship or even great devotion, but it is not tantamount to the typical kind of religious feelings of people towards God, deities or occult, oracular and religious beliefs.[19]

Is this really so? Why should one accept the categorical distinction that Shariati makes between these two types of emotions, i.e. religious and social? The entire disciplinary tradition of sociology of religion is based on the notion of similarity of these two types and Durkheim has clearly demonstrated the categorical resemblance of the religious and the social. Why then does Shariati insist on another decoding of this complex issue? Certainly, one needs to inquire into the entire cosmos of Shariati's work. In doing so, I think the answer can be found in his two volume book *Revisiting the History of Religions*, where he states that these two types are categorically different, and gives his reasons as such,

> It is impossible that a person could change his religion in his own society, unless we assume that religion is not of identical nature to that of the soul of collectivity. Therefore, I have two reasons for judging Durkheim's theory invalid; the first critique is that the worshipping of the collective soul, which manifests itself in a totem, is not of a religious kind because there are many instances where individuals within a single society or in a single clan, without having their collective soul changed, have taken the religion of other society. The second critique which one could construct to falsify the Durkheimian position on sociology of religion, is the

---

19   Ibid., 71.

fact that there are cases where within a single community everybody be-lieves in their own totem, but while the majority believes in one religion, nevertheless there are minorities of the same clan or tribe who believe in other religions. Namely, in a particular community there is one totem and one single kind of ancestral worship, but simultaneously, one can see the existence of various religions in the same society. Therefore, one could assume that the collective soul cannot be identical with the reli-gious soul. Apart from this, it should be clearly indicated that totemism is not the only exclusive form of primitive religion; all kinds of religions could be traced back to this totemic form of religiosity.[20]

After laying out his arguments, Shariati moves even further by arguing that not only is totemism not the *only form* of religiosity, it is not even the *primary form* of religion. In other words, if we are looking for primary forms of religion then we should consider, 'fetishism and animism, which, in according to many scholars, are earlier forms of religion, and thus it is wrong to assume that to-temism is the only primary form of religion.'[21]

Why is this important? To state it differently, why is it important to talk about other early forms of religions such as animism or fetishism rather than totem-ism? How does it assist Shariati in his critique vis-à-vis Durkheim? If one could discredit Durkheim's thesis on archetypicality of totemism, then, in Shariati's view, the whole sociological edifice of Durkheim would crumble down as,

fetishism and animism, as early forms of religion, are configurations of worship of various innumerable forces, indistinctive magical powers, and the spirits of objects or nature in general. [If this could be established then one could easily argue that these early forms of religion] cannot be manifestations of the collective soul of a tribe or a clan, and also spirits and magical forces in these types of religions have nothing to do with the concrete personification of society or the social.[22]

With this in mind, we should then ask what these early forms of religion are if they are not manifestations of collective souls derived from particular societies or communities. For Shariati, they are most often,

a kind of primitive interpretations of the world, nature, or even ... archaic forms of analysis and explanation of world's phenomena, as well as their

---

20   Ibid.
21   Ibid.
22   Ibid.

relationships to human beings. [Thus, they have] nothing to do with an individual's relationship with his/her own society.[23]

Conclusion

In this chapter, I did not intend to work on Durkheim's sociology of religion as there are ample studies on this aspect of Durkheim. What I wanted to demonstrate is the importance of Shariati's interpretation of Durkheimian sociology of religion which seems to be absent in mainstream sociological and theoretical debates.[24] Of course, one could argue that it would have been better to study Durkheimian sociological studies of religion, and based on the existing literature appraise Shariati's intervention. However, I think this would have been another study where the authenticity of perspective is attached to the Eurocentric form of cognition. Here, I have attempted to demonstrate the significance of alternative approaches to the classics of sociology as far as sociology of religion is concerned. In other words, the Iranian sociological tradition views the world from a different perspective and this vector itself is based on a distinct historical, cultural and political context. For me to elaborate on this vector has been the lietmotif of this study.

Bibliography

Durkheim, Emile. *The Elementary Forms of Religious Life*. Translated by Karen E. Fields. New York: The Free Press 1995.

Miri, Seyed Javad. *Intercivilizational Social Theory: Complementarity and Contradiction in the Muslim and Western Intellectual Tradition*. Bloomington, IN: Xlibris Corporation, 2007.

Miri, Seyed Javad. *Reflecting upon Theoretical Poverty of Human Sciences in Iran*. Tehran: Publishing House of Sociologists, 2015.

Miri, Seyed Javad. *Revisiting Farabi: Overcoming Clerkish Perspectives in Human Sciences*. Tehran: Publishing House of Sociologists, 2015a.

Shariati, Ali. Collected Works 14 *Tarikh ve Shenakht Adyan* (Revisiting the History of Religions). Tehran: Sahami Enteshar Publication, 1399/2009.

---

23   Ibid., 72.

24   Miri, *Intercivilization Social Theory*, 190–213.

CHAPTER 6

Ali Shariati and Critical Theory: From Black Affirmation to Red Negation

Dustin J. Byrd

The year 2017 not only marks the inauguration of America's first crypto-fascist president, Donald J. Trump, but also marks the anniversary of various watershed moments in the history of humanity, especially man's capacity to revolt against injustice, oppression and the diminishment of the human being to a mere *thing-of-manipulation*, and/or *homo consumens*.[1] Within these conditions, each individual bears little to no value outside of the use-value for those who use and exploit them. Yet, through these explosive *jetztzeit* (now-time) moments of protest and revolution, segments of humanity have shown not only their capacity, but also their willingness, to risk their existence in order to liberate themselves from such oppressive conditions. Five hundred years ago, on October 31, 1517, Martin Luther, an Eremite Augustinian monk and professor of Biblical Studies in Wittenberg, Germany, protested against the corruption of the Roman Catholic Church by hammering his *95 Theses* to the doors of the Wittenberg Castle-Cathedral. Luther stood in protest of the blatant corruption of the Medici successor of St. Peter, Pope Leo x. Although this act was preceded by similar actions by men like Girolamo Savonarola, the rebellious Dominican monk who temporarily ousted the Medici from Florence and fought against the Borgia Pope, Alexander vi, Luther's singular act of protest sparked what would become the Protestant Reformation – a movement that rose up against the nefarious, simony-infested and extremely "worldly" church. In the name of a more-true, and from their perspective "purified" Christianity, Luther rebelled against the mendacity and hypocrisy of the Medieval Catholic Church.

Four hundred years later, in 1917, in the name of a vision of society free from capitalist exploitation and monarchical oppression, the Bolsheviks, led by Vladimir Ilyich Ulyanov, better known by his alias "Lenin," stormed the stale edifies of state power, demanding "all power to the soviets." For these Marxist-Leninist proletarians, neither a long-entrenched aristocracy nor the bourgeoisie (as exemplified by the short-lived government of Alexander Kerensky) should rule a nation of peasants and workers, but rather the precariat and proletariat

---

1 Roger Griffin, *The Nature of Fascism.* (New York: Routledge, 1993), 1–55.

should rule themselves through the democratic worker councils (*soviets*). The Romanov dynasty, which kept themselves in power by systematic oppression and exploitation of the Russian populace, having exploited and appropriated the wealth and labor of their people for centuries, was overthrown by an uprising of the hungry and war-weary masses. Under the slogan, "bread, peace, and land," they proclaimed that never again would the people grovel at the feet of the wealthy and privileged. Thus, they rejected the stale ideology that the Romanovs were their "natural" masters; the monarchy's rule was only the result of history – a history which could be overthrown via revolutionary class struggle.

Just fifty years later, in 1967, the revolutionary Commandante Ernesto "Che" Guevara, the Argentinian medical doctor who was instrumental in the overthrow of the American-backed Cuban dictator Fulgencio Batista in 1959, was executed in Bolivia – an act orchestrated by the Bolivian military government and the Central Intelligence Agency, and captained by the Cuban ex-pat Félix Rodríguez. Still defiant in the face of an expansive imperial power, Che's last words to his Bolivian executioner were, "Shoot, coward, you are only going to kill a man." Indeed, Che's complete identification with his revolutionary cause, the cause of human emancipation, has forever cemented his defiant image with that of liberation, justice, and the end of capitalist exploitation and imperial tyranny. No face in the West has ever become more associated with the Third World's struggle against oppression then Che Guevara, and thus his image appears wherever humanity finds itself in a left-wing revolt, as his disobedience to the status quo was his obedience to a vision of a society worthy of all human life.

We in the West are familiar with the names of Martin Luther, Vladimir Ilyich Lenin and Ernesto "Che" Guevara, even if contemporary western society is blissfully unaware of the prophetic and Socratic nuances of their life and work. In many ways, the memory of rebellious individuals like Luther, Lenin and Che, are like phantoms – ghosts with familiar names – somehow lingering around, their presence eerily felt, but thoroughly ignored as they don't seem to impact the routinized lifeworld of the given market-driven consumer society – the society of *ghafla* (mindlessness/distractedness).

While these names force some of us to recall what we learned (or did not learn) in our all-too-shallow history classes, many revolutionaries who have made enormous impacts on the lives of millions remain completely unfamiliar to those of us in the somnambulant West. Their names are no more familiar to us than the random Uber driver, restaurant server, or bank teller. This, coming from the perspective of the Frankfurt School, is unforgiveable; for if the *freedom of all* is to supplant the *freedom of the few*, which is the current condition of much of the world, then we much understand those same (or similar) revolutionary forces that animate the struggle for liberation outside of the West. The liberation of the proletariat and precariat in the West is predicated on liberation of those same people outside of the West. Those of us in the western world must begin to cultivate a world-consciousness, which entails leaving behind our occidental-narcissism. As Malcolm X attempted to do, we must become international in scope, so that the cause of liberation can create allies among the entire span of the world's wretched and oppressed.

One such revolutionary we must study is Dr. Ali Shariati, the revolutionary sociologist, intellectual, author and activists who was instrumental in the overthrow of the Shah of Iran, Mohammad Rezā Pahlavi. This American puppet regime was installed by the CIA and MI6 in a coup d'état in 1953, overthrowing the democratically elected socialist Prime Minister, Dr. Mohammad Mosaddegh. This illegal act of imperial power ushered in one of the most brutal dictatorships in the modern Middle East. Just ten years after the murder of the Che Guevara, in 1977, Ali Shariati's struggle against the "Peacock Throne" came to an abrupt end, as he died under "mysterious circumstances" in a foreign hospital in Southampton, Britain, shortly after he had been released from the Shah's prison.[2] His premature death ended the life of one of the most important modernizers and reformists in Islam – who, by all accounts, was a sincere (and desperately needed) *mujaddīd* (renewer of Islam).[3] Unlike those phantom revolutionaries mentioned before, whose names and ideas linger as specters in the western air, Shariati's contribution to the liberation of his country from western dominance, both politically and economically, remains evident even today. Although his face does not adorn the walls of government buildings and the inner-sanctums of personal homes in Iran, as does the images of Ayatollah Khomeini and his successors, the language and ideals of Ali Shariati so fertilized the once stale traditionalism of the Shi'a clerics, that it's hard to fathom modern Shi'a Islam without his revolutionary influence. His impact on the most important of all modern Iranian Shi'a clerics, Ayatollah Khomeini, is undeniable.[4] In many ways, it is through Ayatollah Khomeini, and his appropriation of an Islam saturated with revolutionary class-consciousness, *Red Shi'ism*, that Shariati's influence can still

---

2   Ali Rahnema, *An Islamic Utopian: A Political Biography of Ali Sharī'ati.* (London: I.B. Tauris Publishers, 2000), 330–370.

3   Ali Rahnema (Ed.), *Pioneers of Islamic Revival.* (London: Zed Books, 2008), Chapter 9.

4   Dustin Byrd, *Ayatollah Khomeini and the Anatomy of the Islamic Revolution in Iran: Towards a Theory of Prophetic Charisma.* (Lanham, MD: University Press of America, 2011), 77–107.

be witnessed today.[5] Amidst the reign of the Shah, Shariati taught a whole generation that resistance was indeed a fundamental principle within Islam, and that to embody this principle – to disobey the unjust status quo – was not only a revolutionary duty for those seeking national liberation, but an act of religious faith. *To be Muslim is to revolt, and to revolt is to be Muslim.*

Purpose

The purpose of this chapter is to explore Ali Shariati's attempt to recover the revolutionary core of Islam – resurrecting the prophetic, emancipatory and liberational core that once animated the Islam of the 7th and 8th century, which, by the 20th century, had become uninspiring, static, non-dialectical and/or even oppressive, and thus incapable of realizing the very mission it was tasked to do by Muhammad himself: to create the social, political and economic conditions that were worthy of the divine's dearest creation: mankind. This chapter seeks to demonstrate how Ali Shariati's marriage of class-conscious western philosophy – born out of the struggle to emancipate the West from its own class-confinements and abuses of power – and Shi'a Islam, reinvigorated the slumbering core of Prophet Muhammad's religion. With the help of the Frankfurt School's Critical Theory of Religion and Society, I will demonstrate that Ali Shariati not only came to agree with the Frankfurt School's *dialectical* approach to religion, which rejected Feuerbach's, Marx's, Lenin's, Freud's and Nietzsche's *abstract negation* of religion, but that he also followed a similar process in regards to western critical philosophy: he engaged in a *determinate negation* of such philosophy, thus delivering its emancipatory potentials to religion. For Shariati, this meant that the "affirmative" Black Shi'ism of the Safavid dynasty was negated in favor of the "negative" Red Shi'ism/Islam of Muhammad ibn 'Abdallah, 'Alī ibn Abī Ṭālib, Al-Ḥussein ibn 'Alī ibn Abī Ṭālib and Abū Dhār al-Ghifarī. In this sense, Ali Shariati, like the Frankfurt School, created a Critical Theory of Religion, wherein religion struggles not only against secular oppression, but against religious oppression as well. Thus, Shariati's revolutionary Islam will struggle against the degrading idols of modernity just

---

5   Clerical detractors of Shariati pleaded with Khomeini to condemn Shariati's work as being "unIslamic." However, according to the biographer Ali Rahnema, having read the available works of Shariati, Khomeini refused to be pitted against one of the most influential critics of the Shah, even if he was also critical of the clerical establishment. Rahnema, *An Islamic Utopian,* 275.

as the Frankfurt School's Critical Theory of Religion struggles against the idols of neo-liberal capitalism, nationalism, ethno-superiority and all other ideologies that legitimate human oppression. Lastly, unlike the secular Frankfurt School, who translated religious elements into secular philosophy, Ali Shariati consciously did the opposite: he translated secular philosophy into religion. In an era of increased secularization, where many critics of religion expect it to soon come to its end, Shariati's religious approach proved to be more appropriate for the national liberation of 20th century Iran, which still held fast to its Shi'a identity.

The Frankfurt School's Critical Theory of Religion: Determinate Negation

The Frankfurt School for Social Research has long been viewed as a neo-Marxist school of thought, which also has deep roots in the works of Kant, Hegel, Freud and Nietzsche. To their critics, these left-wing Jewish intellectuals of the mid-20th century represent an invasive "cultural Marxism," which is claimed to be responsible for the modern "evils" of multiculturalism, political correctness, and the erosion of the Christian foundations of the West.[6] To their supporters, they are non-conforming intellectuals who questioned the foundational ideologies of capitalism, consumerism and bourgeois democracy. Within their broader critical theory of society, these scholars, including Theodor W. Adorno, Max Horkheimer, Hebert Marcuse, Walter Benjamin, Erich Fromm and Leo Löwenthal, developed a critical theory of religion.[7] While their work on religion saturated a variety of their larger works, the development of such constellational thought was pioneered most concretely by the scholar of the second generation of critical theorists, Rudolf J. Siebert. Later, following the September 11, 2001, attacks on New York and Washington D.C., religion became a serious subject of inquiry for other philosophers such as Jürgen Habermas, Jacques Derrida, Slavoj Žižek, Judith Butler and Martha Nussbaum. The Frankfurt School faithfully followed the dialectical logic of the historical materialist Karl Marx, which he learned from his teacher G.W.F. Hegel. While negating, preserving,

---

6　Although these accusations against the Frankfurt School have had a long life in the West, especially among the "alt-right," they recently motivated one of the worst hate crimes in Europe: the white nationalist Anders Behring Breivik's lone wolf terrorist attack on Oslo and Utøya Island in 2011, which resulted in the deaths of 77 individuals.

7　See Eduardo Mendieta, *The Frankfurt School on Religion: Key Writings by the Major Thinkers.* New York: Routledge, 2005.

fulfilling and elevating Aristotelian logic, Hegel's dialectical logic attempted to go beyond the realm of the given, the structures of the *world-as-it-is*, offering us insights into the *world-of-becoming* – the *world-as-it-should-be* – beyond the world of appearances and beyond the ideological world of "necessary appearances."[8] Hegel's metaphysics, philosophy of history and dialectical logic thereby created the intellectual space necessary to imagine a world in which the arc of history is bent towards reedom for all. This dialectical method, which Hegel described as *determinate negation (bestimmte negation)*, seems perfectly obvious to dialectical philosophers today, but when it was first articulated in his *Science of Logic (Wissenschaft der Logik)* in 1816, it proved revolutionary, especially in the hands of the Young Hegelians, including Ludwig Feuerbach and Karl Marx. Marx would later turn Hegel "upon his head," by dialecticizing the left-wing materialism that was becoming increasingly prevalent in his day. Such materialism gave primacy to the material world in history's development and its current state-of-being.

But before there was Marx, there was Hegel's dialectical logic, and in order to better understand the central claim of this argument, that Hegel's dialectical logic is essential for both the Frankfurt School's and Ali Shariati's critical theory of religion, we should examine the relevant passage wherein Hegel articulates his understanding of dialectics. Attempting to explain the nature of *determinate negation,* as opposed to *abstract negation*, Hegel defines his logic as such,

> All that is necessary to achieve scientific progress – and it is essential to strive to gain this quite *simple* insight – is the recognition of the logical principle that the negative is just as much positive, or that what is self-contradictory does not resolve itself into a nullity, into abstract nothingness, but essentially only into the negation of its *particular* content, in other words, that such a negation is not all and every negation but the negation of a specific subject matter which resolves itself, and consequently is a specific negation, and therefore the result essentially contains that from which it results; which strictly speaking is a tautology, for otherwise it would be an immediacy, not a result. Because the result, the negation, is a *specific* negation, it has a *content*. It is a fresh Notion but higher and richer than its predecessor; for it is richer by the negation or opposite of

---

8   I use the word "ideology" or "ideological" in the Marxian sense, as the necessary camouflaging of reality behind statements, systems of thought, political propaganda, etc., meant to conceal the reality of class exploitation, racism, sexism, and the structure of domination by which the powerful continue to dominate the powerless.

the latter, therefore contains it, but also something more, and is the unity of itself and its opposite. It is in this way that the system of Notions as such has to be formed – and has to complete itself in a purely continuous course in which nothing extraneous is introduced.[9]

G.W.F. HEGEL; *Hegel's Science of Logic*, 54.

From this important quote, we have identified the dialectical processes that will animate the Frankfurt School's relationship to religion as well as Shariati's relationship to western philosophy. The Frankfurt School does not *abstractly negate* religion in the same way that their predecessors Feuerbach, Marx, Lenin and Nietzsche did, wherein all of religion is negated into "abstract nothingness," but rather they grasp elements within religion that they wish to preserve, elevate and fulfill within their own secular philosophy, which serves as a "fresh notion" that is "higher and richer than its predecessor." It is the "unity" of the prophetic elements within religion with critical secular philosophy. As such, the Frankfurt School has *determinately negated* religion, or even sublated (*aufheben*) religion, which allows certain semantic and semiotic material to migrate from the depth of the Abrahamic religions, especially Judaism and Christianity, into Critical Theory – an emancipatory process that Shariati will similarly follow but in the opposite direction; philosophy will be determinately negated, or sublated, into critical prophetic religion.[10]

This being the case, it cannot be claimed that these mainly secular philosophers are hostile to religion, unlike some of their immediate predecessors, for if they were, they would engage religion via *abstract negation* – an attempt to cancel religion altogether. On the contrary, they remained open to religion, witnessing the liberational and emancipatory potentials that dwelled just behind its public façade and its historical crimes. Thus, the first generation of the Frankfurt School saw both those elements within religion that aided in man's emancipation as well as those elements that contributed to man's continual enslavement, debasement and oppression. Thus, in his insightful *Notizen*, the first director of the Frankfurt School, Max Horkheimer, gives us his dialectical

---

9   G.W.F. Hegel, *Hegel's Science of Logic*. Trans. A.V. Miller. (Atlantic Highlands, NJ: Humanities Press International, 1993), 54. The emphases are in the original.

10   Hegel defines "sublation" as having two meanings, 'on the one hand it means to preserve, to maintain, and equally it also means to cause to cease, to put an end to. Even "to preserve" includes a negative element, namely, that something is removed from its immediacy and so from an existence which is open to external influence, in order to preserve it. Thus what is sublated is at the same time preserved; it has only lost its immediacy but is not on that account annihilated.' See, G.W.F. Hegel, *Hegel's Science of Logic*, 107.

definition of religion. He begins with what he determines to be the "good" aspects of religion, which we will later define as being the philosophically and historically *negative* aspects of religion, writing,

> What is religion in the good sense? To sustain, not to let reality stifle, the impulse for change, the desire that the spell be broken, that things take the right turn. We have religion where life down to its every gesture is marked by this resolve.[11]

For Horkheimer, "good religion" is the religion that rebels against the reality that stifles the humanity's longing for a different reality; "good religion" is the religion that preserves and acts upon the "impulse for change" within a world-condition that is unworthy of the dignity of human existence; "good religion" is predicated on the desire to break the spell of the given – the social conditions that foreclose on biophilia in favor of necrophilia; "good religion" longs to unlock the iron cage built by man's domination of man, man's domination of nature, man's exploitation of man, man's exploitation of nature, and man's alienation from himself, his fellow man, and his natural surroundings. According to Horkheimer, when religion is saturated with this longing for change, it embodies the original impetus that birthed the historical Abrahamic traditions.

What then is religion in the bad sense? Horkheimer writes,

> It [bad religion] is the same impulse but in its perverted form, as affirmation, prophecy, that gilds reality in the very act of castigating it. It is the lie that some earthly or heavenly future gives evil, suffering, horror, a meaning. The lie does not need the cross, it already lives in the ontological concept of transcendence.[12]

Here, one can see where Horkheimer's critique of religion takes on its dialectical form. First, he identifies those elements within "good religion" that should remain preserved within secular philosophy: the longing for a world without man's debasement via imperialism, capitalism, racism, sexism and all other forms of oppression and exploitation. Second, he identifies precisely those elements in "bad religion" that must be negated: its affirmation of the status quo, the sophistic appearance of "castigating" the unjust reality while secretly strengthening its already-existing coordinates, and the ideological claim,

---

11   Max Horkheimer, *Dawn & Decline: Notes 1926–1931 & 1950–1969.* Trans. Michael Shaw. (New York: The Seabury Press, 1978), 163.

12   Ibid.

which often takes on a metaphysical stature, that unnecessary suffering has an imminent and inherent meaning – thus justifying its existence. What Horkheimer's dialectical definition of religion is articulating here is that religion itself can either be a social force in service to man's liberation, or it can be functionalized as an ideological cover, a legitimation, for man's enslavement, exploitation, debasement. Thus, from the standpoint of the early critical theorists, because religion is in opposition to itself, *religion therefore must oppose religion*; it must fight against its own tendencies to become the handmaiden of the dominant classes – the *mala'* (wealthy aristocrats) and *mutrif* (the insatiate who live in ease and luxury), as Shariati described them. Religion's inner-contradictions, its own inner-logic, impels it to struggle against its tendency to sacrifice its *negativity* (its prophetic or *contra-mundi* elements) at the altar of earthly power, causing it to degenerate into mere *affirmative* ideology. Thus, in order to rescue religion from itself, it must resist its own functionalization as a means to give permanence to social statics.[13]

However, from the perspective of the Frankfurt School, rooted deeply within the western Enlightenment, the idea that religion itself will emancipate itself from its own self-imposed chains is wishful thinking. Western religion, which abandoned, for the most part, its emancipatory potentials in favor of a world-affirming type of "winner" religion (not a "loser" like the battered and abused Jesus on the cross), may have already nailed itself in its own historical coffin. For Critical Theory, the only substantive way to rescue those irreplaceable revolutionary potentials which formed the core of "good religion," is to forcibly rescue them from their *affirmative*, or "bad" forms; to emancipate those potentials via *determinate negation* of religion as a whole, thus allowing those materials to find new dwellings in secular critical philosophy – the emancipatory language of the modern prophetic voice, especially in the West. As the critical theorist Theodor W. Adorno wrote, 'nothing of theological content will persist without being transformed; every content will have to put itself to the test of migrating into the realm of the secular, the profane.'[14] From a secular western perspective, those aspects of religion that cannot pass the test of secularization must be left in the ditch of history, for without migration "into the realm of the secular," such religious language falls upon theologically-deaf ears.

Once rescued from the distorted form of affirmative Judaism and affirmative Christianity, such semantic and semiotic materials congealed within the

---

13   Ali Shariati, *Religion vs. Religion*. Trans. Laleh Bakhtiar. (Chicago: ABC International Group, Inc., 2003), 40, 47, 59.

14   Theodor W. Adorno, "Reason and Revelation" in *Critical Models: Interventions and Catchwords*. (New York: Columbia University Press, 2005), 136.

Frankfurt School's Critical Theory, serving as important sources of ideology critique. In this way, religion is no longer inhibited by the straightjacket of its historical betrayal of its own emancipatory nature. Through its dialectical negation, preservation and fulfillment, it comes to fertilize and propel critical philosophy to take on the mantle of the prophets, thus becoming "prophetic." Wherein the prophet once was the voice of the divine, the critical philosopher becomes the voice of *al-ḥaqq, veritas, aletheia, emet* (the Truth). Thus, a *determinate negation* of religion releases the revolutionary aspects of religion from the exoskeleton that strangles it, and gives them new life. It is no longer encumbered by the heavy shackles it placed around its own neck throughout the historical process. However, it no longer is religion per se, but rather religion's prophetic spirit that lives on within Hegel's "fresh Notion": a theologically-induced secular philosophy. In this role, critical philosophy serves as the grand inquisitor of the stifling reality produced by capitalist modernity, just as Socrates once questioned the wisdom of the Athenian slave-supported "democratic" state. As it looks to the *present* unjust and unsatisfactory conditions that limit man's flourishing, it interrogates the mendacity of the *past* and prepares for the horrors of neo-fascism(s) sure to come in the *future*.

With the Frankfurt School's *determinate negation* of religion in mind, it is entirely untrue to say that religion has been *abstractly negated* from western civilization, as some of the non-western critics have charged. Even though it appears to be thoroughly secular, it has not abandoned all forms of religious morality and/or ethical considerations: residue of the theological remains within the secular. Thus, Christian care (*caritas*) for the needy has been translated into social solidarity, which manifests itself in universal healthcare and the robust welfare state; the *Imago Dei* (man made in God's image) has been translated into the *Universal Declaration of Human Rights*; and the idea of *monogenesis* (the idea that all mankind shares common parentage) has been translated into movements against racism, sexism and xenophobia – as all humanity constitutes a single family. While such social policies no longer claim explicit theological justification, they do preserve their genealogical roots in religion.

However, just as Ali Shariati saw that religion fought against religion for the very soul of religion, so too secularity is split within itself and therefore fights against itself. There is a *negative* form of secularity, which has learned from emancipatory religion, rescued and appropriated the prophetic aspects of emancipatory religion, and elevates them in their struggle against all form of social oppression. On the other hand, there is an *affirmative* form of secularity, which like affirmative religion, serves as an apologist for the unjust conditions of the status quo, the given, the *world-as-it-is*. Just as affirmative secularity

abandoned the emancipatory potentials inherent within the original impulse behind the western Enlightenment, which at its beginning was meant
to liberate 'human beings from fear' and install 'them as masters' of his own
fate, it has also abandoned any attempt to *determinate negate* the emancipatory potential of revealed religion. Affirmative secularity has rather *abstractly
negated* religion precisely because it – whether in its neo-fascist, neoliberal or
neoconservative forms – witnesses prophetic forms of religion as viable and
potent threats to its class-dominated vision of the world – a Nietzschian vision
in which the *übermenschen* of society naturally dominate the *untermenschen* –
the *Aristocratic Law of Nature* universalized as a constitutional principle of
social organization, or, as expressed in the world of capitalist politics, the neo-
liberal utopia realized.[15]

Ali Shariati as Critical Theory of Religion

In Ali Shariati's book, *Religion vs. Religion*, he developed an Islamic form of
liberation theology, one that has strong resemblance to the Latin American
theologians and their struggle against North American imperialism. Applied
to Islam, Shariati follows closely the theological orientation of the Peruvian
theologian Gustavo Gutierrez, the initiator of Christian Liberation Theology,
and brings together a penetrating class analysis with the eschatological and
social claims of traditional theology – dragging calcified religion back down
to the muck and mire of the oppressed, the wretched, the discarded and the
excluded. In what is essentially two lectures, Shariati claims that religion's
primary struggle throughout history has not been between it and non-belief,
but rather between what he distinguishes as (1) the "religion of revolution,"
and (2) the "religion of legitimation." To his mind, the antagonism between
these two fundamentally different forms of religion have continued to propel
history forward, much like Marx's theory of class struggle. It was only in the
modern period, most especially in the 19th century West, that religion had
been forced to struggle against those who did not believe in some form of
divinity – the atheists.[16] Although the struggle between religion and secularity

---

15   Max Horkheimer and Theodor W. Adorno. *Dialectic of Enlightenment: Philosophical
        Fragments.* Ed. Gunzlin Schmid Noerr. Trans. Edmund Jephcott. (Stanford, CA: Stanford
        University Press, 2002), 1; Also see Dustin J. Byrd, *A Critique of Ayn Rand's Philosophy of
        Religion: The Gospel According to John Galt.* (Lanham, MD: Lexington Books, 2014), 51–67,
        145–167.
16   Shariati, *Religion vs. Religion,* 21. For Shariati, *kāfirūn* (disbelievers) are not atheists, as
        even *kāfirūn* believe in some form of divinity. Rather, they attempt to cover up that belief

is the predominant struggle in the West, Shariati demonstrated that the struggle between religion and non-religion is fairly new in the history of mankind, and only came to the rest of the world via European imperialism and the neo-imperialism of neoliberal globalization, which has exported western culture and economics to most of the non-western world. Until modernity, the predominant struggle taking place in the man's civilizations was between *al-muwaḥḥidun* (the unitarians) and *al-mušrikūn* (the polytheists). More specifically, between the prophetic religion of the Jews, Christians and Muslim, against the pagans and idolaters.[17] For Shariati, the religion of Islam, which has *determinately negated,* or *sublated (aufheben)*, its forebears, i.e. Judaism and Christianity, is the purest form of monotheism – at least as it was formulated and practiced by the Prophet, his companions, and his family.[18] As the purity of monotheism has been crystalized in the Abrahamic faith of Muhammad, Islam stands at the forefront against the modern world's descent into cultural, political and economic idolatry, the materialistic *shirk* (polytheism) of the consumer society, and moral vacuity of nihilism, i.e. *al-Jāhilīyah al-Jadīd* (the new age of ignorance). As such, modern Islam has a revolutionary, emancipatory, and liberational mission that not only has been inherited from the life of Prophet Muhammad (*al-sīra al-Nabawiyya*), but must be, according to Shariati, rediscovered, resurrected and reloaded against the modern backslide into a polytheistic and idolatrous state – especially in the *dar al-Islam*, where *gharbzadegi* (westoxification) has increasingly become entrenched in the family, civil society, and the state.[19] In order for that rejuvenation to occur, one must critically examine the same antagonistic dialectic within Islam that the

---

for their own selfish reasons. Additionally, Shariati's understanding of atheism is relatively common, and he seems to accept atheism as simply those who do not believe in any kind of divine being. The philosophical idea that the most concentrated form of theism has been preserved within the theological silence of the atheist – who say nothing about the divine – as if it's apophatic atheism – is missing from his analysis. For the philosopher Ernst Bloch, only the atheist could be a true believer, for it was only in the atheist's theological silence that the divine was not made a mockery of through cataphatic and reified language.

17   Ibid., 23.
18   Ibid., 31.
19   First coined by the Iranian philosopher Ahmad Fardid, the concept of "gharbzadegi" was made popular by Jalal Al-e Ahmad in his 1962 book *Occidentosis: A Plague from the West.* This term indicates the non-western person's infatuation, blind acquisition, and submission to all things western, so much so that the individual forgets their own cultural identity and their own history. Whatever is western is irrationally elevated to the status of good; whatever is domestic is denigrated to the status of bad. The person who has been stuck by "occidentosis," has been, in essence, mentally colonized by a foreign entity, and in effect is incapable of critique of that which colonizes them.

Frankfurt School discovered in both Judaism and Christianity: the dialectic between *affirmative* and *negative* religion, and the entrenched struggle between
the two. From this vantage point, we see where and how Ali Shariati developed
a critical theory of Islam along the same lines of the Frankfurt School's critical theory of Judeo-Christian religion – thus rescuing the most recalcitrant,
non-conforming and prophetic form of religion from its priestly penitentiary,
returning it to the struggle for a more peaceful, just and reconciled society.

Restorative Determinate Negation and the Recovery of the Social-Sacred

In terms of Hegel's dialectical logic, the negation of the negative is the positive;
the specific content of that which is negated vacates the specific content of
that which is preserved, i.e. the positive that remains, thus preserving, elevating and reformulating the positive into a new or "fresh notion." Such logical
movement forces that which is negated to resolve itself into nothingness – the
dustbin of history. In terms of Ali Shariati's *determinate negation* of the *Black*
Shi'ism of the *clerical* Safavid state, he attempts to negate the dynasty's original betrayal of the authentic Islam of the *Prophet*. Their betrayal was their
unwise abandonment of the prophetic and messianic nature of Muhammad's
Red religion of protest for the *Black* religion of worldly affirmation. Thus, they
chose to elevate an Islam congruent with the power-structures of the class-
stratified given society: the rule of the few over the many. For Shariati, they did
not *abstractly negate* Islam, for they could not do so without losing political legitimacy as Muslims rulers. Rather, they abandoned its *geist*; Islam became the
ideological cover by which they ruled Muslims *as Muslims in name only,* similar
to that of the opportunistic Umayyad clan (*al-'Umawiyyūn*), whose nepotism
births the imperial Umayyad dynasty and split the *ummah* (community) in
two. Those *negative* (world-defying) aspects of Islam, which aim at the unrav-
eling of the unjust and exploitative conditions humanity labors under, were
revoked in favor of a *religion of affirmation*, i.e. positive religion, or in Shariati
parlance, a "religion that legitimates."[20] This religion of faux-harmony seeks to
reconcile the victims of society to their victimization instead of elevating consciousness of the unpleasant dissonance of unnecessary suffering. The religion
of affirmation deodorizes the putrid stench of class warfare and class domination; the religion of the affirmative "Priest," as opposed to that of the revolting
"Prophet," seeks to incorporate more fully those who find themselves the
abused of history, on Rome's cross, the torturer's rack, or the impaler's spikes,

---

20   Shariati, *Religion vs. Religion,* 32–33.

into the harmonizing worldview of the oppressor – the ideology of reified class relations – by which the victims accept their condition as inevitable, natural, or the way it *must* be. In this sense, Ali Shariati's critical theory of religion attempted to turn the clock on history – reversing it to a time when the *zeitgeist* of Muhammad still animated the community of believers. Theoretically, his was a *restorative determinate negation* of Black Shi'ism, which aimed at the recovery of the prophetic *animus* of Red Islam.

The dialectical tension inhibiting the religion of Islam from realizing its *social-sacred* mission, its Janus-faced and seemingly impassible dialectic between the affirmative and the negative, was overcome by Shariati's own *determinate negation* of the Safavid's worldly sublation of Islam to the worldly dictates of the *mala'* and *mutrif*, their power-nexus, and insatiability. Speaking about those Muslims who perverted Islam into an ideology of legitimation, Shariati said,

> It is they who guarded and confirmed the wealthy aristocrats (*mala'*) and the insatiable people who live in ease and luxury (*mutrif*), oppression, suppression, exploitation, hardships, discriminations, ignorance and the killing of human talents, throughout history and theses pauses, stagnations and killing of great heroes, the killing of great spirits throughout history; it was they who neutralized all of the benefits which should have been gained from the efforts, *jihad* and struggles of the rightful prophets and the rightful religion in history.[21]

In order for Red Shi'ism/Islam of the Prophet, his companions, his family, and the Muslim "socialist" Abu Dhār al-Ghifarī, to reappear, the historical betrayal of the emancipatory elements of the Prophet's religion, as perpetrated by the Black Shi'ism of monarchical clerics and the hypocrites (*munāfiqun*), which turned Islam from a "good religion" to a "bad religion," had to be reversed. Their *determinate negation* of the prophetic elements of Islam had to be *determinately negated* in order to rescue those prophetic and emancipatory elements. Returning Islam to its rightful place as a religion of emancipation is precisely what Shariati aimed to do in his critical theory of religion.

Against the Idols – Bilderverbot and Tawḥīd

Although Ali Shariati and the first generation of the Frankfurt School came from two different religious traditions, Shi'a Islam and Judaism, they both, in

---

21   Shariati, *Religion vs. Religion*, 59.

their attempt to create a critical theory of religion, turned to similar theological concepts: The *Bilderverbot* and *Tawḥīd*, as animating notions that oppose the unjust *world-as-it-is*. The *Bilderverbot* is the 2nd Commandment of the Jewish Decalogue. It states,

> You shall not make for yourself a graven image, or any likeness of anything that is in heaven above, or that is on the earth beneath, or that is in the water under the earth; you shall not bow down to them or serve them; for I am the Lord your God am a jealous God.[22]

Tawḥīd, understood in Islam as the radical oneness of the Divine, is described in the *Qur'ān* numerous times, as it is the essential message of the revelation. *Sūrat al-Ikhlāṣ*, which is often described as *Sūrat al-Tawḥīd*, described the divine (*Allāh*) as such:

> Say, 'He, God, is One. God, the Eternally Sufficient unto Himself. He begets not; nor was He begotten. And none is like unto him.'[23]

Both of these concepts are intrinsically tied to worldviews that reject the idolization of anything temporal or created: in a phrase – anything *less than the divine*. In both Judaism and Islam, it is commonly understood that the concepts of *Bilderverbot* and *Tawḥīd* belong exclusively to the theological realm. However, both Ali Shariati and the Frankfurt School argue that their meaning can be, and should be, and in some cases are originally meant to be, exported into the social sphere, thus deploying them within a social struggle against the already existing society and all its gross disfigurements.

It is evidenced from their own writings on religion that the Frankfurt School does not only root itself in the Enlightenment thought of Kant, Hegel, Marx, Freud and Nietzsche, but also in the Hebrew figure of Moses, the emancipatory prophet of the Torah. More specifically, the Critical Theory is anchored in the second commandment found in the Hebrew Bible, the *Bilderverbot,* or "image ban." Take for example Max Horkheimer's 1969 letter to Otto O. Herz of Vienna. In this letter, Horkheimer attempts to explain why the Jewishness of

---

22   *The Holy Bible.* Deuteronomy 5:8. Revised Standard Version (New York: Thomas Nelson Inc., 1972), 161.

23   *Al-Qur'ān. Sūrat al-Ikhlāṣ* 112: 1–4. Seyyed Hossein Nasr (Ed.), *The Study Quran: A New Translation and Commentary.* (New York: HarperOne, 2015), 1579.

his recently deceased friend and collaborator, Theodor W. Adorno, did not appear in his funeral.[24] Horkheimer writes,

> I have a keen understanding of your regret that there was no acknowledgement of his Jewishness at the burial of my friend Adorno. The *external* reasons are obvious. His father was of Jewish heritage. His mother, née Calvelli-Adorno della Piana, and her sister were both Catholics and artists who were important in Adorno's education. Teddie Adorno was baptized a Catholic and confirmed a Protestant due to the influence of a Protestant religion teacher.[25]

From this passage, it appears that the funeral for Adorno was thoroughly Christian or maybe at best nominally Christian. It appears his Jewish heritage was not considered despite the fact that it was his father's ethno-religious heritage. Nevertheless, Horkheimer is attempting to assuage the confusion of Mr. Herz, saying that this was only the "external" façade to Adorno's complicated relation to religion; what was really important about Adorno was his life's work, i.e. Critical Theory. Although it didn't appear in his funeral, what lay at the core of his life's work was thoroughly Jewish. In fact, it was the most radical aspect of all of Judaism. Horkheimer continues,

> I am telling you this in order to help you understand the complicated attitude of the decease to religion and to a specific faith. On the other hand, I may say that Critical Theory, which we both developed, has its roots in Judaism. It derives from the idea that *thou shalt make no image of God*.[26]

For the secular skeptic, it may be difficult to accept the idea that the theological prohibition on idolatry lay at the very foundation of Critical Theory. However, from the standpoint of secular philosophy, we must ask a different question: why were these supposedly "neo-Marxist" philosophers harkening back to the biblical account of Moses for their modern struggle against the barbarity of modernity, especially fascism. What kind of conceptual material did Moses provide Critical Theory, especially considering that Critical Theory is a thoroughly modern philosophy – understood to not only be rooted in the

---

24   Max Horkheimer, *A Life in Letters: Selected Correspondence.* Ed. and Trans. by Manfred R. Jacobson and Evelyn M. Jacobson. (Lincoln, NE: University of Nebraska Press, 2007), 361.

25   Ibid. Emphasis is mine.

26   Ibid. Emphasis is mine.

Enlightenment, but also understood to be that which attempted to rescue and preserve the Enlightenment in the face of its collapse into a new oppressive and totalizing myth?[27] Clearly, for Horkheimer and Adorno, the "image-ban" provided some kind of foundation from which they could build their Critical Theory of Society as well as their Critical Theory of Religion, which is concerned not entirely with theological questions, but rather with social, political and economic questions.

The power of the *Bilderverbot* lies in its *negativity*: its resistance towards anything temporal or created being absolutized into a false-divinity – an idol. Whether it is a nation, a leader, or an ideology, the negativity of the "image-ban" forbids – both religiously and philosophically – the adherent from submitting to anything other than that which creates the created – the a-temporal, the eternal, the ever lasting. The positivity of images, their immanence as reality, is the lie that they are anything other than the creation of man's own hands or mere nature, and therefore subject to the same decay as the rest of matter. In other words, they are but temporal objects falsely raised to the level of the atemporal – the eternal. When thinking about physical icons, this ban on worshipping the non-divine as if it were the divine seem theologically sound within the context of Abrahamic faiths. In the Bible, Abraham himself was the original idol-destroyer.[28] However, for the Frankfurt School, the anti-idolatry of the *Bilderverbot* has an additional export to the social-realm; nothing in *society* can be falsely elevated to the level of an absolute, to which absolute submission is due. Since this is the case, all things that augment themselves to the level of an absolute, must be rejected, criticized, and deconstructed until they are shown to be what in reality they are: lies parading as Truth. As such, the *Bilderverbot* lies at the heart of the Frankfurt School's secular ideology critique – for it too brooks no confidence in the claims of anything falsely absolutized.[29]

---

27   See Max Horkheimer and Theodor W. Adorno's *Dialectic of Enlightenment: Philosophical Fragments.*

28   *Al-Qur'ān*, 21: 51–70.

29   Ali Shariati was well aware of the anti-idolatry of the western Enlightenment. He wrote, "the mission which European intellectuals and seekers of liberation undertook in their struggle with the church, the religion of the Middle Ages in Europe resulted in the liberation of European thought after 1000 years of stagnation. They struggled against this deviated religion and religious deviation, that is, multitheism (*shirk*). They developed a resistance movement against a religion ruled by an arrogant despot who, in the clothes of the Prophet Jesus, rebelled against God's commands. The mission of theirs was a continuation of that very mission which the divinely-appointed prophets continuously undertook against the reactionary, deviated religion which opposed the people, which

Some may say that the image ban seems to work for the religious, as they are the ones who willingly submit to the unseen divine being. It should be very different for the secular philosopher who does not accept the existence of a divine being and is therefore free to attach his loyalties to whatever humanly-constructed edifice he wishes to. This may be the case for some philosophers, such as the fascist Martin Heidegger and others who absolutized German *blut und boden* and the Führer.[30] However, this is not the case for the Frankfurt School. This is due to two reasons; first, they determinately negated Judaism, thus sublating its image ban into secular philosophy, which they personally and theoretically attached themselves, not only as a singular philosophical principle, but more precisely as a guiding-spirit that animated their entire corpus. In other words, the image ban was translated from its original theological context into philosophy, by which its anti-idolatry negativity continued within secular form – against any form of social, political and/or economic idolatry. Second, since Kant demonstrated reason's limitations, that reason cannot penetrate the *thing-in-itself,* including, and most especially, the divine being – which eludes all positive articulations – the Frankfurt School has remained silent on the existence of the divine. Within that silence, the possibility of the divine remains preserved – for the silence itself is apophatic theology. In a sense, the *mysterium tremendum* that accompanies the totally otherness of the divine within Abrahamic faiths, which renders positive utterances about the divine as being false, untrue, and lies, or at best semblances, is preserved in their Critical Theory. Therefore, they need not be personally committed to the whole of Judaism to embody the negativity of Judaism's *Bilderverbot* in their critical political theory and dialectical religiology.

Turning to Shariati's political-social understanding of Islam's notion of *Tawḥīd*, we see something very similar to the Frankfurt School's sublation of Judaism's Bilderverbot, albeit in a different direction within a dialectical movement. As I previously mentioned, in his book *Religion vs. Religion,* Shariati reminds his listener that *Tawḥīd* (divine oneness) has struggled throughout history with *shirk* (polytheism). However, this struggle has not simply been

---

opposed human rights, which legitimates or justifies the position of those who hold the power, wealth and/or means by which to deceive, which stupefies and narcotizes people. The European intellectual did this in order to *destroy all idols* and all signs of the religion of multitheism although they did not explain things in these terms." Emphasis added. See Shariati, *Religion vs. Religion,* 59–60.

30   Victor Farías, *Heidegger and Nazism.* Ed. Joseph Margolis and Tom Rockmore. Philadelphia: Temple University Press, 1989.

between two mere theological ideas, but rather this antagonism takes concrete form in the struggle for human emancipation in history. He writes,

> This religion of monotheism, while it invites humanity to submit before God, in the same way and for this very reason, *it invites humanity to rebel against anything that is other than He*. Opposed to this, the religion of multitheism [polytheism] or *shirk* invites humanity to rebel against this great Beloved of Existence, before this invitation of Islam to God, who is the meaning of all of existence and the eternal goal of all life, and to rebel against the religion of Islam and [its call to] "surrender." It terminates automatically in surrender and slavery to hundreds of other powers, to hundreds of other polarizations and forces, where each pole, each power, each class and each group has a god.[31]

For Shariati, the oneness of the divine, which testifies to the oneness of his creation, including the human family, is the foundation by which the believer rejects all forms of idolatry – the absolutization of not only a created thing, but a given social structure, political ideology, etc. In the mid-20th century, the structure that determined the political-economy of Iran was the capitalist system and the neo-liberal imperial power that both supported it and was supported by it, i.e. the United States and their client, the Shah of Iran. The *negativity* inherent within the notion of divine oneness dissolves all attempts to elevate anything in the *dunyā* (world) from proclaiming itself to be the Truth (*al-ḥaqq*) – for only the divine being, which can only be articulated adequately in silence or *via negativa*, as in negative theology, can be considered absolute Truth, and thus engender absolute obedience.[32] In this sense, absolute obedience to the divine manifests itself in disobedience to that which contradicts the *tawḥīdic* principle of Islam itself, as Prophet Muhammad's Islam is understood to be the "perfected religion" that the divine has chosen for mankind.[33] While

---

31   Shariati, *Religion vs. Religion*, 30.

32   From a traditional Islamic perspective, apophatic (negative) theology becomes preferable to cataphatic (positive) theology when positive theology treads too close to defining the divine within the limits of man's species language. However, it is also clear that Islam prefers to speak of the divine from within the language of the divine, i.e. the *Qur'ān* itself, in the Arabic language. It is understood that while man's understanding of the full capacity of divine reality is limited, and that the *full* meaning of the *Qur'ān* escapes even the most knowledgeable of scholars, *Qur'ānic* language is preferable to either apophatic silence or cataphatic distortions.

33   *al-Qur'ān*, 5: 3.

this creates potential *fitnah* (division) within the community of believers, who have no choice but to interpret the *Qur'ān* and the Islamic tradition within the confines and laws of reason, grammar, and logic, even with which errors can be made, it nevertheless secures the believer from conflating the *given* with the *ought*, the *world-as-it-should-be* with the *world-as-it-is*, as well as *dunyā* and *ākhira* (the hereafter).

For Shariati, the diminishment of *Tawḥīd* to a mere theological category, even as central as it is, does violence to the notion itself. This deflation robs the notion of its social-political and economic elements. In other words, it turns *Tawḥīd* into a category for academic discourse, a subject of theologians (*mutakallimūn*), a simple matter of cognition, rather than a *way-of-being-in-the-world* that is modeled after the praxis of Muhammad, which inevitably includes communicative rationality and *moral-practical* concerns. For Shariati, polytheism is not only a positivistic description of a given theology of multiple gods, but is an active form of religion that justifies, sanctifies and legitimates injustice, exploitation, and continual degradation of humanity. It is an affirmative political-theology of the status quo, the ruling class, the *mala'* and *mutrif*.[34] This is the same critique Muhammad leveled at Mecca's pagan religion and society in the 7th century Arabia; its polytheist theology legitimated its unjust poly-perverse society.

With the dichotomy of *Tawḥīd* and polytheism in mind, Shariati reminds us that the *oneness of humanity* is inextricably tied to the *oneness of the divine*. When the singular concept of the divine is falsely divided, it inevitably legitimates the false – and historically bloody – divisions championed by classism, racism, ethnocentricity, and feelings of racial superiority, etc. He writes,

> It is the development of a society based upon a [philosophy] and based upon a social school in which an arrogant leader who rebels against God's Command, who is the legitimizer of discrimination, is destroyed and *replaced by monotheism* which signifies the *unity of society and humanity*.[35]

Opium Religion

It may come as a surprise to some to hear a deeply religious figure, such as Ali Shariati, agree with the 18th and 19th century Enlightenment philosophers'

---

34   Shariati, *Religion vs. Religion,* 32–33.
35   Ibid., 31. Emphasis added.

and Historical Materialists' claim that religion is the "opiate of the masses," a seemingly anti-religion statement, formulated by Marx as such,

> Religious suffering is at the same time an expression of real suffering and a protest against real suffering. Religion is the sigh of the oppressed creature, the sentiment of a heartless world, and the soul of soulless condition. It is the opium of the people.[36]

While it is clear that Marx sees religion as an epiphenomenon – a result of the material conditions in which the abased masses finds themselves – he does not place the blame for the misery of those masses upon religion per se. He rather sees religion as the sincere expression, sigh and sentiment of genuine suffering: suffering that is translated into consoling thoughts, ideas and practices. For Shariati, the historical materialists' critique of religion, especially the polytheistic religion that is born from the suppression and/or extraction of the prophetic, is correct. Shariati agrees that religion is too often functionalized simply as a narcotic for the masses, assuaging the pain, suffering, and alienation they experience within their lifeworld. In such a functionalized state, religion fails to motivate such suffering individuals to change the coordinates that impose unnecessary suffering upon them – it rather reconciles them to what they perceive as their "fate." Shariati stated unequivocally in *Religion vs. Religion* that Marx's analysis is right, saying that opiate religion helps 'surrender' people 'to their abjectness, difficulties, wretchedness and ignorance, surrender to the static situation which they are obliged to have' and even 'surrender to the disgraceful fate which they and their ancestors were obliged to have and still have – an inner, ideological surrender.'[37] Thus, opium religion has the effect of evaporating the emancipatory potential of the maligned classes, dulling down their willingness to stand upright and "walk tall" in the face of opposition, to use the expression of the theologian-philosopher Ernst Bloch.[38] Such

---

36   Karl Marx, *The Marx-Engels Reader*. Ed. Robert C. Tucker. (New York: W.W. Norton & Co., Inc., 1978), 54.

37   Shariati, *Religion vs. Religion*, 35.

38   Jürgen Habermas, *Autonomy and Solidarity: Interviews with Jürgen Habermas*. Ed. Peter Dews. (New York: Verso, 1992), 144. Before Marx, Kant opined about the opiate form of religion, writing in his book *Religion within the Boundaries of Mere Reason*, that "the aim of those who have a clergyman summoned to them at the end of life is normally to find in him a comforter, not on account of their physical sufferings brought on by the last illness or even by the natural fear in the face of death (for on this score death itself, which puts an end to life, can be the comforter) but because of the moral sufferings, the reproaches of their conscience. At such time, however, conscience ought rather to be stirred up and

opiate religion convinces the victims of the status quo to accept their abasement not only because it assuages their suffering, and makes them "feel good," but also because it comforts them to think that their suffering is the divine's will, which, no matter how painful, imparts inherent "meaning" into their suffering. Shariati says,

> It is the opium of the people so that people find belief in the idea that whatever happens is in God's hands. It is because of God's will and any efforts to try and change the situation, to try to improve the life of the people is to oppose God's will.[39]

Shariati is fully aware that the form of religion that the western Enlightenment itself rebelled against was either (1) the religion that appeared on the outside to be monotheistic but was in reality polytheistic, worshipping the false-gods of wealth, power and prestige, and therefore a betrayal of Christianity's elevation of the poor, powerless and excluded, or, (2) bourgeois religion – which was merely functionalized in Bourgeois society as a pattern-maintenance system, which serves to integrate the materially impoverished masses into the already-existing society of class domination. In such a society, religion becomes mere *ideology* (false consciousness) – an ideology the bourgeois themselves didn't – and still don't – believe in.

Nevertheless, Shariati's surmises that philosophers such as Marx fail to penetrate the reality of Abrahamic religion: its *dialectical* nature, or, as he states, the ongoing inner-struggle within religion, i.e. the historical conflict between 'human-based multitheism and divinely based monotheism.'[40] In other words, Marx and his followers failed to adequately differentiate the dialectic of religion: the *positive religion* of the Bourgeois and the *negative religion* of the Prophets, i.e. the priestly religion that legitimates the status quo and the prophetic religion that rebels against the status quo; the "bad religion" of enslavement

---

sharpened, in order that whatever good yet to be done, or whatever consequences of past evil still left to be undone (repaired for), will not be neglected, in accordance with the warning, "Agree with thine adversary" (with him who has a legal right against you) "quickly, while thou art in the way with him" (i.e. so long as you still live), "lest he deliver thee to the judge" (after death), etc. But to administer *opium* to conscience instead, as it were, is to be guilty of a crime against the human being himself and against those who survive him, and is totally contrary to the purpose for which such support given to conscience at life's end can be held necessary." See Immanuel Kant, *Religion within the Boundaries of Mere Reason and Other Writings.* (New York: Cambridge University Press, 1998), 93.

39   Shariati, *Religion vs. Religion*, 36–37.
40   Ibid., 60.

and the "good religion" of emancipation. Without an adequate understanding of religion's dialectical nature, and its struggle against itself, the abstract negation of religion advocated by many materialists would vacate religion from the humanity's struggle against injustice, poverty and imperialism. When the opium side of religion is universalized, it forecloses on the prophets and the prophetic voices who resist the status quo, thus leaving religion to those who functionalize it for maintaining social statics. Like the first generation of critical theorists, especially Theodor W. Adorno, Max Horkheimer, Erich Fromm, Walter Benjamin and Leo Löwenthal, who weren't prepared to reject the negativity of the *Bilderverbot*, Ali Shariati was not prepared to abandon the prophetic within religion, the recalcitrant negativity of *Tawḥīd*, but rather he attempted to recover, reload, and redeploy it in the struggle for human emancipation, in his case, against the social, political, and economic polytheism of the Shah of Iran.

Context Matters: Shi'i Iran and the Secular West – Recovery or Sublation

So far I have argued that both the first generation of critical theorists of the Frankfurt School and Ali Shariati attempted to rediscover and recover those negative and prophetic elements of Abrahamic religion and redirected them towards the emancipation of the suffering and oppressed masses. However, there is one important differentiation that should not be overlooked: the *social* and *historical context* in which these two streams of radical thought came to be, i.e. twentieth century Iran and the increasingly secularized modern West. These contexts impinge on the direction in which such emancipatory material is rescued and translated. Specifically, does the recovered material find its home in philosophy or in religion?

As Ali Rahnema's comprehensive biography *An Islamic Utopian* suggests, Ali Shariati was essentially a modern religious man; he was a man of both reason and Shi'i faith. He lived within a country where religion remained an integral part of the life of the individual, family, and society.[41] In this context, the dominant interpretation of reality and orientation of praxis was safely guarded within the arms of religion, even if much of the Shi'i tradition had capitulated to the demands of the Pahlavi status quo, thus delivering to its adherents an emasculated faith: affirmation via political quietism. Although Iran had gone through the Shah's so-called "White Revolution" (*Enghelāb-e Sefīd*) (1963–1968), which was meant to modernize and westernize Iran, and

---

41   Rehnema, *An Islamic Utopian,* 1–103.

had consequently been ensnared in the ravages of *gharbzadegi*, the nation was still at its core a religious one.[42] The thin veneer of western secularity, which was strongest amongst the western educated ruling elites, did not penetrate far enough into the spirit of the Iranian people that it could dislodge Shi'i Islam from their being and civilization.

On the other hand, for the first generation of Critical Theorists, growing up as assimilated Jews within the earliest decades of 20th century Europe, especially Germany, the secularization process had already removed religion as a meaningful social force within the lives of the majority of the people. At best, religion, especially Christianity, was a faint shadow of what it used to be. Western Europe was content to claim itself a "Judeo-Christian" civilization without taking the substantive claims of Christianity seriously. Although a self-declared religious identity remained engrained within certain segments of society, and in some geographical locations more than others, the Enlightenment for the most part had neutralized religion as the true guiding light within the civilization's lifeworld, thus leaving an existential void – the "triumph of nihilism" that Friedrich Nietzsche foresaw.[43] In search of something to replace that which was missing with the demise of religion, Europe in the early 20th century gravitated to the next transcendental cause that could provide the masses with meaning, purpose, and sense of mission. Although not entirely the "new values" Nietzsche had in mind, both international communism and/or palingenetic nationalism, i.e. fascism, consumed the void left by the collapse of traditional Christianity.[44] Additionally, both of these political philosophies were born in response to the false promises of the bourgeoisie, which failed to deliver material prosperity for all. Its foundational principles, *liberté, égalité*, and *fraternité*, proved to ring hollow for the poor, the wage laborer, the colonized and the marginalized, who remained hopelessly without *liberté*, without *égalité*, and without *fraternité*. Rather, in the name of such lofty values, the Bourgeois Enlightenment brought a stringent class hierarchy, economic exploitation, imperialism and a modern form of tribalism. Although its values remained potent, transformative, and even revolutionary, the bourgeoisie itself failed at its task – to make men free and masters of their fate – thus opening space for a return to neo-pagan tribal alliances (nationalism) or a "new Christianity," i.e.

---

42   Mohammad Reza Pahlavi Aryamehr, *The White Revolution*. Tehran: The Imperial Pahlavi Library, 1967. Also see Jalal Al-i Ahmad, *Occidentosis: A Plague from the West*. Trans. R. Campbell. Ed. Hamid Algar. Berkeley: Mizan Press, 1984.

43   Friedrich Nietzsche, *The Will to Power*. Trans. Anthony M. Ludovici. (New York: Barnes & Noble, 2006), xvii.

44   Ibid., xviii.

Marxism – messianism without the *heavenly* messiah. As such, both Marxism and fascism can be understood as the Bourgeoisie' inner-criticism.

For our two schools of thought, Shariati's and the Frankfurt School's, these contexts determined the relationship of their political philosophies to religion. For Shariati, the still religious context of Iran would not allow him to follow the Frankfurt School in their sublation (*aufheben*) of the emancipatory, prophetic, liberational and revolutionary aspects of religion into non-conformist secular philosophy, which rescued religion's core values while simultaneously allowed its public face to move into the background of history. In essence, religion was *determinately negated* into philosophy, sociology, and secular revolutionary praxis, which was appropriate for a modern secular society, such as Europe. Yet, what the Frankfurt School did, Shariati could not do; he was bound to a very different society. For him, there was no way to abandon Shi'i Islam for secular philosophy, despite his thorough knowledge of the latter. Rather, secular philosophy, especially that of Marxism, neo-Marxism, and other forms of radical third world liberation philosophy, had to be *determinedly negated,* or sublated, into revolutionary religion; it had to shed its secular garb and offer its most revolutionary semantic and semiotic materials to religion, so that religion may once again come into contact with that which was suppressed within itself: the prophetic and *tawhīdic* way-of-being of Prophet Muhammad.[45] In a sense, Shariati created an *Islamic liberation theology*, not a *secular revolutionary philosophy*.[46] Thus, the revolutionary elements of Judaism and Christianity, which had been determinately negated into secular political philosophy in the West, where integrated into Shi'i Islam by Shariati, in effect fertilizing the grounds for the revolution in Iran with oppositional thought. This does not mean that the Iranian revolution relied on what was essentially a secular form of Christianity (if we can see Marxism and other leftist liberational thought in that way), but rather those revolutionary semantics and semiotics born out of secular liberational philosophy *reawakened* materials *already dwelling within Islam*, and in particular Shi'i Islam – the Islam of the martyrs 'Ali and Ḥussein: the spirit of Karbalā.[47]

---

45   In terms of the history of revolution, Muhammad's liberational revolt against the oppressive and unjust conditions of Arabia's *Jāhilīyah*, continued the same *geist* that animated both the intellectual/political revolt of Socrates in Athens and the slave revolt of Spartacus in Rome.

46   See Hamid Dabashi, *Theology of Discontent: The Ideological Foundation of the Islamic Revolution in Iran.* (New Brunswick, NJ: Transaction, 1993/2006), Chapter 2.

47   See Hamid Dabashi, *Shī'ism: A Religion of Protest.* (Cambridge, MA: The Belknap Press of Harvard University Press, 2011), Chapter 3.

The articulation of man's aspiration towards freedom, rationality, wholeness, and peace found in both secular revolutionary philosophy and revolutionary Islam remains the common ground and common source of solidarity between these two sometime-complimentary sources of radical change. This can be witnessed within the Iranian revolution itself, as those who attempted to liberate Iran from the oppression of the Shah were mainly those who embraced some form of radical left-wing liberation thought, i.e. anti-imperialism, Marxism, neo-Marxism, Trotskyism, and Critical Theory, etc., or those influenced by Shariati's class-conscious Islam, including Ayatollah Khomeini. Even outside of Iran, those secular intellectuals who had sympathy for national liberation struggles saw something in the Iranian revolution that was genuinely emancipatory, overruling their general suspicion of religion. Although the particularities of the Shi'i tradition remained mysteries to many of them, they nevertheless could recognize the hallmarks of an oppressed people attempting to overthrow an unjust and corrupt puppet regime imposed upon them by a neo-liberal capitalist superpower. For example, the French philosopher, Michel Foucault, enthusiastically embraced the Iranian revolution, despite the many western critics that pointed to the revolution's more brutal aspects and its ties to clerical authority, which Foucault himself could not embrace.[48]

Critical Theory of Religion and Revolutionary Islam in an Age of Neo-fascism

Both in Islam and the Critical Theory of Religion, or "dialectical religiology," as developed by the Frankfurt School for Social Research, prophetic voices remain vital for the welfare of society. In Islam, the "seal of the prophets" (*khātam al-nabīyīn*), Prophet Muhammad, has come, fulfilled his mission, and in doing so ended the possibility of another prophet sent directly from the divine to engage in theological clarification and social transformation. Nevertheless, the post-Prophet "prophetic" remains important for believers, because it is the prophetic followers of the Prophet who speak the truth of the prophet, even though they do not consider themselves directly commissioned to deliver the divine's message. Similarly, Critical Theory embraces the "prophetic," even though it is skeptical of the idea of an apophatic divinity amidst the imminent

---

48   Behrooz Ghamari-Tabrizi, *Foucault in Iran: Islamic Revolution after the Enlightenment*. Minneapolis: University of Minnesota Press, 2016; also see Janet Afary and Kevin B. Anderson, *Foucault and the Iranian Revolution: Gender and the Seductions of Islamism*. Chicago: University of Chicago Press, 2005.

godlessness of secular modernity. This is especially true in light of modernity's horrific catastrophes, which have only sharpened the painful contradictions of the theodicy problem. Yet for the critical philosopher of religion, the prophetic represents the unrelenting Socratic spirit – in religious form – that stands in opposition to unaccountable power, identifies the lies, and boldly proclaims the truth concealed behind the necessary appearances of the already existing society. Thus, as *ahl al-nabīyīn* (people of the prophets), the Muslims and the Critical Theorists can both humbly take upon themselves the mantle of the prophets, and *enjoin what is right and forbid what is wrong* (*al-Qur'ān* 3:110). Thus, they can cooperate in the struggle for the creation of a society rooted in justice, equality, brotherhood, and reconciliation, as both *responsible intellectuals* and *responsible believers*.

However, just as there were prophets in antiquity, there were false-prophets in antiquity. Likewise, just as there are those who are prophetic in modernity, there are those who are falsely-prophetic in modernity. Modernity, especially in an age of rising tensions between the West and the Muslim world, between the religious right and the secular right (alt-Right and New Right), between global neo-liberalism and political Islam, between fascism and the world, breeds false-prophets. They are the ubiquitous spawn of the *al-Jāhilīyah al-Jadīd* (new age of ignorance), who traffic in the gods of palingenetic nationalism, Wiedergänger consumerism, invasive capitalism, and neo-fascist tribalism. Their gods are those of money, the market, race, power and greed.[49] However, unlike in a religious age, where the false-prophets could be readily identified, we now live in an age of religious illiteracy, which is so desperate for transcendent guidance that the false-prophets of modernity suffice as legitimate leaders of nations. They sell the illusion of genuine prophetic religion and the emancipatory power of the Enlightenment to their unwitting purchasers, who do not realize they're buying existential, political, and economic "snake-oil." This has been a catastrophe for both the West and the Muslim world, as the masses have been left in the hands of those who only seek their own self-aggrandizement, their own self-interest, and their own self-satisfaction, at the expense of those who have unwittingly invested themselves into the very status quo that has brutalized and debased them for generations.

49　Against the Huntington "Clash of Civilization" thesis, the Argentinian Pope Francis claims that the calamities of the modern world are not religiously-inspired, but are rather the result of the deification of money. See Joanna Berendt, "Pope Francis says World is at War, but it's Not a Religious Conflict." https://www.nytimes.com/2016/07/28/world/europe/pope-francis-poland-world-youth-day.html (Accessed 2/25/2017).

Since the terror attacks of September 11th, 2001, and the subsequent "war on terror" that has brought terrorist violence to the streets of major western cities, there has been an ever increasing rise of neo-fascism, which threatens to swallow up the progress made by nations following the devastation of World War II. Additionally, in the Muslim world, among the ashes of Islam's civilizational peak and the ruins of colonialism and imperialism, many Muslims have turned to authoritarian political ideologies camouflaged under a false veneer of Messianic-Islam. From the perspective of the Socratic and prophetic, both ideologies make mockeries out of the real Enlightenment movements they claim to support. *Takfīrī*-religious extremism, especially in the Muslim world, betrays the progressivity, revolutionary, and emancipatory basis upon which Prophet Muhammad created his egalitarian community in Medina. The West, having long since abandoned any substantive attachment to Christianity, has throughout the 20th century abandoned much of the Enlightenment as well, transforming it into a tool of domination and legitimation for its continuous economic colonization of the globe: the *dialectic of Enlightenment*. For example, in the name of western modernization, Iran was economically colonized by the United States and their puppet the Shah.[50] In the name of women's liberation, agrarian reform, and technological advancement, the Shah imposed a repressive worldview and *way-of-being* that was alien to the majority of the population – forcing many to adopt the colonized mind or be marginalized within their own country. While the Shah spoke in the "name of the people," he stole the people's future in the name of the ideological promises of the western Enlightenment.

While the Shah extolled the benefits and values of westernization, he not only failed to embody those values, but he also failed to translate the Enlightenment's ideals into Islamic language, through which deeply religious people could understand. Ali Shariati himself demonstrated that such translation could be done. The Enlightenment's quest to make man the master of his fate could find articulation within Islam's *tawḥīdic* parlance, as Islam itself was against slavery (bondage) to others and to the desires-of-self (*nafs*). Through his recalcitrant speeches and lectures, Shariati demonstrated that the Shah was not interested in those liberational values, principles, and ideals, expressed in the Enlightenment's core language. Rather, he was solely interested in the functionalization of such language to legitimize actions taken to benefit himself and those connected to him. In other words, the language of the western enlightenment was ideological camouflage for pure greed and power – which only diminished the veracity of the Enlightenment's verbiage in the

---

50   John Perkins, *The New Confessions of an Economic Hit Man.* (Oakland, CA: Berrett-Koehler Publishers, Inc., 2016), 117–121.

perspective on many. For Shariati, as a devout Muslim as well as someone who was rooted firmly in the revolutionary aspects of the Enlightenment, both in its Bourgeois and Marxian forms, such a distortion of language, as practiced by the Shah, could not stand unopposed. If prophetic and revolutionary language was to mean anything, it had to be in support of man's substantive emancipation, not an ideological project that either preserved the unjust status quo or furthered man's exploitation. Such bold moves by *responsible intellectuals,* as Shariati called them, are desperately needed in a time wherein many in the West are turning towards neo-fascism to solve their existential and economic crises, and many in the Muslim world are embracing an Islam detached from the concept of justice and mercy as a way of "defending" the *dār al-Islam*. If forms of nihilistic destructiveness are to triumph, it is precisely because those who have the ability to act against it, the mind to understand it, and the desire to confront it, fail to translate and mobilize such capacities into political action, in the way the first generation of Critical Theorists and Ali Shariati did.

Bibliography

Adorno, Theodor W. "Reason and Revelation" in *Critical Models: Interventions and Catchwords*. New York: Columbia University Press, 2005.

Adorno, Theodor W. and Horkheimer, Max. *Dialectic of Enlightenment: Philosophical Fragments*. Edited by Gunzlin Schmid Noerr. Translated by Edmund Jephcott. Stanford, CA: Stanford University Press, 2002.

Afary, Janet and Kevin B. Anderson, *Foucault and the Iranian Revolution: Gender and the Seductions of Islamism*. Chicago: University of Chicago Press, 2005.

Ahmad, Jalal Al-i. *Occidentosis: A Plague from the West*. Translated by R. Campbell. Edited by Hamid Algar. Berkeley: Mizan Press, 1984.

Aryamehr, Mohammad Reza Pahlavi. *The White Revolution*. Tehran: The Imperial Pahlavi Library, 1967.

Berendt, Joanna. "Pope Francis says World is at War, but it's Not a Religious Conflict." https://www.nytimes.com/2016/07/28/world/europe/pope-francis-poland-world-youth-day.html (Accessed 2/25/2017).

Byrd, Dustin J. *Ayatollah Khomeini and the Anatomy of the Islamic Revolution in Iran: Towards a Theory of Prophetic Charisma*. Lanham, MD: University Press of America, 2011.

Byrd, Dustin J. *A Critique of Ayn Rand's Philosophy of Religion: The Gospel According to John Galt*. Lanham, MD: Lexington Books, 2014.

Dabashi, Hamid. *Shī'ism: A Religion of Protest*. Cambridge, MA: The Belknap Press of Harvard University Press, 2011.

Dabashi, Hamid. *Theology of Discontent: The Ideological Foundation of the Islamic Revolution in Iran.* New Brunswick, NJ: Transaction, 1993/2006.

Farías, Victor. *Heidegger and Nazism.* Edited by Joseph Margolis and Tom Rockmore. Philadelphia: Temple University Press, 1989.

Ghamari-Tabrizi, Behrooz. *Foucault in Iran: Islamic Revolution after the Enlightenment.* Minneapolis: University of Minnesota Press, 2016.

Griffin, Roger. *The Nature of Fascism.* New York: Routledge, 1993.

Habermas, Jürgen. *Autonomy and Solidarity: Interviews with Jürgen Habermas.* Edited by Peter Dews. New York: Verso, 1992.

Hegel, G.W.F. *Hegel's Science of Logic.* Translated by A.V. Miller. Atlantic Highlands, NJ: Humanities Press International, 1993.

The Holy Bible. Revised Standard Version. New York: Thomas Nelson Inc., 1972.

Horkheimer, Max. *A Life in Letters: Selected Correspondence.* Edited and translated by Manfred R. Jacobson and Evelyn M. Jacobson. Lincoln, NE: University of Nebraska Press, 2007.

Horkheimer, Max. *Dawn & Decline: Notes 1926–1931 & 1950–1969.* Translated by Michael Shaw. New York: The Seabury Press, 1978.

Kant, Immanuel. *Religion within the Boundaries of Mere Reason and Other Writings.* New York: Cambridge University Press, 1998.

Marx, Karl. *The Marx-Engels Reader.* Edited by Robert C. Tucker. New York: W.W. Norton & Co., Inc., 1978.

Mendieta, Eduardo. *The Frankfurt School on Religion: Key Writings by the Major Thinkers.* New York: Routledge, 2005.

Nasr, Seyyed Hossein (ed.). *The Study Quran: A New Translation and Commentary.* New York: HarperOne, 2015.

Nietzsche, Friedrich. *The Will to Power.* Translated by Anthony M. Ludovici. New York: Barnes & Noble, 2006.

Perkins, John. *The New Confessions of an Economic Hit Man.* Oakland, CA: Berrett-Koehler Publishers, Inc., 2016.

Rahnema, Ali. *An Islamic Utopian: A Political Biography of Ali Shari'ati.* London: I.B. Tauris Publishers, 2000.

Rahnema, Ali. (ed.). *Pioneers of Islamic Revival.* London: Zed Books, 2008.

Shariati, Ali. *Religion vs. Religion.* Translated bu Laleh Bakhtiar. Chicago: ABC International Group, Inc., 2003.

CHAPTER 7

Ali Shariati and Ethical Humanism: Conceiving a Perspective of Liberative Social Ethics

Teo Lee Ken

In direct contrast to German philosophy, which descends from heaven to earth, here it is a matter of ascending from earth to heaven ... It is not consciousness that determines life, but life that determines consciousness.

MARX and ENGELS, *The German Ideology*

•••

You knew, you could not but know, this essential mystery of human nature, but you rejected the only absolute banner, which was offered to you to make all men bow down to you indisputably – the banner of earthly bread; and you rejected it in the name of freedom and heavenly bread. Now see what you did next. And all again in the name of freedom! I tell you that man has no more tormenting care than to find someone to whom he can hand over as quickly as possible that gift of freedom with which the miserable creature is born. But he alone can take over the freedom of men who appeases their conscience.

FYODOR DOSTOYEVSKY, *The Brothers Karamazov*

•••

I, on the contrary, chose justice in order to remain faithful to the world. I continue to believe that this world has no ultimate meaning. But I know that something in it has a meaning and that is man, because he is the only creature to insist on having one. This world has at least the truth of man, and our task is to provide its justification against fate itself.

ALBERT CAMUS, *Letters to a German Friend: Fourth Letter*

•••

Introduction: Why Liberative Ethics

I begin with a quote from the publisher's preface in Shariati's *Man and Islam*: 'There is a saying by the Holy Prophet Muhammad that at the beginning of each age, God will send among the people a reformer who will revive His religion after its death.'[1] To some Ali Shariati was such a person. A special individual gifted with 'enormous oratory and literary power.'[2] One 'whose poetic prose was sharper than a sword.'[3] He is unsurpassed in terms of ingenuity of thought, and effortless in his synthesis of various intellectual traditions. Yet few has fiercely divided more opinions than Shariati.[4] On the one hand, he is seen as the intellectual and revolutionary who delivered the moral and political impetus to overthrow the corrupt and unjust regime of the Shah.[5] On the other, he is identified as the person who politicized Islam, having turned it into an ideology, thus providing the basis for the creation of an authoritarian state and political culture. For such critics, he displayed a reactionary intellectual outlook. For example, Shireen Hunter notes how Shariati contributed to the failure of Islamic reformist discourse. She goes as far to argue that it was Shariati who laid the foundations for both the Islamic Revolution and the Islamic Republic.[6]

Others have pointed out Shariati's haphazard and shallow mixing of diverse theories and concepts from both European and Iranian intellectual and cultural traditions.[7] This inability to construct a coherent perspective gave rise to a reactionary and populist intellectual outlook. Syed Farid Alatas for instance critiques Shariati for his narrow reading and sidelining of Marx's ideas. Additionally, Shariati adopts a pedantic binary outlook in his analysis of social phenomena akin to the division of East and West frequently found in

---

1 Ali Shariati, *Man and Islam*. (Houston, TX: Free Islamic Lit. Book Distribution Center, 1981), vii.

2 Ibid., vii.

3 Farhang Rajaee, *Islamism and Modernism: The Changing Discourse in Iran*. (Austin, TX: University of Texas Press, 2007), 131.

4 Ali Mirsepassi, *Intellectual Discourse and the Politics of Modernization: Negotiating Modernity in Iran*. Cambridge, NY: Cambridge University Press, 2000.

5 Ali Shariati, *Religion vs. Religion*. Chicago: Abjad Book Designers and Builders, 1988.

6 Shireen Hunter, ed. *Reformist Voices of Islam: Mediating Islam and Modernity*. New Delhi: Pentagon Press, 2009.

7 Ervand Abrahamian, ed. "The Islamic Left: From Radicalism to Liberalism," in *Reformers and Revolutionaries in Modern Iran: New Perspectives on the Iranian Left*. New York: Routledge Curzon 2004.

Orientalist scholarship. These characteristics that for Syed Farid Alatas mark Shariati as an Occidentalist in relation to his reading of Marx.[8]

I do not intend to engage the merits of such assertions. I highlight them only to demonstrate the sharp criticisms and responses towards the ideas and legacy of Ali Shariati. In this sense, Shariati occupies a position similar to Jean-Jacques Rousseau, G.F.W. Hegel, Friedrich Nietzsche, and Martin Heidegger in the area of social theory, philosophy and the history of ideas. The intense debates over their work are themselves testaments of their importance and influence on contemporary social and political thought. In the case of Shariati, it is specifically the versatility and richness of his ideas that make the study of his works indispensable.

At a general level, such study is significant as it allows us to conceptualize relevant concepts and theories that are both creative and humanistic. This is the process of engaging the contemporary needs of the human condition. Michel Foucault followed closely the Iranian Revolution precisely for this purpose. If European modernity had reached a dead end and the ideals of the European Enlightenment discredited, Foucault saw that 'Iran now offered a new hope.'[9] For him the aim of philosophy is not the Enlightenment-centric Cartesian rationality, but rather it was the inquiry of a critical ontology of the present and an aesthetics of existence.[10] In other words, it was the critique of the limits of thought and the possibility of conceiving a new social and political order for society. Based on this, Foucault perceived the Iranian revolution as opening a new paradigm and an alternative to the "monstrosity of industrial capitalism" and "totalitarian communism" of Europe.[11]

It is in this spirit that I seek to discuss some of Ali Shariati's key ideas, especially in light of the pressing problem of authoritarianism that we confront today. Our attempts to study Shariati's social thought ought not to be distracted by the fierce debates surrounding the intentions and consequences of his perspectives. The critical task is to clarify and refine those ideas, and by doing so conceive a relevant ethical-humanistic vision that engages the human condition. This follows what Dominick LaCapra writes on being 'involved in the

---

8   Syed Farid Alatas, ed. "Alatas and Shariati on Socialism: Autonomous Social Science and Occidentalism," in *Local and Global: Social Transformation in Southeast Asia: Essays in Honour of Professor Syed Hussein Alatas.* Leiden; Boston: Brill, 2005.

9   Janet Afary and Kevin B. Anderson, *Foucault and the Iranian Revolution: Gender and the Seductions of Islamism.* Chicago: University of Chicago Press, 2005), 75.

10   Michel Foucault, *Politics, Philosophy, Culture: Interviews and Other Writings, 1977–1984.* New York: Routledge, 1988.

11   Afary and Anderson, *Foucault*; Foucault, *Politics*, 75.

effort to understand both what something meant in its own time and what it may mean for us today.'[12] Ultimately, it is this relationship between the past and the present that this study modestly seeks to explicate.

Thus against this background I argue that Shariati's core ideas allow us to conceptualize a perspective of liberative social ethics that opposes and seek to inhibit the authoritarian impulse, and its ideology, through a humanistic social-ethical framework. To do this I focus primarily on two key essays by Ali Shariati: *Man and Islam* and *Modern Man and His Prisons.*[13] I start, first, by outlining the nature and characteristics of liberative ethics. Second, I attempt to explain the basis and social origins for such liberative ethics. Finally, I examine how liberative ethics define and challenge authoritarian ethics and authoritarian state ideology in contemporary societies. I conclude by discussing the urgent need for a perspective of liberative social ethics, as well as discuss what is at stake in the encounter between liberative ethics and authoritarianism for the human condition.

However, there are four short points that require clarification. First relates to my selection of texts by Ali Shariati. I have selected two of his essays, *Man and Islam* and *Modern Man and His Prisons,* because they are, at least among his works accessible in the English language, in my opinion his strongest enunciations in support of man as a moral being, as well as the bearer of free will and human autonomy. The idea of man as moral being constitutes the central theme of this chapter.

Secondly, my discussion of Shariati's ideas and ethics is firmly within the scope of a sociological and historical analysis. It is not a reading in theology or religious studies involving hermeneutics or an exegesis of divine scripture. There is a basic need to explain and analyze ethics and authoritarianism in sociological, historical and philosophical terms and concepts. It is vital to explain their social-historical and political-existential nature, origins and implications. By doing so we avoid attributing the origins and implications of ethics and authoritarianism to a metaphysical, divine or mystical entity or source. Here I focus on the social question of good and evil, justice and injustice.

Third, reiterating the need to stay clear of the debates surrounding the original and exact intention, content and legacy of Ali Shariati's ideas, I pursue the following: this chapter is not about what Shariati said, or what I think Shariati said or would say. Rather, it is a modest attempt to explain what I think we can say by reading the texts and understanding the ideas of Shariati, and how we

---

12   Dominick LaCapra, *Rethinking Intellectual History: Texts, Contexts, Language.* Ithaca: Cornell University Press, 1983), 18.

13   Ali Shariati, *Man and Islam.*

can use those texts and ideas to engage the human condition. Accordingly, my chapter is a discussion of the problem of freedom and power along the paths traversed by Shariati.

Finally, this chapter is not an empirical study in the sense of analyzing a specific and concrete event or issue. Rather it is a modest attempt and exploration at the theorization and abstraction of certain themes, ideas, and phenomena. Here it concerns the meaning, the nature, the basis and the implications of firstly, ethics, and secondly, authoritarianism.

Setting the Problem: Freedom and Power

The fundamental problem of freedom and power is my starting point. Here I discuss the nature and characteristics of authoritarianism. For this purpose, I refer to the chapter of "The Grand Inquisitor" in the novel *The Brothers Karamazov*. It is a novel written by the exceptional and perceptive 19th century Russian writer Fyodor Dostoyevsky. *Brothers Karamazov* is considered one of his best works, and this specific chapter is widely recognized as a seminal text in the study of moral philosophy. The Grand Inquisitor presents symbolically and profoundly the predicament of the two opposing ideas of freedom and authoritarianism. In this parable, narrated by the character Ivan to his younger brother Alyosha, the conflict between the ideas of freedom and authoritarianism is illustrated through the pronouncements of the Grand Inquisitor towards Christ. Ivan narrates:

> My action is set in Spain, in Seville, in the most terrible time of the Inquisition, when fires blazed everyday to the glory of God, and in the splendid auto-da-fe evil heretics were burnt.[14]

The next thing that happens is the capture and imprisonment of Christ by the Grand Inquisitor, and his denunciation of Christ. The Grand Inquisitor faults Christ for teaching man the meaning of freedom. Christ was offered the power to change stones to bread, but rejected it. For Christ man desired freedom, and not merely bread, as *man lives not by bread alone*. The Grand Inquisitor mocks Christ for he was wrong in making that choice. He denounces Christ for rejecting the three gifts that were offered to him, which were, (1) the ability to change stone into bread, (2) the chance to be worshipped by men, and (3) to make all

---

14   Fyodor Dostoyevsky, *The Brothers Karamazov*. (New York: Knopf, 1992), 210.

humanity submit to him. It is the three elements of miracle, mystery and authority that man will perpetually seek to fulfill their happiness.

Hence, man is incapable of being free; he fears freedom and dreads the suffering that accompanies a life of freedom. Man will endlessly submit to authority to avoid this suffering, and therefore his freedom. In addition to being obedient to commands, man constantly seek to worship. The Grand Inquisitor reminds Christ that 'there is nothing more seductive for man than the freedom of his conscience, but there is nothing more tormenting either'[15]

A cursory reading might suggest that Ivan opposed and/or critiqued Christianity and the Church, which denied the value of freedom for man. However, the meaning is nuanced. Conversely, we can explain and argue that in using the symbol of Christ, Ivan advocated a belief of Christianity that defends and upholds the freedom of man. It is a deeply religious position. This in contrast to the Grand Inquisitor whose representation of faith and religion is one that is oppressive and dogmatic.

The conflict between freedom and authoritarianism is illustrated in this parable narrated by Ivan to his brother Alyosha. It conveys the moral principle of the freedom of man. Ivan emphasized the primacy of freedom by contrasting it to the idea of authoritarianism. In doing so he explained profoundly and aesthetically the nature of authoritarianism, its characteristics, and the moral and psychological disposition that fosters and perpetuates the authoritarian mentality and ideology. The fundamental nature of authoritarianism is the deprivation and elimination of choice. It entails and demands certainty, ignorance and acceptance, to the extent of death. Authoritarianism comprises the characteristics of, (1) the rejection of human autonomy, (2) the imposition of submission and worship of power, and (3) the exercise and domination of power.

Ethical Humanism and Liberative Social Ethics

After defining the nature and characteristics of authoritarianism, we can then examine its opposing counterpart: ethical humanism. It refers to the humanistic social-ethical framework that underlies liberative social ethics. This conception of humanism derives from the social thought of Ali Shariati. Ethical humanism serves as the framework for the formation of liberative social ethics. Hence, from this humanistic social-ethical framework we can elaborate the nature and characteristics of liberative social ethics, its basis and social origins.

---

15   Ibid., 216.

Ethical Humanism or the Humanistic Social-ethical Framework

This framework is crucial because the conceptualization of liberative ethics rests on two basic premises that ethical humanism sets forth. The first premise is the principle of *social ideal*.[16] It means the pursuance and realization of a better ethical society. Within this principle, there are two key dimensions. The first dimension refers to the striving for moral and humanitarian values. These values include social justice, equality, and freedom. The second dimension is that of *time*; striving for moral and humanitarian values would be intangible without a concept of the past, present and future. The struggle for social justice in the present is (1) due to a social injustice that has occurred in the past, and (2) to ensure that social justice is attainable or realizable in the future. It is similarly for equality and inequality, freedom and unfreedom. Thus, movement is inherent within time.

The pursuance of a better society would not be possible without an understanding or concept of the past, present and future. Simultaneously, movement is not for movement's sake. It is the striving for human values and ideals. The awareness of time and movement in the pursuit of moral and humanitarian values towards a different social order in the future therefore constitutes the meaning of social ideal.

The second premise is *knowledge*. A humanistic framework not only advances the notion of a social ideal, but also requires that it be established on the foundation of knowledge. The idea of knowledge refers to the study and critique of society. It represents the ability to understand how social processes and structures affect society, and in turn, how society, more specifically individuals and social groups, influence the formation of social relations as well as social and political structures. In the absence of a social ideal, attainment of knowledge would be impossible because every inquiry stems from a given moral concern and basis. Nevertheless, without knowledge, moral concern would be futile. The critique of society through the disciplines of history, literature, philosophy, sociology, economics and science, provide the analytical frameworks for moral concern and thus the praxis for social change.

With that in mind, the philosophy of ethical humanism derived from the social thought of Ali Shariati encompasses the twofold foundations of social ideal and knowledge. Shariati explains this symbolically in his essay *Man and Islam*. In a passage, he notes:

---

16   Syed Hussein Alatas, *Cita Sempurna Warisan Sejarah*. Bangi, Selangor: Penerbit Universiti Kebangsaan Malaysia, 2000.

Once man was created, God taught him the names. It is not yet clear what these names were, but every commentator has said something that leaves no doubt that God was talking about education and instruction. In any case, when the creation of man ended, God taught all the names. Man became a possessor of names ... This is what humanism is all about ... superiority depends upon knowledge of the names. Man knows things which angels do not know. This is indicative of the fact that nobility depends upon knowledge and intelligence rather than upon racial superiority.[17]

Ethical humanism opposes authoritarianism, which demands certainty, ignorance and acceptance. It facilitates the formation of liberative social ethics. In the sections that follow, I will discuss the nature and characteristics, and thereafter the basis and social origins of liberative social ethics.

Liberative Social Ethics

Liberative social ethics arises from the commitment to the human condition in pursuit of social change through both the awareness of ideal and temporality, and knowledge as the study and critique of society. The nature of liberative social ethics is therefore the endeavor for a continuous reordering of society based on ethical values. Accordingly, it comprises three main characteristics: (1) the belief in human equality, (2) the affirmation of freedom, and (3) protest and the struggle for social transformation. Furthermore, the basis and social origins of liberative ethics are: (1) human consciousness, (2) human autonomy, and (3) self-sacrifice.

As the first characteristic of liberative ethics, the recognition of *human equality* is the most essential, for it signifies the acceptance of the horizontal relation between individuals in society and various communities. The belief in the universal nature and shared values of humanity underlies this horizontal relation. In a passage on the unity of men, Shariati notes:

Not only are all men equal, they are brothers. The disparity between equality and brotherhood is quite obvious; equality is a legal term while brotherhood is an announcement of the identical nature of all men who have, despite their colors, emerged from a single source.[18]

---

17   Ali Shariati, *Man and Islam*, 4.

18   Ibid., 6.

Human equality is not only the prerequisite for the individual's capacity to determine his or her life, but also presents each individual with the capability to do so. This includes acceptance of the *responsibility* that it entails. The lost or absence of equality entails the elimination of capability and responsibility. It is tantamount to authoritarianism's rejection of human autonomy. Such rejection denies human capability. However, more significantly, it also denies human equality. The rejection of human autonomy means the rejection of human equality. This is destructive because it prioritizes and defends a hierarchal society. Liberative ethics oppose this; it defends the value and recognition of human equality that, (1) contradicts a hierarchical society, and (2) ensures and allows the exercise of both capabilities and responsibility.

The second characteristic is the *affirmation of freedom*. This means two things; it is the recognition of the creative dimension of the human person and recognition of the person's possibility to actualize their highest potential in all spheres of life. The other characteristic is the creation of the environment that allows the cultivation of creativity and self-potential. The former refers to the aspect of agency and the recognition of it, whereas the latter refers to the structural foundations and material conditions that facilitate it. Recognition of creativity and self-potential represents reverence to the human person's sensitivity for unending aesthetic, moral and rational self-expression. Shariati explains and provides the context for this creative bent,

> [mankind] reaches a point when nature alone cannot satisfy him; his needs and feelings evolve beyond the totality of nature's powers, creativities, and possibilities ... Technology is the totality of man's creativity by which he tires to harness the forces of nature which are not within his easy reach ... Man's second creation is of a different kind; it is the artistic creation which is one of the Divine's manifestations of man's soul, and the definition of man as a 'tool-making animal' falls apart here. The art, just like technology, is the manifestation of man's creative aptitude in nature ... So, constructiveness and ingenuity are two of man's characteristics which are the third dimension of his soul.[19]

Authoritarianism, being opposed to such freedom, suppresses this creative aspect of the human person. The imposition to submit to and worship power curtails the dynamism of the personality. At its worst, it destroys and removes entirely both the creative impulse and needs of the human person. In turn, the lost and absence of the creative trait, and the aspiration to realize a higher

---

19   Ibid., 51.

potential, impels a person to become even more dependent on the dictates of power. For only through this way is the person able to have direction and find purpose and meaning in life. This perpetuates the cycle of submission and worship.

Protest and struggle for social transformation is the third characteristic of liberative ethics. Here Shariati's distinction of *bashar* and *ensan* is instructive:

> Bashar is a "being" while Ensan is a "becoming." And the difference between Ensan, Bashar, and all the other natural phenomena such as animals, trees, etc. is that all are 'beings' except Ensan who is a "becoming."[20]

An *ensan* is the constant 'becoming' towards certain ideals:

> But man in the sense of the exalting truth, towards whom we must constantly strive and struggle in becoming, consists of divine characteristics that we must work for as our ideal characteristics. Namely, they are the types of characteristics that do not exist but must become, and the aim of humanity is to become Ensan. Mind you that becoming Ensan is not a stationary event, rather, it is a perpetual process of becoming and an everlasting evolution towards infinity.[21]

It is this idea of the 'perpetual process of becoming' as human persons towards certain ideals that define the meaning of protest and the struggle for social transformation. It is the constant striving for certain ends, in particularly moral values for the betterment of society. The idea of protest is a key element. Shariati invokes and refers to the French writer Albert Camus to emphasize this point. He writes, 'and a third by Camus, "I revolt, therefore I am." All these assertions are correct, but the most exalting becoming, peculiar to man, is referred to by Camus.'[22]

It is this third characteristic of liberative ethics that poses the most dangerous threat to authoritarianism. The exercise and domination of power serves to preserve the status quo. It is thus conservative in nature. It defends and perpetuates the social, political and economic structures, as well as the discourse and ideology that exist in society. As a result, social, political and economic inequalities in society are also maintained. Consequently, it omits the possibility for progress and difference. It precludes the element of movement. To protest

---

20   Ibid., 47.
21   Ibid., 48.
22   Ibid., 49.

is to highlight these inequalities and potential for betterment, and the struggle for social transformation is the movement to change the status quo. It is in this sense that liberative ethics comprises the third characteristic of protest and the struggle for social transformation.

Basis and Social Origins

Earlier I discussed the nature and characteristics of liberative ethics. In this section, I will discuss its basis and social origins. It is crucial to identify the basis and social origins, for they enable the development of three important characteristics, the belief in human equality, the affirmation of freedom, as well as protest and the struggle for social transformation. These comprise of three premises. Liberative ethics arises, first, from *human consciousness*. It refers to the ability of the human person to think and understand man's existence in the world. In other words, it is the questioning of nature, human relations and social phenomena. Consciousness empowers the human person to make philosophical/theoretical evaluations and moral judgments. It also allows man to understand the meaning, and to make sense of, life. It is consciousness that constitutes the human person, or "*ensan*," as Shariati wrote,

> Ensan has three characteristics: (a) he is self-conscious, (b) he can make choices; and, (c) he can create. All of man's other characteristics derived their origin from these three. We are, therefore, ensan relative to the degree of our self-consciousness and our creativities.[23]

And Shariati further adds:

> Ensan is a conscious creature; namely, he is the only creature in all of nature who has attained self-consciousness which I define as; "perceiving one's quality and nature, perceiving the quality and the nature of the universe, and perceiving one's relationship with the universe." We are Ensan to the extent that we are conscious of these three principles.[24]

The denial of and opposition to liberative ethics maintains the human person in their ignorance. As a result, of the process of perpetuating this ignorance is

---

23   Ibid., 49.
24   Ibid., 50.

dehumanization. A social ethics that is liberative reflects both the essence of humanity and upholds human dignity.

Second, liberative ethics has its basis and social origins in *human autonomy*. It refers to the ability to make choices for oneself. It is the recognition that human autonomy is a fundamental constituent inherent in the human person. I noted earlier that as one of the main characteristics of liberative ethics, the belief in human equality preceded or is a prerequisite for choice, in that equality opens the possibility for the exercising of choice. From this perspective, choice is not an outcome, but the foundation of liberative ethics, for it is rooted in human autonomy. Here, it is reversed. The difference is that in the former, choice is a consequence and is manifest through social relations and social structures. The latter instead is a foundational presumption. The understanding and recognition that choice is an intrinsic constituent of the human person makes human equality an imperative. Shariati cites this foundational presumption in his discussion of the ethical and Islamic philosophy of man in the social context:

> Above all, man is located between mud and providence, he is free to choose either as his will dictates. Possession of will and freedom creates responsibility. And so, from the Islamic point of view, man is the only creature who is responsible not only for his own fate but has a mission to fulfill the Divine Purpose in the world.[25]

Two points further affirm the notion that man can make choices. The first is the ability of man to go against his natural needs. The human person can choose not to eat, although biologically, and in accordance with nature, this is how the physical body maintains itself. A person may decide to commit suicide and end their life, though growth and old age is a natural development in the life span of the average individual. Shariati discusses this rebellious side of man in his distinction of man and animal:

> The only superiority that man has over all other beings in the universe is his will. He is the only being that can act contrary to his nature, while no animal or plant is capable of doing so. It is impossible to find an animal which can fast for two days. And no plant has ever committed suicide due to grief or has done a great service. Man is the only one who rebels against his physical, spiritual, and material needs, and turns his back

---

25   Ibid., 6.

against goodness and virtue. Further, his is free to behave irrationally, to be bad or good, to be mudlike or Divine.[26]

Second, the existence of the values of good and evil, and the continuous call for the human person to strive towards goodness, is an affirmation of man's ability to make choices. The standards of good and evil would be implausible without the recognition of this fundamental trait of man. The existence of good and evil implies that man can choose. It discloses an array of possible behaviors, thoughts and actions, and then leaves it to man to decide and judge. Thus, the vocation of man to do good and pursue the ideal of goodness, implies that choice and autonomy is intrinsic in the nature of the human person. For man is a moral being that can commit and pursue both goodness and evil. However, with this capacity for choice follows the idea of human responsibility and accountability.

As a moral being who can go against their own nature, and has the choice to do so,, it follows that the individual can also *revolt*. The idea of revolt, as integral to human autonomy, depicts its rootedness in the constitution of the human person, thereby spurring man's impulse to protest and revolt against the status quo and social order. Man's idealism and his desire for continuous progress stems from this. This is what Albert Camus meant in his affirmation of revolt in the history of men:

> And Ensan is the only creature in nature who can choose (and his dis-obedience is indicative of the fact that he can choose). This is what Camus meant by revolt; either against a social order or against one's own nature.[27]

Lastly, after human consciousness and human autonomy, liberative ethics has its basis and social origins in the idea of *self-sacrifice*. That liberative social ethics exist and uphold the belief in human equality, the affirmation of freedom, and struggle for social transformation stems from this fundamental and most crucial idea. It refers to the understanding of *selflessness*. It is the willingness to give everything up in the pursuit and realization of moral and humanitarian values. It removes any sentiment of self-interest, even when confronting death. It is philosophically a negation of the self for the well-being of others (altruism). It is these elements of negation of the self, in service to others, and in

---

26   Ibid., 5.
27   Ibid., 50.

pursuance of moral values and an alternative vision for society, that constitute self-sacrifice.

The essence of love drives from the phenomenon of self-negation.[28] It is a love that is moral and aesthetic. Neither rational nor logical, this is a process of renouncing the self for a higher ideal and for others, regardless of the consequences. As Shariati wrote,

> But sometimes man destroys all his worldly belongings and ambitions for something more exalting. For instance, he may set himself on fire (without anything in return) so that his society can be saved. This is not a logical act. The roots of such act go to morality. Love is consisted of a power which invites me to go against my profits and well-being and sacrifice myself for others and the ideas that I hold so dear.[29]

Even to the extent of death, because this love is rooted in morality and aesthetics:

> This is ethics and love. When we love someone in order to be loved, or when we are kind to someone so that we can receive a favour, we are business men. Love consists of giving up everything for the sake of a goal and asking nothing in return. This requires one to make a great choice. What is that choice? To choose oneself to die – or some other objective – so another can live and some ideals be realized.[30]

Liberative ethics would be impossible without the idea of self-sacrifice, which is based on the essence of love.

Liberative Social Ethics and Authoritarianism

Thus far I have discussed the nature and characteristics, as well as the basis and social origins, of liberative social ethics. I argue that they emanate from the social thought of Ali Shariati through a critical reading of selected key texts. Here, I will discuss how liberative ethics define authoritarian ethics and

---

28   Erich Fromm, *Man for Himself: An Enquiry into the Psychology of Ethics*. London: Routledge & K. Paul, 1960.; Rajaee, 2007.

29   Shariati, *Man and Islam*, 60.

30   Ibid., 62.

authoritarian state ideology in contemporary society.[31] Furthermore, I will show how liberative ethics challenge both authoritarian ethics and ideology. First, it bears repeating that this not an attempt to establish the claim that liberative ethics develops directly and explicitly from the ideas of Shariati. Rather it is an attempt to derive key themes and concepts from his thinking and texts. Second, in discussing authoritarian ethics and state ideology in contemporary society, I do not intend to highlight any specific events or issues. Instead my discussion is at the conceptual level through the abstraction of authoritarian ethics and state ideology. This is to examine authoritarianism in its fundamental nature at the most basic level.

Basis and Social Origins of Authoritarianism

The defining of authoritarian ethics and state ideology by liberative ethics is vital, as they constitute the basis and social origins of authoritarianism. Therefore, the discussion of how liberative ethics defines authoritarian ethics and state ideology is also a discussion of the basis and social origins of authoritarianism.

Authoritarian Ethics

Two causes impel authoritarianism. The first is authoritarian ethics, which has its roots in man. To understand such form of ethics, and its dimensions, the works of both Erich Fromm and Syed Hussein Alatas are instructive. Erich Fromm (1900–1980) was born in Frankfurt, Germany in 1900. A psychoanalyst and philosopher, Fromm was of the most important thinkers and public intellectuals of the 20th century. He was a brilliant, passionate and eloquent proponent of an ethics-based humanistic philosophy. The Talmudic tradition, psychoanalysis, Marxism and socialist ideas influenced him greatly in the development of this philosophy. He was a member of the *Institute of Social Research*, commonly known as the *Frankfurt School*, under the direction of Max Horkheimer, having joined it in 1930.

Fromm's unique combination of Marxist and Freudian thought brought new theoretical perspectives to the field of philosophy and critical theory. His other notable contribution lay in the formulation of the concept of "social character." In departing from Freud's focus on libidinal energy, Fromm argued

---

31   By "contemporary society" I refer to society in general and not to a particular society in a given nation-state.

that social processes and structures determined human character or personality. Some of his major works include *Escape from Freedom* (1941), *Man for Himself: An Inquiry into the Psychology of Ethics* (1947), *The Sane Society* (1955), *The Art of Loving* (1956), *Marx's Concept of Man* (1961), *Socialist Humanism* (1965), *The Anatomy of Human Destructiveness* (1973), *To Have or To Be* (1976), and *On Being Human* (1997).

In *Man for Himself*, Fromm notes the interdependence of psychology with philosophy and ethics, as well as sociology and economics. Here he argues that principles of ethical conduct can be found in human nature, and thus from this nature emerges the capacity for goodness. Simultaneously, he points out its opposing traits and explains the concept of authoritarian ethics, 'In authoritarian ethics an authority states what is good for man and lays down the laws and norms of conduct.'[32] Moreover, the source for this authoritarian ethics is *irrational authority*. It is a form of power based solely on power and fear, and compels submission. He writes,

> The source of irrational authority, on the other hand, is always power over people. This power can be physical or mental, it can be realistic or only relative in terms of the anxiety and helplessness of the person submitting to this authority. Power on the one side, fear on the other, are always the buttresses on which irrational authority is built. Criticism of the authority is not only not required but forbidden.[33]

Fromm further explains that authoritarian ethics manifests in two ways. One is formal the other is material:

> Formally, authoritarian ethics denies man's capacity to know what is good or bad; the norm giver is always an authority transcending the individual. Such a system is based not on reason and knowledge but on awe of the authority an on the subject's feeling of weakness and dependence; the surrender of decision making to the authority results from the latter's magic power; its decision can not and must not be questioned. Materially, or according to content, authoritarian ethics answers the question of what is good or bad primarily in terms of the interests of the authority, not the interests of the subject; it is exploitative, although the subject may derive considerable benefits, psychic or material, from it.[34]

---

32   Fromm, *Man for Himself*.
33   Ibid., 9.
34   Ibid., 10.

Authoritarian ethics connotes the human disposition to determine social relations and structures based on pure, which is to say arbitrary and absolute,
authority and power. It seeks to dictate "correct" thought and behavior. As
such, authority and power take precedence over the human personality. It
seeks to establish laws, rules and norms that guide human life and ensure their
conformity.

Elsewhere, the works of Syed Hussein Alatas also capture the essence of
authoritarian ethics. Syed Hussein Alatas (1928–2007) was a prolific Malaysian
sociologist and public intellectual. He obtained his PhD from the University
of Amsterdam in 1963. Alatas held academic positions as lecturer from 1964–
1967 at the Department of Malay Studies in Universiti Malaya (UM), and later
from 1967–1988 at the Department of Malay Studies at the University of Singapore. He returned to Universiti Malaya in 1988 to take up the position of
Vice-Chancellor before taking up positions first at the Department of Anthropology and Sociology and later at the Institute of the Malay World and Civilization (ATMA) in Universiti Kebangsaan Malaysia (UKM).

He authored many books, published numerous articles in journals and
wrote countless essays. He pioneered the field of social sciences and sociology
in Southeast Asia. He wrote extensively on the themes of modernization and
social change, intellectuals and elites, religion, colonialism, corruption, education, and nationhood and nation-building. A remarkable and highly original
thinker, he called for an autonomous social science to define and resolve problems confronting Asian societies and opposed vehemently the imitating of
academic scholarship from Europe and North America. Moreover, he pursued
this relentlessly during his lifetime. It was from this basis and vision that he
developed terms such as "captive mind," "bebalisme" and "colonial capitalism,"
and provided profound and creative insights into the problems of Malaysian
and Asian societies. His key works include *Modernization and Social Change:
Studies in Modernization, Religion, Social Change and Development in Southeast
Asia* (1972), *Islam dan Sosialisme* (Islam and Socialism, 1976), *Intellectuals in
Developing Societies* (1977), *The Myth of the Lazy Native* (1977, 2010), *Kita den-
gan Islam: Tumbuh Tiada Berbuah* (Us and Islam: Unfruitful Growth, 1979), *The
Sociology of Corruption: The Nature, Function, Causes and Prevention of Corruption* (1980), and *Cita Sempurna Warisan Sejarah* (The Ideal of Excellence as His-
torical Legacy, 2000).

In a public lecture in 2000, Alatas reflected on the conflict between the values
of good and evil. He expressed them through two different concepts. The first,
representing goodness and virtue, is the ideal of excellence (*cita sempurna*),
and the second, representing evil and corruption, is the ideal of destruction
(*cita bencana*). The ideal of excellence refers to the human endeavor to pursue

social ideals and the ideal society. This is a historical endeavor that stretches back to the French and American Revolution, and further to the classical Islamic period during the time of Saidina Ali, who emphasized the importance of a just government.[35] In direct conflict with the ideal of *excellence* is the ideal of *destruction*. Opposing everything that the ideal of excellence upholds and pursues, it espouses corruption, abuse of power, and exploitation.[36]

Thirteen years earlier, Alatas had discussed this relationship between good and evil in a lecture titled *Iman Hussein and the Islamic Faith*, delivered in 1987. Referring to the commemoration of 'Āshūrā and the event of Karbalā, he explained how the resistance and subsequent death of Hussein, the son of Saidina Ali, the fourth caliph and husband of Fāṭimah, the daughter of Prophet Muhammad (PBUH), at the hands of Yazīd ibn Mu'āwiya, represented the 'conflict of two opposing ideals of life.'[37] Hussein personified the values of self-sacrifice and justice, whereas Yazīd embodied tyranny and injustice. The history of man is therefore the history of these opposing values.

> The tragedy of Karbala was the dialectical highpoint of conflict between two extremely opposite forces, alien to each other, negating each other, going back deep into history, representing the interest of opposing classes and human types. Behind the tragedy of Karbala was the contest between Ali and Muawiyah. Behind this was the contest between the Prophet Muhammad and Abu Sufyan in the early period of Islam, and behind this, the fountain of it all, was the affair of Hashim and his nephew Umayyah.[38]

Therefore, the nature and origin of good and evil stems not simply from metaphysics and divine scripture. Instead, they involve social conflicts that arise out of the contestation of moral and ethical values. In other words, man, as well as good and evil, are historical. History, or the history of man, is the history of the contestation of good and evil, justice and injustice, and this conflict has endured to this day.

Identifying the key aspects of human disposition, as well as the ethical or moral temporal conflicts, in the writings of both Erich Fromm and Syed Hussein Alatas, allows us to arrive at two salient points. First, we see the human inclination for pure power and authority, and consequently the quest to

---

35   Alatas, *Cita Sempurna Warisan Sejarah,* 2000.
36   Ibid.
37   Alatas, *Imam Hussein and the Islamic Faith,* 2.
38   Ibid., 6.

impose 'correct' thought and behavior. Second, we recognize the existential and historical-sociological nature as well as consequences of good and evil. These elaborations by Fromm and Alatas offer a contemporary perspective to the meaning and qualities of authoritarian ethics, for those aspects are the cornerstones of authoritarian ethics, which form one of the bases and social origins of authoritarianism. Thus, the writings of Fromm and Alatas serve as a guide to illustrate how liberative ethics defines authoritarian ethics and simultaneously assist to explain the cause of authoritarianism.

Authoritarian State Ideology

In addition, liberative ethics define the ideology of the authoritarian state; ideology being the second cause of authoritarianism. The authoritarian state's ideology gives rise to and maintains authoritarianism in two ways; it is first the use of state structures to impose authoritarian political ideology on society. Authoritarian political ideology emerges when authoritarian ethics becomes political. It is the process of seeking to preserve a particular social order, or alter an existing social order, in accordance with authoritarian ethics. This process further involves the mass mobilization of society, and it ends with the capturing of the State. Thus, authoritarian state ideology connotes or represents the use of State institutions, the bureaucracy, the national legal system and mechanisms, its law and enforcement and/or security machinery to expand and enforce authoritarian political ideology.

Secondly, and more critically, is the capability and function of authoritarian state ideologies to nurture authoritarian ethics in man and consequently in society. In other words, it creates and defends the social conditions fertile for the growth of authoritarian ethics in man and society. This is because, whereas authoritarian ethics, which is the human impulse for pure power and authority and its imposition, has its roots in man, it is also on the other hand the outcome of social processes impinging on the human psyche and nature. Fromm explains this social-psychological interaction through his conceptualization of *social character*. Here character structure is 'the result of the basic experiences and mode of life.' He continues,

> The social character necessarily is less specific than the individual character. In describing the latter, we deal with the whole of the traits which in their particular configuration form the personality structure of this or that individual. The social character comprises only a selection of traits, the essential nucleus of the character structure of most members of a

group which has developed as the result of the basic experiences and mode of life common to that group ... The concept of social character is a key concept for the understanding of the social process. Character in the dynamic sense of analytic psychology is the specific form in which human energy is shaped by the dynamic adaptation of human needs to the particular mode of existence of a given society. Character in its turn determines the thinking, feeling, and acting of individuals.[39]

Social Character is different in comparison to the imposition of the authoritarian political ideology in that here man imbibes and internalizes the authoritarian political ideology. Through internalization, authoritarian ethics are cultivated and amplified, so much so that man comes to identify with the qualities of authoritarianism, which are, (1) the rejection of human autonomy, (2) the imposition of submission and worship to power, and (3) the exercise and monopoly of power, as not only valid, but also the sole articulation of truth. As the only truth, man and society believe and conform to such ethics.

Thus, we encounter the two sides and implications of authoritarian ethics and the authoritarian state's ideology. The first is positive and direct, while the second is negative and indirect. It is positive and direct to the extent that man is inclined to pursue and seize pure authority and power. While in pursuance of, and upon attainment of that force, man rejects human autonomy, imposes submission and worship of power, and dominates through such power. Conversely, it is negative and indirect to the extent that it inculcates in man's nature a willingness to accept in totality the rejection of his own autonomy, a submission to and worship of power, and he believes such power to be unitary and exclusive. In the following sections, I will discuss the implications of authoritarianism and the challenge that liberative ethics poses to authoritarianism.

Implications of Authoritarianism

Authoritarianism entails two basic implications. First is the formation of a hierarchical society. In such a society, those who occupy the pinnacle of the hierarchy determine the social life of those at the base. They define "correct" thought, speech and behavior, and they decide what constitutes truth and falsehood, right and wrong. In doing so only they acquire the privileges of, and the right to maintain, political and economic decision-making, and thereby they alone acquire the benefits that follow it. The effect of which is a society

---

39   Erich Fromm, *Escape from Freedom.* (New York: Henry Holt & Co., 1969), 277–278.

with enormous economic, political and social inequality. However, the biggest casualty in this situation is human autonomy and the exercise of choice, for such inequalities become obstacles to autonomy and eliminate the ethical concept of choice.

The creation of a society based on arbitrariness and myth is the second implication of authoritarianism. By *society based on arbitrariness* I mean a society ruled and governed by the random discretion of the state, its institutions, bureaucracies and officials, as well as social and political groups. The structuring of its social order is not based on the forming and implementation of a set of predefined and consented laws, rules and policies. Consequently, it resembles the concept of *irrational authority* that Erich Fromm cites. Here, arbitrariness is the manifestation of such an authority. In such conditions, there is no ethical and social framework or set of values that guide society. Stable categories of value and language are impossible and unknown, resulting in uncertainty in the public and private spheres of everyday life.

On the other hand, by *society based on myths* I mean the maintenance and directing of a society in accordance with abstract and metaphysical ideals. Such ideals are not grounded in the historical and sociological processes and realities of the society. Rather these principles and aims mislead society and mystify the socio-political, economic and cultural problems of society. This involves the process of producing and defending fiction as well as drawing the picture of an illusory future. It is also related to the notion of utopia. Utopian thought is a form of thinking that is unable or unwilling to comprehend an existing social reality, but is intent on changing an existing or particular condition.[40] Consequently, that intent or desire to change is based on inaccurate and/or false assumptions. Such thinking also leads individual and groups to pronounce a false and romantic future.

Therefore, the two implications of authoritarianism that I have just discussed are first, a hierarchical society, and second, a society based on arbitrariness and myth. To review, so far in this chapter I have done the following: I have provided the fundamental problem that preoccupies this chapter – the problem of *freedom* and *power*, and here I defined and explained the basic nature and characteristics of authoritarianism. Then I discussed the definition and nature of ethical humanism or the humanistic social-ethical framework. It is founded on the two premises of *social ideal* and *knowledge*, which provides the framework for liberative social ethics.

---

40   Maruuf Shaharuddin, ed. "Religion and Utopian Thinking among the Muslims of Southeast Asia," in *Local and Global; Social Transformation in Southeast Asia: Essays in Honour of Professor Syed Hussein Alatas.* Leiden: Brill, 2005.; Karl Mannheim, *Ideology and Utopia: An Introduction to the Sociology of Knowledge.* London: Routledge & Kegan Paul, 1936.

In my discussion of liberative social ethics, I argue that it can be derived from the ideas and selected texts of Ali Shariati. Based on these two texts, *Man and Islam*, and *Modern Man and His Prisons*, I argue for a conceptualization of liberative social ethics that upholds the belief in human autonomy, affirms freedom, and advocates for protest and struggle in pursuit of social transformation. Liberative ethics has its basis and social origins in human consciousness, human autonomy, and the idea of self-sacrifice. Next, I discuss the basis and social origins of authoritarianism from a contemporary perspective. I argue that authoritarian ethics and the authoritarian state ideology constitute the two bases and social origins of authoritarianism. In the last section before my conclusion, I will attempt to discuss how such liberative ethics stand as a challenge to authoritarianism.

The Challenge of Liberative Ethics: Liberation vs. Authoritarianism

Authoritarianism encompasses three characteristics: (1) the rejection of human autonomy, (2) the imposition of submission to, and worship of power, and (3) the exercise and domination of power. Liberative ethics opposes authoritarianism by rejecting these qualities. In its place, it advocates for: (1) the belief in human equality, (2) the affirmation of freedom, and (3) it advocates for the struggle for social transformation. Both authoritarianism and liberative ethics arise from the human disposition. Still there are fundamental differences between the two that result in different values, and these values have different implications for man and society. Authoritarianism links the need to constrain autonomy as well as the affirmation of power to a metaphysical and divine source. However, liberative ethics, because of its social nature, sees constraints on autonomy and the affirmation of power as having its source in a social-temporal agency and phenomenon. In other words, it stems from human thought and actions. Hence, liberative ethics espouses human autonomy and freedom as existential and social-temporal values. These values originate in man, and likewise arise from his existence in and relation to the world.

In addition, authoritarianism develops and intensifies the negative traits in man. It cultivates and derives its basis from authoritarian ethics that also have their origins in man. Through authoritarian state ideology, it further utilizes state institutions, bureaucracies and mechanisms to nurture, internalize and impose this ethics on man and society. Liberative ethics, on the other hand, identifies and recognizes the positive, constructive and humanitarian traits in man, and accordingly strives to cultivate and develop these traits and other ethical values within man and his society. These traits include consciousness, autonomy, love, and the values of compassion, and human dignity. In doing so, the outcome is a society that is founded on the moral values of social justice, equality and freedom. It rejects and opposes the hierarchical, arbitrary and myth-driven society that authoritarianism produces.

Above all, the emphasis on moral and ethical values differentiates liberative ethics from authoritarianism. These moral and ethical values represent the point of its strongest resistance and opposition. This differentiation, though seemingly self-evident, has to be made emphatically, for it counters the criticism that liberative ethics itself has authoritarian inclinations, which contributes to the rise of authoritarianism. The fundamental tenet and greatest strength of liberative ethics is its unwavering insistence on the indispensability of a moral and ethical center for society. This moral center is located in the reservoir of values and ideals that society is immersed in, which guides the building of social relations in such society. These values include social justice and human dignity. Philosophy, religion, culture and political thought, among others, are the sources of these values and ideals. These sources and their values and ideals transcend all intellectual and cultural traditions. Related to the idea of a *moral center* is the idea of *moral vision*. This refers to a particular ideal or set of ideals that a society strives to achieve. This striving is a perpetual process. It endeavors to conceive of and attain a better future in line with those ideals. Thus, society is guided by a moral center in the present, and a moral vision towards the future.

In the absence of both a moral center and a moral vision, society is unable to function, and it ceases to exist, as there are no moral or ethical standards that guide the thought, actions and behavior of man. In its place, society is governed by power and coercion. Now authoritarian ethics and authoritarian state ideology prevails, and that can lead to the rise of authoritarianism. It is this development that liberative ethics seeks to inhibit and oppose. It is a statement and reaffirmation of human equality, freedom and the need to struggle for constant social transformation. Beyond everything else, it is the endeavor to seize, return and defend the moral center in society. Liberative ethics is an intervention in the grand historical struggle between ethics and values against power and authority, it demarcates the polar centers of morality and absolutism, and it is a commitment to the human condition.

Conclusion: The Stakes

I began the central discussion of this chapter by highlighting the fundamental problem between freedom and power. From that starting point, I have attempted to explain this problem through the perspective of ethical humanism and/or a humanistic social-ethical framework. In doing so I demarcated this problem along the lines of liberative social ethics on one side, and authoritarianism on the other. More importantly, I argued for a conceptualizing of a perspective of liberative ethics derived from the ideas and selected key texts of Ali Shariati. Such conceptualization both defines and challenges authoritarianism.

Here I want to end by discussing what is at stake in the conflict between freedom and power in general, and liberative ethics and authoritarianism in particular. Albert Camus' *The Stranger* narrates the life of Meursault, the main character, who is indifferent to the world. To him whatever he feels, thinks or does is inconsequential. In the novel Meursault is condemned for not crying at his mother's funeral, as he showed no anguish over her death. He is later sentenced to death by a judge for failing to demonstrate remorse for his shooting and killing a man on a beach. It is noteworthy that the two events are linked in such a way that Meursault is subsequently sentenced to death for both his indifference at the funeral and to the murder. The novel seems to highlight the point that the consequence of and punishment for indifference to the world is death. This appears to be the intended meaning. For at the end, Meursault comes to the realization that he is given a death sentence not because of his behavior towards his mother or for his actions on the beach. Rather, it is for his indifference to the world and his misunderstanding of the insignificance of everyday life decisions and events. In a telling passage, Meursault recounts this realization in a conversation with a priest in his cell before his death sentence:

> I had been right, I was still right, I was always right. I had lived my life one way and I could just as well have lived it another. I had done this and I hadn't done that. I hadn't done this thing but I had done another. And so? It was as if I had waited all this time for this moment and for the first light of this dawn to be vindicated. Nothing, nothing mattered, and I knew why. So did he. Throughout the whole absurd life I'd lived, a dark wind had been rising toward me from somewhere deep in my future, across years that were still to come, and as it passed, this wind leveled whatever was offered to me at the time, in years no more real than the ones I was living. What did other people's deaths or a mother's love matter to me; what did his God or the lives people choose or the fate they think they elect matter to me when we're all elected by the same fate, me and billions of privileged people like him who also called themselves my brothers?[41]

This novel portrays, in an in-depth and aesthetic manner, the absurdity and meaninglessness found in the human condition. Camus' brilliance lies in his ability to weave a narrative that captures the human condition in simple and

---

41   Albert Camus, *The Stranger*. (New York: Vintage International, 1989), 121.

clear prose without losing the intensity, complexity and philosophical mean-ing of the situation in question. This phenomenon, or situation of the absurd and meaningless, is relevant for our present purpose.

I argued that the causes of authoritarianism are authoritarian ethics and an authoritarian state ideology. However, to go further and inquire into a deeper layer, both authoritarian ethics and authoritarian state ideology per-sists because of man's inability to confront what he perceives as an absurd and meaningless world. In such a world, his thoughts, feelings, speech, actions and expressions are insignificant, and therefore have no consequences, whether it is ethical or political, economic or social, cultural or philosophical, on the social-temporal world and human condition. Neither does it affect the past, present and future. Erich Fromm offers a profound description of this predicament in his formulation of the fundamental question confronting man in the contemporary human condition. He writes,

> The awareness of human separation, without reunion by love – is the source of shame. It is at the same time the source of guilt and anxiety. The deepest need of man, then, is the need to overcome his separateness, to leave the prison of his aloneness. The absolute failure to achieve this aim means insanity, because the panic of complete isolation can be overcome only by such a radical withdrawal from the world outside that the feeling of separation disappears – because the world outside, from which one is separated, has disappeared. Man – of all ages and cultures – is confronted with the solution of one and the same question: the question of how to overcome separateness, how to achieve union, how to transcend one's own individual life and find at-onement.[42]

Similarly, Ali Shariati offers an eloquent depiction of this contemporary situa-tion in his explanation of one's self as prison, writing,

> The last prison, one's self, is the worst of all since it is the one which has rendered man the most helpless prisoner ... Why has today's man, who has freed himself from the prison of nature, history and society, reached absurdity ... Why can't man come out of his cell? It is too hard. In the past, the aforementioned prisons had four walls around my existence and I was aware of my own incarceration. For instance, when man was primi-tive, he was aware of the existence of a river or a jungle next to him; he

---

42   Erich Fromm, *The Art of Loving.* (New York: Harper Perennial Modern Classics, 2006), 9.

had to become a fisherman or a hunter. He felt the presence of such determinisms in the past, but with respect to this last one, there is no wall around man's existence. It is a prison that I carry with myself. This is why becoming self-conscious and familiar with this one is the hardest task of all. Here, the prison and the prisoner are the same; that is he disease and the patient have merged together.[43]

A consistent thread linking both of these passages, and the ideas and condition they capture, is the alienation and estrangement of man first from himself, and second the world that he lives in. It is this "separateness" and "self-prison" that results in an absurd and meaningless world. More important and severe are the implications of this human situation, for they lead to the emergence of authoritarianism both in its direct and positive, and indirect and negative forms. Authoritarianism in turn creates the environment for the formation and further maintenance of an absurd and meaninglessness world. A vicious cycle leads one to the other. Thus, the urge for liberative ethics is compelling. So that man may regain a relation to himself and his world, he must first overcome the situation of living in an absurd and meaningless world. Second, he must oppose and eliminate authoritarianism. It is this that is at stake in the fundamental problem and grand conflict between freedom and power, between liberative social ethics and authoritarianism.

To reiterate, only by embracing liberative ethics can we end the dangerous cycle of an absurd and meaningless world filled with authoritarianism. Ali Shariati, in *Man and Islam,* calls for love and ethics as the only way to exit from this human condition. Building on his ideas and the parameters for this fundamental problem he has identified, I argue for the creation of liberative social ethics. It is an ethics that espouses, (1) belief in human equality, (2) the affirmation of freedom, and (3) the struggle for constant social transformation on the basis of, (1) human consciousness, (2) human autonomy, and (3) self-sacrifice. It follows closely Shariati's reminder that *life is conviction and struggle, and nothing more.*

Bibliography

Abedi, Mehdi. "Ali Shariati: The Architect of the 1979 Islamic Revolution of Iran." *Iranian Studies,* Vol. 19, No. 3/4 (1986): 229–234.

---

43   Shariati, *Man and Islam,* 58.

Abrahamian, Ervand. "Ali Shariati: Ideologue of the Iranian Revolution." *MERIP Reports*, No. 102, Islam and Politics, (1982): 24–28.

Abrahamian, Ervand. "The Islamic Left: From Radicalism to Liberalism." In *Reformers and Revolutionaries in Modern Iran: New Perspectives on the Iranian Left*, edited by Stephanie Cronin, 268–279. New York: Routledge Curzon, 2004.

Afary, Janet. and Kevin B. Anderson. *Foucault and the Iranian Revolution: Gender and the Seductions of Islamism*. Chicago: University of Chicago Press, 2005.

Akhavi, Shahrough. "Islam, Politics and Society in the Thought of Ayatullah Khomeini, Ayatullah Taliqani and Ali Shariati." *Middle Eastern Studies*, Vol. 24, No. 4 (1988): 404–431.

Alatas, Syed Farid. "Alatas and Shariati on Socialism: Autonomous Social Science and Occidentalism." In *Local and Global; Social Transformation in Southeast Asia: Essays in Honour of Professor Syed Hussein Alatas*. Edited by Riaz Hassan, 161–180. Leiden: Brill, 2005.

Alatas, Syed Hussein. *Imam Hussein and the Islamic Faith*, (No publisher given), 1987.

Alatas, Syed Hussein. *Cita Sempurna Warisan. Sejarah*. Bangi, Malaysia: Penerbit Universiti Kebangsaan, 2000.

Arendt, Hannah. *On Revolution*. New York: Penguin Books, 2006.

Arendt, Hannah. *Eichmann in Jerusalem: A Report on the Banality of Evil*. New York: Penguin Books, 2006.

Arendt, Hannah. *The Origins of Totalitarianism*. San Diego: Harcourt, 1994.

Arendt, Hannah. *The Human Condition*. 2nd ed. Chicago: University of Chicago Press, 1998.

Axworthy, Michael. *Revolutionary Iran: A History of the Islamic Republic*. London: Allen Lane Penguin Books, 2013.

Baehr, Peter. *Hannah Arendt, Totalitarianism and the Social Sciences*. Stanford, Calif.: Stanford University Press, 2010.

Bayat, Assef. "Shariati and Marx: A Critique of an 'Islamic' Critique of Marxism.'" *Alif: Journal of Comparative Poetics*, No. 10, Marxism and the Critical Discourse, (1990): 19–41.

Camus, Albert. *Resistance, Rebellion and Death: Essays*. New York: Vintage Books, 1974.

Camus, Albert. *The Stranger*. New York: Vintage International, 1989.

Crooke, Alistair. *Resistance: The Essence of the Islamic Revolution*. New York: Pluto Press, 2009.

Dabashi, Hamid. *Theology of Discontent: The Ideological Foundations of the Islamic Revolution in Iran*. New York: New York University Press, 1993.

Dostoyevsky, Fyodor. *The Brothers Karamazov*. New York, Knopf: Distributed by Random House, 1992.

Fischer, Michael M.J. *Iran: From Religious Dispute to Revolution*. Cambridge, Mass.: Harvard University Press, 1980.

Fromm, Erich. *Man for Himself: An Enquiry into the Psychology of Ethics.* London: Routledge & K. Paul, 1960.

Fromm, Erich. *Marx's Concept of Man.* New York: F. Ungar Publishing, 1961.

Fromm, Erich. *Escape from Freedom.* New York: Henry Holt & Co., 1969.

Fromm, Erich. *The Art of Loving.* New York: Harper Perennial Modern Classics, 2006.

Foucault, Michel. *The History of Sexuality: Volume I, An Introduction.* New York: Pantheon Books, 1978.

Foucault, Michel. *Power/Knowledge: Selected Interviews and Other Writings, 1972–1977.* New York: Pantheon Books, 1980.

Foucault, Michel. *The Foucault Reader.* New York: Pantheon Books, 1984.

Foucault, Michel. *Politics, Philosophy, Culture: Interviews and Other Writings, 1977–1984.* New York: Routledge. 1988.

Ghamari-Tabrizi, Behrooz. "Contentious Public Religion: Two Conceptions of Islam in Revolutionary Iran: Ali Shariati and Abdolkarim Soroush." *International Sociology,* Vol. 19(4) (2004): 504–523.

Hunter, Shireen, ed. *Reformist Voices of Islam: Mediating Islam and Modernity.* New Delhi: Pentagon Press, 2009.

Jahanbegloo, Ramin. and Nojang Khatami. "Acting Under Tyranny: Hannah Arendt and the Foundations of Democracy in Iran." *Constellations,* Volume 20, Issue 2, (2013): 328–346.

Jebnoun, Noureddine., Mehrdad Kia, and Mimi Kirk, (eds). *Modern Middle East Authoritarianism: Roots, Ramifications, and Crisis.* New York: Routledge, 2014.

Kamrava, Mehran. *Iran's Intellectual Revolution.* Cambridge: Cambridge University Press, 2008.

LaCapra, Dominick. *Rethinking Intellectual History: Texts, Contexts, Language.* Ithaca: Cornell University Press, 1983.

Lee, Robert D. *Overcoming Tradition and Modernity: The Search for Islamic Authenticity.* Boulder, CO: Westview Press, 1997.

Machlis, Elisheva. "Ali Shariati and The Notion of Tawhid: Re-exploring the Question of God's Unity." *Die Welt Des Islams* 54 (2014): 183–211.

Mahdavi, Mojtaba. "One Bed and Two Dreams? Contentious Public Religion in the Discourses of Ayatollah Khomeini and Ali Shariati." *Studies in Religion,* Vol. 43(1) (2014): 25–52.

Mannheim, Karl. *Ideology and Utopia: An Introduction to the Sociology of Knowledge.* London: Routledge & Kegan Paul, 1936.

Marx, Karl. and Fredrick Engels. *The German Ideology.* Amherst, N.Y.: Prometheus Books, 1998.

Miri, Seyed Javad. "Humanism and Sociological Imagination in a Frommesque Perspective," In *Reclaiming the Sane Society: Essays on Erich Fromm's Thought,* Edited by Seyed Javad Miri, Robert Lake and Tricia M. Kress, 31–36. Rotterdam: Sense Publications, 2014.

Mirsepassi, Ali. *Intellectual Discourse and the Politics of Modernization: Negotiating Modernity in Iran*. New York: Cambridge University Press, 2000.

Mirsepassi, Ali. *Political Islam, Iran and the Enlightenment: Philosophies of Hope and Despair*. New York: Cambridge University Press, 2011.

Pasaoglu, Mehmet Talha. "Nationalist Hegemony over Islamist Dreams in Iran and Pakistan: Who were Shariati and Maududi?" *Asian Politics & Policy*, Volume 5, Number 1 (2013): 107–124.

Rahnema, Ali. (ed.), *Pioneers of Islamic Revival*. London: Zed Books, 1994.

Rahnema, Ali. *An Islamic Utopian: A Political Biography of Ali Shariati*. London: I.B. Tauris, 1998.

Rajaee, Farhang. *Islamism and Modernism: The Changing Discourse in Iran*. Austin, TX: University of Texas Press, 2007.

Rawls, John. *Lectures on the History of Political Philosophy*. Cambridge, MA: Belknap Press of Harvard University Press, 2007.

Shaharuddin Maaruf. "Religion and Utopian Thinking among the Muslims of Southeast Asia," In *Local and Global; Social Transformation in Southeast Asia: Essays in Honour of Professor Syed Hussein Alatas*, Edited by Riaz Hassan, 315–330. Leiden: Brill, 2005.

Shariati, Ali. *On the Sociology of Islam*. Berkeley: Mizan Press, 1979.

Shariati, Ali. *Culture and Ideology*. Houston, TX: Free Islamic Literatures, 1980.

Shariati, Ali. *Marxism and Other Western Fallacies: An Islamic Critique*. Berkeley: Mizan Press, 1980.

Shariati, Ali. *Man and Islam*. Houston, TX: Free Islamic Lit. Book Distribution Center, 1981.

Shariati, Ali. *What is to be Done: The Enlightened Thinkers and an Islamic Renaissance*. Houston, Texas: The Institute for Research and Islamic Studies, 1986.

Shariati, Ali. *Religion vs. Religion*. Chicago: Abjad Book Designers and Builders, 1988.

Solomon, Robert C. *Existentialism*. New York: Oxford University Press, 2005.

Taleqani, Mahmud, et al. *Jihad and Shahadat*. Houston, TX: The Institute for Research and Islamic Studies, 1986.

CHAPTER 8

The Liberties of a Transmitter: Frantz Fanon According to Shariati

Georg Leube

The perception of poverty is different from poverty itself, as the perception of ignorance is different from ignorance. The perception of poverty and backwardness has a social price, not poverty alone. This is the mission of the intellectual (*rawshanfikr*) and his place is the following: Between reality and the perception of reality.[1]

∴

Introduction

In theses short phrases, Shariati sketches a domain of intellectual intervention that stands between reality and perception. Intellectuals, literally *enlightened thinkers*, are neither exclusively concerned with factual matters at hand, nor with theoretical inquiry in a sphere of perception detached from social, economic or other "worldly" considerations. Intellectuals are those who, by constantly re-considering and re-framing our world, decisively contribute to its shape. This concept of a *rawshanfikr* or intellectual strongly grounded in the reality of his surrounding world is clearly informed by the *intellectuel engagé*, a

---

1 *Iḥsās-i faqr ghayr az khūd-i faqr ast mithl-i iḥsās-i jahl ke ghayr az jahl ast. Iḥsās-i faqr wa-'aqab māndegī arzish-i ijtimāʿī dārad, na khūd-i faqr.*

    Risālat-i rawshanfikrān īn ast wa-jāyishān hamīnjā ast: Bayn-i wāqiʿīyat wa-iḥsās-i wāqiʿīyat. Ali Shariati, "Frānts Fānūn (Frantz Fanon)," in: *Majmūʿe-yi Āthār-i Muʿallim-i Shahīd-i Duktur ʿAlī Sharīʿatī* vol. 31, *Vīzhegīhā-yi qurūn-i jadīd* (Tehran: Shirkat-i Intishārāt-i Chāpkhash, 1370/1992), 420.

    This article has become possible thanks to the generous support of my esteemed teacher, Professor Abbas Poya, who also granted me access to his copy of Shariati's collected works.

concept developed decisively in the existentialist circles of France in the 20th Century.[2]

In presenting this vision of the engaged thinker to an Iranian audience, Shariati acts as translator of a concept *en vogue* in the Paris of the early 1960s, when he studied at the Sorbonne, propagating the engaged intellectual to his readers and listeners in Iran in the 1960s and 1970s. Like any other translation of ideas and concepts to a new audience, Shariati's presentation of this stimulating concept was deeply shaped by interventions of its translator, who actively restructured his topic to ensure a favorable reception to the concepts transmitted by him. Starting with the – in the context of 1960s Paris possibly somewhat unexpected – choice of Frantz Fanon as his example for the concept of an engaged intellectual, Shariati comprehensively appropriated not only the theory of French existentialism, but also the biography of Frantz Fanon himself, which he fundamentally transformed in order as to turn him into a suitable vehicle for the demonstration of ideas he wished to convey to his Iranian audience.

The concept of the engaged intellectual is, as will be shown in the course of this chapter, only one of a plethora of concepts, ideas and theories that Shariati attributed and connected to Frantz Fanon in a presentation of barely over 7 pages. While the interdependency between Shariati as an "original thinker" and Shariati as a "transmitter of ideas" is vexingly elusive in most of his other work, this chapter argues that his choice of the literary genre of a biography of Frantz Fanon resulted in a field where Shariati's method of intervention becomes visible in an exemplary fashion. Detailed analysis of Shariati's strategies of appropriation both of 1960's intellectual Paris and Fanon's biography itself reveals how freely Shariati switched between the cumbersome conventions of "mere transmission" and "original thought," composing a largely counterfactual, yet coherent alternative biography of Frantz Fanon. The liberty of Shariati in diffusing literary conventions specific to the genres of fictional and academic writing thus emerges as the main original contribution of Shariati as the transmitter of the biography and thinking of Frantz Fanon to an Iranian audience.

Biographical Background: A Short Biography and Chronology of Ali Shariati's Stay in Paris

To follow the interplay between transmission and appropriation in Shariati's short presentation of Frantz Fanon, some information on the biographical

---

2   See for instance Jean-Paul Sartre, *L'existentialisme est un humanisme* (Paris: Gallimard, 2011), 31, 50–51.

background of Shariati is necessary. In this short sketch, I mainly follow the authoritative biography by Ali Rahnema, while paying special attention to Shariati's stay in Paris and his correspondence with Frantz Fanon.[3]

Having finished the single degree available at the Faculty of Literature at Mashhad at that time as first in his class, Alī Shariati was as surprised as his classmates were by the Shah's decree that gave a state scholarship to study abroad to "those graduating university students who had ranked first in their respective faculties."[4] His eventual destination, Paris, was determined quite prosaicly by the fact that his foreign (European) language was French.[5]

Leaving his family and wife, who was in her sixth month pregnant, behind, Shariati arrived in Paris in late May 1959.[6] While ostensibly writing his PhD on the *Faḍāyil-i Balkh*, a topic that his doctoral father recalled Shariati was not overly interested in, Shariati soaked up the intellectual atmosphere of Paris. Among the individuals who most impressed him was – alongside Louis Massignon, George Gurvitch, Jacques Berque and Jean-Paul Sartre – also Frantz Fanon.[7] While the other teachers, whom Shariati is later said to have canonized as "his idols," were in Paris during his stay there, his contact with Fanon was more indirect, partially from a lecture of Sartre on Fanon's "Les Damnés de la Terre," partially from Shariati's work on a translation of some of Fanon's books into Persian.[8] According to Rahnema, direct contact between Fanon and Shariati only took place in the form of three letters between both, which Fanon probably sent from Tunis, where he served for the Algerian *Front de Libération Nationale* (National Liberation Front, FLN), editing the FLN's journal entitled *al-Mujāhid*.[9] According to Akhavi, Shariati himself also published some articles in this journal.[10] In his presentation of Fanon, Shariati mentions neither his work as a translator of Fanon's books, nor their correspondence or any articles he himself may have published in Fanon's journal *al-Mujāhid*.

Deeply impressed by his stay in Paris, Shariati returned to Iran with a doctoral degree from the Sorbonne in June 1964.[11] His subsequent career was characterized by an almost notorious influentiality as a public intellectual,

---

3   Ali Rahnema, *An Islamic Utopian: A Political Biography of Ali Shari'ati* (London: I.B. Tauris, 2014). See Ervand Abrahamian's review of this book, *Science and Society* 64, 2 (Summer 2000): 261–264.

4   Rahnema, *An Islamic Utopian*, 69, 86.

5   Ibid., 87.

6   Ibid.

7   Ibid., 120.

8   Ibid., 119, 127.

9   Ibid., 127.

10 Shahrough Akhavi, "Sharī'atī,'Alī," in *The Oxford Encyclopedia of the Modern Islamic World*, ed. John L. Esposito (Oxford: Oxford University Press, 1995), IV, 47.

11 Ibid., 131.

overshadowing his changing affiliations with different state and private institutions. It is in this phase of what Rahnema called his prolific teaching
between 1966 and 1976 that Shariati probably composed the text presenting
Frantz Fanon to an Iranian audience.[12] Before turning to the text, however, a
short inquiry into the literary strategies employed by Shariati in recounting his
formative years in France is necessary.

The *Fictive Mind*

Confronted with the perplexing amount of counterfactual arguments and
misattributed quotations in Shariati's collected works, especially in the passages dealing with Shariati's time in France, Rahnema dedicated a special
chapter to what he describes as Shariati's *Fictive Mind*.[13] Rather than see this
counterfactual aspect of Shariati's writings as unintentional mistakes attributable to slips of pen and memory, Rahnema argues that Shariati not only played
a game of association and allusion, blurring the distinction between autobiographic reminiscences and fictional writings, but also went as far as to invent
references in scientific contexts. What appears as errors and mistakes on the
first glance is shown by Rahnema to be the product of an elaborate strategy
of literary association used by Shariati to structure, frame and interpret his
ideas. Profiting from Rahnema's investigative diligence, we can thus build on a
solid foundation to examine Shariati's literary techniques in his presentation
of Frantz Fanon.

In diffusing autobiography and fiction, Shariati made extensive use of as-
sonances and dates, leaving "us to grapple with and guess at the true meaning
and significance" of the names and relations contained in his writings.[14] In
constructing this world of mirrors, Wiedergänger and double meanings, Shariati repeatedly conforms to narrative archetypes into which he molds his recol-
lections and phantasies. While the structuring of Shariati's mystical beloved
encountered, lost and resurrected in the Paris of his later writings is compared
to Dante Alighieri's Beatrice by Shariati himself, the relevant archetype underlying some of the counterfactual information provided about Frantz Fanon
appears to be Shariati's depiction of himself, moulded into an archetypic lost
searcher of meaning.[15]

---

12   Ibid., xiv.
13   Ibid., 161–175.
14   Ibid., 167.
15   Ibid., 173.

That Shariati did not hesitate to switch between fact and fiction in the context of academic writing and presentations is demonstrated by Rahnema's analysis of the eminent scientist Chandel, who is frequently quoted by Shariati.

> In a lecture to students at the Petroleum University in Abadan, Shari'ati descussed an ascending group of intellectuals [...]. In the middle of it was a man called Professor Chandel [...]. Chandel is the product of Shari'ati's fictive mind [...] the twin which Shari'ati created for himself to say what he could not say outright, give further authority to his views and help him out when he needed the intellectual support of one who would say exactly what Shari'ati wanted him to say. [...] Shari'ati had conceived of his own pen-name, Sham', the Persian for candle. [...] Inspired by his own Persian pen-name, Shari'ati cloned another candle, this time in French; Chandel. Typical of Shari'ati, instead of using some [sic] else's name or any already-existing name, thereby operating under a stranger's mask, his double was a transparent image of himself.[16]

This chapter argues that Shariati did not exclusively restrict his imagination to the fictive mask of Professor Chandel, but also used historical figures like Frantz Fanon as speakers of whatever he needed them to say. By focusing specifically on counterfactual information contained in Shariati's presentation of Frantz Fanon, the narrative strategies and possibly the underlying motives of Shariati's appropriation of the mask of the Antillean-Franco-Algerian theoretician of decolonization become visible. It is now time to turn to this presentation itself.

Frantz Fanon and His Adaptation by Ali Shariati: A Short Presentation of Shariati's "Frānts Fānūn"

The text that forms the basis for this chapter has, as far as I see, not been discussed in the research concerned with Shariati. It is contained on pages 416–423 of Volume 31 of the collected works of Shariati, containing mostly a collection of short, unconnected texts and entitled *Vīzhegīhā-yi qurūn-i jadīd*, which can tentatively be translated as *Features of the Modern Centuries*. I have not been able to find any further information about this volume or the presentation of Frantz Fanon contained in it. Abrahamian's hint that Shariati's lectures were "almost all recorded, transcribed and published by his disciples, first in separate pamphlets and then in a collected works numbering 38 volumes" may be applicable for this short presentation, which accordingly would have been

---

16   Ibid., 161–162.

part of a lecture.[17] There is a very basic chart on page 419 and a note correcting counterfactual information about Fanon's family background. While the latter almost certainly was included by an editor other than Shariati himself, as will be argued below, the former may represent some rudimentary illustration used by Shariati during his lecture to illustrate the span from six to seven years of age to adulthood.

Starting with a short biography of Frantz Fanon, the text mainly purports to represent the main arguments of three of Fanon's most famous books in chronological order, starting with *Peau Noire, Masques Blancs*, continuing with *L'An V de la Révolution Algérienne* and concluding with *Les Damnés de la Terre*.

In keeping with the inquiry in Shariati's narrative strategies in appropriating the historical figure of Frantz Fanon, I will in the following passages focus on three distinct levels, on which this appropriation becomes visible in the form of counterfactual information given by Shariati. Level 1 will discuss changes to Fanon's biography, level 2 adaptations of Fanon's writings and level 3 the attribution to Fanon of concepts developed by other intellectuals, which were *en vogue* in Paris of the early 1960s.

Level 1: Changes in the Biography of Frantz Fanon

The first level, on which the information given by Shariati sharply differs from the factual life of Frantz Fanon, concerns elementary parameters of Fanon's biography, which is sketched on the first page of Shariati's presentation. While these counterfactual aspects in Fanon's biography as narrated by Shariati at first glance seem to be the result of simple errors on the part of Shariati or – if indeed the text under examination derives from a transcript of a lecture by Shariati – due to misunderstandings on the part of the anonymous listener of Shariati, the scholarly renown of Shariati makes it unlikely that Shariati himself would confuse details as pertinent as Fanon's familiar background. An argument against errors due to a faulty transcript of a lecture lies in the fact that many of the details given in the text are precise and correct. Why should a listener have wrongly noted Fanon's familiar background, while correctly noting dates concerning the Algerian revolution and the titles of Fanon's books?

As closer examination reveals, the counterfactual details contained in Shariati's presentation of Fanon do not result in a chaotic or confused narrative, as one would expect random errors to be. The picture emerging from the counterfactual details is in the contrary very coherent. Rather than explain these discrepancies as mere errors caused by slips of pen and memory, this chapter

---

17   Abrahamian, "Review," 262.

accordingly argues that the coherence of the counterfactual information given by Shariati is evidence of a conscious strategy of narrative appropriation by which Shariati mobilized the historical figure of Frantz Fanon as a second Professor Chandel saying precisely what he wished him to say.

In this context, the obvious changes to Frantz Fanon's biography can be interpreted as "guideposts and signals to get him [Shariati] through the maze he conjures."[18] Contrary to Shariati's claims, Frantz Fanon by no means came from a Berber background from North Africa and this false information is duly corrected in a footnote by the editor.[19] However, this adaptation of Fanon's family background draws Fanon closer to Shariati, who frequently frames himself as a foreign-educated student who duly returns home to alleviate his country's plight.

This counterfactual intervention also serves to counter possible objections to the justification of Fanon's stand on behalf of the Algerian revolution. As Frantz Fanon himself remained painfully aware, his Antillean familiar background and subsequent studies in France made him an outsider to the Algerian revolution. By counterfactually furnishing a Berber background to Fanon, Shariati presents Fanon as an intellectual firmly grounded in his personal heritage. This may have been seen as especially significant by his audience in the context of an Iran deeply concerned with matters of "Westoxication" following Āl-i Aḥmad's influential essay on the detrimental influence of the West on non-Western traditions of society and learning.[20] Rather than be forced to discuss the complicated question of whether the nascent movements of emancipation from the overpowering influence of "the West" could include foreign idealists, Shariati thus presents Fanon as an entirely uncomplicated case of a native Algerian of Berber background idealistically returning to his home country.

Narrative assimilation of Fanon's and Shariati's biographies may also explain the curious description of Fanon as a student of 32 years in Paris.[21] While historically Frantz Fanon studied at Lyon, Shariati himself was enrolled at the Sorbonne at Paris. I am not sure what to make of the age of 32 at which Fanon is said to have studied in Paris, however, this age is closer to Shariati's age of 31, at which he returned to Iran from France, than to Fanon's 28 years at which he took up his first post at the hospital of Blida-Joinville in Algeria in 1953.[22] If one explains the mistakes contained in Fanon's biography as motivated by a

---

18   Rahnema, *An Islamic Utopian*, 166.

19   *Frānts Fānūn az Barbarhā-yi Shamāl-i Āfrīqā būd*, Sharī'atī, "Frānts Fānūn," 416.

20   See Jalāl Āl-i Aḥmad, *Gharbzadegī (Westoxication)*, Volume 8 of Jalāl Āl-i Aḥmad's collected works (Tehran: Intishārāt-i Jāmedarān 1384/2006).

21   Shariati, "Frānts Fānūn," 416.

22   Ibid.

narrative strategy of assimilating Fanon to Shariati, the description of Fanon's status as a foreigner, *khārijī*, in Algeria on the same page could accordingly be interpreted as one of Rahnema's "signposts," alerting the reader – or for that matter Shariati himself – of the counterfactual adaptation of Fanon's family background.[23]

Compared with this surprisingly obvious discrepancy between Fanon's actual life and the – in itself mutually contradictory – information given in Shariati's presentation, the other chronological mistakes are more difficult to interpret. Contrary to Shariati's statement, Fanon's arrival in Algeria in 1953 preceded the outbreak of the Algerian War; rather than return to his home country in time of war, Fanon took position in a French hospital.[24] After his emigration to Tunis, Fanon neither worked as a doctor, nor did he write his first book, *Peau Noire, Masques Blancs*, which had already appeared in France in 1952, there.[25]

Level 2: Adaptation of Fanon's Writings

If the changes to Fanon's biography to a certain degree assimilate the biography of Fanon to the life of Shariati, it is now time to turn to the counterfactual adaptations to Fanon's writings, which Shariati included in his presentation. In his extensive presentation of Fanon's *L'an V de la revolution algérienne*, Shariati focuses especially on Fanon's analysis of the impact of the revolution on the traditional family structures inside Algerian society. While Fanon, however, analyzes in detail the subversion of the traditional relationships of son and father, daughter and father, brothers and couples, Shariati only mentions the change revolution brings to the relationship of a daughter to her father.[26] The following discussion of the different timespans of childhood in the West and *"countries that are behind"* is, on the contrary, not to be found in Fanon's *L'an V*.[27]

Interpretation of this rather striking selectiveness and accretion may possibly start from some other curiously counterfactual details, which appear to

---

23   Ibid.
24   Ibid.
25   Ibid., 417.
26   Frantz Fanon, *Oeuvres* (Paris: La Découverte, 2011), 335–338, 338–342, 343, 343–346; Shariati, "Frānts Fānūn," 417–418.
27   *Kishwarhā-yi ʿaqab mānde*, Shariati, "Frānts Fānūn," 419. The whole passage runs over pages 418–420.

be narrative interventions of Shariati himself. While the supposedly traditional Algerian custom of the daughter veiling herself in front of her father does not appear in Fanon's writings, in the context of this presentation it arguably serves to bring an Iranian audience to the side of Fanon / Shariati in asserting the laudability of a revolution in family relations.[28] In a similar way, the trade of carpet weaving as an example of a trade by which children had to support their families in backwards countries is not mentioned by Frantz Fanon, but would have been a quite logical example when adressing an Iranian audience.[29] A similar adaptation of Fanon for an Iranian audience may motivate Shariati's change of Fanon's famous appeal concluding *Les Damnés de la Terre* not to aim at turning Africa into a new Europe into an appeal not to turn Africa into a new America, arguably more in line with the growing Anti-Americanism in pre-revolutionary Iran.[30]

If one chooses to follow this line of argumentation, the Fanon whom Shariati uses as a mask to speak to his Iranian audience does not only have a biography which is structured on Shariati's, but he also teaches concepts and ideas, which Shariati may have been believed to fall on fertile ground with his Iranian audience. Provocative aspects of Fanon's writings were accordingly left out and some details adapted to tune the message ascribed to Fanon to Shariati's presumable audience.

Level 3: Attribution to Fanon of Concepts Developed by Others

The last level on which Shariati counterfactually modifies the historical figure of Frantz Fanon and his works is the attribution to Fanon of concepts, plans and theories developed by others. While the discussion of children's development and its different speeds in First and Third World countries does not, as indicated above, feature in Fanon's *L'an V*, to which it is attributed by Shariati, I cannot at the present indicate any specific source from which Shariati may have drawn this concept instead. Another case of a theory not to be found in Fanon's writings is the economic theory of development voiced by Shariati's Fanon.

It is not at all possible for a country with light industry to become industrialized, for it will still be dependent on other countries. Therefore, the

---

28   Shariati, "Frānts Fānūn," 418.

29   Ibid., 419.

30   Fanon, *Oeuvres*, 676; Shariati, "Frānts Fānūn," 421.

first step must be on the path of heavy industry [...]. But the social condition of these countries (in the state which they are currently in) is limited from two sides, by the scarcity of the accumulated consumption and by the nature of the accumulated consumption [...]. The only possible way lies in the [cooperation of] a geographical region in the sale, production and consumption [of a given product] to one country of the Third World. This means that the economic conditions, the mines and the savings, which exist in all countries and which amount to a heavy industry, will be developed and that the other countries of the Third World do not further develop [this particular industry]. The market of this country therefore lies in the other countries of the Third World, which thereby also become the owners of heavy industry and do not need to buy products from Europe (every [country] specializes in one specific industry). In this way, [Third World countries] can both own heavy industry and take their needs out of the grasp of European capitalists.[31]

This crash-course in development economics comes as somewhat of a surprise when seen in the context of the published works by Frantz Fanon, especially in the context of *Les Damnés de la Terre*, to which Shariati attributes this passage. Difficult though it is to pinpoint precisely the factual source from which Shariati is drawing – as we have seen above it is quite possible that some of the thoughts which Shariati lets Fanon voice are really the ideas of Shariati himself – it seems that the influence of Che Guevara's theory of development can be detected in this passage. Guevara's speech at the second economic meeting of the afro-asiatic solidarity in Algiers in particular describes the problems attached to the development of heavy industry in Third World countries in a way quite parallel to the analysis ascribed to Fanon by Shariati in the above passage: The uniform deployment of investments in the development of the industry of Third World countries leads to an oversized production compared to its possible markets.[32] The solution suggested also resembles Shariati's conclusion: Investion in a mutually synergetic way opens the way to a more efficient use of resources.[33] While these brief remarks of Guevara do not go into as much detail as Shariati's deliberations and accordingly cannot have served as the direct source, it is nonetheless suggestive that one of the

---

31   Shariati, "Fränts Fänün," 422.

32   Ernesto Che Guevara, *Ausgewählte Werke in Einzelausgaben, Band 3: Aufsätze zur Wirtschaftspolitik* (Köln: Weltkreis, 1988), 168.

33   Guevara, *Aufsätze*, 168.

concepts attributed by Shariati to Fanon may be traceable to Guevara, another leftist intellectual very much *en vogue* in Paris during Shariati's sojourn there.

Conclusion

Shariati's presentation of Fanon on the first glance seems to adhere to the expected standards imposed by the biographical genre according to the basic conventions of academic writing. After a short biographical introduction, Fanon's alleged writings are discussed and summarized book by book. Shariati as the author of this review of Fanon's work ostensibly stays out of his discussion, limiting his visible personal intervention to the occasional use of the 1. person plural pronoun "we."[34]

The extent and possible motivation of Shariati's intervention contained in his presentation of Fanon only become visible through a comparison of his summaries with Fanon's factual biography and writings. Shariati's contrafactual information does, when read and analyzed in the light of Rahnema's findings on the use of fictional elements by Shariati in his autobiographic works, present a surprisingly coherent picture, modifying Fanon's biography and his books to a remarkable extent and thereby turning him into a mask or *alter ego* which Shariati could use to voice arguments which he believed needed to be received as backed by Fanon's authority by his Iranian audience. This coherence of much of the counterfactual information forms a strong argument against the first impression of the reader that the text is "full of errors." Even if we were to doubt Shariati's memory, difficult as this seems in itself in the light of his scholarly career, errors would in all likelihood not result in a picture as coherent as that drawn in this presentation of Frantz Fanon.

In not adhering to his audiences' expectation that he present some sort of "factual truth," Shariati's liberties place their author outside his ostensible stance of a biographer working according to standards of academic writing, which would have him limited to quotations of others while clearly labelling any original thoughts as his own. Some of the liberties taken by Shariati as a transmitter appear to be motivated by what Shariati may have seen as the "greater good" of enabling a smooth reception of Fanon's work. A good example of this is the omission of Fanon's analysis of the near-total dissolution of traditional familiar relationships in times of revolution, which has been analyzed above. Rather than shock his audience with the disturbing idea of revolution dissolving family as so far understood, Shariati narrowed Fanon's analysis

---

34   Shariati, "Frānts Fānūn," 421.

to the sole example of the relationship between father and daughter. Even in this example, however, he changes Fanon's criticism of the father's uncomfortability in front of the developing sexuality of his daughter, which he may still have thought too problematic for his Iranian audience, to the counterfactual assertion that Fanon criticized the supposed Algerian custom of a daughter's need to wear the *ḥijāb* in front of her father. This – entirely fictional – tradition would likely have been seen as sufficiently absurd by his Iranian audience to justify Fanon's challenge to traditional relations inside the Algerian family.

Motivated by a "greater good" as some of Shariati's interventions may be, the compelling phantasm which this presentation so gleefully depicts clearly goes beyond what can be justified as a "political necessity" dictated by Shariati's Iranian audience. Instead, Shariati seems to enjoy this game of mirrors built on his implicit disavowal of standards of academic discourse, associating freely and even leaving "signposts" in the form of internal contradictions in his presentation, alerting the attentive reader that just as Fanon cannot be an Algerian and a "foreigner" at the same time, there may also be further contradictions between the presentation and the factual life and works of Frantz Fanon.

Shariati's elusive mockery of the genre- and discourse-related expectations that a quotation actually refer to where the cited passage originally occurred instead places him in the category of post-modern literary authors similarly blurring the lines between transmission, critique and original thought. It is in Orhan Pamuk's famous *Kara Kitap* (The black book), published in 1990 for a Turkish audience in search of its lost non-European traditions, that we find the second chapter, *When the Waters left the Bosporus*, introduced with a quote ascribed to a certain İbni Zerhani: "Nothing can surprise as much as life. Other than writing."[35] In his meticulous – and largely reliable – reference list containing the quotes opening the different chapters of his book, Pamuk traces this quotation to a *"Kitap-al Zulmet"* or *Book of oppression*, "of the obscure book (Bottfolio), translated into Arabic by İbni Zerhani."[36] This book, its suggested author and the supposed translator into Arabic are equally obscure. While it is doubtful whether Pamuk actually read Shariati's writings and was influenced by his compositional methods, both use their freedom as intellectuals seen as transmitters across cultural, linguistic and scriptural boundaries to play with their audiences' expectations and emancipate their role as writers from the genre-bound laws of correct quotation.

---

35   Orhan Pamuk, *Kara Kitap* (Istanbul: Yapı Kredi Yayınları, 2013), 24.
36   *2. Bölüm: Kitap-al Zulmet, Obscuri Libri'den (Bottfolio), Arapçaya çeviren: İbni Zerhani.* Pamuk, *Kara Kitap*, 467.

It would be unfair to hold the genre-related expectations of a reliable use of citations to Shariati, as he loudly warnes his readers that he is not to be judged according to these standards by including obviously contrafactual information in the beginning of his biography of Frantz Fanon. Rather, this chapter argues that we as readers of Shariati need to question our expectations: Where we assume Shariati to be writing as somewhat of a split personality, scientifically detached in his "academic output" and personally involved in his "fictional writing," Shariati shapes a genre for himself, as an engaged intellectual ever so succesfully fusing transmission and adaptation with his original thought.

Bibliography

Abrahamian, Ervand. "Review of An Islamic Utopian: A political biography of Ali Shari'ati by Ali Rahnema" *Science and Society* 64, 2 (Summer 2000): 261–264.

Akhavi, Shahrough. "Sharī'atī, 'Alī," in *The Oxford Encyclopedia of the Modern Islamic World*, edited by John L. Esposito. Oxford: Oxford University Press, 1995.

Āl-i Aḥmad, Jalāl. *Gharbzadegī (Westoxication)*, Volume 8 of Jalāl Āl-i Aḥmad's collected works. Tehran: Intishārāt-i Jāmedarān 1384/2006.

Fanon, Frantz. *Oeuvres*. Paris: La Découverte, 2011.

Fanon, Frantz. *L'an V de la révolution algérienne*. Paris: La Découverte / Poche, 2011.

Guevara, Ernesto Che. *Ausgewählte Werke in Einzelausgaben, Band 3: Aufsätze zur Wirtschaftspolitik*. Köln: Weltkreis, 1988.

Pamuk, Orhan. *Kara Kitap*. Istanbul: Yapı Kredi Yayınları, 2013.

Rahnema, Ali. *An Islamic Utopian: A Political Biography of Ali Shari'ati*. London: I.B. Tauris, 2014.

Sartre, Jean-Paul. *L'existentialisme est un humanisme*. Paris: Gallimard, 2011.

Shariati, Ali. "Frānts Fānūn (Frantz Fanon)" in *Majmū'e-yi Āthār-i Mu'allim-i Shahīd-i Duktur 'Alī Sharī'atī* vol. 31, *Vīzhegīhā-yi qurūn-i jadīd*. Tehran: Shirkat-i Intishārāt-i Chāpkhash, 1370/1992: 416–423.

CHAPTER 9

Understanding Ali Shariati's Political Thought

Chandra Muzaffar

I began reading Ali Shariati in the early 1980's. I was a young academic at that time, teaching at a university in the northern part of Malaysia. *On the Sociology of Islam* was the first of his writings on my menu. After that, I devoured his *Marxism and other Western Fallacies*, then moved on to his *Hajj*. Over the years, I have had the opportunity to consume many of his other works. Because of this, my students in various political science courses have been introduced to Shariati's books and ideas as well.

Shariati, needless to say, has had a profound impact upon my thinking. I feel that he captured the essence of the message of Islam. In addition, that essence is the crux and core of God's eternal message to humanity. It is a message that has to be translated into reality. Shariati tried to do this. Because he tried, he suffered the agony and the pain that accompanies all such endeavours. Indeed, he sacrificed his life as he sought to uphold that eternal message. This is what enhanced his appeal to me as a person. He was an intellectual who lived and died for his ideals. It explains why I made it a point to pay my humble respects to this noble human being by visiting his grave at *Behishte Sayyeda Zainab* in Damascus during my trip to Syria in 2007.

Perspective on Tawḥīd

In this essay, I am focussing upon Shariati's thoughts in relation to politics. In a sense, it is not possible to separate his thinking on politics from his ideas on other aspects of society. They are all inter-connected and inter-linked. One should therefore begin with his larger vision of life itself and the meaning and purpose of human existence and then zero in upon politics as an important dimension of life.

As Shariati puts it,

> My world-view consists of *tawḥīd*. *Tawḥīd*, in the sense of oneness of God, is accepted by all monotheists. But *tawḥīd* as a world-view in the sense I intend in my theory means regarding the whole universe as a unity,

instead of dividing it into this world and the hereafter, the natural and the supernatural, substance and meaning, spirit and body. It means regarding the whole of existence as a single form, a single living and conscious organism, possessing will, intelligence, feeling and purpose. There are many people who believe in *tawḥīd*, but only as a religious-philosophical theory, meaning nothing but 'God is one, not more than one.' But I take *tawḥīd* in the sense of a world-view, and I am convinced that Islam also intends it in this sense.[1]

He further elaborates,

Tawḥīd, then, is to be interpreted in the sense of the unity of nature with metanature, of man with nature, of man with man, of God with the world and with man. It depicts all of these as constituting a total, harmonious living and self-aware system. I have said the very structure of *tawḥīd* cannot accept contradiction or disharmony in the world. According to the world-view of *tawḥīd*, therefore, there is no contradiction in all of existence: no contradiction between man and nature, spirit and body, this world and the hereafter, matter and meaning. Nor can *tawḥīd* accept legal, class, social, political, racial, national, territorial, genetic or even economic contradictions, for it implies a mode of looking upon all being as a unity.[2]

A consequence of *tawḥīd*, Shariati notes,

is the negation of the dependence of man on any social force, and the linking of him, in exclusivity and in all his dimensions, to the consciousness and will that rule over being. The source of support, orientation, belief, and succour of every individual is a single central point, a pivot around which revolves all the motions of the cosmos. All beings move in a circle described by the luminous radii equidistant from the centre, which is the powerful source of all being, the only will, the only consciousness, the only power that exists and rules over the universe. The position of man in this world is an objective embodiment of this truth, as is, more obviously, his circumambulation of the Ka'ba.'[3]

---

1 Ali Shariati, *On the Sociology of Islam*. trans. Hamid Algar, (Berkeley: Mizan Press, 1979), 82.

2 Ibid., 85–86.

3 Ibid., 87.

It follows from this notion of man's relationship to that central point – that pivot – that in 'the world-view of *tawḥīd*, man fears only one power, and is answerable before only one judge. He turns to only one *qibla*, and directs his hopes and desires to only one source. And the corollary is that all else is false and pointless – all the diverse and variegated tendencies, strivings, fears, desiresand hopes of man are vain and fruitless.'[4]

Shariati concludes, '*tawḥīd* bestows upon man independence and dignity. Submission to Him alone – the supreme norm of all being – impels man to revolt against all lying powers, all humiliating fetters of fear and of greed.'[5]

There is no need to emphasize that belief in the oneness of God – an engaged surrender to God – and living and acting in accordance with the values and principles that constitute that consciousness of God, is God's eternal message to humankind. In his numerous lectures, letters and essays, Shariati tried to convey this message to his fellow human beings. He elaborated and adumbrated this message in his worldview of *tawḥīd*, that as we have seen, is a philosophical exposition of the oneness of God, but he did not develop that worldview further in terms of what it means specifically to politics or economics or culture or ethnic relations or family life. In other words, Shariati did not construct in any detail a *tawḥīdic* politics or a *tawḥīdic* economics or a *tawḥīdic* culture or a *tawḥīdic* perspective on ethnic relations or family life.

The Nexus to Politics

Based upon Shariati's *tawḥīdic* worldview, I shall attempt to establish a nexus between certain ideas in this worldview and politics. Because submission to God is central to *tawḥīd*, any ideology or political system that demands total, absolute loyalty to a leader, or an elite, or a cabal would be anathema to Shariati. Besides, power is one of God's attributes. It is a reminder to us that whatever power we human beings exercise is temporal and transient. It is wrong therefore for us to aggrandize power or to monopolize authority. It follows from this that political authoritarianism, the centralization of power or any form of dictatorship, would be completely unacceptable to Shariati. He was very much aware of the oppression that often results from harsh authoritarianism and how the suppression of dissent emasculates society.

Although an ardent opponent of authoritarianism and the aggrandizement of power, Shariati did not develop a concept of power, its characteristics, its

---

4   Ibid.
5   Ibid.

limits, its legitimate uses, and its underlying ethical foundation. Neither did he concern himself with the institutions and structures related to power. Nor did he offer any thoughts on how a prevailing culture could shape and sustain an ethical political order or conversely, degrade and destroy it.

Khalifah and Trust

One gets the impression that instead of delving into culture and structure in trying to fathom the exercise of power, Shariati sought to empower the human being, the human being as vicegerent – *khalifah* – on earth. As vicegerent, the human being,

> has accepted the heavy Trust of God, and for this very reason, he is a responsible and committed being, with the free exercise of his will. He does not perceive his perfection as lying in the creation of a private relationship with God, to the exclusion of men; it is rather in the struggle for the perfection of the human race, in enduring hardship, hunger, deprivation and torment for the sake of the liberty, livelihood and well-being of men, in the furnace of intellectual and social struggle, that he attains piety, perfection and closeness to God.[6]

Applied to politics, this would mean that for Shariati, it is the position of the human being as the bearer of the divine trust that is the essence of his pursuit of power – since power is the pivot of politics. He has to fulfil this trust with a profound sense of responsibility. His exercise of freedom is to enable him to fulfil this trust. However, in the process he will have to struggle and suffer. Suffering thus becomes an indispensable component of Shariati's idea of politics.

Shariati felt that suffering, even if it led to the renunciation of life itself, to martyrdom, was worthwhile if it resulted in justice for the human family. An essential aspect of justice was preserving and enhancing the dignity of all, of the whole of creation. Justice and dignity were noble goals that could only be achieved if we employed noble means. It is because means shaped ends in politics that Shariati emphasized the liberation the self from its ego. It is only through such liberation that the human being, determined to fulfil God's trust, would succeed in delivering justice, unsullied by personal ambition, and glory to the people.

---

6 Ibid., 123.

In emphasizing the deliverance of justice to the people, Shariati is actually focusing upon leadership and the primary responsibility of the ruler. There are various passages in his writings where he alludes to the sort of qualities that leaders should possess. His eloquent reflections on Prophet Muhammad, Imam 'Ali, Imam Hussein and Abu Dhār Ghifārī for instance, bear testimony to this. Writing of the Prophet, he notes, 'Until the end of his life, when Islamic rule was established throughout Arabia, he did not change his lifestyle. He was the absolute ruler of a country and he ate barley bread. He would sit with the poor upon the ground at their meal just like a humble slave. He would ride a donkey bareback and, most of the time, he would sit another person behind him.'[7] He adds, 'Half of the floor of the Prophet's house was carpeted with sand.'[8] It is said that the Prophet 'tested himself with hunger by often tying a stone around his stomach so that he could bear the causticity of hunger.'[9] Simplicity and humility were the outstanding attributes of the Prophet; attributes that Muslims through the ages have always expected their rulers to emulate.

Although noble traits in leaders were recognized as laudable, Shariati, as we have seen, gave greater weight to the status of the human being as vicegerent on earth. In this, he was different from the classical Muslim scholars from Al-Fārābī and Al-Mawardī to Al-Ghazālī and Ibn-Khaldūn.[10] For them the virtues of the ruler were what guaranteed the success of a society. Shariati went beyond rulership and brought to the fore the empowerment of the human being. By constantly reminding the human being of who he is, why he is on earth, and what the ultimate purpose of life is, Shariati compels us to view politics from a spiritual-moral perspective that is not debased by the politics of power or the power of politics.

Communism and Capitalism

If Shariati's view of politics differed in some respects from classical Islamic political thought, it was also at variance with the two great political systems produced by the West in the last three centuries. We shall first look at communism, as a system at the root of which is Marxism, a subject on which Shariati

---

7   Ali Shariati, *Shariati in English*. Year of Publication not known; Place of Publication not known; Name of Publisher not known, 123.

8   Ibid., 140.

9   Ibid.

10   The writings of these and other thinkers can be found in M.M. Sharif, *A History of Muslim Philosophy*: Vol. 1 and 11. Wiesbaden: Otto Harrassowitz, 1963.

had a lot to say. Shariati was critical of Marxism for many reasons. Its denial of the transcendent and the sacred and its exposition of life as a force, a process that finds expression solely on the material plane was unacceptable to believers like Shariati. He saw dialectical materialism, the intellectual fulcrum of Marxism, which presents itself as 'the only completely scientific description of reality,' as a dogma with fanatical tendencies, which was elevated to the level of 'the absolute and exclusive truth.'[11] It is because of Marxism's dogmatic character that the communist system, convinced that it was the only true system for humankind, has often been utterly ruthless towards ideas and institutions outside its orbit. The experience of communist societies has also shown that it utilized centralised power to increase industrial production that served the interests of the state rather than the well-being of the working-class. As the 1960's and 1970's unfolded, Shariati was exposed to these and other grave flaws in communism both as theory and as practice.

The monumental weaknesses in capitalism also became obvious to Shariati early in his intellectual journey. If certain dimensions of liberal thought constituted the intellectual underpinning of the capitalist system, it may be argued that the glorification of individual freedom and its manifestation in the market economy sometimes lead to gross acts of selfishness and greed, and it's selfishness and greed that are largely responsible for the concentration of wealth in the hands of a few and the ever widening gap between the very affluent and the abjectly poor within individual nations and at the global level. Capitalism, Shariati also observed, had enslaved the human being to the machine whose overriding goal was the continuous maximisation of profit.[12] The human being in turn in capitalist societies was driven by the desire for unending consumption.[13] For it is untrammelled consumption which keeps the wheels of production rolling – and the margin of profits expanding.

As ideology and system, capitalism, it is understood, is preoccupied with wealth acquisition and material success. The transcendent and the sacred count for little in its scheme of things. However, capitalist societies, as a whole, do not adopt an aggressive and antagonistic attitude towards formal religion as such – unlike a number of communist states. Shariati was cognisant of this difference.[14]

---

11   Ali Shariati, *Marxism and Other Western Fallacies: An Islamic Critique.* trans. R. Campbell. (Berkeley: Islamic Foundation Press, 1979), 26.

12   Ibid., 16.

13   Ibid., 17.

14   Ibid., 25.

Religious Ideology

Nonetheless, Shariati knew that capitalism, like communism, was inhospitable to the nourishing of a society inspired by *tawḥīd*, the oneness of God, which views the human being as *khalifah*, a vicegerent on earth, devoted to the pursuit of justice and dignity. Would it be possible to bring such a society to fruition in an environment in which *tawḥīd* and vicegerency were part of the vocabulary of the elites and the people? There is no guarantee. Shariati laments that there have been many Muslim societies where Islamic rituals and forms are faithfully observed, where loyalty to God and love for the Prophet are eulogized day and night, and yet *tawḥīdic* justice, that seeks to close the gap between the rich and poor, is banished and the dignity of a vicegerent uttering a word of truth before a ruler is crushed mercilessly. This had been so even in the early decades of Islamic history.

Shariati brings this out dramatically in his narration of the struggle of the pious companion of the Prophet, Abu Dhār, during the reign of the third Caliph, Uthmān ibn 'Affān. Abu Dhār spoke out with courage and honesty against the excesses and the wrongdoings of the Caliph. Because he developed a significant following, the Caliph felt threatened, punished, and persecuted him, leading eventually to his tragic death in the isolation of a desert.[15] This conflict between the wielders of power, who have deviated from truth and justice, and those who are opposed to them on the basis of principle and righteousness, has happened right through time.

Nevertheless, those who have betrayed the essence of a religion – in this case, Islam – often use and exploit religious symbols and practices to legitimate their misdeeds. As Shariati wrote,

> These guardians of Islam who were responsible for the glorification of the Islamic rites and rituals, for propagating the traditions of Islam, who were entrusted with enhancing its power, and who attempted to expand and inseminate its civilisation, sciences, culture and mysticism – and not the infidels and the materialists – destroyed Islam from within and made it lifeless, directionless and motionless.[16]

By identifying aspects of communism and capitalism and the distortion of religious teachings as impediments in the quest for a *tawḥīdic* society, Shariati was actually pinpointing certain underlying causes of injustice and

---

15   See Shariati, *Shariati in English op. cit*, 144–145.
16   Ali Shariati, *What is To Be Done*. (United States of America: The Institute for Research and Islamic Studies, 1986), 38.

inhumanity that has been present right through the history of civilisation. The Pharaoh – the symbol of political power – *Qarun* (*Croesus*) – the embodiment of economic power – and *Bal'am bin Ba'ura'* – the representative of religious authority – are three human types who invariably stand in the way of justice and dignity.[17] These forces often collude and conspire with one another in order to preserve and perpetuate their dominance and control. Confronting and overcoming them is the sacred duty of all those who care for the well-being of present and future generations.

Resistance

This underscores the significance that Shariati attached to resistance in his vision of politics. His admiration for Abu Dhār was a manifestation of how much he valued the politics of resistance. However, it was more than Abu Dhār. He saw resistance in the Prophet's noble struggle for justice and peace; in the sufferings that the fourth caliph 'Ali ibn Abī Ṭālib had to endure; in the life of virtue exemplified by Fāṭimah; in Ḥussein's martyrdom.

Resistance is inextricably intertwined with sacrifice. Resistance, as we know, demands huge sacrifices from those who have chosen this path. Sacrifice, Shariati reminds us, is central to Islam. This is why it is at the heart of one of the most important practices in the religion: the performance of the *hajj*. It explains why the hajj is known as the rite of sacrifice.[18]

What one has to sacrifice is one's selfishness. The ultimate expression of this is reflected in Prophet Ibrāhīm's willingness to sacrifice his own son, 'Ismā'īl, because of his love for God. It is mainly around this principle of 'sacrificing 'Ismā'īl' that the hajj is constructed.'[19] Curbing selfishness and becoming selfless is expected of all Muslims. For politicians in particular, it is imperative that they set aside their own selfish interests and genuinely seek to serve a larger cause rooted in God Consciousness. This is what *tawḥīdic* politics is all about.

The Contemporary Ethos

If Shariati were alive today, what would he regard as some of the major challenges to the sort of politics of selflessness that he envisaged? I shall single out

---

17   Ibid., 48. See also Ali Shariati, *On the Sociology of Islam op. cit*, 115–116.

18   For an in-depth exposition on the real meaning of the hajj, see Ali Shariati. *Hajj.* Trans Dr. Ali A. Behzadnia and Najla Denny. Houston, Texas: Free Islamic Literatures INC., 1980.

19   Ibid., especially the chapter entitled 'The Sacrifice of Ismail.'

a major challenge within the domestic politics of a number of Muslim societies and an even more formidable challenge in the arena of global politics and economics to illustrate the obstacles present in the contemporary world to the realization of *tawḥīd* in politics.

Aggressive, violent sectarianism has emerged as a colossal threat to the unity and solidarity of the Muslim *ummah* in countries such as Iraq and Syria, Lebanon and Bahrain, Yemen and Pakistan, among others. Sunnis are pitted against the Shi'a and the Shi'a are pitted against the Sunnis. A schism that has existed within the *ummah* for more than a thousand years has in recent years taken an ugly turn for the worse largely because of politics and power dynamics within nation-states, within regions and at the international level. Tens of thousands of both Shi'a and Sunni have been killed, maimed and tortured because of the continuing conflict between the two. The root causes of the conflict seem to be connected to the desire of elements within one group to perpetuate their power and influence in the face of what they perceive as the rise of the other group, with some of its own distinct ideas and practices, and with the potential to challenge the dominance of the former. Forces outside the Muslim *ummah* have exacerbated the conflict within the *ummah* by backing one side against the other in pursuit of their own agenda. Various attempts to end the killings have not succeeded so far[20] – although there has been one serious endeavour to bring influential figures from the Sunni and the Shi'a communities together through the adoption of a common pledge.[21] Shariati would have endorsed these efforts.

The other challenge is a global one closely related to the politics and economics of hegemony. In spite of the end of the colonial epoch in the formal sense, the centres of power in the West, led by Washington D.C., continue to seek to dominate and control the world. Their drive for global hegemony is the main reason why wars and chaos prevail in certain parts of the world.[22] In the

---

20 One such attempt was an appeal to Sunnis and Shi'a by two leaders, Dr. Mahathir Mohamad, a former Prime Minister of Malaysia and a Sunni, and Seyyed Muhammad Khatami, a former President of the Republic of Iran and a Shia. The appeal that I had initiated on behalf of the International Movement for a Just World (JUST) was announced on 22 May 2013 from Putrajaya, the administrative capital of Malaysia. See Mahathir bin Mohamad and S. Muhammad Khatami (2013) "A Joint Appeal to Sunnis and Shi'as' Putrajaya."

21 This is a reference to the well-known Amman Message that unfortunately has now been relegated to the back burner. For a reflection on the Message in the context of the current Sunni-Shia friction, see Chandra Muzaffar 2016. *Critical Concerns from East to West* (e-book), 127–131 Available at: https://issuu.com/juste-books/docs/critical_concerns_from_east_to_west (Accessed 5/21/2016).

22 I have explored global hegemony in a number of my writings. See for instance Chandra Muzaffar, 2008. *Hegemony, Justice; Peace.* Shah Alam, Malaysia: Arah Publications.

1960's and 1970's it was Vietnam and Indo-China, the Congo and Chile. Today, it is Afghanistan, Iraq, Syria, Libya, Yemen and Somalia. Even global terrorism stands in a paradoxical relationship with hegemony. On the one hand, some of the groups resorting to acts of terror may be challenging the United States and Western hegemony. On the other hand, terrorism itself is being manipulated by hegemonic actors themselves and their allies to perpetuate their control and dominance.[23] For Shariati, a principled critic of imperialism, the continuing power of Washington D.C. helmed hegemony, and the opportunistic manoeuvres of hegemonic actors, would be an utter travesty of justice.

Adding to that injustice would be another dimension of the pursuit of global hegemony, which has a direct bearing upon the oneness of the human family and therefore upon the concept of *tawḥīd*. This is the economic dimension of hegemony that in the last few decades have witnessed the increased expansion of global capitalism. Even in Shariati's time, in the 1960's and 1970's, the impact of capitalist transnational corporations was growing rapidly. Today, with the entrenchment of financial capitalism at the global level – investment banks, money markets and hedge funds running into trillions – the overwhelming power of capital has become even more pronounced. It has led to the concentration of wealth in the hands of a small coterie and subsequently widened further the yawning gap between the obscenely opulent and the mass of humanity left at the very bottom of the heap.[24] It has been estimated that the 1% at the apex of the global hierarchy owns and controls as much wealth as the rest of the human family put together![25] Such a massive chasm – there is no need to emphasize – makes a mockery of *tawḥīd* and of the oneness of the human family.

---

23   This is analysed in a few of my recent publications. See for instance Chandra Muzaffar, 2016. Religious Loyalties, Shared Humanity and Global Citizenship in *Critical Concerns op. cit* (e-book), 338–365, and also Chandra Muzaffar, 2013. "The Global War on Terror – and The Prawn Behind the Stone" in *A World in Crisis: Is There A Cure?* (e-book), 28–40. Available at: https://issuu.com/justebooks/docs/world_in_crisis_is_there_a_cure (Accessed 5/21/2016).

24   This is discussed in Chandra Muzaffar, 2013, "A World in Crisis: The Relevance of Spiritual-Moral Principles" in *A World in Crisis op.cit* (e-book), 9–28. It is further probed in Chandra Muzaffar 2015, "From Unipolar to Multi-Polar" in *The Long Journey to Human Dignity and Global Justice* (e-book), 78–95 Available at: https://issuu.com/juste-books/docs/the_long_journey_to_human_dignity_a (Accessed 5/21/2016).

25   An Economy for the 1% (https://www.oxfam.org/en/research/economy-1) (Accessed 5/21/2016).

What is to be Done?

It is apparent that both in the domestic arena and at the global level, the imperative to translate Shariati's central political ideas into action is even more urgent than before. Young Muslims and non-Muslims alike should strive to give meaning and substance to *tawḥīd* and the position of the human being as vicegerent on earth. What this demands are not just education and *awareness building* – a task that Shariati performed so well in his short life – but also mobilization and networking right across the continents.

If the young inspired by the word and the work of Shariati succeed to enhance justice and dignity, even on a modest scale, in some corner of the earth, they would have lived up to the legacy of one of the greatest intellectual activists of the 20th century.

Bibliography

Muzaffar, Chandra. *Hegemony, Justice; Peace*. Shah Alam: Arah Publications, 2008.

Muzaffar, Chandra. *Critical Concerns from East to West*. Petaling Jaya: International Movement for a Just World, 2016. https://issuu.com/justebooks/docs/critical_concerns_from_east_to_west.

Muzaffar, Chandra. *A World in Crisis: Is There a Cure?* Petaling Jaya: International Movement for a Just World, 2013. https://issuu.com/justebooks/docs/world_in_crisis_is_there_a_cure.

Muzaffar, Chandra. The Long Journey to Human Dignity and Global Justice. Petaling Jaya: International Movement for a Just World, 2015. https://issuu.com/justebooks/docs/the_long_journey_to_human_dignity_a.

Shariati, Ali. *On the Sociology of Islam*. Berkeley: Mizan Press, 1979.

Shariati, Ali. *Sharīʿati in English*. Place of Publication not known: Name of Publisher not known, Year of Publication not known.

Shariati, Ali. *Marxism and other Western Fallacies an Islamic Critique*. Translated by R. Campbell. Berkeley: Islamic Foundation Press, 1979.

Shariati, Ali. *What is to be Done*. United States of America: The Institute for Research and Islamic Studies (IRIS), 1986.

Shariati, Ali. *Hajj*. Translated by Ali A. Behzadnia and Najla Denny. Houston: Free Islamic Literatures INC, 1980.

Sharif, M.M. *A History of Muslim Philosophy Vol I & II*. Wiesbaden: Otto Harrassowitz, 1963.

CHAPTER 10

The New Islamism: Remembrance and Liberation

Sophia Rose Arjana

Islamism, Orientalism, and the Post-Islamist Milieu

Islamism, which can be broadly defined as *a political vision that has Islam as its foundational ethic*, has largely failed on its promise to deliver Muslims from oppression, poverty, and suffering. New Islamism offers a vision of reform that relies on a conscious, engaged and activist Islam. It restores Islam's intended path of human transformation from the inside out through the remembrance of Allah and meditation on the Islamic value of justice, which leads to personal and social liberation. In contrast, much of Islamist discourse has called for a transformation from the outside inward, and that is a significant reason for the failure of Islamism. This article argues that liberation can only be won through reclaiming an ethic that has been largely forgotten. As the Qur'ān reminds us, 'Remember me, I shall remember you.'[1]

Throughout the twentieth century, Islamic thinkers have offered a complex set of responses to the economic, political, and social realities that Muslims who are living in colonial and postcolonial spaces must negotiate. Today, poverty, war, colonialism, neocolonialism, occupation, and political oppression mark the lives of millions of Muslims and most articulations of Islamism have not eliminated these problems. Prophet Muhammad said it was a person's duty to solve these ills, instructing, 'If one of you sees an abhorrent action, let him correct it with his hand; if he cannot, let him do it in words; if he cannot, let him do it in his heart – which is the weakest degree of faith.'[2] Because all moral action comes from the heart, these acts are intimately related.

Islamist articulations have been aligned with two main positions. The first is represented by Islamist movements that look to the West as a model for systems and institutions. They typically rely on American or European models and fail in an Islamic society due to their over-reliance on foreign ideologies and values. One alternative to this approach comes from Tariq Ramadan, who suggests that instead of using the West to reform Islam, Islam should be used

---

1 Qur'ān 2: 152.

2 Tariq Ramadan, *Western Muslims and the Future of Islam* (New York: Oxford University Press, 2004), 94.

to reform social conditions in Muslim and non-Muslim societies. As he writes, 'what matters is to know that Muslims – reforming their understanding – can contribute, without dogmatism and in collaboration with other traditions, to the ethical reform of the contemporary world.'[3]

A second type of Islamism reflects religious concerns but fails to satisfy the needs of Muslims living in modernity, often ignoring ethical dilemmas that affect individuals and communities. These ideologies have at times resulted in a misreading of Islam and therefore advocate violence and destruction, such as we see today in the Taliban movement that has contributed to a seemingly unending cycle of anxiety, horror, and misery for Afghans. As Kuovo and Mazoori argue, 'the suffering endured by Afghans over the course of the past three decades knows no geographic, temporal or ethnic bounds.'[4] The Taliban, while not wholly responsible for this violence, certainly contributed to the overall malaise experienced by men, women, and children living inside the country.[5] While scholars continue to argue over whether the Taliban should be classified as Islamist or Jihadi, it is certainly a political and Islamic entity.

This essay points to an Islamist vision that offers a third way – presenting an antidote to the current state of moral despondency plaguing much of today's world. Curing the masses from moral affliction is the main focus of Islamism, for if the systems in force were adequate there would not be a need for an Islamic social and political superstructure different from what currently exists. New Islamism is, in this way, an indictment of two competing meta-systems – Western liberalism and modern Islam. Islam is viewed as the antidote to the problems of the world, or at least a way to deal with the challenges of greed, oppression, pain, and suffering. Islamism builds upon the foundations of these concerns as found in the Qur'ān and other foundational texts and expresses them politically. At root, these concerns are central to the Islamic tradition, as the American Shaykh Hamza Yusuf explains here,

> According to commentators of the Qur'ān, the one who was dead refers to having a dead heart, which God revived with the light of guidance that one may walk straight and honorably among human beings. Also, the

---

3 Tariq Ramadan, *Radical Reform: Islamic Ethics and Liberation* (New York: Oxford University Press, 2009), 148.

4 Sari Kuovo and Dallas Mazoori, "Reconciliation, Justice and Mobilization of War Victims in Afghanistan," *The International Journal of Transitional Justice* 5 (2011): 500.

5 See Kevin J. Ayotte and Mary E. Husain, "Securing Afghan Women: Neocolonialism, Epistemic Violence, and Rhetoric of the Veil," *NWSA Journal* 17, no. 3, States of Insecurity and the Gendered Politics of Fear (2005): 112–133.

Prophet Muhammad said, "The difference between the one who remembers God and the one who does not is like the difference between the living and the dead." In essence, the believer is someone whose heart is alive, while the non-believer is someone whose heart is effectively dead.[6]

The purification of the heart leads to the health of the body, community, and world. In this way, Islam offers a cure for the diseases of the heart, which are intimately connected to the problems of the world. Yusuf argues, 'Every criminal, miser, abuser, scoffer, embezzler, and hateful person does what he or she does because of the diseased heart.'[7] It also may be true that some of these afflictions are due to the system of domination in which we live that creates limited options for survival. Nonetheless, Islam offers a process of spiritual recovery – a cure for these diseases of the heart. Islamism has failed because it has overturned the order of things. Instead of focusing on moral behavior – *adab* – and allowing it to heal society, the reverse has been advocated. This is an inversion of the movement from inside out to outside in – *adab* has been reconstructed as the consequence of political Islam; instead, transformation must begin at the core and radiate outward like the sun's warmth. This inversion is precisely why Islamism has failed.

Islamism has focused less on the causes of spiritual and social decay and more on the outward effects of moral disease. For the generation of Muslim reformers active in the eighteenth and nineteenth centuries, two central concerns – oppression and stagnation – were seen primarily as the results of colonialism, European systems of dominance, and Muslim apathy. Less attention was placed on the failure of Muslims to execute the mandate they were given. The figures active during this era – Shah Waliullah, Jamāl al-Dīn al-Afghānī, Muḥammad Rashīd Riḍā, Muhammad Iqbal, and others – generated a nationalistic consciousness among Muslims living under colonial and neo-colonial rule.[8] During this initial phase of reformist activity, we see a concern with the blind imitation (*taqlīd*) of Islam at the direction of clerics who were intellectually impotent and, in many cases, in the service of a colonial government or some other inept system that might or might not have had Muslims in positions of power. Today, we see this problem in the native informant or

---

6   Hamza Yusuf, *Purification of the Heart: Signs, Symptoms and Cures of the Spiritual Diseases of the Heart. Translation and Commentary of Imam al-Mawlud's Mathart al-Qulub* (Chicago: Starlatch Press, 2004), 2.

7   Ibid., 8.

8   Ameer Ali, "Islamism: Emancipation, Protest and Identity," *Journal of Muslim Minority Affairs* 20. No. 1 (2000): 12.

intellectual who serves the interests of the colonizer in sneaky and pernicious ways. Hamid Dabashi argues that these individuals, in service to the emperors of capitalism, are new versions of old collaborators, 'Uncle Tom has evolved into Auntie Azar and Uncle Fouad, well-educated and sophisticated enough to disguise their obsequiousness towards their white employers and audiences.'[9]

The Islamist indictment of contemporary Muslims is broad and can be found in the work of thinkers like al-Afghānī whose critique of the *ulama* is well known. Al-Afghānī saw 'religious stagnation (*jumūd*), and blind imitation (*taqlīd*)' as 'the enemy of true Islam.'[10] Reformers often saw the first of these as situated in the second due to the intransigence of the *'ulamā'* and the development of *ta'asub al-madhhab*, or "*madhab* fanaticism."[11] *Taqlīd* is, from the viewpoint of Sunni jurisprudence, necessary because of the absence of *mujtahids*.[12] The position of Shi'a clerics, it should be pointed out, is radically different due to the Imamate, a system that includes Imams and their teachings as well as *ayatollahs* and other scholars who are not only permitted but encouraged to engage in *ijtihād* – the effort to exercise independent reasoning in questions of law – which was discouraged in Sunni circles from the tenth century forward.[13]

The classical Islamic reformers, often called "modernists," expressed a number of shared concerns in their work, including the formulation of Islamic solutions to challenges posed by Western hegemony, the embrace of certain philosophical and scientific aspects of modernity, the construction of new institutions of learning to meet the challenges posed to Islamic societies, the revival of *kalām* (theology), and the revival of Islamic languages, in particular Arabic.[14] Despite the importance of these great minds, they failed to instigate a global recovery of Islam. They did, however, inspire a number of Islamic movements, intellectual and political, from the *Ikhwān al-Muslimūn* in the early part of the twentieth century (better known in the West as "the Muslim

9   Hamid Dabashi, *Brown Skin, White Masks* (New York: Pluto Press, 2011), 15–16.

10   Sukidi, "The Traveling Idea of Islamic Protestantism: A Study of Iranian Luthers," *Islam and Christian-Muslim Relations* 16, no. 4 (2005): 404. Also, see Albert Hourani, *Arabic Thought in the Liberal Age, 1798–1939* (Cambridge: Cambridge University Press, 2002), 127.

11   Rudolph Peters, "Idjtihād and Taqlīd in 18th and 19th Century Islam," *Die Welt des Islams* 20, no. 3/4 (1980): 141.

12   Ibid., 139.

13   Ibid., 135.

14   Ibrahim M. Abu-Rabi, "Contemporary Islamic Intellectual History: A Theoretical Perspective," *Islamic Studies* 44, no. 4 (2005): 512.

Brotherhood") to the work of Amina Wadud, who are both situated in the call for *ijtihād* voiced by early Muslim modernists.[15]

The lack of Muslim engagement with Islam's ethical imperative was later expounded upon by thinkers in the twentieth century and often expressed as the blind imitation of supposed norms. One of the results of this Muslim apathy is forgetfulness. As Omid Safi notes, 'if Muslims are to be worthy of the name "Muhammad's people," if the adjective "Muhammadi" is to be meaningful, then it is incumbent on Muslims to embody the qualities of mercy and justice that Muhammad so perfectly embodies.'[16] Anything else is *aghfala* – the forgetfulness that leads to social decay. Politically, this is expressed in unjust rule, corruption, greed, and scandal. Ali Shariati, the Iranian sociologist and philosopher who passionately argued that there were two Islams – one of the palace and one of the people – was keenly interested in resurrecting the "Muhammadi spirit," as elucidated in this commentary on "true Islam." He wrote,

> It is not enough to say we must return to Islam. We must specify which Islam: that of Marwan or that of Marwan the ruler. Both are called Islamic, but there is a huge difference between them. One is the Islam of the Caliphate, of the Palace, of the Rulers. The other is the Islam of the people, of the exploited, and of the poor. Moreover, it is not good enough to say that one should be 'concerned' about the poor. The corrupt Caliphs said the same. True Islam is more than 'concerned.' It instructs the believer to fight for justice, equality, and elimination of poverty.[17]

The return to this conscious, engaged, and activist Islam is my foremost concern in this chapter, but first we must explore why this is the direction Islamism must take. Islamism voices a fairly strong indictment of modernist Islam. However, Western modes of progress are equally unsatisfactory. As 'Shariati writes, 'It [democracy] was caught in a hard-line capitalism in which democracy turned out to be as disappointing as theocracy. Liberalism is revealed as a regime in which liberty exists only for the titans that fight to outdo each other in

---

15   Amina Wadud, *Qur'an and Woman: Rereading the Sacred Text from a Woman's Perspective* (New York: Oxford University Press, 1999), XIII.

16   Omid Safi, *Memories of Muhammad: Why the Prophet Matters* (New York: HarperOne, 2009), 303.

17   Ali Shariati, "Islamology: Lesson 3, 7–8," quoted by Ervand Abrahamian, "Ali Shariati: Ideologue of the Iranian Revolution," *MERIP Reports* 102/Islam and Politics (1982): 27, quoted in Sukidi, 406.

plunder.'[18] For 'Shariati, humanism is not the problem – a humanism alienated from all religion and spirituality is the problem. This concern over alienation is rooted in the Islamic concept of *tawḥīd* – the unity of God – that orders Islamic cosmology, constructs the world, and defines ethics. *Tawḥīd* is related to a number of other Islamic concepts, including *wujūd* (all existence and non-existence), *tanzīh* (transcendence) and *aḥad* (unity). For an understanding of how these ideas construct the Muslim's world, we turn to these words from Ibn al-'Arabī.

> The *aḥad* does not accept association, and no worship is directed toward it. On the contrary, worship belongs to the Lord, so pay attention to giving the station of Lordship its full due and leaving unity in the *tanzīh* to which we have alluded. The *aḥad* is exalted, forbidden through its unreachability, and it forever remains in obscurity. There can never be any self-disclosure through it, for its reality forbids that. It is the 'face' that possesses the 'burning glories.'[19]

Oneness and Unity are core Islamic principles that cannot be stated emphatically enough and as we shall see, they are necessary to any Islamist vision that is true to the faith.

'Shariati voiced concern over modern statehood's lack of a moral compass, and this can be stated even more emphatically today. The use of coercive but sometimes difficult-to-detect methods of force, including torture, present challenges to social justice movements that exist under repressive regimes.[20] The cruelty inflicted on human bodies by the modern secular state exemplifies the failure of modernity to value all humans. This very concern – the sanctity of human life – is at the forefront of many Islamist projects, even more so today due to the mass punishments inflicted on Muslim men and women at sites ranging from GTMO to Abū Ghraib. Scholars, alarmed at these developments, have described the new world order as a 'new ideological environment [that] promotes 'a police concept of history,' that is the reframing of historical process into the divisions of ideal safe space and duplicitous, dystopic and

---

18   Ali Shariati, *Marxism and Other Western Fallacies* (Kerala: Islamic Foundation Press, 1988), 59.
19   William Chittick, *The Self-Disclosure of God: Principles of Ibn al-'Arabī's Cosmology* (Albany: State University of New York Press, 1998), 168.
20   James Ron, "Varying Methods of State Violence." *International Organization* 51, no. 2 (1997): 298–299.

risk-laden space.'[21] Under this vision, Muslims occupy these dystopic and risky spaces and are expendable. The Muslim is Giorgio Agamben's *homo sacer*, 'the person who can be killed because of the sole virtue of the fact that he is alive and because it is the will of the sovereign power to put an end to his life with impunity.'[22]

However, the fact that Islamism is primarily about these types of issues is obfuscated by the meta-narrative about Muslims as violent, less developed, and anti-modern. In their effort to characterize the Islamist project as a re-turn to pre-modernity, some critics claim that Muslims are inherently opposed to logic and rationalism and are anti-modern and anti-democratic. Such nar-ratives about Muslim *otherness* are situated in Orientalism, an ideology that began in the eighteenth century and continues to be in force, which requires an almost ridiculous level of reductionism regarding what Islam is and what Muslims believe. Islamism is thus often described as a natural result of the Muslim condition, which is developmentally behind that of the American or European. Salwa Ismail explains how this view has resulted in a category of Islamism that is essentalized and static. As she explains,

> Some explanations of Islamism posit Islam as the determining factor, and view it as embodying some unchanged, essential beliefs and ideas that motivate the believers to act. From this perspective, Islamists are moved by the ideal of the early Muslim society and a belief in the unity of reli-gion and politics. Such an account is problematic, however. It gives rise to a central question about the terms in which inquiry into the subject is conceptualized and framed: what is the basis for privileging religion over class, nation or gender in the constitution of an individual's identity? In the case of Muslims, this account rests on an ontological principle that constructs Muslims as different to most other social beings.[23]

Such arguments are used to argue that Muslims are a religious type and that Islamism is a natural result of this typology – a logical fallacy that relies on

---

21   Allen Feldman, "On the Actuarial Gaze," *Cultural Studies* 19, no. 2 (2006): 209. Also see Jacques Rancière, "Politics, Identification, and Subjectivization," *October* 61 (1992): 78–82.

22   Steven C. Caton, "Coetzee, Agamben, and the Passion of Abu Ghraib," *American Anthro-pologist* 108, no. 1 (2006): 118. Also see Giorgio Agamben, *Homo Sacer: Sovereign Power and Bare Life*. Palo Alto: Stanford University Press, 1998.

23   Salwa Ismail, "Being Muslim: Islam, Islamism and Identity Politics," *Government and Op-position* 39, no. 4 (2004): 617.

the claim that Muslims are different, alien, and alienated from normative humanity. Among the problems with this view is that Islamism, at least today, is often used to determine one's identity and to effectively form a link between Islam and modernity.[24] Despite the use of Islamic objects and symbols in modern projects, an effort exists to portray political Islam as anti-modern. For instance, critics of the veil often describe it as an ancient relic – a symbol of the refusal of Muslims to join the modern world. However, Leila Ahmed has shown that it is very much part of modernity – a way for women to express agency in disparate contexts by choosing to veil or unveil. Despite these moves, there is an insistence that Islam is the sole determining factor in political choices.

> They [Muslims] are primarily determined by their religion that itself is understood in narrow terms as embodying fixed principles, key among which is the idea of the shari'a. Further, it is argued that Muslims are comparatively more devout than the adherents of other religions, and that their religiosity is intimately tied up with their politics. This sort of account is often countered by a related, but equally misleading, historicist view. Islamist politics are worked into a meta-narrative according to which religion declines in salience/importance with economic development and industrialization. Muslims are thus seen as existing at a lower stage of development and will experience secularism once they have advanced to a higher stage.[25]

Such a construction relies on the argument that Muslims live in a space that is separate and distinct from our space. This *denial of coevalness*, using Johannes Fabian's words, sanctions 'an ideological process by which relations between the West and its Other, between anthropology and its objects, were conceived not only as difference, but as distance in space and Time.'[26] Talal Asad also challenges the notion that Muslims occupy a different reality by arguing that we are all "conscripts of modernity," cogs in the machine of capitalism with little agency. As he puts it, modernity has created "refugees" that 'may adopt the standards of the more potent society in order to survive as individuals" – these are "conscripts of civilization, not volunteers.'[27]

---

24   Ibid., 622.

25   Ibid., 617.

26   Johannes Fabian, *Time and the Other: How Anthropology Makes Its Object* (New York: Columbia University Press, 2002), 31.

27   Talal Asad, "Conscripts of Western Civilization," in *Dialectical Anthropology: Essays in Honor of Stanley Diamond, Vol. 1, Civilization in Crisis*, ed. Christine Gailey (Gainesville:

Like many subjects discussed under the ideology of Orientalism, Islamism is far more complicated than it is made out to be. Asef Bayat offers the descriptor of "religious activism" as a way to get around some of the issues with terminology that have resulted in the overuse and misuse of words like "fundamentalism."[28] Islamism is perhaps best understood as a wide variety of ideologies and movements that, while not necessarily anti-modern or violent, can exhibit these characteristics. Islamists often take the position that Islam should be a foundation of the social contract, but this stance can be worked out in radically different ways. At its most basic level, Islamism is 'the belief that the Koran [Qur'ān] and the Hadith (Traditions of the Prophet's life) have something important to say about the way society and governance should be ordered.'[29] More liberal readings of this position see Islam as part of modern statehood (such as Iran), whereas more stringent readings perceive Islam as the only replacement for government (e.g. *al-Qa'eda*). In fact, Islamism includes organizations that reject the notion of an Islamic state altogether (or are not interested in such a proposal) such as Pakistan's *Tablighi Jammat* and Indonesia's *Nahdatul Ulama* movements.[30]

The failure of Islamism, however, does not lie solely at the feet of Orientalism. If Islamism had broader appeal, it would have more successes outside the Iranian example. While this essay is not focused on Islamism's greatest success – the 1979 Iranian revolution – I would suggest that the success of Khomeini's message was at least in part due to its universalistic message, a message that came in part from 'Shariati as the "Voltaire of the Revolution."[31] While situated in very Persian notions about the good, this revolutionary message nonetheless offers a path to liberation that is global in scope. As Mackey writes,

In the political theology of Ayatollah Khomeini, it was God's will that a revolution unique to Iran's own political history and cultural environment reach out to bring oppressed people everywhere into its folds. The roots of this certainty that the Islamic Republic constituted the universal

University Press of Florida, 1992), 333, quoted in David Scott, *Conscripts of Modernity: The Tragedy of Colonial Enlightenment* (Durham: Duke University Press, 2004), 8.

28   Asef Bayat, "Islamism and Social Movement Theory," *Third World Quarterly* 26, no. 6 (2005): 893–894.

29   Graham E. Fuller, "The Future of Political Islam," *Foreign Affairs* 81, no. 2 (2002): 49.

30   Ibid., 49.

31   Mansur Farhang, "Resisting the Pharaohs: Ali Shariati on Oppression," *Race & Class* 21 (1979): 31, quoted in Brad Hanson, "The 'Westoxication' of Iran: Depictions and Reactions of Behrangi, al-e-Ahmed, and Shariati," *International Journal of Middle East Studies* 15, no. 1 (1983): 18.

model of justice for Muslims and non-Muslims lay in Iran's Persian-Islamic culture. A fundamental feature of that culture is the incessant quest for an ideal society, defined primarily in terms of universal justice. In Persia, the hope for the ideal society resided in Ahura Mazda, the cosmic of 'Force of Good.' In Islam, it found conformation in the tenet that religion is the primary advocate for justice.[32]

Today, Islamism is experiencing a self-inflicted decline. As scholars have noted, the use of violence – indiscriminate and at times on a massive scale – is at least partially responsible for the failure of Islamism as a viable ideological system. September 11, 2001, and other such attacks have only hastened the decline of Islamists.[33] A combination of apathy, disapproval, and revulsion has hastened the end of terrorist groups in the past.[34] In fact, 'Violence in itself has proven to be a death trap for Islamists.'[35] While pockets of support for violent jihādis exist, most Muslims are fatigued, exhausted, and disgusted by the killing of men, women, and children, whether Muslim, Hindu, Christian, Jew, or other. The violence that marks much of Islamist activism is symptomatic of the disease of "unmindfulness" (aġhfala), a point I shall return to when discussing 'Shariati's political theology.

Post-Islamism is a response to the failure of traditional Islamist programs. As a reactive process situated in the desire for social change, it represents a shift away from the purely theological to the practical. Asef Bayat describes it as both a condition, in which 'the appeal, energy, and sources of legitimacy of Islamism get exhausted even among its once-ardent supporters' and as a project that is 'a conscious attempt to conceptualize and strategize the rationale and modalities of transcending Islamism in social, political, and intellectual domains.'[36]

Post-Islamism has emerged from this fatigue, and in many ways is a very modern project, situated in a kind of universalism that sees Islam as a broad category rather than a strict, closed identity focused on ethnicity, race, or country of origin. In the revolutions that erupted in several Arab states in December

---

32   Sandra Mackey, *The Iranians: Persia, Islam and the Soul of a Nation* (New York: Plume, 1996), 309.

33   As Kepel argues, 'Sept. 11 was an attempt to reverse a process in decline, with a paroxysm of destructive violence.' See Giles Kepel, *Jihad: The Trail of Political Islam* (Cambridge: Belknap Press, 2002), 4–5.

34   Audrey Kurth Cronin, "How Al-Qaida Ends: The Decline and Demise of Terrorist Groups," *International Security* 31, no. 1 (2006): 28.

35   Kepel, *Jihad,* 376.

36   Asef Bayat, "What Is Post-Islamism?" *ISIM Review* 16 (2005): 5.

of 2010, protest slogans reflected a sense of despondency about the government that were often rooted in Islamic cultural norms, but most protestors did not embrace Islamist parties. In Egypt, the failure of the *Ikhwān al-Muslimūn* to govern effectively has only solidified the sense among many Egyptians that military dictatorships, secularism, and Islamism have all failed at one level or another.

One of the hallmarks of post-Islamism is its looking within Islam for the answers to problems formerly seen as having solutions in Western neoliberal secularism. When a former CIA official argued, 'democratic values are latent in Islamic thought if one wants to look for them, and [that] it would be more natural and organic for the Muslim world to derive contemporary liberal practices from its own sources than to import them wholesale from foreign cultures,' he was simultaneously right and wrong.[37] The answers are to be found in Islam, not in an ostensibly superior Western ideology. One of the central problems raised by post-Islamism is that political Islam has relied too heavily on ethnic and cultural norms in its articulation of the need for social justice, liberation, and morality. Roy is one of several thinkers who argue that post-Islamism differentiates itself from Islamism on this point – the solution is to be found in the foundations of the tradition rather than in later expressions of it.[38] These foundations, however, must be recovered and internalized before radical change is possible. Salvation through the act of remembrance is the first step in this process. Only *dhikr* will lead us out of forgetfulness and awaken us to Allāh's presence, to the realization of *tawḥīd*.[39]

The Political Theology of Remembrance: Ali 'Shariati

The work of Ali 'Shariati has left an indelible mark on the consciousness of Iranians. Many identify him – along with Ayatollah Ruhollah Khomeini – as an intellectual and spiritual father of the 1979 Revolution. Ervand Abrahamian has called him 'the main ideologue of the Iranian Revolution.'[40] Even though

---

37   Fuller, *The Future of Political Islam*, 52.

38   See Olivier Roy, *Globalized Islam: The Search for a New Ummah* (New York: Columbia University Press, 2004).

39   Julia D.E. Prinz, "The Relationship between the Inner and Outer Dimensions in Islam as a Foundation for Inter-Religious Dialogue," *Islam and Christian-Muslim Relations* 15, no. 2 (2004): 177.

40   Ervand Abrahamian, "'Ali Shariati: Ideologue of the Iranian Revolution," *MERIP Reports* 102 [Islam and Politics] (1982): 24.

his ideas are concerned with the salvation of Iranian society, they have universal appeal and are the focus of the remainder of this chapter.[41] His ideas offer one vision of how Islamism can work to alleviate the malaise experienced by many in the world today.

'Shariati is often described as an Islamic socialist due to the Marxist themes that permeate some of his writings. For example, he believes in a classless communal society. However, he differs from Marx on several points relating to the role of power in patterns of ownership and capitalism.[42] The most significant difference between the two intellectuals is situated in the question of a way out of the capitalist dilemma – the source of the misery 'Shariati wants to alleviate. While Marx advocates a socialist agenda to the exclusion of other alternatives, 'Shariati presents Islam as the only possible solution. Religion [Islam] is the vehicle through which human agency is possible, 'Religion is, therefore, a road or a path, leading from clay to God and conveying man from vileness, stagnation and ignorance, from the lowly life of clay and satanic character, toward exaltation, motion, vision, the life of the spirit and divine character.'[43] In this articulation, Islam functions as an exalted moral vision – for Muslim and non-Muslim alike.

For 'Shariati, the recovery of Islam is critical for the resurrection of human potential and recovery from the sad state of society. His work is strongly situated in Shi'a theology, albeit a modernist reading of it that insists on just, ethical rule inspired by the examples of Imam 'Ali, Imam Hussein and other martyrs whose deaths symbolize the goals of the *ummah* and *nezam-i tawhīd* – the activist community and a unitary society.[44] Reform is only possible through human agency, martyrdom, and revolution: 'Shariati's Islamic ideology insisted on religious grounds that in order to be a good Muslim one must fight to overthrow the existing social order, and condemned both secular radicals and conservative clerics within the religious establishment who might oppose his revolutionary plans.'[45]

The revitalization of humanity can only occur through the implementation of a tripartite Islamic system that includes (1) *ijtihād* (the exercise of

41   Hanson, *The Westoxification of Iran*, 14.
42   Shahrough Akhavi, "Islam, Politics and Society in the Thought of Ayatollah Khomeini, Ayatullah Taliqani and Ali Shariati." *Middle Eastern Studies* 24, no. 4 (1988): 412.
43   Ali Shariati, *On the Sociology of Islam: Lectures by Ali Shariati*, trans. Hamid Algar (Oneonta, NY: Mizan Press, 1979), 94.
44   Abrahamian, *Ali Shariati*, 26.
45   Ali Mirsepassi, *Political Islam, Iran, and Enlightenment: Philosophies of Hope and Despair* (New York: Cambridge University Press, 2011), 125.

independent judgment by qualified persons on questions of law); (2) *al-amr bi al-ma'ruf wa al-nahy 'an al-munkar* (a general principle of commanding the good and forbidding evil); and (3) *muhājirat* (emigration).'[46] For 'Shariati, *ijtihād* should be engaged by each individual in order to bring him or her clarity about the prophetic message contained in the Qur'ān and in other Islamic sources. From his perspective, leaving this up to the *'ulamā'* has resulted in a weakened Islam that serves the state and those in power instead of the man, woman, and child. 'Shariati is often characterized as "anti-clerical," but he actually focuses his criticism on the narrow thinking of the Shi'a religious class and elements he sees in their preoccupation with ritual prescription and other matters that from his perspective, have little or nothing to do with the renovation of human society.[47] In his work there is also a sense of despondency over the numb state of Shi'i religiosity, something Shariati sees as a result of the clerical establishment's lack of passion for justice and social change.

The direct apprehension of the Qur'ān is a hallmark of Islamic modernism and it is not surprising that it finds its way into Shariati's writing. What is most important here, however, is that the Qur'ān functions in his vision of social change in a particularly bold way. The reason that *ijtihād* is so key is because the Qur'ān is a tool of liberation, because it 'puts a minimum of restrictions on human freedom and allows human beings the largest measure of liberty, while exactly the reverse is the case with intermediate authorities.'[48]

The second action – commanding good and forbidding evil – must also be required by each individual, as reflected in the call for social action: 'Every day is "Āshūrā, Every place is Karbalā".'[49] The requirement to be constantly and actively engaged in social struggle is not optional – it is a moral imperative for every Muslim that will transform the world. The last act necessary for social transformation is emigration – a double-pilgrimage to the unified human community (for Muslims, this would be the *ummah* or *Shi'a 'Ali*, followers of 'Ali) and to Allāh.[50]

In this movement toward God, we find one of many expressions of 'Shariati's identification as a mystic. His ultimate rejection of Marxism is explained in part by the importance placed on mysticism within the Shi'a tradition. Marxism only gets us so far; in 'Shariati's view, 'Islam combines the keen

---

46   Akhavi, *Islam, Politics and Society*, 412.

47   Hanson, *The Westoxification of Iran*, 17–18.

48   Mazheruddin Siddiqi, "Islamic Modernism," *Islamic Studies* 12, no. 3 (1973): 183.

49   See Shariati's exact wording of this quote below.

50   For Shi'as, prophetic leadership is found in the Imams, who in Shariati's view are likened
      to anti-colonial leaders as individuals who fought against tyranny and oppression.

sense of social responsibility of socialism with two other key dimensions, the spirituality of mysticism and the primacy of existence/freedom of existentialism, in balance.'[51] In Ali Rahnema's definitive biography, we find the most extensive examination of his mystical beliefs and practices in a close reading of *Kavir, Descent in the Desert*, and *Dialogues of Solitude*.[52] In Dialogues of Solitude (*Guftygūhā-yi Tanhā'ī*), 'Shariati provides a recollection of one of his mystical experiences. 'Whatever it was, [if] I could keep myself on my feet I could still stay alive. There was groaning, there was a secret drop of tear, there was complaint, but mostly inside myself.'[53]

An internal movement of the spirit is fundamental to 'Shariati's vision of change and is likely a reflection of his mystical orientation. The heart's pilgrimage toward God is a focus of Sufi teachings, perhaps best known in the saying, "Die before you die," an instruction that is Sufic but situated in many Islamic sources. One ḥadīth reports Prophet Muhammad saying, 'The true Flight (*hijrah*) is the flight from evil, and the real holy war (*jihād*) is the warfare against one's passions.'[54] The pilgrimage of the heart is also essential to the religious transformation necessary for social change. *Dhikr*, the remembrance of Allah, is the path to this altering of the current state of the world. Like other mystical traditions, Islam sees change as a result of inner devotion – the human is the agent of change. The Qur'ān states the importance of *dhikr* in numerous places. In Surah 2:152, 'Remember me, I will remember you.' The focus of one's heart on Allah, then, is the foundation of change. 'It is the practice of remembrance that leads the inner dimension to expression in the exterior dimension and it is the practice of remembrance that draws the outer dimension toward the inner dimension.'[55]

'Shariati's call for social transformation is both prophetic and revolutionary, and it is also universal. Despite its broad applicability, this vision of human renewal requires a very Islamic process of remembrance (*dhikr*), consciousness (*vojdan*), activism (*fa'aaliyyat*), and liberation (*azaadi*).[56] Each of these

---

51   Hanson, *The Westoxification of Iran*, 16. Also, see Ali Shariati, *Marxism and Other Western Fallacies: An Islamic Critique*, trans. Robert Campbell (Berkeley: Mizan Press, 1980), 122.

52   Ali Rahnema, *An Islamic Utopian: A Political Biography of Ali Shariati* (New York: I.B. Tauris, 2000), 144–145.

53   Ali Shariati, *Guftygūhā-yi Tanhā'ī* (Tehran: Muna Publications), quoted in Abdollah Vakily, "Ali Shariati and the Mystical Tradition in Islam," (PhD diss., McGill University, 1991), 54.

54   Todd LeRoy Perreira, "'Die Before You Die': Death Meditation as Spiritual Technology of the Self in Islam and Buddhism," *The Muslim World* 100 (2010): 252.

55   Prinz, *The Relationship between Inner and Outer Dimensions*, 177.

56   I use Farsi here instead of Arabic because Shariati was an Iranian intellectual. The Islamic concept of *taqwā*, or God-consciousness, is discussed in the following section, where I argue that it serves as the fundamental principle of "the new jihad."

is rooted in *taqwā*, God-consciousness, which is not coincidental, for the possibility of social change always first requires a change within. For 'Shariati, this occurs in each human who is individually (and collectively) the causal agent of social transformation.[57]

The remembrance of Allāh is a key part of the religious life of Muslims in daily prayers, optional supplications (sometimes called *du'a*), and other rituals. In the Qur'ān, we find numerous references to the meditation, or thoughtfulness, directed toward Allāh. As mentioned above, verse 2:152, 'Remember me, I shall remember you,' is an instruction that suggests a personal relationship with God. This is not simply a duty; like other Islamic teachings, it provides relief – an expression of Allāh's mercy and compassion. In 13:28, we find these words: 'It is through remembrance of Allāh that hearts find rest.' Remembrance, then, is an act that serves as a relief, expressed in the *ḥadīth* where Prophet Muhammad asks Bilal to give the call to prayer as a mercy. Remembrance is the act that helps the revolutionary focus on the struggle ahead by meditating on the past.

The remembrance of Allāh activates the individual to be conscious about the world in which he or she lives, of its potential for beauty, love, and transformation alongside the realities of horror, pain, suffering, and loss. As fellow scholar Omid Safi has suggested, 'This life is and is not the garden. This life is an exile.'[58] This condition of humanity is due in part to the capitalist project, which in the words of Martin Luther King has created a 'suffering, poverty-stricken humanity.'[59] For 'Shariati, it is represented theologically in the struggle between good and evil, 'The wing represented by Abel is that of the subject and the oppressed; i.e. the people, those who throughout history have been slaughtered and enslaved by the system of Cain, the system of private ownership which has gained ascendency over human society.'[60] For him, the struggle against oppression is as old as the prophetic tradition, for even Abraham destroyed the idols and Moses stormed the palace of the Pharaoh.[61]

Remembrance is what brings about the consciousness (*vojdan*) that serves as the foundation for change; its primary example is found in Karbalā'. For 'Shariati, this was the very essence of consciousness – the act that revealed the corrupt and sinister behavior of the enemy. As he puts it, 'The blood of the

---

57   Akhavi, *Islam, Politics and Society*, 413.

58   Omid Safi, lecture at Iliff School of Theology, Denver, CO, April 5, 2014.

59   King, Martin Luther Jr., *A Testament of Hope: The Essential Writings and Speeches of Martin Luther King Jr.*, ed. James M. Washington (New York: HarperOne, 1986), 629.

60   Shariati, *On the Sociology of Islam*, 108.

61   Ali Shariati, "Shahādat," in *Jihād and Shahādat: Struggle and Martyrdom in Islam*, ed. Mehdi Abedi and Gary Legenhausen (North Haledon, NJ: Islamic Publications International, 1986), 156.

martyrs removed all the masks and drew all the curtains of deception,' cancel-
ling 'the grand conspiracy forever.'[62]

'Shariati's activism (*fa'aaliyat*) is situated in Shi'a liberation theology. An
Islamist revival grounded in 'Shariati's liberation theology represents a reading of Islam that is emancipatory. It asserts a broad ethical imperative that
re-orients myopic Islamist entropy to better account for the tradition's integration into wider systems, allowing for the engagement of Islam with the problems caused by capitalism, liberalism, militarism, and materialism.

The promise of an Islam that restores the human spirit and offers solace
and relief for the Muslim as well as the non-Muslim exists in the acknowl-
edgement of injustice and the act of witnessing that is required to change it.
'Shariati describes this act in theological terms, connecting it with the sacrifice
of Ḥussein – the proto-martyr of the Shi'a tradition – and identifying it as a
program for individual and social transformation. *Shahādat* is the active witnessing that sheds light where there is none, revealing the wrongs committed
in the name of capitalism and tyranny. '*Shahādat* is not war – it is mission. It is
not a weapon – it is a message, It is a word pronounced in blood.'[63] The reference to blood, however, is not necessarily an open call to violence. It is an act
of remembrance, implying, in his words, 'that something has been covered and
is about to leave the realm of memory, being gradually forgotten by people.'[64]
It is the *shahīd* that serves as the witness, and only the "most sublime" of these
individuals are martyred.[65]

'Shariati's vision of liberation (*azaadi*) can result in political change, but it
is more fundamentally a spiritual change – one that transforms the individual
from inside out. This is why he writes that a "revolutionary self-formation" or
"revolutionary puritanism" is the path to social revolution.[66] The first part of
this formation is prayer, which is joined by manual work (to train the body)
and social struggle (to train the spirit).[67] Together, they represent an attitudi-
nal change that is directed toward Allāh's unity, which Muslims call *tawḥīd*.

Tawḥīd is not only important for Shariati, however; it also ties much of
Islamic theology together. Not only the belief of a singular deity, it is the sense

---

62   Shariati, *Shahādat*, 208.
63   Shariati, *Shahādat*, 209.
64   Ali Shariati, "A Discussion of Shahīd," in *Jihād and Shahādat: Struggle and Martyrdom in
       Islam*, ed. Mehdi Abedi and Gary Legenhausen (North Haledon, NJ: Islamic Publications
       International, 1986), 236.
65   Shariati, *A Discussion of Shahīd*, 236.
66   Rahnema, *An Islamic Utopian*, 361.
67   Ibid.

that everything is connected. When 'nothing – not even yourself – exists at all save through the existence of One, then you will have truly realized the unity of Allāh.'[68] For Shariati, *tawḥīd* is the key to liberation, 'The Prophet of Islam came to confirm the universal doctrine of *tawḥīd*, and to bring that unity into human history, to all races, nations, groups, families and social classes, and to eliminate the discord brought by polytheistic religions.'[69] This *tawḥīdic* impulse has the potential to create a community of witnesses, what Shariati calls the *ummatan wasatan*.[70] Such a community is reframed as a movement, one that has the potential to "do something" – to create 'light and heat in the world and in the cold and dark hearts.'[71] This reference to creating light where there is darkness is an allusion to the state of unconsciousness that characterizes modern man, where Islamic values are turned upside down, where power is 'dressed in piety and sacredness.'[72] It is only when this undressing occurs that liberation will be won.

Bibliography

Abrahamian, Ervand. "Ali Shariati: Ideologue of the Iranian Revolution." *MERIP Reports* 102 [Islam and Politics] (1982): 24–28.

Abu-Rabi, Ibrahim M. "Contemporary Islamic Intellectual History: A Theoretical Perspective." *Islamic Studies* 44, no. 4 (2005): 503–526.

Agamben, Giorgio. *Homo Sacer: Sovereign Power and Bare Life*. Palo Alto: Stanford University Press, 1998.

Al-Jerrahi al- Halveti, Shaikh Tosun Bayrak. *Inspirations on the Path to Blame: Shaikh Badruddin of Simawna*. Putney, VT: Threshold Books, 1993.

Akhavi, Shahrough. "Islam, Politics and Society in the Thought of Ayatollah Khomeini, Ayatullah Taliqani and Ali Shariati." *Middle Eastern Studies* 24, no. 4 (1988): 404–431.

Ali, Ameer. "Islamism: Emancipation, Protest and Identity." *Journal of Muslim Minority Affairs* 20. No. 1 (2000): 11–28.

Asad, Talal. "Conscripts of Western Civilization." In *Dialectical Anthropology: Essays in Honor of Stanley Diamond, Vol. 1, Civilization in Crisis*, edited by Christine Gailey, 333–51. Gainesville: University Press of Florida, 1992.

---

68   Shaikh Tosun Bayrak al-Jerrahi al-Halveti, *Inspirations on the Path to Blame: Shaikh Badruddin of Simawna* (Putney, VT: Threshold Books, 1993), 132.

69   Shariati, *Shahādat*, 157.

70   Ibid., 237.

71   Shariati, *A Discussion of Shahīd*, 240.

72   Ibid., 191.

Ayotte, Kevin J. and Mary E. Husain, "Securing Afghan Women: Neocolonialism, Epistemic Violence, and Rhetoric of the Veil," *NWSA Journal* 17, no. 3, States of Insecurity and the Gendered Politics of Fear (2005): 112–133.

Bayat, Asef. "What is Post-Islamism?" *ISIM Review* 16 (2005): 5.

Bayat, Asef. "Islamism and Social Movement Theory." *Third World Quarterly* 26, no. 6 (2005): 891–908.

Caton, Steven C. "Coetzee, Agamben, and the Passion of Abu Ghraib." *American Anthropologist* 108, no. 1 (2006): 114–123.

Chittick, William. *The Self-Disclosure of God: Principles of Ibn al-ʿArabī's Cosmology.* Albany: State University of New York Press, 1998.

Cronin, Audrey Kurth. "How Al-Qaida Ends: The Decline and Demise of Terrorist Groups." *International Security* 31, no. 1 (2006): 7–48.

Dabashi, Hamid. *Brown Skin, White Masks*. New York: Pluto Press, 2011.

Fabian, Johannes. *Time and the Other: How Anthropology Makes Its Object*. New York: Columbia University Press, 2002.

Farhang, Mansur. "Resisting the Pharaohs: Ali Shariati on Oppression." *Race & Class* 21 (1979): 31–33.

Feldman, Allen. "On the Actuarial Gaze." *Cultural Studies* 19, no. 2 (2009): 203–226.

Fuller, Graham E. "The Future of Political Islam." *Foreign Affairs* 81, no. 2 (2002): 48–60.

Hanson, Brad. "The 'Westoxication' of Iran: Depictions and Reactions of Behrangi, al-e-Ahmed, and Shariati." *International Journal of Middle East Studies* 15, no. 1 (1983): 1–23.

Hourani, Albert. *Arabic Thought in the Liberal Age, 1798–1939*. Cambridge: Cambridge University Press, 2002.

Ismail, Salwa. "Being Muslim: Islam, Islamism and Identity Politics." *Government and Opposition* 39, no. 4 (2004): 614–631.

Kepel, Giles. *Jihad: The Trail of Political Islam*. Cambridge: Belknap Press, 2002.

King Martin, Luther Jr. *A Testament of Hope: The Essential Writings and Speeches of Martin Luther King Jr.* Edited by James Melvin Washington. New York: HarperOne, 1986.

Kuovo, Sari and Dallas Mazoori. "Reconciliation, Justice and Mobilization of War Victims in Afghanistan." *The International Journal of Transitional Justice* 5 (2011): 492–503.

Mackey, Sandra. *The Iranians: Persia, Islam and the Soul of a Nation*. New York: Plume, 1996.

Mirsepassi, Ali. *Political Islam, Iran, and Enlightenment: Philosophies of Hope and Despair*. New York: Cambridge University Press, 2011.

Perreira, Todd LeRoy. "'Die Before You Die': Death Meditation as Spiritual Technology of the Self in Islam and Buddhism." *The Muslim World* 100 (2010): 247–267.

Peters, Rudolph. "Idjtihād and Taqlīd in 18th and 19th Century Islam." *Die Welt des Islams* 20, no. 3/4 (1980): 131–145.

Prinz, Julia D.E. "The Relationship between the Inner and Outer Dimensions in Islam as a Foundation for Inter-Religious Dialogue." *Islam and Christian-Muslim Relations* 15, no. 2 (2004): 171–184.

Rahnema, Ali. *An Islamic Utopian: A Political Biography of Ali Shariati*. New York: I.B. Tauris, 2000.

Ramadan, Tariq. *Western Muslims and the Future of Islam*. New York: Oxford University Press, 2004.

Ramadan, Tariq. *Radical Reform: Islamic Ethics and Liberation*. New York: Oxford University Press, 2009.

Rancière, Jacques. "Politics, Identification, and Subjectivization." *October* 61 (1992): 78–82.

Ron, James. "Varying Methods of State Violence." *International Organization* 51, no. 2 (1997): 275–300.

Roy, Olivier. *Globalized Islam: The Search for a New Ummah*. New York: Columbia University Press, 2004.

Safi, Omid. *Memories of Muhammad: Why the Prophet Matters*. New York: HarperOne, 2009.

Scott, David. *Conscripts of Modernity: The Tragedy of Colonial Enlightenment*. Durham: Duke University Press, 2004.

S'Shariati, Ali. *On the Sociology of Islam: Lectures by Ali Shariati*. Translated by Hamid Algar. Oneonta, NY: Mizan Press, 1979.

S'Shariati, Ali. *Marxism and Other Western Fallacies*. Translated by Robert Campbell. Kerala: Islamic Foundation Press, 1988.

Siddiqi, Mazheruddin. "Islamic Modernism." *Islamic Studies* 12, no. 3 (1973): 179–192.

Sukidi. "The Traveling Idea of Islamic Protestantism: A Study of Iranian Luthers." *Islam and Christian-Muslim Relations* 16, no. 4 (2005): 401–412.

Vakily, Abdollah. "Ali Shariati and the Mystical Tradition in Islam." PhD diss., McGill University, 1991.

Wadud, Amina. *Qur'an and Woman: Rereading the Sacred Text from a Woman's Perspective*. New York: Oxford University Press, 1999.

Yusuf, Hamza. *Purification of the Heart: Signs, Symptoms and Cures of the Spiritual Diseases of the Heart. Translation and Commentary of Imam al-Mawlud's Mathart al-Qulub*. Chicago: Starlatch Press, 2004.

CHAPTER 11

Ali Shariati on the Question of Palestine: Making a Sacred Symbol for Uprising against Injustice and Domination

Mahdi Ahouie

Dr. Ali Shariati was one of the most influential intellectuals of the Islamic Revolution. The impact and popularity of his writings and teachings continue to be felt throughout Iranian society. Holding a post-graduate degree in sociology from the University of Paris, Shariati was a major advocate for the cause of the revolution during late 1960's and early 1970's. As an intellectual, he attempted to explain and provide solutions to the problems faced by Muslim societies through traditional Islamic principles interwoven with and understood from the point of view of modern sociology and philosophy. Shariati gave his most famous speeches between 1969 and 1972 at the *Hosseinieh-ye Ershad*, a major religious-cultural center in the north of Tehran. These lectures proved to be hugely popular amongst his students, producing a great intellectual force for the Iranian revolution of 1978–1979. As a result, and through word of mouth, his popularity spread rapidly throughout all sectors of society, including among the middle and upper classes, where interest in Shariati's teachings began to grow immensely.[1]

One of Shariati's first commentaries on the Palestinian question dates back to July 1967, a few weeks after the Six Day War. In a very critical tone, he criticized certain leftist intellectuals for their support of Israel.[2] He regretted that, according to some Iranian Marxists,

---

1   For an in-depth discussion of Shariati's political life, see Houchang E. Chehabi, *Iranian Politics and Religious Modernism, The Liberation Movement of Iran under the Shah and Khomeini*, Ithaca and New York: Cornell University Press, 1990.

2   Shariait's reaction was mainly provoked by an article by Daryoush Ashouri, one of the disciples of Khalil Maleki, in the monthly *Ferdowsi*, in which he had revealed his support for Israel, blaming the majority of Iranian intellectuals for confusing anti-imperialism with anti-Zionism and even anti-Semitism. For Ashouris' article, see Daryoush Ashouri, "Zedde Sahyunism va Zedde Amperialism dar Sharq!" *Ferdowsi*, Issue 820, 11 July 1967, 6–7. For more on Khalil Maleki's faction of Iranian Marxists, see Homayoun Katouzian's introduction to Khalil Maleki, *Khaterat-e Siyasi* (*Political memories*), 3rd edition, Tehran: Ravaq Publications,

whoever feels sorry for the Arabs' defeat and the misery of thousands of poor homeless Arabs of Jerusalem and Sinai and Syria is called bourgeois ... Whoever says Israel is a Western creature is bourgeois ... Whoever feels sympathetic for the Palestinian refugees who have been expelled from their home cities and houses and lands into the burning deserts of Jordan ... their sympathy derives from the bourgeoisie! ... Whoever feels hatred and revengeful for seeing that after all those [Muslim] glorious conquests in history, Jerusalem has now fallen to the hands of [Zionist] Jews and that the Muslims have become defenseless victims of a Jewish-Christian [alliance] and are being expelled form that sacred land in the most brutal way, has been affected by the lowest bourgeois feelings![3]

As evident in this paragraph, he summarizes the reasons for his hostility towards Zionism as follows: (1) Israel is a Western creature in the Middle East; (2) Israel treats the Arab people unjustly and brutally; and finally (3) Palestine is an inseparable part of the Muslim world.

Rejecting the idea that Israel was 'a free and democratic and socialist and anti-imperialist government,' as claimed by some leftist writers, he accused them of being ignorant of the real nature of Israel.[4] Highlighting Israel's "injustice" even towards Jewish people, he wrote,

There are a lot of human-loving and broadminded Jews who consider Zionism and the state of Israel a betrayal to both Judaism and humanity ... The behavior of the Israeli government is so beyond brutality and ultra-fascist, that even Hitler and Mussolini would renounce it. I have heard from many intellectual Iranian and Egyptian and Syrian and Iraqi and North African Jews, who are living in large numbers in Paris and Italy and Britain, that not only does the Israeli government look down at the Arabs – whose home had been there for centuries – like the Indian untouchables, but it even considers those Jews, who have been manipulated by the Zionist propaganda and have left Iran and Egypt and Morocco and

1360 (1981), pp. 35–80. See also Mehrzad Boroujerdi, *Iranian Intellectuals and the West: The Tormented Triumph of Nativism*, Syracuse: Syracuse University Press, 1996, 53.

3   Ali Shariati, *Asaar*, 617–618.

4   This is again in reference to Ashouri's article mentioned earlier. Khalil Maleki and Jalal Al-e Ahmad had also expressed similar ideas in admiration of Israeli "democracy" and "real socialism." However, Al-e Ahmad later turned against Israel after 1967. For examples of Maleki's supportive comments about Israel, see *Elm va Zendegi*, Farvardin 1332 (March–April 1953), 87; *Nabard-e Zendegi*, Day 1337 (January 1959), 32–33.

other Arab and Islamic countries to the Promised Land ... as aliens and strangers.[5]

Shariati continued his discussion concerning the discrimination he perceived between the Western and the Eastern Jews in Israel by arguing that the Eastern Jews had become a humiliated minority, who are viewed as being inferior to the American and European Jews because they were thought to have been "Arabized" and "Muslimized" during the long history of coexistence between Muslims and Jews in the East. They were, according to Shariati, considered nothing but a burden for Israeli society, and being so were deprived of any political and economic progress.[6]

On the combination of anti-Zionism and anti-imperialism in the Middle East, which was criticized by some leftist writers, Shariati argued that such a combination was quite natural and understandable, because imperialism was not 'an abstract and metaphysical notion similar to concupiscence or devil and likewise.'[7] However, imperialism, he added, 'is always exposed through an objective facade, like the former [British] Oil Company in Iran, the East India Company, the Mines Union in Congo, and Zionism in the Arab countries.'[8] According to Shariati, those who wondered why the Iranian people were so appalled by Israel's aggression in the Arab lands, whereas they had not shown the same feelings on the Indo-Pakistani war or the Greek offensive against the Muslim Turks, were simply ignorant of the real reasons behind Iranian opposition to Israel. He emphasized that Iranian intellectuals were not opposed to Zionism in Palestine, and its aggression against Egypt, Syria and Iraq, only out of their religious connection to Palestinian people, but their objection had, first and foremost, derived from a 'rejection of imperialism and Western colonialism.'[9]

Shariati defined Zionism as a creature of Western colonialism whose role would be to create a basis for imperialism in the heart of the unstable Muslim nations.[10] In his opinion, Israel represented a fascist state,

A regime, occupying a land by the force of weapons made in Britain and America and France, bringing capitalists from all over Europe to a poor Arab country and expelling its native people into the burning deserts of Sinai

---

5   Shariati, *Asaar*, 628.
6   Ibid., 629.
7   Ibid., 623–624.
8   Ibid.
9   Ibid.
10   Ibid., 631–632.

and Jordan and all over Africa and the Middle East, imprisoning Muslim peasants in their villages, crushing any Arab country which would want to release itself from the domination of Western colonialism upon an order from the imperialists, wildly torturing the prisoners of war, expelling people from their houses, and putting its political and social basis on the Jewish race and religion; how is such a regime not fascist? ... Zionism, not the idea of Arab solidarity against colonialism, is equal to fascism.[11]

Shariati refused to compare the Arab-Israeli conflict to other usual cases of territorial disputes in the world. He was outraged by the idea expressed by some Iranians Marxists, who had suggested that Iranian intellectuals should reject any sign of anti-Semitism by considering the Arab-Israeli conflict as a normal territorial dispute. He emphasized,

Israel is not a question of class and economy, which would relate to revolutionary socialism, and has nothing to do with being progressive or backward. This is the question of aggression towards the nationality of a people as a whole and the occupation of a part of their homeland. Here, every Arab person, from right to left, feudal to socialist, and Muslim to materialistic, is hurt.[12]

Responding to the accusation of anti-Semitism, he compared the Israeli occupation of Palestine with the Nazi occupation of France, by which every French citizen was humiliated and distressed. He asked Iranian leftist intellectuals what they would have thought of a French intellectual in Montpellier, who had become furious by the Nazi occupation of Paris during the Second World War, aroused with a sense of revenge,

Would [they] blame him ... for following the feelings of the masses and giving up his essence of intellectuality, and for not considering the occupation of Paris a normal territorial dispute, and for being affected by racist anti-German hatred, and for mixing French nationalism with anti-Nazism and anti-Germanism?[13]

Shariati continued this argument by asking if the creation of Israel in Palestine was compensation for the West's crimes against the Jewish people, including

11   Ibid., 630–631.
12   Ibid., 634–635.
13   Ibid.

the persecution in Germany, Poland, France, Spain, and Russia. If so, he wondered why this compensation should be paid at the expense of the Muslims of the Middle East. He wrote,

> Why should the West and Christianity give up Islamic Palestine as payoff? Why shouldn't they give up a part of Poland where they put the Jews under the most terrible torture? Why don't they give one state of the Federal Republic of Germany as compensation for the Holocaust? Why should Christianity compensate for its torture of the Jews during the past two-thousand years from the pocket of Islam? Why should the West pay for its crimes from the empty pockets of the Middle East nations? Why should the houses and lives of some hundred thousands of homeless Muslim Arabs be given to the Jews as reparation for the church's crimes, Europe's sins, and the Nazis' Holocaust? The Jews have been living in Islamic countries for centuries as if in their homelands and have been enjoying all their social and economic rights.[14]

Shariati concluded this long piece of writing by regretting that, instead of compensating for its past injustice against the Jews out of its own resources, Western powers had put the fate of the Jewish people in the hands of some adventurous militarist leaders and used them as its means to torture the Muslims of the Middle East in the same way that the West had persecuted the Jews for the past two thousand years.[15] This way, Shariati implied that both Muslims and Jews had become victims of Western imperialism.

In his *Rereading the Iranian-Islamic Identity*, Shariati dedicated one part of his analysis to the discussion of nationalism. He argued that Western perceptions of nationalism were the results of pervasive racism and anti-Semitism, which eventually led to the emergence of Zionism as a defensive reaction. Zionism, he argued, provoked ethnic Arab nationalism in the Islamic societies. Shariati concluded that on this basis all nationalist movements derive from, and strengthen each other, despite the fact that they may appear politically opposite.[16] He continued to claim that nationalism in Iran had never had a racist component, and thus, it was never anti-Jewish,

> One of the most honorable characteristics of our society is that our culture and religion have never provided fertile grounds for racist

---

14   Ibid., 635.

15   Ibid.

16   Shariati, *Bazshenasi-ye Hoviyat-e Eslami va Irani*, 89.

humiliations to grow. The example of [Iranian] Jews is the best evidence for that. They had for centuries been assimilated in our society while they also kept their religious and racial distinction; however, they did not face any trouble in accommodation to their surroundings, and they were even easily accepted in our Islamic bazaar which was always the major source of strong religious emotions [of Muslim Iranians]. They often enjoyed a humane and intimate relationship with their Muslim colleagues. It was therefore quite natural that they were not dreaming about the Promised Land and were not tempted to return to Zion and never thought of racial superiority and the creation of an independent polity and government. In contrast, if we witnessed the rise of aggressive Zionism in the West, that is because it was a reaction to their brutal and ruthless anti-Semitism, which started as early as seventy years before Christ by the Romans and was followed by the Christian church and most recently, by Fascism and Nazism in Europe and America, under which the Jews were considered the "low race," "murderers of god," and "inherent traitors," and had to go through all kinds of stunning torture and humiliation. It is not accidental that no single Zionist has risen from within the Jewish population of all the Islamic countries.[17]

In Shariati's opinion, Fascism, Nazism, and Zionism were all products of Western racist nationalism. Although Zionism was a reaction to Christian anti-Semitism in the West, it had inherited its very same racist essence.[18] On other occasions, he referred to Zionism as 'the second biggest tragedy after Nazism.'[19] For example, he wrote,

Do you think these Western movies which are constantly and tirelessly showing to the world the crimes of the Fascist and Nazi Germans are false? No, they are all true! But the question is why they only show so much sensitivity about 'some part of the truth' and ignore the rest?[20]

Shariati harshly criticized those, who according to him, were trying to justify Israel's occupation of Palestine by saying that the Palestinians could enjoy a better life in Israel than under any Arab country. Although he acknowledged that Israel was perhaps more democratic than the Arab regimes, he emphasized

17   Ibid., 113.
18   Ibid., 114.
19   Shariati, *Ali*, 248.
20   Shariati, *Nameha*, 93–94. Quoted from Shariati's letter to Jalal Zarrini Monfared.

that his opposition to Israel related to its very existence and had nothing to do with Israel's political behavior,

> They have made this argument and put it in the mouths of the European and American people like a sandwich. They used the same argument to justify colonialism in the past – like for instance, that British rule over India was much better than the government of the Muslim Indian rulers prior to the era of Western colonialism ... In regard to Israel's rule over Palestine, it would be a "fallacy" to compare the regime of Ben Gurion and Golda Meir with that of [King] Faisal and [King] Hussein in terms of their behavior with their citizens. It is true that the former is definitely more democratic and more liberal than the latter. But here, we are not talking about the type of political regime and its behavior; we are talking about colonialism, occupation, and the takeover and the right of independence in the relationship of one country with another. Otherwise, everybody knows that the behavior of the British rulers and the British people in general were far more democratic and more civilized and more whatever than the local governments of the African tribes ... But so what? Why should we make this comparison anyways?[21]

Shariati believed Western imperialism and Zionism had formed a "united front" against the Muslims.[22] He once enumerated all the enemies of Islam and Muslims as follows,

> Our enemies in this time include imperialism, materialism and capitalism, the spirit of bourgeoisie, exploitation, machinism, class differences, fascism, Zionism, nihilism, greediness for welfare, madness of consumption, cultural colonialism, self-alienation, permissiveness, historical disintegration, cultural metamorphosis, decline of moral values, and rule of money.[23]

He also named "world Zionism," "international imperialism," "old and new colonialism," together with "tyranny," "racism" and "Westoxication" as the biggest troubles of the current time.[24]

---

21   Ibid., 94.
22   Ibid., 114.
23   Ibid., 176. Quoted from Shariati's letter to his wife.
24   Shariati, Shi'eh, 77.

Shariati suggested that Muslims unite against what he called 'the alliance between imperialism and Zionism.'[25] He especially concentrated on the Palestinian question after the Six-Day war of 1967 and the occupation of Jerusalem by Israel.[26] Referring to the Shi'a-Sunni dispute, he wrote,

> There is a plot to make a split behind the [Muslims'] front lines, and this is the best way to distract them from the threat of Zionism. That is, to frighten the Sunnis about Shi'a Islam and to intimidate the Shi'a people about the danger of Sunni Islam. And what would be a better relief for the enemy to see that the two soldiers in the opposite front are fighting with themselves ... Beyond the noisy wrangles of these two brothers trying to settle the accounts of the early years of Islam, one can easily hear a victorious laughter from the West Bank of the river.[27]

Shariati held that amidst both Shi'a and Sunni people, there were hard-line extremist clerics who provoked the feelings of these two major groups of Muslims against each other and fuelled a futile dispute among them.[28] He argued that this way would result in both sides consciously or unconsciously serving the interests of Zionism and world imperialism. He repeatedly referred to the Shi'a-Sunni arguments as a "plot" by the enemies,

> [They] want to intimidate us from each other so that we won't be afraid of the danger of imperialism; [they] want to mobilize us against each other so that we will be distracted away from Zionism; [they] want to draw us into fighting with each other so that we forget where the real warfront is. It is not accidental that all these arguments and provocations and discussions and debates from both sides end up with the same conclusion, and both sides issue the same fatwa against each other: According to one side, 'Shi'a is worse than Israel,' and according to the other side, 'Sunni is worse than Israel.' Logically, the outcome of these two arguments is that 'Israel is better than all Muslims.' Who could imagine how much money has been spent to make Muslims acknowledge this by themselves?[29]

---

25   Ibid., 168. He also referred to 'the united front of Colonialism-Church-Israel' in another place. See Shariati, Shi'eh, 269.

26   Ibid., 269. See also Shariati, Tashayo', 52.

27   Ibid., 244.

28   Shariati, ba mokhatabha, 189–190.

29   Shariati, Tashayo', 252.

Shariati expressed his regret that just after the Six-Day war and the occupation of Jerusalem, some forces had provoked the Shi'a-Sunni dispute within the Islamic world. He urged the Shi'a intellectuals openly reject the comments by some traditionalists that viewed the Sunnis to be more dangerous than Israel for the Shi'a people.[30] While criticizing the Sunni extremists for fuelling the hostility between Shi'a and Sunni Muslims, he urged the Sunnis to align with the Shi'a people against Zionism, which he thought was the most threatening enemy of all Muslims. He wrote,

> The Sunni Muslim intellectuals who are well aware of Islam and the situation of Muslims in today's world should enlighten their people not to be manipulated by the [anti-Shi'a] propaganda. They should not replace the hatred of colonialist Jews and Christians, who have penetrated into the heart of the Islamic world with hostility against Shi'a people who are in fact their friends.[31]

Shariati claimed that he was under pressure from different direction due to his views on two specific topics: Zionism and Islamic solidarity.[32] Referring to these two topics as "overly sensitive" subjects in Iranian society, he explained in detail what he meant by unity between the Shi'a and Sunni Muslims, writing,

> The kind of unity that I advocate for Islamic society is the unity among people from different branches of Islam, who are resisting the same anti-Islamic enemies: A unity against the external enemy – that is, imperialism and Zionism. The [theological] unification of Shi'a and Sunni is meaningless; it is not wise, nor is it feasible ... What I mean by "unity" – as I have said several times – is the unity of Shi'a and non-Shi'a Muslims against imperialism and Zionism, not the unification of Shi'a and Sunni branches, not that Shi'a and Sunni become one entity. Whoever says this – unification of Shi'a and Sunni – does not know anything about Shi'a and Sunni, nor is he aware of history and religion as well as intellectual and scientific matters.[33]

The *Hosseinieh-ye Ershad* Institute, where the most famous intellectual of the revolution, including Ali Shariati and Ayatollah Motahhari, gave many of their

---

30   Ibid., 249.
31   Ibid., 248.
32   Shariati, *Ali*, 130.
33   Ibid., 179.

most important speeches, was shut down in the early 1970's because of the government's pressure and some internal administrative difficulties. In one of his last lectures before the closure of the center, Shariati warned his young fans about the influence of the enemy's propaganda in splitting the Muslim camp and referred to what he called 'the alliance of Jews and Christians' as 'the black force of Western colonialism.'[34] He stated that, in his opinion, the Zionists had an unarguable control over the world media and that they could manipulate even the most intellectual of people,

> During the years 1961, 1962, and 1963, when I was in France, I could see that the biggest political, ideological, philosophical, and social character in the West, or at least in France – Jean Paul Sartre – who was considered in the West the major mastermind and ideologue of Humanism and Existentialism... the most important founding Father of the contemporary philosophical school, and the most respected political, social, and revolutionary figure, was totally influenced by the manipulating propaganda of World Zionism. His thoughts, words, interviews, writings, and behavior were all dedicated freely to defending the power of Zionism as he referred to it as 'the sole experience of Socialism in the Middle East,' 'the symbol of Western democracy among the Arab countries,' and 'the manifestation of human liberalism in the traditionalist and backward societies.' However, many Jewish intellectuals later realized that the Zionists were the worst fascists in the world and a disgrace to the Jewish religion and people.[35]

As a revolutionary intellectual, Shariati was determined to provide a new interpretation of Islam, which would be useful in combating the problems of contemporary Iranian society. In his discussion of Imam Ali, he stated that the teachings of the Shi'a Imams were perfectly applicable to modern life, 'as if they are present in front of us today and can teach us what we should do now.'[36] He continued,

> Ali is not just a 'sacred image' which we are only supposed to praise ... Being a Shi'a to Imam Ali is not an abstract notion, but it is a 'practical fact.' That is because 'Shi'a' means 'following' and this is an 'action' – an objective and specific purposeful action – not just a 'feeling,' not just a

---

34   Ibid., 283.
35   Ibid., 283–284.
36   Ibid., 175–176.

'saying,' and not an 'emotional subjectivity' ... The main three chapters of Ali's life can be summarized as: 'ideology, unity, and justice.' These are three big lessons for all times and all places. These are three vivid mottos which the Muslims of the world badly need today in order to combat [their] intellectual decline, lack of ideology, class differences, domestic exploitation and tyranny, and external enemies – imperialism and Zionism. This is the meaning of vividness of the Imam; this is why the Imam is always present, and why Ali always remains our guide and Imam.[37]

In late 1973, when Shariati became immensely popular among young university students, he was captured by the Shah's secret police (SAVAK) and put in jail for eighteen months. This was his second time in prison after being taken into custody upon returning from Paris in 1964. Eventually, widespread pressure from the populace and an international outcry led to the end of his prison term, and he was released on March 20, 1975, under special circumstances, whereby he would not be allowed to teach, publish, or hold gatherings, whether in public or private. The state security apparatus, SAVAK, would also maintain close scrutiny of his every movement. Shariati rejected these conditions and decided to leave the country for England. Three weeks later he died of what was announced as a heart attack.

Concluding Remarks

Throughout the 1960's and 1970's, many new concepts such as anti-imperialism were introduced into the Iranian religious discourse. The influence of Jalal Al-e Ahmad's works on religious thinkers and the role of such scholars as Ali Shariati were decisive in this process. After 1967, Iranian religious thinkers started to use a line of reasoning – as reflected in Shariati's discourse – that held that Israel was the representative of Western colonialism and imperialism in the Middle East. A suitable ground was maintained for reinforcing religious opposition to Israel on the basis of such modern concepts as "freedom-seeking" and in the context of the general global clash between the "oppressors" and the "oppressed." In the 1960's and 1970's, when several Third-World nations in Africa and Asia were striving for independence from Western colonialism, such a portrayal of the world as being divided between the oppressors and the oppressed appealed to so many religious thinkers in Iran, who were opposed to the Shah's foreign and domestic policies on the one hand and to the interference of Western powers in Iran on the other. In this context, Palestinian

---

37   Ibid.

resistance against Israel was taken by many Iranian Islamist revolutionaries as a scared symbol and an example of the struggle against oppression both domestically and globally. The question of Palestine was an issue over which leftist and Shi'a concepts of justice-seeking and opposition to oppression perfectly matched.

Shariati contributed to the Iranian political discourse on Israel and Zionism by bridging the perspectives of the earlier anti-Israeli religious forces such as Ayatollah Kashani and those of the Iranian socialists such as Jalal Al-e Ahmad. By providing a type of leftist interpretation of Islam, they borrowed the idea of "Israel as the puppet of imperialism" from the left and the concept of "standing for justice" from the Shi'a.[38] The outcome was a heated anti-Zionism based on a combination of Islamic and socialist ideas. In sum, Shariati's perception of the Palestinian question can be summarized in the following phrase of his own: 'We are not hostile to the Jews, but we are hostile to Israel. And that is not because of its religion, but because it is fascist and because it is a basis for Western colonialism and imperialism.'[39]

Bibliography

Ashouri, Daryoush. "Zedde Sahyunism va Zedde Amperialism dar Sharq!" *Ferdowsi*, Issue 820, 11 July 1967.

Boroujerdi, Mehrzad. *Iranian Intellectuals and the West: The Tormented Triumph of Nativism*. Syracuse: Syracuse University Press, 1996.

Chehabi, Houchang E. *Iranian Politics and Religious Modernism, The Liberation Movement of Iran under the Shah and Khomeini*. Ithaca and New York: Cornell University Press, 1990.

Shariati, Ali. *Ali*. Tehran: Nashr-e Azmun, 1384/2005.

Shariati, Ali. *Asaar-e Goonegoon*. Vol. II, Tehran: Agah Publication, 1384/2005.

Shariati, Ali. *Ba Mokhatabhaye Ashna* Tehran: Hosseinieh-ye Ershad, n.d.

Shariati, Ali. *Bazshenasi-ye Hoviyat-e Eslami va Irani*. Tehran: Elham Publications, 1381/2002.

Shariati, Ali. *Nameha*. Tehran: Qalam Publications, 1384/2005.

Shariati, Ali. *Shi'eh*. Tehran: Elham Publication, 1378/1999.

---

38   Shariati even clearly stated that he believed in a 'sort of leftist and progressive interpretation of Islam' (Shariati, *Nameha*, 91). However, it did not mean at all that he believed in Marxism. In contrast, Shariati was explicitly opposed to Marxism and/or Communism. His "sort of leftist" interpretation of Islam simply meant a socialist and revolutionary approach to religion, but Islam still constituted the core of his thoughts.

39   Shariati, *Shi'eh*, 267.

CHAPTER 12

Shariati on Islamic and Western Philosophy of Education

Khosrow Bagheri Noaparast

Introduction

This chapter concentrates on a rare work of Ali Shariati titled *Philosophy of Education* (1979). This book is a comparative study of education philosophies in which the traditional Islamic system of education is compared to modern western forms of education. In this study, I argue that Shariati was an advocate of traditional Islamic education and additionally was a critic of modern western education.

In the first part of what follows, classifications are suggested pertaining to the specific characteristics Shariati assigns to the two philosophies of education. These classifications make it possible to systematize his views. In addition, having been borrowed from systematic orientations in philosophy of education, this classification gives a façade to his views more suited to the specific vocabulary of philosophy of education. These classifications include two sections of (1) philosophical foundations and, (2) educational implications. The philosophical foundations of education include the ontological, anthropological, epistemological, and axiological, while the educational implications include the aims, principles and slogans of education and educational activities.

In the second part of the chapter, an evaluation of Shariati's view is advanced. In evaluating Shariati's work, this chapter takes three steps. In the first step, it is argued that the sharp contrast between Islamic and Western philosophy of education is too sharp. There are many overlaps between the two education philosophies that need to be taken into account. In the second step, it is argued that "the West" is not a unified whole; but at most, it is an anomalous monism. In the third step, Shariati's attempt to revive traditional Islamic education is appreciated, but the difficulties in doing so will be highlighted.

Classification of Islamic and Western Philosophies of Education

Shariati emphasizes certain characteristics that pertain to Islamic and Western philosophies of education, arguing that such characteristics need to be classified. As I previously alluded, these classifications are comprised of philosophical foundations and educational implications.

Philosophical Foundations

The philosophical characteristics Shariati mentions as the underlying parts of Islamic and Western educational systems are introduced here in terms of the ontological, anthropological, epistemological, and axiological foundations of education. In a comparative manner, these foundations are as follows: From an ontological foundation, Shariati holds that the Islamic view deals with the universe while the western view concentrates on nature, which is often associated with materialism. From the Islamic perspective, the monotheistic worldview is the pivotal point according to which the universe is understood as being God's unique creation and under his guidance. Even though nature and its observable realities matter, and are dealt with in this view, the whole universe is not confined to nature, rather nature is subordinated to the divine sphere of the world. Thus, Shariati refers to this Islamic ontology as being idealism, and in a more comprehensive phrase, as a 'realism based on idealism.'[1] By realism, he refers to the realm of nature and its objective and empirical entities. By idealism, as the building block or core of Islamic ontology, he means the divine sphere. Thus, according to him, the Islamic view does not deal with spirituality at the cost of rejecting the material world, nor does it concern itself with the material world by ignoring the spiritual or divine sphere. The latter position, namely naturalism, is exactly what Shariati takes as the western view. As such, he refers to this view interchangeably as realism, naturalism, and materialism.[2]

In his anthropological foundation, Shariati argues that the central concern of the Islamic view is the human being, whereas the hallmark of the modern western view is society. In other words, in the Islamic view, humans are humans in terms of their basic characteristics, and are thus not confined to any particular society. These basic characteristics define the humanity of the human; and consequently such characteristics are not dependent on any particular sort of society. Rationality, truth-seeking, and moral consciousness might be mentioned as prime examples of such characteristics. Yet society, as the pivotal point of anthropology in the modern Western view, takes the human to be a member of modern society. In this functional view, people are defined in terms of the function they play in the whole of society. Engineers, teachers, and workers each have their own functions in the organism of the society and

---

1   Shariati, *Philosophy of Education*, 116, 119.
2   Ibid.

they are not defined, or even definable, outside of the terms of the functions they perform. The upshot of this view is that the human individual is understood to be a social animal, whereas in the Islamic view the human individual has universal and met-social dimensions. Thus, Shariati holds that in the Islamic view, humanity is justified within the world system, whereas in the western view, humanity is justified within the social system.[3]

Referring to Durkheim, Shariati attempts to make it clear that there is no contradiction between deeming modern societies individualistic and at the same time socialistic and functionalistic. Durkheim, according to Shariati, holds that in traditional societies, social conscience (*consciane sociale*) was strong and the individual was under its dominance.[4] Whereas in modern societies the individual is more rational and independent, and there is no dominant social conscience. Shariati holds that Durkheim's point is correct from an internal and emotional point of view; that is to say, in modern societies, people feel that they are independent.[5] However, from an external and objective viewpoint, individuals are under the pressure of society and are limited to their own functions within such society. He writes, 'That is, in the road of societies' evolution and perfection toward modernism, humans become more isolated from the inside and more social from the outside.'[6] One might say that in this way, Shariati can put both liberalism and socialism on par when he advocates the idea that society is dominant in the modern western view. This is because he interprets individualism, being the core of liberalism, as an internal emotional feeling that is compatible with a functional view of society.

From the epistemological angle, the difference between the Islamic and western viewpoints is as follows: Shariati holds that the slogan of the ancient science, including the Islamic view, was, in a word, "truth," whereas the slogan of the modern view of science is "power," as epitomized by Bacon's famous statement that science is serves to dominate nature.[7] In an Islamic view, truth has its roots over and beyond the human mind, and the problems of humanity are the basic realities of the world. To the extent that humans can capture these realities, determines whether or not they achieve the relevant truths and when. On the other hand, Shariati understands modern epistemology as a form of instrumentalism, in which science becomes a tool for taking power. This statement needs to be qualified in order to meet the different features of

---

3   Ibid., 116.
4   Ibid., 111.
5   Ibid., 113.
6   Ibid.
7   Ibid., 115.

western epistemology. The qualification needed is based upon the differentiation between two types of instrumentalism: "weak" and "strong."

In the weak version, instrumentalism is attributable to a certain level of scientific activities, namely the level of application rather than explanation. This version can be seen in the case of logical positivism, which adheres explicitly to truth as the defining feature of science, in contrast to values that are taken to be subjective. The fact/value distinction, parallel to the objective/subjective distinction, indicates that for positivists, science has instrumental characteristics, particularly in application. Whereas in explanation, science deals with objective facts and truths.

In the strong version, however, instrumentalism comes to the fore even in explanation. This means that scientific constructs have instrumental characteristics and they should not be taken as representative of facts. Pragmatists take this position, among others. Shariati holds that the overwhelming spirit of the western view is pragmatic.[8] According to pragmatists, science is for problem solving and a theory is tested for its efficacy, not for its truth unless truth is taken to be relevant to its efficacy. Even Willard Quine, who attempted to distance himself from the instrumentalism of classical pragmatists, has strong affinities with instrumentalism. He wrote,

> as an empiricist I continue to think of the conceptual scheme of science as a tool, ultimately, for predicting future experience in the light of past experience. Physical objects are conceptually important to the situation as convenient intermediaries – not by definition in terms of experience, but simply as irreducible posits comparable, epistemologically, to the gods of Homer. For my part I do, qua lay physicist, believe in physical objects and not in Homer's gods; and I consider it a scientific error to believe otherwise. But in point of epistemological footing the physical objects and the gods differ only in degree and not in kind. Both sorts of entities enter our conceptions only as cultural posits. The myth of physical objects is epistemologically superior to most in that it has proved more efficacious than other myths as a device for working a manageable structure into the flux of experience.[9]

As this quotation demonstrates, concepts used in science are tools for prediction and therefore they should be judged in terms of their efficacy and workability rather than their truth. In this endeavor, there is no difference between our

---

8   Ibid., 116.
9   Quine, *Two Dogmas of Empiricism*, 314.

concept of electron and Homer's gods. The crucial point is that the workability of a hypothesis does not necessarily indicate its being true, as there is ample evidence in the history of science for false, and at the same time, workable hypotheses. An example of such is the flat earth theory, which historically worked well, and still works contrary to the fact that the earth is round. The workability of this theory is due to what Nikolas Rescher calls the *error-tolerance of nature*.[10] Thus, a workable theory can be erroneous, but its workability derives from its being within the realm of nature's error-tolerance. Thus, the upshot in the comparison between the Islamic and western views in epistemology is that the former is truth-oriented while the latter is power-oriented.

Some may be confused as to why Shariati assigns the attributes of realism and pragmatism to the whole of the western view and not to two different parts. While it makes sense to hold the notion that there are two separate but defining parts in the West – realism and pragmatism – it would be contradictory however to attribute both of them at the same time to the West as a whole. This is because realists are concerned with representing reality, whereas pragmatists reject it and even, as Richard Rorty holds, take such a rejection as the core of pragmatism.[11] In order to resolve this contradictory point in Shariati's statements, it might be said that in dealing with the western ontology, Shariati identifies it with realism, which is associated with materialism and naturalism. However, when it comes to epistemology, he uses the term pragmatism, and it is clear that pragmatism is compatible with materialism and naturalism in ontology.

As for axiology, Shariati deals with it implicitly; he briefly mentions the top priorities of Islamic and western values. Axiology is about the nature of values, but listing the values is not enough for axiology. By making explicit what is implicit in the list of values one might show what position Shariati takes regarding axiology. The top values he derives from the Islamic view, which stand in contrast to the western view, are, among others: human morality vs. social behavior, beauty vs. welfare, and perfection vs. happiness. These contrasting ideals indicate that the nature of values in the Islamic view have their roots in *universal realities*, whereas the western values have a *human-oriented nature*, as the values of social behavior, welfare and happiness, deal primarily with human affairs. By contrast, Islamic values are concerned with basic and absolute characteristics. For instance, human morality, in contrast to social behavior, is to be understood as absolute morality parallel to basic human characteristics beyond a certain society's particular conventions. In addition, beauty

---

10   Rescher, *Scientific Realism*.
11   Rorty, *Objectivity*, 65–66.

and perfection are God-oriented values, as it is mentioned in the Islamic traditions, which states that "God is beautiful and likes beauty."[12] Furthermore, God is introduced as the final point of perfection. Thus, relativism would be the hallmark of western axiology, whereas absolutism can be understood as the hallmark of Islamic axiology.

Educational Implications

Having formulated the philosophical foundations of Shariati's view, I now turn to organizing his educational views according to these foundations. The first and most important question education is concerned with regards its own nature. In fact, all the philosophical foundations of an educational approach are reflected in the basic concept of education that the approach suggests. Even though Shariati does not give an explicit definition of education from either an Islamic or western perspective, he regards it implicitly in the picture he gives of the educated person. According to Shariati, the educated person, or the aim of education in the Islamic view, is the virtuous person.[13] Whereas in the western view, it is the competent person. The contrast between "virtue" and "competency" is indicative of the contrasts between the relevant philosophical foundations.

On the one hand, the concept of "virtue" retains trace elements of the philosophical foundations of Islam. As far as ontology is concerned, virtue is associated with the main sources of perfection and beauty in the world, namely God. Thus, a virtuous person is a God-like entity. In terms of anthropology, virtue references basic human characteristics that go beyond a certain society's particular conventions. Similarly, virtue goes beyond a value theory in which values are human or society oriented.

On the other hand, the concept of "competence" retains trace elements derived from the philosophical foundations of the West. Competence presupposes a naturalistic ontology in which the dominance of nature is at issue. Furthermore, competence presupposes an anthropology in which the human individual is a member of a certain society with its particular needs and conventions, and thereby is a society-oriented concept rather than a universe-oriented one. Likewise, competence references an epistemological foundation in which science is associated with power and problem solving. Finally, as for axiology, competence presupposes a human-oriented nature of values.

---

12   Kolaini, *Al-Usule al-Kafi*, Vol. 6: 438.

13   Shariati, *Philosophy of Education*, 115.

In order to highlight the difference between the two views concerning an educated person, I offer this example: a competent engineer is a person who has acquired all the functional skills needed to work as an engineer in an industrial society, whereas a virtuous person should have characteristics, such as truth-telling, that are not confined to a certain society. Using another pair of contrasting words, Shariati refers to a person educated in Islam as a "good human," and to the western educated person as a "powerful human."[14]

The impact of these philosophical foundations can be traced back in other segments of the educational system of both Islam and the West. This appears obvious when observing the content, or curriculum, of the education program. According to Shariati, in an Islamic education system, empirical sciences are welcome alongside spiritual or theological materials, in which values are central.[15] However, their places are different in that the superior place is devoted to the spiritual endeavors and/or values. Thus, wisdom, insight, and the "science of guidance" are sought in an Islamic education. In contrast, western education gives a central position to knowledge, information, and the "science of facts."[16] Thus, Shariati uses the words "culture" and/or "value" as the pivotal point of Islamic education, whereas he uses "civilization" or "utility" as the main concern of western education.[17] Such curriculum demonstrates the traces of their relevant ontologies, anthropologies, epistemologies, and axiologies.

In terms of educational methods, Shariati puts forward this pair of contrasting words: cultivation vs. instruction.[18] According to him, the Islamic view puts *cultivation* at the center of education, whereas the western view takes *instruction* as the main vehicle for education. This is in parallel to the above-mentioned centrality of *values* in the curriculum adopted by Islamic education, and the centrality of *knowledge* in western education. According to Islamic education, in order to provide pupils with values, instruction is not enough, but living with pupils and dealing with their daily issues and giving them a role model is required. Thus, Shariati admires the traditional Islamic education for providing pupils with the opportunity for having informal access to their teachers.[19] In traditional Islamic seminaries, there was a chamber (*hojrah*) for the teacher alongside the chambers for pupils. The teacher's

---

14   Ibid., 116.
15   Ibid., 118.
16   Ibid., 116.
17   Ibid., 115–116.
18   Ibid., 115.
19   Ibid., 31–32.

chamber was without any privileges so that the pupils could have sincere relationships with their teachers.

On the other hand, according to Shariati, western education is *technology-oriented*.[20] Such an orientation has given birth to the phrase "techniques of instruction," which is widely used in the literature of modern education. By introducing such techniques into education, it turns into a mechanical endeavor by which changes in pupils' behavior are taken as predictable. In contrast to this technology-oriented education, Shariati advances an *ideology-oriented* Islamic education.[21] Even though ideology is too ambiguous a word to be expected to make good sense, the contrast might help to capture the meaning that Shariati intends. Ideology, in contrast to the mechanical character of technique, indicates that understanding and choice is a central issue in the methods of education. If ideology is taken as indoctrination – to impose some beliefs on pupils, similar to brain-washing – then the contrast Shariati holds between ideology and technique would be irrelevant. Thus, as far as ideology – in terms of method – is concerned, it should mean using proper procedures for understanding and choosing one's beliefs and values.

Again, the affinities between the methods used in the two educational systems and their underlying philosophical presuppositions are clear: In terms of an Islamic education, procedures of understanding and choice of values are affixed to a world that contains the roots of values and truths, by which the individual is taken as a discoverer of these values and truths. As for western education, the technique-orientation is affixed to a naturalistic ontology, in which nature is waiting to be dominated, the individual is a truth-maker rather than a truth-discoverer, whose needs and interests serve as the criteria of values.

Evaluation of Shariati's Comparative Philosophy of Education

So far, I have attempted to formulate Shariati's comparative philosophy of education in regards to its Islamic and western characteristics. In this part, an evaluation of this comparative philosophy of education is forwarded. This will include three segments; (1) I will highlight Shariati's sharp distinction between the two philosophies of education and offer a critique; (2) I will evaluate his unified conception of western philosophy of education, and (3) I will address his urge for reviving the Islamic tradition.

---

20   Ibid., 115.

21   Ibid.

A Sharp Contrast

As the first part of the chapter shows, Shariati draws a sharp contrast between the two philosophies of education in terms of their philosophical foundations as well as their educational implications. However, one might find out some overlapping areas in the two philosophies of education based on Shariati's own clarifications. This is because Shariati holds, on the one hand, that an Islamic philosophy of education is comprised of two concerns: one empirical and the other spiritual. On the other hand, he introduces western philosophies of education solely as an empirical and technological-oriented endeavor. This demonstrates that the two seemingly opposing views have commonalities as far as the empirical and technological aspects are concerned. Even though, according to Shariati, the western view is reductionist in dealing with nature and empirically confrontational with it, but this does not indicate that there are no overlapping areas between the two views. Even if we deny the neutrality of procedures and techniques, and hold some affinities between them and the underlying philosophical approaches, again it does not follow that there are no overlapping areas between the two viewpoints. This is because the impact of certain philosophical foundations on methods, procedures, and techniques are not so absolute and exclusive, to the point that those methods, procedures, and techniques cannot at all be used by other viewpoints. Thus, the logical implications of Shariati's own project negates the sharp contrast he draws between the two views.

After all, the alleged paradigmatic relationship among systems of thought, in general, and systems of philosophy of education, in particular, are self-defeating. This is precisely the case because of the following: by such a relation, none of the paradigms would be tenable as there is no criterion for their validity unless there is an internal criterion that leads to solipsism. This is the logical dead-end of paradigmatic relations. Politically speaking, this relation will have no other consequence other than a war among incommensurable paradigms. This is because there are no conceptual commonalities between the two paradigms that make it possible for them to find a solution for their conflicts. What remains is only physical elimination. As for the relationship between Islam and the West, there are attempt nowadays to make it a paradigmatic relation that justifies a war between them.

If the paradigmatic relationship is logically, as well as politically, a dead-end, then the hard contrast between Islamic and western philosophies of education needs to be undermined, and commonalities between them thus sought.

Is the Western Philosophy of Education a Unified Whole?

Shariati's other presupposition is that western philosophies of education are a unified whole. This presupposition can be challenged as well. As it was shown in the first part, Shariati considers the educated person in the Islamic view to be the "virtuous person," while this ideal in the western view is posited as the "competent person."

However, it is interesting to note that in the West there is at least one rival for the competence approach, which is called "capability approach." This approach was introduced by Amarta Sen (1979) and expanded by others such as Martha Nussbaum (1997, 2011) and Melanie Walker (2003, 2007). This approach is in fact a return to Aristotle and his teleological view of human nature. According to this approach, humans, by way of being human, have potentialities that need to be actualized by education. From among the human capabilities, the following are identified: capability of self-criticism and criticism of social tradition; capability of seeing oneself not only as a citizen but also as a human in a reciprocal relationship to others; and the capability of seeing things from others' points of view.[22] As it is clear, cultivating these capabilities would lead to an educated person who is beyond a certain society's requirements.

In a broader sense, going back to Aristotle again, there have been attempts in recent times to revive virtue ethics and virtue epistemology. Virtue ethics have been revived by Elizabeth Anscombe (1958) and followed up by Alasdair MacIntyre, Philipa Foot, and John McDowell among others. Anscombe maintained that concepts used in ethics, such as "right," "wrong," and "moral oughts," are derived from the discipline of law, which presupposes the existence of a lawful authority, whereas moral concepts should have a moral basis. According to virtue ethics, at issue in morality is first the imperative to deal with the question "what kind of person should one be," rather than "what should be done?" In other words, virtue ethics gives the priority to moral persons and the basic characteristics they should embody rather than moral acts.

There is also a return to Aristotle, in what is called "virtue epistemology."[23] Parallel to virtue ethics, in which there is a focus on change from the deed to the doer, in virtue epistemology, so too there is a focused change from belief to the believer. This is to maintain that the truth of a belief is not related merely to the belief itself, but to the process through which the belief is acquired. By extending the term "virtue" to the intellectual realm, parallel to

---

22   Nussbaum, 2011.
23   Sosa, 1991; Zagzebski, 1996.

moral virtue, intellectual virtues are introduced in virtue epistemology. Some examples of intellectual virtues are intellectual courage, intellectual fairness, and intellectual humility.

These views in the West show that western philosophies of education cannot be confined to the competence approach in contrast to the virtue approach, being devoted to the Islamic view. The virtue approach has not only a long history in the West, going back to Aristotle, but also has been revived in the recent times in western ethics and education.

Reviving the Islamic Philosophy of Education

The comparison that Shariati makes between Islamic and western philosophies of education derives from an urgent need to decide which to follow. Referring to the western philosophies of education, Shariati states, 'we are now unwillingly faced with it and are obliged to decide about it.'[24] It is also evident that Shariati, in his comparative philosophy of education, is an advocate of the Islamic philosophy of education and a critic of the western philosophy of education. It follows that the choice of Muslims should be to reject the western option and embrace the Islamic one. This is to say that Shariati invites us to revive an Islamic philosophy of education.

The challenge that Shariati feels is understandable. This is in fact the challenge facing all traditional systems of education that are confronted with modernity. This confrontation threatens the procedures that we are accustomed to as well as the invaluable elements of our tradition.

Now, the question is this: Is it possible to revive the basic orientations of traditional education and resist the philosophical requirements of modern education, while simultaneously dealing with the fact that certain forms and procedures of modern education are being imposed on our traditional system of education? It is worth noting that Islamic seminaries in Iran, such as *Jameat al-Mustafa* and *Houzeh Elmiah* in Qom, Iran, have used some of the procedures of modern universities, such as summative examinations, classification in terms of undergraduate and graduate levels, dissertation and chapter writing, and so on and so forth. While this is the case in seminaries, the story of universities in Iran and other Muslim countries is an almost wholesale acceptance of the modern university system. These facts show that the wholesale rejection of the modern system of education seems to be impossible, and thus the only options are, (1) a wholesale acceptance of modern education, or (2) at most an

---

24   Shariati, *Philosophy of Education*, 114.

amalgamation of traditional and modern education. From these two, the latter option would be preferable if it is shown that the positive elements of traditional education can be harmoniously synthesized with modern education.

Thus, the question turns out to be, what types of synthesis between the elements of the two systems of education are harmonious and acceptable, and what types are eclectic and unacceptable? The straightforward answer to this question would be to synthesize the higher elements such as the aims, ideals, and basic values from traditional Islamic education, with the lower elements, such as means, procedures, and techniques from modern systems of education. However, the matter is not that simple. This is precisely because some of the lower elements would have long term and expansive effects that might encompass the higher elements and make them neutral and ineffective.

Let's mention an example: the *marketization of knowledge*. This is apparently a lower element in contemporary western education. At face value, it might be taken as a useful procedure for extending the effects of the educational system to the whole nation, or even the world. Perhaps it was for this reason that this element was absorbed in the educational system of Iran. The term "marketization of knowledge," and the associated term "knowledge-based economy," are used in Iran's official state documents.[25] However, this element seems to have a penetrating effect that can extend itself into the ideals and aims. As some scholars have pointed out, this slogan of neoliberalism is a node in the network of an extensive discourse which has relationships with other nodes, such as "stakeholder," "entrepreneurship," "accountability," "competence," "science and technology parks," "knowledge economy," etc.[26] This grand discourse could replace the market economy with a market society, in which the whole society turns into a market in which every social affair would be defined by market-exchange. This would inevitably lead to the degeneration of higher values. It is worth saying that the term "Qur'ānic business" is currently used in a prestigious congress in Iran.[27] By this term it is meant that the Qur'ān can provide us with a good and extensive business; it encourages individuals to look for new ways by which they could generate income by means of the Qur'ān. Ironically, this reminds us of a verse in the Qur'ān in which God urges the Prophet to abstain from asking for money for his mission.[28]

One might think that the marketization of knowledge has become a necessary element in educational systems so that appealing to it is inevitable.

---

25   The Fourth Program of Development, 2005.
26   Olssen and Peters, *Neoliberalism*, 2005.
27   Qur'anic Research, 2015.
28   Qur'ān, 6: 90.

However, this is not the case. As Salberg, among others, has pointed out, the marketization of knowledge, as an element in the "Global Education Reform Movement," is not inevitable for an educational system to develop.[29] On the contrary, according to him, there are other ways for an educational system in the modern world to develop. He has analyzed the case of Finland's educational system and has shown how this system has succeeded in educational endeavors by using procedures other than the marketization of knowledge.

Conclusion

In support of traditional Islamic education, Shariati, in his *Philosophy of Education*, emphasizes elements of that system, such as the different forms of freedom the students had; the comprehensive structure of curriculum – including the subjects that required rational contemplation, as well as the subjects based on revelation; amalgamation of freedom and responsibility of students, etc. The main claim of the book is that there is a sharp contrast between the Islamic and western philosophies of education. According to Shariati, the hallmark of western philosophies of education is to educate an individual based on the needs of society, whereas the main characteristic of Islamic philosopheies of education is to educate the human, not merely as an atomistic selfish individual, or as a functional *member* of society, but as a human whose potentialities are actualized. In other words, modern philosophies of education take knowledge as a means to dominate nature, thus putting an emphasis on students' *competences*, whereas Islamic philosophies of education, having accepted realistic and experimental aspects, transcend educational endeavors seeking to dominate nature and the whole universe. Rather they attempt to provide students with 'virtues.'

It has been argued in this chapter that Shariati's sharp contrast between Islamic and western philosophies of education is neither logically nor politically defensible. Looking for overlaps between the two views is particularly important for providing a dialogical relationship between the Islamic and western world, whereas the sharp contrast would inevitably contribute to a "clash of civilizations." It is argued further that the unified nature Shariati holds for western philosophies of education can be challenged on the grounds that the virtue approach attributed to Islamic philosophy of education has a long history in the West, and has been recently revived. Finally, Shariati's call for the revival of an Islamic philosophy of education is shown to be a difficult endeavor. It is argued that this revival can only go one way; we must look for a

---

29   Salberg, *Finnish Lessons*.

harmonious synthesis between the higher elements of an Islamic philosophy of education and the lower elements of western philosophies of education. All things considered, this synthesis is not a straightforward endeavor.

Bibliography

Kolaini, Mahnaz. *Al-Usule al-Kafi*. Tehran: Dar al-Ketab al-Islamiyah, 1984.

Olssen, Mark and Michael Peters. "Neoliberalism, higher education, and the knowledge economy: From the free market to knowledge capitalism," *Journal of Education Policy*, 20 (2005): 313–347.

Nussbaum, Martha. *Cultivating humanity: A classical defense of Reform in Liberal Education*. Cambridge, MA: Harvard University Press, 1997.

Nussbaum, Martha. *Creating capabilities. The Human Development Approach*. Cambridge, MA: The Belknap Press of Harvard University Press, 2011.

Quine, Willard. "Two dogmas of empiricism." *Meaning*, edited by Mark Richard, 295–316. Oxford: Blackwell Publishing, 2003.

Qur'anic Research. *The Congress of Qur'anic Research*. Held in The Ministry of Science and Technology of Iran. Tehran: San'at Square, 2015.

Rescher, Nicholas. *Scientific realism*. Dordrecht: D. Relde, 1987.

Rorty, Richard. *Objectivity, Relativism and Truth: Philosophical Chapters I*. Cambridge: Cambridge University Press, 1991.

Sahlberg, Pasi. *Finnish Lessons: What can the world learn from educational change in Finland?* New York: Teachers College Press, 2011.

Sen, Amartya. *Equality of what? The Tanner Lecture on Human Values*, 22 May, Stanford University, 1979.

Shariati, Ali. *Philosophy of Education*. Tehran: Be'sat, 1979.

Sosa, Ernest. *Knowledge in Perspective: Selected Essays in Epistemology*. Cambridge: Cambridge University Press, 1991.

The Fourth Program. *The Fourth Program of Islamic Republic of Iran's Economic, Social and Cultural Development 2006–2010*. Tehran: Sazman Mudiriat va Barnamehrizi Keshvar, 2005.

The Holy Qur'an.

Walker, Melanie. "Framing Social Justice in Education: What does the Capability Approach offer?" *British Journal of Educational Studies* 51 (2003): 168–187.

Zagzebski, Linda. *Virtues of the Mind: An inquiry into the Nature of Virtue and the Ethical Foundations of Knowledge*. Cambridge: Cambridge University Press, 1996.

CHAPTER 13

Ali Shariati and Anti-Americanism in the Persian Gulf Region

Fatemeh Shayan

Introduction

In this chapter, Shariati's viewpoints on the Islamic Revolution of Iran and its adopted Islamic identity are examined, as it is posited that these phenomena encouraged anti-American sentiment by highlighting the threat of the United States to Islamic identity. In addition, this analysis of Shariati's views is extended to the wider Persian Gulf region, by which I examine anti-American sentiment between 2000 and 2011.[1] More than a century ago, Bismarck declared the Persian Gulf to be a region he hoped God would never allow him to fall victim to.[2] However, in the last three decades, security of the Persian Gulf region has been influenced by American geopolitical strategies and the American military presence. Issues such as the invasion of Kuwait by Iraq, and the War in Iraq beginning in 2003, have resulted in an unprecedented American presence in the region, which has led to the rise of anti-American sentiments across the entire region.[3]

In examining the issue of anti-Americanism in the Persian Gulf, authors of various studies have mainly focused on the way in which the regional states exercise power in response to the American presence in the region. Concerning anti-American sentiments, in 2002, Barry Rubin examined rising anti-American sentiments as a means for members of the ruling elites to distract the people in the Persian Gulf.[4] Following the Iraq War, according to Wesley,

---

1   This time period was chosen due to the effects of globalization, which have become more apparent in the Persian Gulf since 2000. The 2003 US War in Iraq brought again the US policy into the forefront of attention in the region, which is still influential, despite the US army withdrawal from Iraq in 2011.

2   J.E. Peterson, "The Historical Pattern of Gulf security," in *Security in the Persian Gulf, Origins, Obstacles and the Search for the Consensus*, ed. Lawrence G. Potter and Gary G. Sick. (New York and Basingstoke: Palgrave, 2002), 7.

3   Mohammed Ayoob, "American Policy towards the Persian Gulf." In *International Politics of the Persian Gulf*, ed. Mehran Kamrava. (New York: Syracuse University Press, 2011), 120–123.

4   Barry Rubin, "The Real Root of Arab Anti-Americanism." *Foreign Affairs*, 81/6 (2002): 73–85.

the unilateral American policy resulted in the exacerbation of anti-American sentiments. Wesley further noted that unilateral American policies had led to an overreach, while arrogantly ignoring the rest of the world, where a series of reactions ranging from terrorism to anti-American viewpoints have emerged.[5] Although these have been the subject of extensive analyses on anti-American perspectives, at a general level, the viewpoints of Ali Shariati on anti-Americanism in Iran and their connection to the developments in the wider Persian Gulf region have remained largely unexplored.

At the same time, it is important to note Lynch's analysis of Arab politics and their anti-American viewpoints. The authors explain that, following the events that took place between 1999 and 2004, American presence in the Arab world has increased, resulting in the Arab states politically aligning themselves against American policies toward Iraq. Thus, Lynch suggests that anti-Americanism has become a unifying force for the Arab states, whereby satellite television and other mass media are utilized to disseminate their viewpoints. Lynch's perspective, however, is broad and does not extend to the examination of the phenomenon that specifically pertains to the Gulf Cooperation Council (GCC) states. According to Lynch's analysis, the Arab states in the Middle East allegedly exercise power vis-à-vis the United States. These broad generalizations are made, even though Lynch limits anti-American sentiments to the viewpoints of the regional states, while excluding the perspectives of other actors. Accordingly, his examination is insufficient when exploring the relationship of power in the context of anti-Americanism in the Persian Gulf post-Iraq War, where the transnational actors of al-Qaeda and the regional public are involved in the process of forming anti-American sentiments.

To provide a new perspective, the work presented in this chapter aims to answer the question: *How is Shariati's viewpoint on anti-Americanism interrelated with the rise of anti-American sentiments in the Persian Gulf?* To gain such an understanding, two phenomena, globalization and American policies in the region, are examined. To analyse them, I will utilize the *Regional Security Complex Theory* (RSCT) developed by Barry Buzan and Ole Wæver, while specifically drawing upon its constructivist aspect. Taking the constructivist perspective allows, for example, us to discern how globalization and American policies in the region are securitized by regional states, which has led to anti-Americanism. I will limit my examination to the period between 2000 and 2011.

---

5 Michael Wesley, "The Consequences of Anti-Americanism: Does It Matter?" in *Anti-Americanism: in the 21st Century (Volume 4)*, ed. O'Connor, Brendon and Martin Griffiths. (Oxford: Greenwood Press, 2007), 221.

In the next section, I first address Ali Shariati's viewpoint on anti-Americanism, before adopting the theoretical approach by which I will examine the securitization of the American threat to the Islamic identity in the region, which has led to a rise in anti-Americanism. Moreover, I study specific anti-American sentiments that emerged in 2000–2003, which coincides with the period of extensive American globalization. This allows American policy, which increased anti-Americanism from 2004 to 2011, to be examined in detail. This discussion will culminate with some concluding remarks. In essence, the analysis of Shariati's viewpoints on anti-Americanism and its connection to the wider region indicates that American policies in the region since the Iraq War have resulted in more of a rapid rise of anti-Americanism than has American-led globalization.

Ali Shariati and Anti-American Perspective

Ali Shariati was one of the most prominent Iranian intellectuals in the 1960's and 1970's. When he returned to Iran after obtaining a doctorate in Paris, he lectured on various Islamic issues at the religious meeting halls in Tehran. Ali Shariati believed that Islam was the appropriate response to the evils of capitalism and imperialism. He connected Islam to Third Worldism, as well as political and cultural anti-Americanism in particular.[6] The combination of inflation, resource shortages and income inequalities among Iranian people exacerbated the discontent with rapid modernization especially among the young as well as the society at large. Anti-Americanism was challenged by new Shia interpretation of Shiism, associated with Ali Shariati. Consequently, Shariati was able to initiate a social movement among young people that mobilized them against the US[7] Additionally, Amr Sabet argued that the Iranian Revolution represented a desire among Shia Iranians to find justice in the face of the suffering caused by the Shah's Government.[8] This perspective is in line with that of the then Supreme Leader of Iran, Ayatollah Ruhollah Khomeini, who openly voiced his anti-American stance, 'our [nation] and other Islamic

---

6   Patrick Clawson, "The Paradox of Anti-Americanism in Iran," *Middle East Review of International Affairs* 8/1 (2004): 20.

7   Ali Shariati, "Expectations from Muslim Women." (1997). http://www.shariati.com/english/woman/woman3.html, (Accessed 9/25/2016).

8   Amr Sabet, *Islam and the Political: Theory, Governance, and International Relations*. (London: Pluto Press, 2008), 49–58.

[nations] know their enemy [the US], who is also the enemy of God, Islam and [the] Quran. And the US is our enemy who wants to obliterate the world.'[9]

Like Ayatollah Khomeini, his successor, Ayatollah Sayed Ali Khamenei depicts the United States as a threat. He states that 'today ... the US openly threatens the Muslim [Islamic] world and talks of a crusade against it.'[10] Shariati's anti-American message provided new religious standards for moral references, which were opposed to secular judgments. It constituted a basic rejection of the modern American message. Thus, Shariati was successful in striking a sensitive chord in the subjective make-up of the Iranian Islamic identity. In this context, it was possible for Shariati to present a religious framework for the Iranian nation, which brought Islam and Islamic identity to the forefront of the collective consciousness. The emphasis was placed on the contrast between good and evil, embodied in the confrontation between Iran with Islamic identity and the United States. This approach resulted in the emergence of new meanings and definitions of identity, such as those specific to Iranians and Shia, which resulted in a new focus within the Islamic Revolution of Iran.[11]

This perspective of Shariati, which emphasized the Islamic identity of Iran and the threat that the US posed to its survival, is examined below by extending the analysis towards the wider Persian Gulf region and the way in which the US has threatened Islamic identity since the 2003 Iraq War.

The Approach: Theoretical Framework – Regional Security Complex Theory and Securitization

In this study, I draw upon the *Regional Security Complex Theory* developed by Buzan and Wæver in 2003 to conceptualize and evaluate the American threat to Islamic identity, which has led to the rise of widespread anti-Americanism in the Persian Gulf. Although the RSCT provides a blend of materialist and constructivist approaches, its constructivist perspective is utilized in this article.

Using the constructivist approach, RSCT builds on securitization theory by referring to a process within which political communities treat something as

---

9   Ayatollah Khomeini, "Speech by Ayatollah Rouhollah Khomeini, Former Supreme Leader of Iran, at the massive crowd of people in Jamaran," *Testament: The Current Message and the Future Generation.* Jamaran, 1982.

10 Ali S. Khamenei, "Address by the Iranian Supreme Leader Ayatollah Ali Khamenei at the Opening Session of the Third International Conference on Quads and Support for the Palestine People," *Palestine Issue at the Focal Point.* 14 April, 2006.

11 Sabet, *Islam and the Political*, 250–257.

an existential threat to a referent object and call for an exceptional measure. In this chapter, I apply securitization to examine how the key leaders of the regional states securitized threats imposed by another state (the United States of America), which called for urgent measures prior to and after the 2003 Iraq War. Within this framework, Buzan et al. (1998) recognized three processes of securitization, based on the entity that alerted the region to the threat (the securitizer, in this context the leaders in the Persian Gulf region), entities that have been threatened (the referent object, here referring to the Islamic identity of the states and societies in the Persian Gulf region), and the source of the threat (the US).[12]

This characterization is problematic, as Buzan et al. failed to consider the importance of audiences as evaluators of the perceived threats. Therefore, the theoretical framework adopted in this article builds upon that which was utilized by Buzan et al., in an attempt to shed light on the role of audiences in the securitization process. This weakness in Buzan et al.'s theory was conceptualized by Sarah Leonard and Christian Kaunert, who highlighted the relationship between the securitizing actor and the audience in the securitization process. According to these authors, audiences must agree with the claims made by the securitizing actor in order for a successful securitization to occur. As audiences vary, securitizers could experience formal support from members of the ruling elites and members of parliament, while failing to persuade the citizens. Certain members of the public could also be a source of moral support.[13] Among different audiences, for example, the regional states contributed to securitization and have become increasingly anti-American, owing to the perceived threat to Islamic identity. The securitization process examined in this chapter considers the United States as a threat to the referent object, the Islamic identity of the regional states, and the Iraqi society in particular. Thus, the leaders of the regional states have securitized the threat of the US.

The Analysis

US-led globalization has posed a threat to the Persian Gulf regional societies between 2000 and 2003, and has led to rise in anti-American sentiments. However, the threat of globalization did not disappear after 2003. Rather, other

---

12   Buzan et al., *Security: A New Framework for Analysis*. Boulder, Co: Lynne Rienner, 1998.

13   Sarah Léonard and Christian Kaunert, "Reconceptualizing the Audience in Securitization Theory" in *Securitization Theory: How Security Problems Emerge and Dissolve*, ed. Thierry Balzacq. (New York: Routledge, 2011), 60–65.

threats, such as the US policy-driven War in Iraq, were prioritized. In considering the belief that globalization leads to Americanization, one important factor of this perceived threat is how globalization threatens the identity of the regional nations. However, a counterfactual analysis will be presented to address the positive effects of globalization in the region. The purpose of this counter perspective is not to dismiss the threat of globalization in the region, but to demonstrate the benefits, as well as the disadvantages, of the US-led globalization in the region.

Globalization is Not a Threat: A Counterfactual Analysis

Globalization has affected the region in more ways than just through its threat to an Islamic identity (see below). We can pose a counterfactual question of what would happen in the Persian Gulf region if globalization was not considered a threat. This question is addressed in an interview with a Kuwaiti professor:

> Globalization is a complicated phenomenon. American values are neo-liberalism, free economy and market. Those values of globalization are shared in the Persian Gulf region. It holds a new liberal economic policy, and the majority of those policies come from the US. When it comes to other values such as individualism, family and collective identity, there are great differences between the Persian Gulf region and the US.[14]

The Kuwaiti professor compares the optimistic and pessimistic aspects of globalization in the Persian Gulf region, and his viewpoint represents the opinion of the majority of experts and scholars in the region (see below). Additionally, his viewpoint supports the positive impacts of globalization in the region through the promotion of a free market economy. To connect the interviewee's viewpoint about the positive impacts of globalization to the events in the region, the states of the Gulf Cooperation Council (GCC) launched the Custom Union law in the 23rd session of the GCC Supreme Council held in Qatar in 2003. They abolished the procedures and regulations restricting trade and implemented unified custom taxes and regulations for non-member states.[15]

---

14   Interview with Kuwaiti professor on the security in the Persian Gulf, June, 2012.
15   Gulf Cooperation Council, "Implementing procedures for the Custom Union of the GCC,"
      1 January, 2003, http://www.gcc-sg.org/eng/index9038.html?action=Sec-Show&ID=93,
      (Accessed 1/17/2013).

This evidence is in line with the speech of the Secretary General of the GCC states, Abdollatif Al-Zayani, in December of 2012, at the opening session of the Forum on Sustainable Development between the GCC states and China. He endorsed the effects of globalization on the GCC states' and the region's economies by affirming that they play an essential role in the global economy, thus, creating an imperative to maintain the security and stability of this vital region of the world.[16]

Globalization Threatens the Islamic Identity of the Nations in the Region

American-led globalization has had a profound impact on Islamic identities in the region. The process has reinforced existing securitization measures taken by religious leaders, such as Ayatollah Khamenei. In other words, several regional leaders have securitized the threat of American-led globalization to the referent object – the Islamic identities of societies in the region. A threat framed by Ayatollah Khamenei, the Supreme Leader of Iran, describes the nature of this perceived threat to Islamic identity as such,

> Cultural threat and cultural invasion [by the US] covers the whole world. But on this front, Iran is the focus of attention of the threat. We stand against it by expanding moral, social attitudes of individuals and strengthening religious and political belief.[17]

Similar statements are prevalent across the region. For example, in a 2001 speech commemorating the commencement of the works of the second year of the third session of the Shura National Council, the former Saudi Arabian King, 'Abdullah 'Abdulaziz stated,

> The world of today with all its civilizations and cultures is stepping towards increased proximity [globalization], and towards more mutual

---

16   Abdulatif bin Rashid Al-Zayani, "Address by the Secretary General of the GCC, at the opening session of the Forum on Sustainable Development between the GCC Member States and the Republic of China organized by the Ministry of Foreign Affairs, the United Arab Emirates, in cooperation with the Emirates Center for Strategic Studies and Research," Abu Dhabi, 12 December, 2012.

17   Ayatollah Khamenei, "Remark by Ayatollah Ali Khamenei to the Members and the Director of the Supreme Council of the Cultural Revolution in Tehran." 15 June, 2011.

cooperation among countries and societies. We realize this but we still abide with commands of Islam.[18]

Preserving Islamic identity in the face of the United States-led globalization was also a priority articulated by Tariq Khaddam Al-Fayez, the Second Secretary for Saudi mission at the UN:

> In light of globalization, the human community becomes one unit or one small village. It also means openness and recognition of the other, while at the same time, poses a threat due to the pressure it exerts upon [identity] ....[19]

For regional leaders, the Islamic identity of the regional societies represents the main referent object to be protected from the American-led globalization threat. The public is reminded of how 'the US intends to Americanize the youths and change the Islamic identity.'[20] In their interviews, participants from the region acknowledged the societal threat posed by the US-led globalization process, especially to the Islamic identity of youth from a range of different perspectives. According to one Kuwaiti interviewee:

> Media and media products extensively project American values in the Persian Gulf region via television (TV) programs, music and films. There is certainly a case to be made that values are embedded in this media. For example, issues related to sex and homosexuality, which are commonly found in the US media, make people in the region critical of American cultural products. In the Persian Gulf, it is bad taste for such topics to be openly discussed. Regional governments try to exclude those programs from the media, ban harmful political messages and prevent people that watch satellite TV from being exposed.[21]

This viewpoint is in line with the political leadership in the region, who also present American media as a societal threat. General Ismael Ahmadi-Moghaddam,

---

18 (Abdullah) Abdulaziz Al Saud, "Speech by Abdullah Abdolaziz, the King of Saudi Arabia, at the Consultative of Saudi Arabia 3rd Term 2nd Year," Riyadh, 2001.

19 Tariq Khaddam Al-Fayez, "Speech by Tariq Khaddam Al-Fayez, Saudi Arabian Second Secretary in the UN, at the Second Committee, General Assembly – 64th Session, 'Globalization and Economic Independence,'" New York, 21 October, 2009.

20 Ibid.

21 Interview with Kuwaiti Professor on the Security in the Persian Gulf, June 2012.

the Iranian Head of the National Security Force, has made specific references to the threat posed by satellites bringing American media into Iranian society. In particular, he criticized youth exposure to criminal acts and violence portrayed in satellite programs. Consequently, he argued that people must be prevented from watching foreign satellite programs, recommending that Iranian culture should be promoted instead, through a greater variety of local TV programs. One of the commitments of the Iranian police forces is to limit access to satellite content. According to Ahmadi-Moghaddam, the measures taken to avoid exposure to American media have been effective.[22] Such viewpoints are common in the region. They support the notion that American media is perceived as a threat to the societal security of the regional societies.

To recall the securitizing move of Ayatollah Khamenei and King Abdullah, the Parliamentary Union of the Organization of Islamic Cooperation (PUOIC) and Islamic scholars serve as one audience, and have responded with a variety of actions. As previously discussed (see Section 3), audiences can be classified as either the general public, who provide moral and policy makers, or as political bodies and authority figures, who provide formal support for a securitizing move. PUOIC is in direct contact with representatives of member states and have offered formal support to the securitizing move of regional leaders as well as the adoption of extraordinary measures. These categories are notably flexible, as actors and audience can easily overlap.

PUOIC members include Kyrgyzstan, Chad, and the Persian Gulf countries, among others, and represent an important audience for securitizing moves in the Persian Gulf. The organization seeks to '[defend] of the true image of Islam' and '[the protection] of the interests of the Muslim world.'[23] Importantly, PUOIC calls for 'desisting from the imposition of any form of restrictions on cultural and religious rights in the era of globalization.'[24] Preserving the

---

22   Ismaeel Ahmadi-Moghaddam, "Remark by Ismaeel Ahmadi Moghaddam, Chief Policemen of Iran," in BBC Persian, 6 December, 2012. For more information on the threat of the US to the cultural identity of the regional nations, see also Sabet, *Islam and the Political*, 84–88.

23   Parliamentary Union of Organization of Islamic Cooperation Member States, "About the OIC." (2013) http://www.oic-oci.org/oicv2/page/?p_id=52&p_ref=26&lan=en, (Accessed 12/30/2013).

24   Parliamentary Union of Organization of Islamic Cooperation Member States, "Resolution No. 8-WSC/6-CONF on Promoting the Position of the Youth in the Islamic Countries," June 2010. http://www.puic.org/english/index.php?option=com_content&task=view&id=1396 &Itemid=0#Res8, retrieved 16.9.2010.

uniqueness of Islamic cultural identities and rejecting Americanism[25] continues to be one of the major points of concern for the PUOIC.

In addition to illuminating the societal threat of American-led globalization
in the region, the PUOIC also fears the effects of globalization on the youth
in Muslim countries, which is perceived as leading to a deeper penetration
of American influences.[26] The PUOIC has urged members of parliaments and
governments to establish centres devoted to curbing the American influence
among young people and preserving Muslim identity. The PUOIC was not
only formed as a reaction to increased American influences in Islamic societies; Islamic scholars – with overlapping roles as actors and audiences –
particularly in the GCC, states have also called for boycotts of American
products, which represents a spill-over of anti-American sentiment. For example, Yūsuf al-Qaraḍāwī, the Qatar-based chief religious scholar and the
chairman of *Islam Online*, saw the US-led globalization as 'the old imperialism
presented under a new name [...] to build a specific model.'[27] Furthermore, he
has stated that, in order to preserve Islamic identity in the region, the US threat
(and influence) must be removed from *their* societies.[28]

Al-Qaraḍāwī also encouraged the boycott of American products in the GCC
states in 2002, and later issued a fatwa in 2003 forbidding the advertising of
American goods.[29] Rawhi Abeidoh, a trading company manager in Dubai, has
acknowledged that the boycotts had the desired effect, while enabling the
public to demonstrate its anti-American beliefs. Several American fast-food
restaurants in Saudi Arabia were almost deserted during the boycott. The cam-
paigner for this initiative also 'boycotted US household items, vehicles, food
and beverages, and tobacco.'[30] Abeidoh also quoted Charley Kestenbaum, the
U.S. embassy's commercial officer in Saudi Arabia in 2000, 'The fact is that the
impact of the boycott is very significant [...] yes, we are concerned. But exactly

25   Farah Naaz, "Impact of Globalization on the GCC States, Cultural Dimension" in *Global-
      ization and the Changing Role of the States: Issues and Impacts*, ed. Basu, Ramki, (Randall,
      Berkshire and New Delhi: Sterling Publishers, 2008), 160, 163.

26   Mohamed El-Shibiny, *The Threat of Globalization to Arab Islamic Culture*. (Pittsburgh:
      Dorrance Publishing, 2005), 84.

27   Qaradawi quotes in Lynch, "Globalization and Arab Security" in *Globalization and Na-
      tional Security*, ed. Jonathan Kirshner. (New York: Routledge, 2006), 189.

28   For example, see Ivan Krastev, "The anti-Americanism Century," *Journal of Democracy*
      15/2 (2004): 8, 14.

29   For example, see Yusuf Qaradawi, Qatar-Based Chief Religious Scholar and the Chairman
      of Islam Online, Interview in Mecca, 30 April, 2002.

30   Rawhi Abeidoh, "Popular Boycott Hits U.S. Exports to Saudi Arabia." *Common Dreams*, 20
      June, 2002.

how big this impact is, very hard to determine without a detailed study.'[31] Islamist activists have also used mosques, cassette sermons and widely distributed books[32] to persuade the youth to preserve their cultural identity and encourage anti-American thinking.

> Globalization is a threat to identity in the [Persian Gulf region]. There is a fear that certain aspects of globalization, particularly the increasing dependency of Arab countries cultural sphere, will lead to social fragmentation, more negative effects on cultural character.[33]

It seems clear that while regional actors have enjoyed the economic benefits of the American-led globalization process, they have also felt threatened by political and socio-cultural encroachments by the US. In summary, the American-led globalization is perceived as a threat to the referent objects – regional states and their nations. Political authority figures have generally adopted the viewpoint that political reforms would prepare the ground for a partial loss of power. Increased demands for political reform during this period have been inextricably linked to the American-led globalization phenomenon, and thus the US, which pressured the GCC states to establish representative parliaments that would not only reduce elite political power, also cede it to Shia minorities. The spread of American culture in the region was thus characterized as presenting a threat to the Islamic social fabric.

Anti-American Sentiments in Iran since the 2003 Iraq War

Prior to the Iraq War, representatives of the Iranian government made considerable efforts to prevent the war. Iran feared that the US would install a client regime in Iraq, which would pose a strategic threat to the Iranian state. Put briefly, it was posited that, as an occupying force, the US would be positioned right at the western border of Iran.[34] Thus, while Iran had successfully neutralized the threat of Saddam, the US presence in Iraq represented a newer,

---

31   Kestenbaum quoted in Abeidoh, *Popular Boycott*, 2002.

32   Lynch, *Voices of Arab New Public*, 206.

33   Ahmad Shboul, "Islam and Globalization: Arab World Perspectives," in *Islamic Perspectives on the New Millennium*, ed. Virginia Hooker and Amin Saikal. (Singapore: ISEAS Publishing, Institute of Southeast Asian Studies, 2004), 56.

34   Kamran Taremi, "Iranian Foreign Policy Towards Occupied Iraq, 2003–2005." *Middle East Policies* 12/4 (2005): 33–35.

perhaps even more serious threat.[35] It is important to note that the Shia Iranian state represents the referent object. Given that the Iranian state characterized the American threat as not merely strategic, the Shia identity of Iran can also be treated as a referent object. In this context, it was characterized as such by an American interviewee, who noted,

> The US was not happy with Iran. During the Iran and Iraq War, our initial effort was to provide considerable assistance to Sunni Iraq in order to prevent the consolidation of the Shia Iranian state. In the 1980's, Saddam was also afraid of Shia Iran because of the Shia population in Iraq and Sunni minority being narrowly bunched together.[36]

Another American interviewee pointed to the direct American presence in the Persian Gulf since the Iraq War,

> What we have is the removal of one of the regional poles of Sunni power in Iraq, with Shia Iran benefiting in terms of relative power, and a very heavy American involvement during this period through the occupation of Iraq. The US is withdrawing from Iraq in 2011, but not from the region as a whole.[37]

From these excerpts, it is evident that American foreign policy was perceived as being primarily aimed at neutralizing the power of the Iranian state in the region. According to the Iranian leadership, however, the United States was viewed as not just a threat to Iran; given its status as the "protector" of Shia Islam, the American threat to Iran was also viewed as a threat to Shia Islam itself.

From the viewpoint of Iran, the United States has gradually become as an increasing threat. Indeed, at several points since 2003, military conflict between the two nations seemed likely. Yet, the possibility of war was not the only way for the US to threaten Iran. For example, the Bush administration exerted political pressure through its support of democratic reforms, which was viewed as an immediate threat to the state. The report by the American State Department on *Advancing Freedom and Democracy* describes the US's

---

35   Kayhan Barzegar, "The New Balance of Power: The Iranian Perspective." *Middle East Security Council* 17/3 (2010): 52–53.

36   Interview with American academic expert on the security in the Persian Gulf 12, July, 2012.

37   Interview with American academic expert on the security in the Persian Gulf 10, December, 2011.

efforts to support those pushing for democratic reforms in Iran.[38] According to Grace Nasri, many Iranian activists remain sceptical of the benefits of democracy. It is still very risky to openly campaign for reform. Activists allege that Iranian political leaders perceive them as agents and spies of the United States within Iran and many have been imprisoned following such accusations.[39] Nevertheless, funding pro-democracy groups has been one way in which the US threatens the Iranian establishment since the Iraq War. The threat of a possible US-led invasion has been prominent in Iranian public discourse since 2003.[40] According to Ali Yunesi, Minister of Intelligence during the 2000–2005 mandate, while the US possesses political and military means to attack Iran, it should keep in mind the experience of the Iraq War.[41] Abdullah Ramazanzadeh, the Iranian government spokesperson during the war, acknowledged the threat, but also argued that 'Iran has to adopt a policy that would prevent a war with the US.'[42]

Viewed in this way, for example, Akbar Hashemi Rafsanjani, the Expediency Council Chairman since 1989, sought to securitize the US by characterizing it as "a savage wolf." However, he has also stated that Iran's armed forces are the strongest forces in the region and can combat the American threat.[43] This widespread belief in Iran of a possible US attack persisted until an agreement was reached between Iran and the P5+1[44] in 2013 over its nuclear energy program. Mahmoud Ahmadinejad, then President of Iran, stated regarding the threat of the US,

> The United States and Israel seek world support for a military strike on Iran and warn against such attacks. We have been hearing such threats since the time [then US President George] Bush was in office.[45]

---

38   United States Department of State, Advancing Freedom and Democracy, 2008.

39   Grace Nasri, "Iran: Island of Stability or Land in turmoil," *Digest of Middle East Studies* 18/1 (2009): 64–66.

40   Taremi, *Iranian Foreign Policy*, 44.

41   Ali Yunesi, "Remark by Ali Yunesi, Former Minister of Intelligence of Iran," at *Jame Jam*, Tehran, 25 July, 2003.

42   Ramenzadeh quotes in Taremi, *Iranian Foreign Policy*, 39.

43   Ali Akbar Hashemi Rafsanjani, "Remark by Ali Akbar Hashemi Rafsanjani, the Expediency Council Chairman of Iran," in *Ettela'at*, International Persian Daily Newschapter. Tehran, 16 April, 2003. Almost all Iranian leaders perceive the US as a threat.

44   The five permanent members of the UN Security Council, together with Germany, (known collectively as the P5+1) have been negotiating with Iran since 2006.

45   Mahmoud Ahmadinejad, "Statement by Former President of Iran, Mahmoud Ahmainejad, in Tehran," 4 October, 2011.

Presently, Iran has the largest deployed ballistic force in the Middle East. Since 2006, Iran has demonstrated its ballistic capacity in four highly publicized exercises.[46] Beyond these advances, Iran has also developed medium-range ballistic missiles and continues to increase the range, lethality and accuracy of these systems.[47] While Iran has increased its military power as a response to the perceived US threat, former President Ahmadinejad, has characterized its military capabilities as primarily defensive, saying,

> Our military policy is based on deterrence. We never use our military strength to conquer lands. We want to prevent injustice and aggression. We would plan in a way [to destroy] the defensive equipment of enemies [at the starting point].[48]

Representatives of the state (see above) have repeatedly emphasized Iran's expected reaction to any possible US attack. Consequently, military expenditure escalated from $7,195 million in 2003 to $9,109 in 2004, $11,296 in 2005 and $12,233 in 2006.[49] As a result, security forces and the Revolutionary Guard bolstered their number of troops, and numerous military exercises have been performed in the Persian Gulf to demonstrate Iran's military power. These exercises have continued to the present day. The military exercise 'Velayat 90' [State 90], in December 2011, covered an area of 2,000 kilometres, from the Strait of Hormuz in the Persian Gulf to the Gulf of Aden, close to the Indian Ocean. The purpose of the exercise was to demonstrate Iran's newest military equipment and missile technologies. The possibility of a US attack on Iran was highly topical in Iran in the early aftermath of the Iraq War. The perception that war with the United States was possible led to a number of attempts by political figures to securitize the perceived threat to the Iranian state, and by extension, Shia Islam.

---

46   For example, see, Iranian Armed Force, "Offensive Pahbad with Capacity to Carry Missile and Bomb," 12 October, 2013. http://www.aja.ir/portal/Home/ShowPage.aspx?Objec t=News&CategoryID=b8789b0b-9886-4e12-94fb-8ecaaa0f102e&WebPartID=5f839c92-0f3f-44f6-b8e5-54f8133dd762&ID=ebfdad26-eb24-45fa-ac6a-09a0a08a4320,   (Accessed 11/1/2013); Ronald Burgess, "Report to Congress: Before the Senate Armed Services Committee on Iran's Military Power," 14 April, 2010. http://www.armed-services.senate.gov/ statemnt/2010/04%20April/Burgess%2004-14-10.pdf, (Accessed 10/12/2012).

47   Burgess, *Report to Congress*, 13.

48   Ahmadinejad, *Statement by Former President*.

49   Carina Solmirano and Pieter Wezeman, "SIPRI Factsheet: Military Spending and Arms Procurement in the Gulf States." (2010) http://books.sipri.org/files/FS/SIPRIFS1010.pdf, (Accessed 9/26/2013).

How did the Iraq War intensify anti-American sentiments within Iran? Anti-American sentiments could not only be found in the statements of Ayatollah Khamenei, representatives of the state and parliament, but also during Friday Sermons, a forum for religious leaders to address the faithful on recent political, social and economic issues in Iran and globally. Friday Sermons continue to be one of the key venues used by religious leaders and the Iranian public to present anti-American sentiments. Tehran's provisional Friday Sermons leaders, Ahmad Jannati and Ahmad Khatami, are strongly anti-American. Yet, their viewpoints appear only slightly different. Jannati emphasizes that anti-American sentiment in Iran does not pertain to personal disputes with the United States; rather, such views represent a fight to support the principles of the Islamic Revolution in Iran. He further elaborates on how the US continues to threaten Iran, both politically and militarily, because it fears Iran's power in the region. However, he claims that these threats have been ineffective.[50] In contrast, in a 2008 speech before the Parliamentary election, Khatami stated that Iranians with anti-American perspectives are preferred candidates for senior state positions and advised the public to vote for anti-American candidates in the parliamentary election.[51] The scholars Alidad Mafinezam and Aria Mehrabi describe the extent of such sentiment in Iran:

> Iran's government has been one of the most stridently anti-American anywhere in the world ... if Iran can be conceived to drop its anti-American posture this will send the signal to many countries that the US has flexibility and will-power to turn its relationship around even with one of the most hitherto anti-American states in the world.[52]

Anti-American Sentiments in the GCC States

An unintended consequence of the war in Iraq has been the regional rise of sectarian conflict between Shia and Sunni states. In other words, the Iraq War has widened the Shia-Sunni conflict. From the perspective of one Saudi Arabian interviewee,

---

50   For example, see Ahmad Jannati, "Remark by Ahmad Jannati, Tehran's Provisional Friday Prayers Leader," at *Fars News Agency of Iran*. Tehran, 24 August, 2007.

51   Ahmad Khatami, "Remark by Ahmad Khatami, Tehran's Provisional Friday Prayers Imam," at the *Fars News Agency of Iran*. Tehran, 8 March, 2008.

52   Alidad Mafinezam and Aria Mehrabi, *Iran and its Space among Nations*. (Westport: Praeger, 2008), XIV.

Leaders of the GCC states were not happy that they supported the US against Saddam during the Iraq War; however, Sunnis were marginalized in the new Iraqi government in the war's aftermath. Radical Wahhabis pushed some Arab people to Iraq to fight the US and some leaders of the GCC states expressed anti-American sentiment more forcefully as a means to put pressure on the US. *It is ironic that while GCC leaders are US allies, they support anti-Americanism in the media and are considered by the public as heroes of anti-American sentiment.*[53]

Leaders in the GCC states consider the United States as a threat to their Sunni identity. The GCC states and Sunni identity are treated as referent objects in this process. As such, GCC leaders consider themselves protectors of both national identities and collective Sunni identity. This understanding represents a modified application of the "Westphalian straitjacket." This further suggests that regional socio-political dynamics differ from those of Western democracies. While states in the Persian Gulf have historically played a prominent role in establishing stability within their territories, they have also reinforced and aggravated internal divisions. The GCC states practicing Sunni Islam promote the Sunni identity while marginalizing Shia minorities. The opposite is true in Iran and Iraq, which practice Shia Islam. This division has had a significant spill over effect in the region since 2003.

Leaders in the GCC states have argued that the war in Iraq has provided an opportunity for Iran to influence the internal politics of Iraq in new ways. This in turn has led to an increased conflict between Shias and Sunnis. These phenomena represent a societal threat to both the GCC states and Shia Iran and Iraq. In *The Telegraph* article, a daily newspaper in the United Kingdom, Toby Harden referenced the securitizing move of former King Abdullah in relation to the US-led war in Iraq and the ongoing Shia-Sunni conflict:

> King Abdullah states that the US-led Iraq War triggers a conflict between Sunni and Shia states across the region. Saudi Arabia fears that the US might take the side of the Shia, leaving Sunnis at the mercy of Shias intent on vengeance for decades of Sunni domination and oppression.[54]

One piece of purported evidence cited during the securitization process was the alleged use by US commanders in Iraq using covert contacts with a

---

53   Interview with Saudi Arabian Scholar and Think-Tank Expert on Saudi Arabian Political Affairs, January 2012. Emphasis added.

54   King Abdullah cited in Toby Harden, "We'll Arm Sunni Insurgents in Iraq, Say Saudis." *The Telegraph*, 14 December, 2006.

commander of Iran's *Quds Force* – a special unit of the army of the Guardian of the Islamic Revolution – to prevent attacks of Iranian militias in Iraq on US troops.[55] By reducing the threat of attacks on American troops in Iraq, Iran could reap the strategic benefits of having a politically and economically weak neighbour. A similar sentiment was expressed by Ḥamad bin ʿĪsā bin Salmān ʾĀl Ḥalīfah, the King of Bahrain. In 2004, he chaired the twenty-fifth session of the GCC Supreme Council, known as the "Zayed Summit." The Summit presented statements, resolutions and declarations by GCC member states regarding the situation in Iraq. While not directly referring to Iran, he nevertheless emphasized the need to avoid intervention in Iraq's internal affairs and invited 'other sides [Iran and the US] to follow the same principles.'[56]

Michael Eisentadt, Michael Knight and Ahmed Ali, in a publication of the Washington Institute for Near East Policy, have argued that the *Quds Force* has influenced Iraq through funding distributed by Iranian and Iraqi Shia agents. Funds were used to support political proxies in Iraq and contribute to the costs of operating political offices. Yet, as such financial contributions do not represent the totality of Iran's influence in Iraq, other forms of support by Iran to Shia groups also need to be examined. For example, in early 2004, the Quds Force supported covert Shia Iraqi organizations such as the *Badr* group. When the group abandoned the covert policy, Iran expanded its proxy support networks to include radical Shia figures such as Abu Mustafa Al-Sheibani and other radical figures from Muqtadā al-Ṣadr's *Mahdi Army* militia such as Ismail Al-Lami.[57]

Eisentadt, Knight and Ali suggest that the *Quds Force* has trained several thousand fighters through Shia militias to attack US troops.[58] Michael Gordon and Bernard Trainor (2012) cited highly classified American reports in June 2007, which referred to the problem of Iranian support for Shia militias. According to this account, covert discussions nevertheless took place between David Petraeus, the former Commanding General of the *Multi-National Force-Iraq*

---

55   Troops from Iran, other neighbouring states, the US and al-Qaeda participated in Iraq conflict for a wide variety of purposes.

56   Hamad Bin Eisa Al-Khalifa, "Statement by King of the Kingdom of Bahrain and Chairman of the 2004 session of the GCC Supreme Council, at the Closing Statement of the Twenty Fifth Session of the GCC Supreme Council (Zayed Summit)," Manamah, 21 December, 2009.

57   Michael Eisenstadt, Michael Knights, and Ahmed Ali. *Iran's Influence in Iraq Countering Tehran's Whole-of-Government Approach*. Policy Focus #111. (New York: The Washington Institute for Near East Policy, 2011), 7.

58   Ibid., 8.

(MNF-I), and Qasem Soleimani, the Commander of the Quds Force[59] regarding the proposed shelving of the Green Zone,[60] which was a frequent target for insurgents during the Iraq War.[61]

The war has had a profound effect on Iraqi society. According to, Fawzi Shobokshi, the permanent representative of Saudi Arabia to the UN, everyone was aware of the humanitarian harms and devastation that would be unleashed on Iraq as a result of the war.[62] He touched upon the ontological threat the war presented to the Iraqi public in general and Sunnis in particular. An Iraqi analyst interviewee further elaborated on this point:

> The situation of the Iraqi people in the eight years since the war is unpleasant. In the eyes of the people, it is now much worse than prior to 2003. There is an incredible amount of poverty, which has shattered the fabric of the society, and had led to prostitution, dishonesty and crime.[63]

Unemployment increased from 10.4 per cent in 2004[64] to 15 per cent in 2009 and 16 per cent in 2011. Poverty and disease continues to be instrumental in threatening the health and well-being of children.[65] Even prior to the war, the Iraqi public – specifically children – suffered from poverty as a result of economic sanctions imposed by the UN, which remained in effect for the duration of the Iraq War. While economic effects of the war have been devastating, there has also been a complete collapse of social and governmental institutions.

The threatened security of the Iraqi public in general and Sunnis in particular, and increasing conflicts between Shias and Sunnis in Iran and the GCC

---

59   Michael Gordon and Bernard E. Trainor, *The Endgame: The Inside Story of the Struggle for Iraq, from George W. Bush to Barack Obama.* (New York: Random House, 2012), 517–518.

60   Civilian ruling authorities of the US and UK, and the offices of US major companies are located in the Green Zone, the location of a number of Saddam's former strongholds (Global Security 2014).

61   Petraeus quoted in Gordon and Trainor, *The Endgame*, 518.

62   Farwaz Shobokshi, "Remark by the New Permanent Representative of Saudi Arabia in the United Nations at the 4726th Meeting of the Security Council," United Nations, 27 March, 2003.

63   Interview with Iraqi analyst on the security in the Persian Gulf 5, September 2011 and May 2012.

64   World Bank, "Unemployment in Iraq." 17 May, 2006. http://search.worldbank.org/data?qt erm=unemployment+in+iraq+&language=EN&format=html, (Accessed 8/20/2010).

65   United Nations International Children Emergency Fund, "UNICEF Humanitarian Action Update: Iraq." 17 February, 2009. http://www.unicef.org/infobycountry/files/IRAQ_HAU_17_February_2009.pdf, (Accessed 8/20/2010).

states, convinced primary audiences in the GCC states to accept King Abdullah's securitizing move (see above). The acceptance of the United States as an enemy is one possible explanation for increased levels of anti-American sentiment being expressed in the region.

How did the Iraq War intensify anti-American sentiments in the GCC states? Such views have been widely disseminated through state-sponsored news outlets such as *al-Jazeera* and *al-Arabiya*. Through these media, coverage of the war in Iraq, the misery of the Iraqi public and sectarian conflicts has been widely consumed and the views expressed largely embraced by the GCC publics.

In an analysis broadcast by *al-Jazeera*, the analyst Mortaza Hussain argued that the rise in anti-American sentiments in the GCC states and the wider region was closely linked to the US-led war in Iraq. Hussain compared the situation in the Persian Gulf with South Korea, in which the American presence led to widespread anti-American sentiment. He argued that the US initiated the war in Iraq, killed hundreds of thousands of people, occupied Iraq (in contrast to the widely held view in the US that the country was liberated) and stoked simmering sectarian tensions. A significant aspect of his conclusion was that the war in Iraq damaged the ability of the US to find sincere allies in the region.[66] Hussain is likely right and the GCC states do not see any contradiction in maintaining strong economic and political ties to the US while encouraging anti-American sentiments domestically.

In summary, the discussions presented thus far have elucidated how the perceived regional threat posed by the United States to Gulf states as well as Islamic identity has led to a rise in anti-American sentiment. Analyses also revealed how the US has threatened the security of the Iraqi public.[67] This perceived threat to the Sunni identity of the GCC and the Shia identities in Iran and Iraq provides a compelling explanation for the sharp rise in anti-American sentiment in the region since 2003. The basis for anti-Americanism in the post-Iraq War context differs substantially from that of previous periods.

Conclusion

The analyses presented in this chapter are aimed at exploring Shariati's viewpoints regarding the threat that the United States poses to Islamic identity. As was shown, this has given rise to the anti-American sentiments in Iran and the wider Persian Gulf region between 2000 and 2011. The findings reported

---

66   Murtaza Hussain, "The Roots of Global Anti-Americanism." *Al Jazeera*, 11 December, 2012.

67   Michael M. O'Brien, *American Failure in Iraq*. (Bloomington, IN: Author House Press, 2010), 7.

here are derived from a review of the existing studies and the *Regional Security Complex Theory*, specifically its securitization component. In this regard, it was shown that the regional leaders securitized the threat of the US to the referent object of the Islamic identity.

Addressing the main question of the article, the analysis has shown that the youth and their Islamic identity was the major concern of the regional leaders in relation to the threat to the regional societies. The threat to the youth is perceived to be exerted through the widespread usage of American technology, such as satellite television, which is seen as a promotion of a long-term shift to Americanization between 2000 and 2003. Although religious leaders use mosques and other religious places, as well as PUOIC conferences, to alert young people to this threat, modern technology continues to penetrate the region. For example, in Iran, exposure to violent programs on satellite television is one aspect of the perceived threat to the youth, which is linked to the recent increase in social crime. Hence, the securitization of American globalization and the reflection of anti-American attitudes are in line with decreasing this threat.

However, examination of the anti-American sentiments since the 2003 Iraq War has led to some counterintuitive findings. The harsh living conditions in Iraq are a source of great concern for the GCC public. This finding sheds light on the securitization of the American threat and the social aspect of security, Islamic identity in particular. When the analysis is extended to the regional states, it is evident that the Sunni members of the GCC states saw the falling of Saddam as a positive development. On the other hand, the isolation of the Sunni minority in Iraq has infuriated them, resulting in the rise of anti-American sentiment. Iranian leaders perceive the United States as a threat to the state and, because the state has a Shia identity, the threat is interpreted as directed at Islamic identity. At the most general level, the analysis reveals that, although the state actors in the region are not heterogeneous, they share anti-American sentiments.

The analysis also reveals that the American threat to Islamic identity in the Persian Gulf was evident in both analysed periods (2000–2003 and 2003–2011), as the Iraq War deepened the US's influence in the region, resulting in an increased threat to the Islamic identity of the states and societies in the region, which surpassed that caused by globalization. For example, while globalization had a significant influence on the Islamic identity of the youth in the region, the direct influence of the US in the region since the Iraq War has had much more profound consequences. While it threatened both Shia and Sunni identities of the regional states differently, it jeopardized the Islamic identity of the Iraqi public specifically.

According to this theoretical framework, as applied to the analyse of Shariati and the threat to Islamic identity, several directions must be explored simultaneously. Regarding the threat to the Islamic identity of the states and societies in the Persian Gulf, in the analyses performed here, the issue was presented as an identity threat and was thereby merged with the political existence argument. This approach was adopted as threatened states and societies in the region seek the support of their leaders, whom they deem responsible for defending their identity and securitizing the threat. Therefore, it can be concluded that securitization could be utilized to link the political and identity discussions, as these constitute *aggregate security* issues.

Although globalization and the 2003 Iraq War were clearly the catalysts for the rise of anti-American sentiments in the Persian Gulf region between 2000 and 2011, future research is required to examine other causes of growing anti-Americanism since 2012.

Bibliography

Abdulaziz Al-Saud, Abdullah. "Speech by Abdullah Abdolaziz, the King of Saudi Arabia, at the Consultative of Saudi Arabia 3rd Term 2nd Year," Riyadh, 2001.

Abeidoh, Rawhi. "Popular Boycott Hits U.S. Exports to Saudi Arabia." *Common Dreams*, 20 June, 2002.

Ahmadi-Moghaddam, Ismaeel. "Remark by Ismaeel Ahmadi Moghaddam, Chief Policemen of Iran," in BBC Persian, 6 December, 2012.

Ahmadinejad, Mahmoud. "Statement by Former President of Iran, Mahmoud Ahmainejad, in Tehran," 4 October, 2011.

Al-Fayez, Tariq Khaddam. "Speech by Tariq Khaddam Al-Fayez, Saudi Arabian Second Secretary in the UN, at the Second Committee, General Assembly – 64th Session, 'Globalization and Economic Independence,'" New York, 21 October, 2009.

Al-Khalifa, Hamad Bin Eisa. "Statement by King of the Kingdom of Bahrain and Chairman of the 2004 session of the GCC Supreme Council, at the Closing Statement of the Twenty Fifth Session of the GCC Supreme Council (Zayed Summit)," Manamah, 21 December, 2009.

Al-Zayani, Abdullatif bin Rashid. "Address by the Secretary General of the GCC, at the opening session of the Forum on Sustainable Development between the GCC Member States and the Republic of China organized by the Ministry of Foreign Affairs, the United Arab Emirates, in cooperation with the Emirates Center for Strategic Studies and Research," Abu Dhabi, 12 December, 2012.

Ayoob, Mohammed. "American Policy towards the Persian Gulf." In *International Politics of the Persian Gulf*, edited by Mehran Kamrava. 22–140. New York: Syracuse University Press, 2011.

Barzegar, Kayhan. "The New Balance of Power: The Iranian Perspective." *Middle East Security Council* 17/3 (2010): 74–87.

Burgess, Ronald. "Report to Congress: Before the Senate Armed Services Committee on Iran's Military Power," 14 April, 2010. http://www.armed-services.senate.gov/statemnt/2010/04%20April/Burgess%2004-14-10.pdf.

Buzan, Barry, Ole Wæver and Jaap de Wilde. *Security: A New Framework for Analysis.* Boulder, CO: Lynne Rienner, 1998.

Central Intelligence Agency. "Predicting the Soviet Invasion of Afghanistan: The Intelligence Community's Record." (2008). https://www.cia.gov/library/center -for-the-study-of-intelligence/csi-publications/books-and-monographs/predicting -the-soviet-invasion-of-afghanistan-the-intelligence-communitys-record/ predicting-the-soviet-invasion-of-afghanistan-the-intelligence-communitys -record.html#link12.

Clawson, Patrick. "The Paradox of Anti-Americanism in Iran," *Middle East Review of International Affairs* 8/1 (2004): 16–24.

Eisenstadt, Michael, Michael Knights, and Ahmed Ali. *Iran's Influence in Iraq.*

Eisenstadt, Michael, *Countering Tehran's Whole-of-Government Approach.* Policy Focus #111, New York: The Washington Institute for Near East Policy, 2011.

El-Shibiny, Mohamed. *The Threat of Globalization to Arab Islamic Culture.* Pittsburgh: Dorrance Publishing, 2005.

Global Security. "Green Zoon." (2014). http://www.globalsecurity.org/military/world/ iraq/baghdad-green-zone.htm.

Gordon, Michael and Bernard E. Trainor. *The Endgame: The Inside Story of the Struggle for Iraq, from George W. Bush to Barack Obama.* New York: Random House, 2012.

Gulf Cooperation Council. "Implementing procedures for the Custom Union of the GCC," 1 January, 2003, http://www.gcc-sg.org/eng/index9038.html?action=Sec-Show &ID=93.

Harden, Toby. "We'll Arm Sunni Insurgents in Iraq, Say Saudis." *The Telegraph*, 14 December. 2006.

Hussain, Murtaza. "The Roots of Global Anti-Americanism." *Al Jazeera*, 11 December, 2012.

Interview with American academic expert on the security in the Persian Gulf 12, July 2012.

Interview with American academic expert on the security in the Persian Gulf 10, December 2011.

Interview with Iraqi analyst on the security in the Persian Gulf 5, September 2011 and May 2012.

Interview with Kuwaiti professor on the security in the Persian Gulf, June 2012.

Interview with Saudi Arabian scholar and think-tank expert on Saudi Arabian political affairs 4, January 2012.

Iranian Armed Force. "Offensive Pahbad with Capacity to Carry Missile and Bomb," 12 October, 2013. http://www.aja.ir/portal/Home/ShowPage.aspx?Object=News&Cat

egoryID=b8789b0b-9886-4e12-94fb-8ecaaa0f102e&WebPartID=5f839c92-0f3f-44f6-b8e5-54f8133dd762&ID=ebfdad26-eb24-45fa-ac6a-09a0a08a4320.

Jannati, Ahmad. "Remark by Ahmad Jannati, Tehran's Provisional Friday Prayers Leader," at *Fars News Agency of Iran*. Tehran, 24 August, 2007.

Khamenei, Ali S. "Address by the Iranian Supreme Leader Ayatollah Ali Khamenei at the Opening Session of the Third International Conference on Quads and Support for the Palestine People," *Palestine Issue at the Focal Point*. 14 April, 2006.

Khamenei, Ali S. "Remark by Ayatollah Ali Khamenei to the Members and the Director of the Supreme Council of the Cultural Revolution in Tehran." 15 June, 2011.

Khomeini, Rouhollah "Speech by Ayatollah Rouhollah Khomeini, Former Supreme Leader of Iran, at the massive crowd of people in Jamaran," *Testament: The Current Message and the Future Generation*. Jamaran, 1982.

Khatami, Ahmad. "Remark by Ahmad Khatami, Tehran's Provisional Friday Prayers Imam," at the *Fars News Agency of Iran*. Tehran, 8 March, 2008.

Krastev, Ivan. "The anti-Americanism Century," *Journal of Democracy* 15/2 (2004): 5–16.

Lynch, Marc. *Voices of Arab New Public: Iraq, Al-Jazeera and Middle East today Politics*. New York: Colombia University Press, 2007.

Lynch, Marc. "Globalization and Arab Security." In *Globalization and National Security*. Edited by Jonathan Kirshner, 171–200. New York: Routledge, 2006.

Léonard, Sarah and Christian Kaunert. "Reconceptualizing the Audience in Securitization Theory" in *Securitization Theory: How Security Problems Emerge and Dissolve*, edited by Thierry Balzacq, 57–76. New York: Routledge, 2011.

Mafinezam, Alidad and Aria Mehrabi. *Iran and its Space among Nations*. Westport: Praeger, 2008.

Naaz, Farah. "Impact of Globalization on the GCC States, Cultural Dimension." In *Globalization and the Changing Role of the States: Issues and Impacts*, edited by Basu, Ramki, 156–170. Randall, Berkshire and New Delhi: Sterling Publishers, 2008.

Nasri, Grace. "Iran: Island of Stability or Land in turmoil," *Digest of Middle East Studies* 18/1 (2009): 57–73.

O'Brien, Michael M. *American Failure in Iraq*. Bloomington: Author House Press, 2010.

Sabet, Amr. *Islam and the Political: Theory, Governance, and International Relations*. London: Pluto Press, 2008.

Parliamentary Union of Organization of Islamic Cooperation Member States. "About the OIC." (2013) http://www.oic-oci.org/oicv2/page/?p_id=52&p_ref=26&lan=en.

Parliamentary Union of Organization of Islamic Cooperation Member States. "Resolution No. 8-WSC/6-CONF on Promoting the Position of the Youth in the Islamic Countries," June 2010. http://www.puic.org/english/index.php?option=com_content&task=view&id=1396&Itemid=0#Res8.

Peterson, J.E. "The Historical Pattern of Gulf security," in *Security in the Persian Gulf, Origins, Obstacles and the Search for the Consensus*, edited by Lawrence G. Potter and Gary G. Sick, 6–15. New York and Basingstoke: Palgrave, 2002.

Qaradawi, Yusuf. Qatar-Based Chief Religious Scholar and the Chairman of Islam Online, Interview in Mecca, 30 April, 2002.

Rafsanjani, Ali Akbar Hashemi. "Remark by Ali Akbar Hashemi Rafsanjani, the Expediency Council Chairman of Iran." In *Ettela'at*, International Persian Daily Newspaper. Tehran, 16 April, 2003.

Rubin, Barry. "The Real Root of Arab Anti-Americanism." *Foreign Affairs*, 81/6 (2002): 73–85.

Sabet, Amr. *Islam and the Political: Theory, Governance, and International Relations*. London: Pluto Press, 2008.

Sabet, Amr. "Religion, Politics and Social Change: A Theoretical Framework," *Religion, State and Society* 24/2–3 (1996): 241–268.

Shariati, Ali. "Expectations from Muslim Women." (1997). http://www.shariati.com/english/woman/woman3.html.

Shboul, Ahmad. "Islam and Globalization: Arab World Perspectives." In *Islamic Perspectives on the New Millennium*, edited by Virginia Hooker and Amin Saikal, 43–73. Singapore: ISEAS Publishing, Institute of Southeast Asian Studies, 2004.

Shobokshi, Fawaz. "Remark by the New Permanent Representative of Saudi Arabia in the United Nations at the 4726th Meeting of the Security Council," United Nations, 27 March, 2003.

Solmirano, Carina and Pieter d. Wezeman. "SIPRI Factsheet: Military Spending and Arms Procurement in the Gulf States." (2010) http://books.sipri.org/files/FS/SIPRIFS1010.pdf.

Taremi, Kamran. "Iranian Foreign Policy Towards Occupied Iraq, 2003–2005." *Middle East Policies* 12/4 (2005): 28–47.

Taremi, Kamran. "Iranian Perspective on Security in the Persian Gulf." *Iranian Studies* 36/3 (2003): 381–391.

United Nations International Children Emergency Fund. "UNICEF Humanitarian Action Update: Iraq." 17 February, 2009. http://www.unicef.org/infobycountry/files/IRAQ_HAU_17_February_2009.pdf.

United States Department of State. "Advancing Freedom and Democracy Report: Iran." (2008). http://www.state.gov/j/drl/rls/afdr/2008/nea/129900.htm.

World Bank. "Unemployment in Iraq." 17 May, 2006. http://search.worldbank.org/data?qterm=unemployment+in+iraq+&language=EN&format=html.

Wesley, Michael. "The Consequences of Anti-Americanism: Does It Matter?" In *Anti-Americanism: in the 21st Century (Volume 4)*, edited by O'Connor, Brendon and Martin Griffiths, 221–238. Oxford: Greenwood Press, 2007.

Yunesi, Ali. "Remark by Ali Yunesi, Former Minister of Intelligence of Iran," at *Jame Jam*, Tehran, 25 July, 2003.

CHAPTER 14

We and Shariati

M. Kürşad Atalar

Introduction

Ali Shariati is one of the most important figures in contemporary Muslim thought due to his unique ideas on Islam and Western philosophy, and his struggle against the colonial powers. For some, he is a man of "action," while for others he was just a "mystic." Some tend to define him as a "true scholar," while others prefer to label him an intellectual who was influenced by the contemporary philosophy of the West. So, who is Shariati and why is he important for us today? In order to give an answer to these questions, we should have a good grasp of the ideas and political stances of Shariati. In this article, I argue that Ali Shariati was a "responsible intellectual" and, in the strictest sense of the word, a "true scholar" who accurately identified the real problems of the Muslim World, and that his particular interest in Muhammad Iqbal stemmed from the fact that Iqbal was a man who epitomized similar "ideals" appropriate for the contemporary age.

Nonetheless, before doing this, it would be better to make a short "period analysis," due to the fact that there is a symbiotic relationship between the views of important thinkers and the historical conditions they find themselves in. There is no doubt that the more we know about the context of the thinker the better we can understand their views. With this in mind, we can easily say that both Iqbal and Shariati were influenced by the Muslim world's contemporary "encounter with the West." Although Iqbal lived in an earlier period of this encounter, the problems produced by it were generally the same in Shariati's life. Therefore, the diognoses and the analyses made by both Muslim "intellectuals" naturally resembled each other. Accordingly, before discussing the views of Iqbal and Shariati, it would be beneficial to analyze the Muslim-West encounter and interpret the various reactions that arose within the Muslim World.

Islam and the West

After centuries of regression and decline, Muslim societies finally hit bottom in the second half of the 19th century. The natural resources of Muslim lands were exploited by western colonial powers, and the heads of the Muslim governments were not able to muster a meaningful resistance. As for the 'ulamā', they often failed to properly fulfill their traditional roles specifically because their knowledge of Islam had eroded over time. Additionally, widespread ignorance among ordinary believers was rampant. Under these conditions, the Muslim world produced a variety of reactions, which we can categorize into three main groups. The first is an "adaptive" response, given by those who tried to *embrace* modernity or reconcile Islam with the West. This group may also be divided into two subgroups, the "secularists," who advocated westernization "from head to foot," and the "modernists," who searched for a way to *reconcile* Islam and the West.[1] The former did by no means justify its stance upon Islamic grounds, while the latter tried to justify its position by arguing that its aim was to update or "modernize" Islamic creeds. The second response came from the "rejectionists," who rejected attempts to justify colonial powers and thoroughly opposed any attempt to embrace modernity.[2] This group too can be divided into two subgroups: the "traditionalists," who totally rejected Western culture, and the "Islamists," who took a more "selective" stand on both western culture and the tradition.[3] The former rejected the main argument of the "adaptive" response precisely because they believed that the responsibility of the Muslims was to obey the *fatwas* of the *'ulamā'*. This was especially important since the gates of *ijtihād* had been closed for centuries. The latter asserted that the most effective solution to the problem is neither to embrace, nor reject, modernity and/or the tradition totally, but rather to embrace a "selective" or a "wise" attitude towards them.[4] According to this latter group, wisdom is the lost property of the faithful, and they have the right to pick it up wherever they find it.[5]

---

1   Ali Shariati, *Biz ve İkbal* (We and Iqbal), trans. Ergin Kılıçtutan. (Bir Yayıncılık, 1985), 70. The later group's primary aim was "Islamization" of modernity. According to Hamilton A.R. Gibb, the group is worthier of praise than the former one in terms of reaching the goal of "embracing" Western modernity (2006: 65).

2   In his well-known article on the typology of revivalists, William E. Shepard cites the name of Ayatullah Khomeini among the "rejectionist neo-traditionalists." (1987: 322).

3   The traditionalists defended the continuation of traditional institutions, schools of thoughts, sects and even religious creeds. They were generally practitioners of sufism and specialists in *'ilm al-Kalām* (theology). They are generally accused of avoiding new problems. Most of the figures that western analysts preferred to label "Islamists" as "Revivalists" belong to this group. Furthermore, it is generally accepted as the group that has a higher capacity to solve new problems that Muslims face in the modern age (Shepard, 1987: 325).

4   Hence, there is no problem, for many of them, to adapt western technology even though adopting its culture is definitely rejected (Yıldırım, 2013: 65).

5   This is also a well-known ḥadīth of the Prophet Muhammad. See *Sunan At-Tirmidhi*, 2687.

Therefore, the problem is not to reject or adapt modernity, but rather to recognize wisdom and know how to obtain it.[6] It may be argued that Iqbal and Shariati belonged to this latter group. Thus, a basic argument can be summarized as follows: (1) religion, specifically Islam, is essentially "political," (2) modernity is incompatible with Islam, (3) the tradition needs to be criticized, and (4) the method, i.e. strategy, must be compatible with the core principles of wisdom.[7]

Iqbal and Shariati have never been far away from "politics" even though each one has strong aesthetic and literary concerns. For instance, Iqbal participated to the talks between his country (then India) and Britain as an official representative, and was the first to advance the idea of Pakistan as a seperate Muslim state.[8] It is sometimes argued that he had nothing to do with "party politics," but this is because he was fully aware of what he was doing: he was trying to construct the ego i.e the strong personality, which he attempts to do in his classic work, *Reconstruction of Religious Thought in Islam*. As to Shariati, he spent his whole life struggling against western colonial powers and their local accomplice, ultimately sacrificing his life for this cause. This shows that both men approached politics in a similar way.[9] Additionally, Iqbal approached the tradition in a "selective" way and asserted that it needed to be criticized. In other ways, he was in search of a "synthesis" between western and Islamic culture.[10] However, this does not mean that he was trying to "justify" modernity. Instead, his aim was to acquire wisdom wherever he found it. This discerning approach

---

6   At this point, the group offers a solution for the whole *ummah*: "returning to the roots." It is the slogan that is embraced by all contemporary revivalist groups. Shariati explains in his book, *Öze Dönüş* (Returning to the Roots), in detail what we should understand by this phrase (2013: 26–35). According to him, "our roots" are not the traditions or perceptions of pre-Islamic ages but should be the Qur'ān and *Sunnah*.

7   Atalar, *Radical Islamism in Turkey*, 44–70.

8   Muhammed Han Kayani. *Felsefe, Siyaset ve Şiir Dünyasıyla İkbal* (Iqbal's Poetry, Politics and Philosophy) (Istanbul: İz Yayıncılık, 2002), 81. In the letter he wrote to Jinnah on 21 June 1937, he explains his idea as such: "A separate Muslim province, reformed on the lines I have suggested above, is the only course by which we can secure a peaceful India and save Muslims from the domination of Non-Muslims. Why should not the Muslims of North-West India and Bengal be considered as nations entitled to self-determination just as other nations in India and outside India are." www.allamaiqbal .com.

9   Shariati, *Biz ve İkbal*, 66–67.

10   M. Kürşad Atalar, *Çağdaş Müslüman Düşünce: Sembol Şahsiyetler* (Contemporary Muslim Thought: Symbolic Figures of Islamic Revivalism) (Pınar Yayınları, 2014), 56–57. See also *Reconstruction of Religious Thought in Islam*, www.allamaiqbal.com.

becomes apparent when he asserts that some concepts[11] and institutions of modernity are incompatible with Islamic principles. Consequently, Shariati too opposses the central concepts of modernity, which also becomes apparent in his criticism of Marxism, existantialism, democracy and other western fallacies.[12] Again, this does not mean that we should totally reject all wisdom of the West. Instead, we should take a wise approach to it and embrace some truths that humanity attained in modern age. Moreover, this is not at odds with Islamic principles but represents indeed a duty that Islam imposed upon Muslims.[13] Finally, both Iqbal and Shariati agree that there is an unbreakable connection between means and ends, and that such a method of discernment must be compatible with Islamic principles.[14] We see that their whole lives attest to their adherence to this principle.

Consequently, keeping the above in mind, we can say that both Iqbal and Shariati were among the "responsible intellectuals" or "enlightened thinkers" (*raushanfekran* in Farsi), who were sensitive to the problems of their times.[15] This is why each of them made an enormous effort to find solutions to the fundamental problems of their age, and this is why their solutions converged on the same principle, i.e. *tajdīd* (renewal) or Islamic "revivalism." Shariati gave particular attention to Iqbal's work because he was aware that Iqbal was not only a good example of Jamāl al-Dīn al-Afghānī's call to resurgence in the twentieth century, but also that Iqbal 'gave ideological consistency and power to his revolutionary uprising.'[16] Nonetheless, Iqbal and Shariati revealed some differences in their approaches, especially in their discourses, or "vocabulary," they used in defense of Islam. This is precisely because they lived at different times, different intellectual milieus and, to some extent, different political climates.[17] Therefore, similarities and differences between these two intellectuals are important, and we should not overlook them.

---

11   For example, he criticized "democracy" as being government by numbers and defined it as a political system for counting noses. (Schimmel, 2012: 114).

12   As is known, one of the well-known works of Shariati is *Marxism and Other Western Fallacies: An Islamic Critique.*

13   Shariati, *Biz ve İkbal,* 72.

14   Sayyid Qutb also emphasized the "principalist attitude" i.e. *minhaj an-nabawi,* as the best road to reach the goal (1980: 20).

15   According to Jean-Paul Sartre, an intellectual should put his skills "directly at the service of the masses." https://intlibecosoc.wordpress.com/2013/06/10/sartre-intellectual-responsibility-is-practical-action-oriented.

16   Shariati, *Biz ve İkbal,* 92.

17   According to Shariati, Islam is now (i.e. in his time) in an offensive position whereas it was in a defensive one in early years of the twentieth century (1985: 132). The intellectuals of a defensive position generally deploy an "apologetic" discourse.

Iqbal and Shariati

Ali Shariati is often recognized as one of the most influential figures in Contemporary Muslim Thought. He is a multi-faceted intellectual who wrote
authoritatively in many fields of social and Islamic sciences. In his various
works, he presented a complex mix of ideas ranging from Islamic radicalism
to mysticism, from Shi'ism to anti-imperialism. Unfortunately, this ecclecticity
caused confusion amongst his readers. Some of them have been left wondering
whether he had a clear system of thought, and while others brought individual
characteristics of his work to the forefront of important discussions. For example, he is, according to those who felt themselves akin to socialism, a "socialist,"
and to those who have strong ascetic concerns, he is a "mystic."[18] These types of
biased descriptions arise short of having a comprehensive view of him and his
ideas. Nevertheless, when we scrutinize his life carefully, having a closer look
at his speeches or writings, we can easily ascertain that there was one singular
characteristics that governed his life/work: being a "responsible intellectual."[19]
He was, in the full sense of the word, a *rushen fikr*[20] who tried to bear witness
to his age, an *alim*[21] who felt himself responsible to his people, to humanity,

18   Cesur, Ertuğrul Cesur, "Batıcılık ve Gericilik Karşısında 'Müslüman Sosyalist' Ali Şeriati"
      ("Muslim Socialist" Ali Shariati Versus Westernism and Reactionarism), in *Bilge Adam-
      lar*, Vol: 30, August (2010): 98–102; Abdollah Vakily, Abdollah, *Ali Shariati and Mystical
      Tradition of Islam*, Abdollah Vakily, unprinted M.A. Thesis, McGill University, Institute of
      Islamic Studies, 1991; David Zeidan, "Ali Şeriati: İslami Köktenci, Marksist İdeolog ve Sufi
      Mistik" (Ali Shariati: Islamic Fundamentalist, Marxist Ideologist and Sufi Mystic), *Bilge
      Adamlar*, Vol: 30, August (2010): 103.
19   Babak Rahimi, "The Rise of Shii Ideology in Pre-Revolutionary Iran," in *Militancy and
      Political Violence in Shiism*, ed. Assaf Moghadam. (Routhledge, London & NewYork, 2012),
      36, 47. See also *Kültür ve İdeoloji* (Culture and Ideology), trans. Orhan Bekin and Bir
      Yayıncılık, 1986: 143–149; *Öze Dönüş*, 76–83, 134–138; *What is To Be Done*, 13–22.
20   The Persian word comes from Arabic word *munawwar al-fikr*, which means "enlight-
      ened" person. But according to Farhang Rajaee, the editor of the book, *What is To
      Be Done*, Shariati attributes to it two different meanings. Sometimes he takes it to
      mean intellectual, but often he considers it to be the attribute of a "social prophet."
      (1986: 27).
21   The Arabic word means simply "the erudite" or "scholar." But according to two verses in
      the Qur'ān, an *"alim"* must be, at the same time, a "responsible intellectual." See Al-Fatir:
      28 (The erudite among His bondmen fear Allah alone) and Al-Jumu'ah:5 (The likeness of
      those who are entrusted with the Law of Moses, yet apply it not, is as the likeness of the
      ass carrying books.).

and above all, to God, the True. And it is generally agreed that he was the "ideo-logue of the Iranian Revolution."[22]

This may be accepted as an accurate description in the sense that he be-lieved that revolutionary ideology is the main tool by which a society can be mobilized and that his passionate ideals had a strong impact on the educated strata of Iranian society, especially on youth.[23] He asserted that every individ-ual had a duty to choose a consciousness-producing ideology through which to change the status quo. As a "responsible" and enlightened member of his society, he tried to do his part. In this sense, he was really an "ideologue," feel-ing himself responsible to "change the world" relative to his ideals, not only in writing on sociology but also in giving speeches on Shi'ism.[24] He is likewise a "responsible intellectual," not only because he wrote about Islamic history, but also because of his work on mysticism. He was both an "ideologue" and a "responsible intellectual" not only in struggling against capitalist exploitation but also in his criticism of the "tradition" itself. That is why he lectured and wrote enthusiastically on many branches of knowledge and on different fields of social and Islamic sciences. What he was trying to do was nothing short of creating awaneress among Iranians and the Muslim *ummah* at large.[25] In doing this, he aimed at "awakening" those who were asleep and/or dead to the world.[26] To him, the Muslim World was in a miserable condition, and as a responsible intellectual who was well aware of this fact, there was no other way to choose except the difficult path i.e. to be a "gadfly" in a Socratic sense.[27] He believed, similar to Iqbal that the real solution to the problems faced in the contemporary age was to awaken people and show them the reality of their condition. He did this by raising their consciousness, molded out of "pain,"

---

22   Ervand Abrahamian, "Ali Shariati: Ideologue of Iranian Revolution," in *Islam, Politics and Social Movements*, eds. Edmund Burke and Ira Lapidus. Los Angeles: University of California Press, 1993.

23   Ali Shariati, *What is To Be Done,* ed. Farhang Rajaee. (Houston, TX: The Institute for Research and Islamic Studies, 1986b), 17.

24   Editor's note: Here, the term "ideologue" is being used in a way that is similar to "theorist" or "intellectual," as opposed to a "blind advocate," which often carries a negative connota-tion in English.

25   For this reasons, we can not call him a typical "academic" in spite of the fact that he taught at Mashhad University.

26   Ali Shariati, *Kendini Devrimci Yetiştirmek* (The Education of a Revolutionary – Persian, Hûdsâzî Enqilâbî), trans. Hicabi Kırlangıç and Derya Örs. (Fecr Yayınları, 2012), 68.

27   See Plato's *Apology of Socrates,* http://www.sjsu.edu/people/james.lindahl/courses/Phil 70A/s3/apology.pdf.

"love" and "action."[28] In his opinion, the one who did not fret about the pains or problems of the people and had no heart to take action to solve them, especially in a time where colonialism and capitalist exploitation prevailed, and obscurantism was at a premium, can not be considered an "intellectual" or "scholar." Indeed, he tried to propose a "solution" to Iran's problems when he cited in his books and speeches the names of Ali, Hussain and Abū Dhar, from the Era of Bliss, and Iqbal and Afghānī from the contemporary age, as good examples of "true Muslims." In sum, the solution was, for him, knowledge of both the Islamic tradition and modernity, that is to say, to have a good grasp of Islam and the West.[29]

Here lies the "originality" of Shariati: Unlike many Muslim scholars and intellectuals in his time, including some well-known Muslim revivalists, he noticed that we, as Muslims, cannot find appropriate solutions to the problems of *ummah* unless we have a sufficient grasp on western thought i.e. modernity.[30] That is why he put a tremendous emphasis on *Husayniyah Irshad*.[31] He did not not see this institution as a *madrasa*, a place where classical learning and studying takes place. Instead, he looked upon it as a center of learning in which he could express himself and his ideas freely, i.e. a place where his revolutionary ideology could be produced. As such, he tried to protect it with might and main.[32] Additionally, he showed a "special interest" in Iqbal on the same ground, thinking that it was Iqbal who recognized the very importance of the matter before him. For instance, when he points to Iqbal as an exemplary character in response to the question, "how would we become a 'true Muslim' in our age," he was, indeed, describing himself, or in another saying, unfolding what he was trying to do. In fact, he wanted to be like Iqbal, thus seeing his own image in him. Hence, he too recognized and believed that the *ummah* could

---

28   Shariati, *Biz ve İkbal,* 111.

29   Ibid., 64–68.

30   For instance, Sayyid Quṭb and Abu'l A'la al-Mawdūdī, who are held as two important figures in Contemporary Muslim Thought, took a close interest in modernity, but their books do not have as much depth or details as Shariati's works in respect to the West. See Atalar, 2014: 85–108, 139–164.

31   Editor's Note: Husayniyahs are religious centers for the commemoration of Husayn's martyrdom.

32   The emotional phrases appearing in the letter (25th November 1971) he wrote to his father when teaching in Husayniyah Irshad proves this very well. He states, in a sentimental tone, that he would bury everything he had, including his whole life, his wife, his children and even his body, if needed, in the base of this institution so as to make it more powerful! (Shariati, 2010, p. 146). When we look at the detailed "practical plan" he prepared for Husayniah Irshad, we can also easily see how much he cared about it (See 1986b: 103–160).

defeat and/or triumph over the West's hegemony 'only if we have a good grasp of it.'[33]

The sense of moral responsibility we witness in both Iqbal and Shariati is not merely rooted in their stated objectives of putting an end to capitalist exploitation and raising the awareness of *ummah*. Rather, they are two like-minded men, both wholeheartedly "seeking truth." We can rightly say that all "symbolic figures" of Islamic revivalism in the contemporary age had such moral responsibility.[34] All of them were ready to sacrifice their lives for the sake of the Truth. They could not stand injustice, and for this very reason they struggled against colonialism or capitalist exploitation. However, they are, above all, "lovers of the Truth."[35] Even if they were at war with western modernity, they were, at the same time, open to any idea or thought deserving to be called "wisdom." This is what Iqbal did when he proposed to "reconcile religion with reason,"[36] and this is what Shariati did when he mentioned in glowing terms those western scholars whom he benefited from.[37] This sensitivity should be distinguished from the "mimetic attitude" ascribed to Muslim modernists.[38] The former loves the

---

33   Shariati, *Biz ve İkbal,* 64.

34   I define "symbolic figure" as a person or a scholar who symbolizes a specific idea or a stance best. To me, there are 12 "symbolic figures" in the history of Contemporary Muslim Thought. They are as follows: Jamāl al-Dīn al-Afghānī, Muhammad Abduh, Muhammed Iqbal, Ayatullah Khomeini, Abu'l-A'la al-Mawdūdī, Malik bin Nabi, Sayyid Quṭb, Ḥasan al-Bannā', Aliya Izzetbegovic, Malcolm x, Ali Shariati and Ercümend Özkan. See Atalar, 2014. We can cite the name of Malcolm x as the best example of how Islam has a great "transforming power" in the modern period, while Shariati symbolizes a responsible Muslim intellectual who put an emphasis on the fact that Muslims should have a good grasp of the West in order to overcome it.

35   The level of sincerity in the hearts of the lovers of truth is so high that they do not refrain from confessing their faults. For example, Shariati confesses, in his book, *Aşina Yüzlerle* (2010: 237), that he committed no sin in his whole life except the one regarding a conditional sale.

36   In the preface of his classical book, *Reconstruction*, Iqbal states that, "the day is not far off when religion and science may discover unsuspected mutual harmonies." www.allamaiqbal.com.

37   Most notables among them are Louis Massignon, Jean-Paul Sartre, Georges Gurvitch and Jacques Berque. He refers to Jean-Paul Sartre and Gurvitch as those "who thought him how to think," while he confessed that Massignon exerted a powerful spiritual influence on his soul. See Shariati, 2012b, 293.

38   By the term "Muslim modernists," I mean those who advocate some sort of accommodationist approach, attempting to reconcile Islam with modernity by using an "apologetic" discourse. Among its leading figures are Fazlur Rahman, Nasr Hamed Abu Zayd, Hassan Hanafi, Muhammad Arkoun and Muhammad Abid al-Jabiri. Indeed, what al-Fārābī,

truth for truth's sake, while the latter simply "imitates" and "admires."[39] What matters most to the lovers of truth is to pay their "debt" to the Truth, not to make a gesture of admiration toward those whom they think they are indebted to. In addition, since the truth is the most valuable thing, they put up a lifelong struggle against falsehood and injustice.

These are the main traits that make Iqbal and Shariati important in Contemporary Muslim Thought. However, there are other significant traits that they have in common. For example, Iqbal is, at the same time, a prominent poet. But poetry, for him, is not an "end" in itself, but rather a "means" to an "end." He is among the proponents of the credo "art for society's sake," and criticized the poets who defended the notion of "art for art's sake."[40] His art is in the service of his faith. Likewise, Shariati too had strong aesthetic and inner spritiual concerns.[41] Such concerns appear in all of his works. But he, as a responsible intellectual, also believed that the highest priority should be given to the problems of his society and the broader Muslim *ummah*. Iqbal and Shariati also share a "method" by which they ascertain the Truth. They both assert that Muslims should fight against colonialism or any form of falsehood by observing Islamic principles and/or moral norms. Both rejected the notion of "ends justifies the means," and thus rejected to use, for instance, of violence to reach a goal.[42] They also abstained from "party politics" because they believed that it was not Islamically justifiable. Instead, they maintained that the real intention behind their activism was aimed at strengthening the "individual," i.e. *merd-i mu'min,* before joining a political party or some kind of an organizational structure. For this very reason, both preferred to stay clear of partaking in political parties or organizational structures, even though they actively took part in the national struggle.[43]

In sum, Iqbal and Shariati can be considered two important figures in Contemporary Muslim Thought who added fuel to the fire of "revival" (*tajdīd*), which was first lit by Jamāl al-Dīn al-Afghānī. Sayyid Jamāl recommended

---

Ibn-Sīnā and Ibn Rushd tried to do in classical age was not so different from what they did in the contemporary. See Atalar, 2013: 538–549.

39   Aristotle may be called a "lover of truth" because he said, "Plato is my friend, but Truth is my better friend!" https://en.wikipedia.org/wiki/Amicus_Plato,_sed_magis_amica_veritas.

40   Shariati, *Biz ve İkbal,* 70. The national poet of Turkey, Mehmet Akif, had a similar idea regarding the matter too. See Şimşek, 2015: 105–120.

41   See *Aşina Yüzlerle,* p. 67. He also says that if the proper conditions existed in Iran he would be a poet or a literary man. (Ibid., 86).

42   Ali Rahnema, *An Islamic Utopion: A Political Biography of Ali Sharīati,* New York: I.B. Tauris Publishers, 1998), 262.

43   The term *merd-i mu'min* was used by Iqbal refers to the "perfect faithful." (Schimmel, 2012: 69; Faruki, 1970: 119–137); See Shariati, 2012: 34, 53; 1985: 95.

to the Muslim *ummah* to "return to our roots," and thought that Pan-Islamic "Unity" was necessary in order to reach this goal. Iqbal too pursued the same goal in his country. However, there is a significant difference in what strategy should be used when achieving the stated goals of these two revivalists. Iqbal realized that self-formation, or the strengthening of the "self," takes priority over the unity of the Muslim *ummah*, and therefore he tried to reconstruct religious thought first. He strongly emphasized that this endeavour would shape the future of the Muslims. While opposing colonialism and attempting to strike a balance between the Shia and Sunnis, Shariati also pursued this goal. Additionally, he was well aware of the pressing need to cultivate a "revolution in mind." In other words, the ways in which Muslims thought had to be transformed before they could transform the world.[44] His attacks on "traditional" or "Black" Shi'ism should be understood within this revivalist context. He criticizes it intentionally because he believed that such criticism of clerical traditionism would play an important role in the future of the revivalist movement.[45]

Nevertheless, there is one more thing, as I have demonstrated; Iqbal and Shariati have similar ideas and similar sentiments with regard to the problems of *ummah*. However, Shariati has a remarkable trait that does not exist equally in Iqbal. Although Iqbal was his source of inspiration, Shariati excelled him in "competence."[46] He knew the West better than Iqbal and his critique of Western Thought was more comprehensive and destructive.[47] That is why his ideas had a greater impact on the intellectuals and educated strata of his society. From this point of view, we may fairly argue that Shariati is the most prominent Muslim intellectual of the contemporary age, representing the "peak point" in Contemporary Muslim Thought. In order to explore more fully what I mean, it would be better to compare him with a well-known historical figure in Islamic history, Imam al-Ghazālī, whose main intellectual traits and cares seem to resemble him in many ways.

Al-Ghazālī and Shariati

As we know, al-Ghazālī was a prominent Muslim scholar in the classical age of Islam. He was keenly interested in all branches of knowledge and represented

---

44   Shariati, *Biz ve İkbal,* 20, 141.

45   See Shariati, 2010: 20, 31, 166; Also Shariati, 1990: 45, 119, 128, 135; Shariati, *Biz ve İkbal,* 62; Shariati, *Aşina Yüzlerle,* 29, 34; Shariati, *Kendini Devrimci Yetiştirmek,* 29.

46   Likewise, Abu Hanifah excelled past his teacher, Hammad ibn Abu Sulaiman, and Aristotle excelled his master, Plato.

47   This is my humble opinion.

the peak of learning in Classical Muslim Thought. Similar to Shariati, he was a multi-faceted individual who contributed to many disciplines.[48] For some, he was a mystic; for others, he was a philosopher. However, to me, he was, above all, a "responsible intellectual" and a "truth seeker," just like Shariati.[49] It is true that he harshly criticized the philosophers, but we should remember that he did it consciously and decisively. He noticed that Greek thought had negatively affected the minds of people and had cast doubt on the reliability of the Muslim scholars. Accordingly, he set about solving the problem, writing his classic text, *Tahafut al-Falasifah* (*The Incoherence of the Philosophers*), a book in which he tried to demonstrate the inconsistency of the philosophers, and eventually charging them with infidelity. He did this because he was aware that the problems that philosophers brought to the forefront could no longer be considered merely "theoretical," they had been transformed into "social" problems. Thus, as a "responsible intellectual," he addressed such issues by writing his *Maqasid* (Aims of the Philosophers) and *Tahafut*, which solved the philosophers' issues effectively. This is precisely what Shariati tried to do when he criticized western thought in the modern age. He too realized that western thought affected the minds of Muslims negatively and the traditional Islamic scholars failed to respond adequately. For Shariati, what the *ummah* needed was for someone to clearly demonstrate the inherent fallacies within modern western ideologies from an authentic Islamic point-of-view. Consequently, this required one to have a good grasp of the West and Islam.

The common point between al-Ghazālī and Shariati is that for each one of them, what is to be done when the *ummah* faces an "external" ideological challenge is first to have a good grasp of it, and then to give an effective response to it.[50] That is why both intellectuals are believed to have reached the highest intellectual position for their times. Al-Ghazālī found all Muslim scholars, including the theologians, in his time insufficient in their responses to the

---

48   Al-Ghazālī wrote authoritatively in four main fields of Islamic sciences: theology, juris-
      prudence, philosophy and sufism. His works were so influential that he was awarded
      by his contemporaries the honorific title *"Hujjat al-Islam"* i.e. Proof of Islam. For many
      Muslims even today, he is a *mujaddīd*, a renewer of the faith. Furthermore, some west-
      ern commentors argue that he is the "single most influential Muslim" after the Prophet
      Muhammad (Watt, 1953).

49   In his *Dalaletten Kurtuluş* (Deliverance from Error – *Al-Munqidh*) he clearly explains what
      he was seeking during his whole life. This is, in his own terms, "the Truth." Even when he
      headed towards mysticism, he was indeed seeking the Truth (al-Ghazālī in Kaya, 2003),
      341–356.

50   Shariati declares this aim in his book, *Biz ve İkbal* (1985: 64) and al-Ghazālī wrote about it
      explicitly in his autobiography, *Al-Munqidh*. (in Kaya, 2003), 348.

challenge coming from Greek thought. His criterion was to "understand the books written by philosophers better than their writers."[51] He was well aware that a Muslim scholar needed to know the arguments of the philosophers in detail in order to triumph over them. This is the most important trait that distinguishes al-Ghazālī from the other theologians of his time. This is why his important treatise, *Al-Tahafut,* became one of the most influential texts in the history of Islamic thought. Likewise, Shariati attempted to do the same in the modern period. He thought that a responsible intellectual should have a good grasp of the West, i.e. should understand the books written by western philosophers better than their writers should in order to respond the challenge.[52] That is why Shariati represents the culminating point of an ongoing ideological struggle waged by Muslim scholars against western thought. Because he strained every nerve in his attempt to understand the West thoroughly, he had the greatest degree of influence over the prevailing intellectual circles in Iranian society. Here, Jean-Paul Sartre's words can be cited as evidence: According to some sources, Sartre, a French existantialist philosopher, said, "I have no religion, but if I were to choose one, it would be Shariati's."[53] It must be noted here that such words signal a hard fact: Shariati duly performed his duty, as was done by al-Ghazālī in the classcial age of Islam.[54] As we know, al-Ghazālī is generally charged with "killing science in Islam," but this accusation also reflects his success in fighting the philosophers. Thus, this is the very point to which we must pay close attention. For sure, al-Ghazālī manage to criticize the philosophers competently, and after him Greek philosophy held little temptation for the Muslim masses, and consequently lost what appeal it already had accumulated with Muslim intellectuals. Even though Ibn Rushd (Averroes) later held firm in his defense of philosophy in his book *Tahafut al-Tahafut* (Incoherence of the Incoherence), his apology too fell short.[55] Likewise, we may fairly consider Sartre's words as evidence of Shariati's success in his intellectual

---

51   Al-Ghazālī in Muhammad Han Kayani, *Felsefe, Siyaset ve Şiir Dünyasıyla* İkbal (Iqbal's Poetry, Politics and Philosophy) (Istanbul: İz Yayıncılık, 2002), 348.

52   See *Biz ve İkbal,* 1985: 23, 106; and *Aşina Yüzlerle,* 2010: 156.

53   See, www.pbs.org/wgbh/pages/frontline/tehranbureau.

54   A similar assesment was done by Subqi, a Shafii scholar, regarding al-Ghazālī. For him, 'if there had been a prophet after Muhammad, al-Ghazālī would have been the man!' See *Tabaqat al-Shafi'iyyah al-Kubra,* Imam Subqi, Cairo, 1324/1906, Vol. IV, p. 101.

55   For example, Mustafa Muslihiddin Bursavi (Khocazade) and Ali Kushji, who are both prominent scholars of the Ottoman period, made a comparision between the *Tahafut's* of al-Ghazālī and Averroes, and mostly acknowledged al-Ghazālī to be correct. See Dölek, 2010: 206.

struggle waged against western thought since they were spoken by a "philosopher" who was among the most influential thinkers in the modern age.

It must be noted here that there is another point in Sartre's words that is usually overlooked. If we look closely, we can see that Sartre "has still no religion." The question we need to ask here is: "why did he not convert to Islam if he was highly influenced by Shariati's religion?" Of course, it may be said that proselytism is a matter of individual choice. However, to me, there is one more thing. We know – and should acknowledge – that Shariati duly performed his duty as a responsible intellectual, but we should also accept that his performance did not suffice to make Sartre a Muslim. Why? Did Sartre act without any reasonable cause in rejecting Islam or did he have a "good reason"? Was it because he found some faults with Shariati's arguments or because he was the victim of his own faulty thinking? Obviously, questions like these may be answered from different perspectives, but if we want to find the "real" answer, we should first, in my opinion, take the "level of knowledge" Muslims reached in this age into consideration, rather than focusing on personal traits or faults. When we measure the Muslims' performance correctly on this matter, we must acknowledge that Contemporary Muslim Thought has evolved into a much more robust ideology with the contributions of Sayyid Quṭb, Abu'l A'la al-Mawdūdī and Ali Shariati, but this is still not enough to "change the world."[56] In other words, it is clearly understood that the "total sum of knowledge" Muslim intellectuals produced in the recent age may perhaps be enough to convert people to Islam on an individual basis, but is not sufficient to win the hearts and minds of people on a global scale. Therefore, the question we should ask here should be 'what is the reason behind this incompetence?' In order to find a plausible answer to this "hot" question, I would like to explain first what I mean when I argue that we should interpret correctly the great wealth of Shariati's legacy that he left us.

"We and Shariati"

First, it should be understood that that title "We and Shariati" is an allegory, and I will use it to express a certain opinion. I can explain this by taking inspiration form the book that Shariati wrote about Iqbal. As is known, the book is entitled *Ma va Iqbal* (We and Iqbal), and it appears that Shariati did it for a

---

56   We see the same implication in Mawdudi's book, *Come Let Us Change the World* (trans. Kaukab Siddique, Washington: The Islamic Party of North America, 1972), but we know that he could not reach the goal, at least to the extent that he wanted to.

specific reason. This can be approached from two particular standpoints. First, we know that the term "we" here corresponds to "Easterners" and "Muslims," and that this implication is directly related to the problem of "identity." For Shariati, "we" are "Easterners" in terms of appreciating spiritual values instead of materialist ones, and "Muslims" in terms of belonging to Islam instead of western ideologies.[57] By naming the book *Ma va Iqbal*, it appears that he wanted deliver a message to Easterners, which can be summarized as follows: only Easterners and Muslims have the potential to resist colonialism and only Islam has the ideological robustness to triumph over western modernity.[58] Second, it is apparent that adding Iqbal's name to the title of the book was deliberate, and meant to send a message. By doing this, he implied that, we, as "Muslims" or "Easterners," must follow the path of Iqbal, for the very reason that it is he who showed us what we should do in the contemporary age.[59] At this very point, I can explain why I named this chapter "We and Shariati." In my opinion, we, as Muslims and Easterners, should make a "situation assessment" once again and try to define "the stage" we have reached at the present time. There is no doubt that today we no longer have a "problem of identity," which our Muslim ancestors had a century ago. Fortunately, we do not need to ask ourselves anymore the question of who we are. We are now well aware that we are "Muslims" and that only Muslims can verily resist and overcome western modernity. However, I think we have something to do with the question of "what should we do?" As is known, people of the world are still being exploited by western powers, and "falsehood" prevails all over the world. It seems that only Muslims can put an end to this, but they seem to be unprepared to take on this difficult task, precisely because they have failed, first of all, to reach the level of knowledge needed to transform Contemporary Muslim Thought into an "ideology of the future."[60] Although it has showed marked improvement, and has evolved into a more robust ideology, especially after the second half of the twentieth century with the contributions of the "trio" of responsible intellectuals i.e. Sayyid Quṭb, Abu'l- A'la al-Mawdūdī and Ali Shariati, it has not yet become an ideology that could win the hearts or minds of people on a global scale. This means that we, as Muslims, still can not reach the goal of "changing the world." The main reason for this is, to me, the *ummah's* incompetence in the sphere of ideology.

---

57   Shariati, *Biz ve İkbal,* 80, 96.

58   Ibid., 93.

59   Here Iqbal is described as a responsible intellectual who is a "witness to his age." (Ibid., 91).

60   Editor's note: the word "ideology" is used here not in the Marxian sense of "false con-
      sciousness" or "false appearances," but rather as a system of ideas, principles, values and
      ideals upon which a political, economic, social and cultural theory is based.

In other words, our knowledge is not sufficient to achieve our ultimate goal. That is why we cannot yet win ideological combat with the West. Having titled this chapter "We and Shariati," I wanted to draw attention to this particular point and argue that we should discuss not only the achievements of Contemporary Muslim Thought but also our "loose ends." To clarify, we should engage in a "situation assesment" once again and ask ourselves at this stage the same question Shariati asked of himself, "what is to be done?"

What is to be Done?

There is no doubt that Shariati, like many other intellectuals or revolutionaries of our age, asked himself this question and answered it competently from his own standpoint.[61] However, we should acknowledge that all the answers given by Muslim intellectuals in the modern period, including Shariati, were not perfect, as Sartre implied in regard to Shariati's religion.[62] In order to give a perfect or "satisfying" answer to this question, we should "systematize" the thought.[63] There is little doubt that Muslim Thought has covered a lot of ground since Jamāl al-Dīn al-Afghānī lit the fire of revival. Although it was, at least in the beginning, a defensive position, and had an "apologetic" discourse, it has evolved into a robust ideology and has hence developed an offensive position over time. Nonetheless, many groups and movements have taken up reactionary positions, which has inevitably led many Muslims to make indefensible mistakes. Of course, there were powerful forces that caused them to do this. Muslims wanted to form "Islamic movements" in order to regain the political power that was lost after the collapse of Ottoman Empire, the last Muslim state of the 20th century. This can be argued as a natural reaction to

---

61   Vladimir Ilyich Lenin is among them. He also wrote a book named *What is to Be Done,* in which he argued that only a vanguard revolutionary party can reach the ultimate aims of socialism. See www.marxists.org.

62   We can pose this argument by considering the verse (*Bani İsrail*: 81) 'Truth hath come, and Falsehood hath vanished away. Lo, Falsehood is ever bound to vanish.' Therefore, if falsehood prevails, this means that the Truth did not, in fact, come there. So the claim of those who argue that they are the true agents or inviters of the cause of the Truth in that period can not be regarded as valid.

63   "Systematization of the thought" means the systematic formulation of a set of ideas, which can be seen as a common feature in all schools of thought. As such, basic concepts are clearly defined and firmly interrelated with secondary ones, and thereby the task of conceptual coherence is done successfully. For details, see www.dusunceninokullasmasi .com.

the catastrophes that happened to the Muslim world in the modern period.[64] But the important point which we should pay close attention to is that these movements were founded in a time of "total collapse," in which intellectual and scholarly activities reached rock bottom. The traditional educational system had already collapsed, and the modern school system was in service to the non-Islamic ideas that had already disseminated throughout the whole Muslim world. Under such circumstances, newly founded organizations would naturally – and necessarily – have problems or ideological shortcomings. In order to meet the urgent need, these movements gave priority to the seizure of political power, and accordingly did not attached much importance to a "revolution of the mind." As a result, they failed, in my opinion, to reach their ultimate goal, even though they succeeded in regaining political power in some regions of Muslim world. Of course, seizure of political power is of great value in meeting particular needs of Muslims, but in determining a more affective strategy, we should give greater importance to the order of priority. First, we are to lay our Islamic foundation firmly, and then build the house. The failure to prioritize the foundation has been the *ummah's* biggest weakness in the contemporary age. In order to overcome this problem, we should "reconstruct religious thought," just as Iqbal and Shariati proposed, which represents *the* very foundation of Islamic revivalism. The firmer we lay this foundation, the more our "building" will be sturdy and capable of resisting the opposition that is sure to come.

Therefore, *what is to be done* at the present time is, first, to know Islam well and second, to have a good grasp of modernity, just as Iqbal and Shariati tried to do in their times.[65] Besides that, we should not bury our head in the sand like "Traditionalists." We will go nowhere while blindly insisting that we have nothing to do with the problems that appeared in contemporary age. What is required is that the *ummah* is sensitive to the current problems and demonstrates a maximum effort to solve them in line with Islamic principles. In building a prototype, we can take al-Ghazālī's ideological struggle waged against Greek philosophy as an example. In his time, such philosophy posed an ideological challenge to the Muslim world, which effected the hearts and minds of people negatively. As a "responsible intellectual," al-Ghazālī noticed the problem and tried to solve it with might and main. He first scrutinized the arguments of philosophers, tried to have a good grasp of Greek philosophy, and only after he was convinced that he understood the books written

---

64   Shariati compares this to the sensitivity best seen in firefighters. (1985: 67).

65   Ibid., 68. This should be our order of priority. Otherwise, there would appear "Muslims Modernists" who are in search of reconciling Islam with modernity.

by philosophers better than their writers, he set about to criticize them. Today, we should do the same thing with regard to secular modernity. It also poses an ideological challenge, which is definitely stronger than the first one, and thus the responsibility of today's intellectuals should be to know it well and criticize it competently in order to remove the doubts that it casts on the minds of the Muslims. Iqbal and Shariati too diagnosed the problem correctly in their particular circumstances and tried to solve it to the fullest extent of their ability and power. Today the same duty rests on our shoulders.

Nevertheless, we have some problems regarding the matter. At first, we should be aware that it would not be easy to solve the problems that have plagued the Muslims long periods. We have a problem of "ideational stagflation" or "ideological deadness," which became apparent between the 13th and 19th centuries in Islamic history and still remains, which is inarguably bigger than the "political problem" we faced when colonial powers invaded Muslim lands. By the early 1800's we hit the rock bottom in respect thereof. Thus, obtaining an ideational dynamism similar to that of the shining era of the first five or six centuries will take a long time, although the revivalist movement has shown some promise in the last two centuries. To put it all in simple terms, we still suffer from a "lack of knowledge," and what is more, this stagflation is widely seen not only among ordinary people but also among intellectuals. Thus, we have to solve it at all costs. We can, for instance, build new institutions like Baghdad's *House of Wisdom* (*bayt al-hikma*) – which was founded by the Abbasid ruler al-Ma'mūn in our classical age – in order to raise the level of knowledge in the Muslim world. Despite the fact that the very aim of this institution was to familiarize the Muslim world to, and appropriate knowledge from, foreign cultures, science, and philosophies, our goal must be primarily to wage an ideological combat against modernity and eventually overcome it. This is because we cannot achieve political success unless we win the ideological battle. Here we should acknowledge that one of the most important requirements for this overcoming is to engage in a "global discourse." The modern world has become globalized, and accordingly the world's problems are being discussed on a global scale. However, Islamic movements still use "local" language in a sense that their target audience is still substantially the people of Muslim world.[66] Thus, the main predicament is that Muslims still use a traditional "religious language" in a globalized postmodern world. They think inside the box, have nothing to do with a contemporary agenda and accordingly cannot reach the global masses.[67] Thus, what should be done in such a case?

---

66   At this point, Shariati's language can be regarded, to a great extent, as an exception.

67   This global discourse includes a variety of topics, such as philosophy of science, contemporary ideologies, postmodern condition, etc.

From my perspective, in a globalized world, we need to change our mind, look outside the box and devise a global language that can potentially address the whole humanity. This is also a requirement for "inviting people to Islam" (*da'wah*). This is a duty, according to Islam, that every believer should perform to the best of their ability.[68] At this point, we should remember the words said by Sartre concerning Shariati's religion and ask ourselves the following question: Why did not Sartre express himself something like this, "I have no religion. But if I were to choose, it would be Sayyid Qutb's or Mawdūdī's!" The answer is clear: he would not say something like that because their "religious language" did not apply to him. Sartre, as a leading contemporary philosopher, can only be convinced by the "ideological language" of Ali Shariati. This is exactly what I mean by arguing that we should use a "global language" in a globalized world, and that it should be capable of addressing the whole of humankind. In my opinion, no one in the Muslim world competently manages to do this so far. Shariati noticed the matter, but under the circumstances of his time, he felt himself compelled to focus on the problem of "content," not that of "language."[69] However, when we have a closer look, even at the "content," we can surmise that he was well aware of the issue and was at pains to solve it. However, this is not sufficient. Today, Contemporary Muslim Thought has still not been systematized in such a way that it could accomplish its goal of transforming into a "school of thought." It has no "systematic" characteristics, and it lacks a concrete or original curriculum. Therefore, it fails to become an "ideology of the future."

In order to accomplish this goal, we should first strive to raise ordinary people's level of knowledge, and then exert every effort to grow "authoritative scholars."[70] Otherwise, there will be an ever-increasing knowledge gap between the ordinary people and the authoritative scholars. The massification or popularization of the accumulated knowledge is very important in the process. Both the "traditional" educational institutions i.e. *madrasas,* and "modern" ones i.e. the universities, are of little use in reaching this goal. They remain substantially incapable of solving our problem. What we need is an ideologically motivated activism, aimed at disseminating knowledge to every strata of the society. We should set our sights on avoiding the marginalization

---

68   See the verse: 'invite to the way of your Lord with wisdom and good instruction, and argue with them in a way that is best.' (*Sūrat an-Naḥl*, 16: 125).

69   Shariati says in his book, *Kendini Devrimci Yetiştirmek,* "our language too should be Islamic!" (2012: 132).

70   I mean by this term simply the competent intellectuals who can write and speak authoritatively on a contemporary agenda, and have a good grasp of ideological matters. Shariati too acknowledges that the *ummah* needs this kind of scholars (2012: 24).

of higher knowledge, especially among the lower segments of society. In order to achieve this goal, we need to organize and carry out a qualifed and "ideologically oriented" reading activity, whose target audience consists of ordinary people as the first stage.[71] Having made significant progress in the process, a "critical mass" will appear in time, and this will ensure that the issues will be discussed more competently.[72] In the long run, the "authoritative scholars" who are capable of solving our problems will come out from among them, and they will ultimately accomplish the goal of giving persuasive answers to the ideological questions of humankind.

Conclusion

Today we are at a "turning point" in a real and substantive sense. Western modernity lost its charm and postmodernity is still far from satisfying the ideological needs and expectations of humanity. At the present time, we are living in a period of, in the full sense of the word, an "ideological vacuum." This gap can only be filled by Islam, which represents the only viable alternative to western modernity. In fact, Shariati already noticed that Islam had a potential to become the "ideology of the future," and in order to reach the goal he considered it necessary to "reconstruct religious thought" in line with Iqbal's proposal. This was a significant and valuable endeavour. Nevertheless, we should admit that this is not enough to "change the world." Even though substantial progress has been made in Contemporay Muslim Thought, it seems clear that there is an enormous amount of work yet to be done. Despite the fact that modernity has lost its chance to become the dominant paradigm once again, we cannot not "see mankind entering the religion of Allah in troops."[73] This is mainly because we cannot systematize the thought yet. In other words, this is because Contemporary Muslim Thought has yet to be transformed into a systematic "school of thought." We should know that only an "ideology" or a "school of thought" that has an internal consistency can charm humankind within contemporary conditions. If we pick up where Shariati left off and "systematize the thought," Islam will no doubt become the "ideology of the future."

---

71 This is a comprehensive "project" that could be actualized by the support of either a nonvolatile fund or a government endorsement. For details, see http://www.dusunceni nokullasmasi.com/tr/dusunce-okulu-proje.aspx.

72 By this term I mean an influential medium-level group who is capable of discussing broader ideological issues, not the critical i.e. "sufficient," number of them needed to make a significant change in a society.

73 See *Sūrat an-Naṣr*, 110: 2.

Bibliography

Abrahamian, Ervand. "Ali Shariati: Ideologue of Iranian Revolution" in *Islam, Politics and Social Movements*, Edited by Edmund Burke & Ira Lapidus. Los Angeles, University of California Press, 1993. First Published in MERIP Reports (January 1982): 25–28.

Al-Ghazālī. *Dalaletten Kurtuluş (Deliverance from Error – Al-Munqidh)*. In *Felsefe Metinleri*, Edited by Mahmut Kaya. Istanbul: Klasik Yayınları, 2003. pp. 341–356.

Al-Mawdūdī, Abu'l-A'la. *Come Let Us Change the World*. Translated by Kaukab Siddique. Washington: The Islamic Party of North America, 1972.

Atalar, M. Kürşad. *Radical Islamism in Turkey: The Cases of Gradualism of Ercümend Özkan and Militanism of Hizbollah*. Ph.D. Thesis, METU. Ankara: Unprinted matter, 2002.

Atalar, M. Kürşad. "80 Sonrası Türkiye'de 'İslam Düşüncesi'nin Problemleri" (The Problems of Muslim Thought in Turkey after 1980s). In *Türkiye'de İslam Düşüncesi ve Hareketi*. Edited by İsmail Kara & Asım Öz. Zeytinburnu Belediyesi Kültür Yayınları, 2013.

Atalar, M. Kürşad. *Çağdaş Müslüman Düşünce: Sembol Şahsiyetler* (Contemporary Muslim Thought: Symbolic Figures of Islamic Revivalism), Pınar Yayınları, 2014.

Cesur, Ertuğrul. "Batıcılık ve Gericilik Karşısında 'Müslüman Sosyalist' Ali Şeriati" ("Muslim Socialist" Ali Shariati Versus Westernism and Reactionarism), *Bilge Adamlar*, Vol: 30, August (2010): 98–102.

Dölek, Haydar. "Ölümsüzlük Problemi Açısından Tehafütler" (Tehafüts in View of the Problem of Immortality). *Fırat Üniversitesi İlahiyat Fakültesi Dergisi*, 15: 1 (2010).

Faruki, M.T. "İkbal'e Göre Mü'min Kişi (*Merd-i Mümin*) Tasavvuru." Translated by Şevket Bulu, *Doğu Dilleri Dergisi*, A.Ü.D.T.C.F. Yay., Vol: 1: 4 (1970): 119–137.

Gibb, Hamilton A. R. *İslam'da Modern Eğilimler* (Modern Trends in Islam). Translated by M. Kürşad Atalar. Ankara: Çağlar Yayınları, 2006.

Iqbal, Muhammad. *Reconstruction of Religious Thought in Islam*. www.allamaiqbal.com.

Kayani, Muhammed Han. *Felsefe, Siyaset ve Şiir Dünyasıyla İkbal* (Iqbal's Poetry, Politics and Philosophy). Istanbul: İz Yayıncılık, 2002.

Lenin, Vladimir Ilyich, *What is To Be Done?* www.marxists.org.

Plato. *Apology of Socrates*, http://www.sjsu.edu/people/james.lindahl/courses/Phil70A/s3/apology.pdf.

Qutb, Sayyid. *Yoldaki İşaretler* (Milestones). Translated by Salih Uçan. Hicret Yayınları, 1980.

Rahimi, Babak. "The Rise of Shii Ideology in Pre-Revolutionary Iran." In *Militancy and Political Violence in Shiism*, Edited by Assaf Moghadam. New York: Routledge, 2012.

Rahnema, Ali. *An Islamic Utopion: A Political Biography of Ali Shari'ati*. New York: I.B. Tauris Publishers, 1998.

Sachedina, Abdulaziz. "Ali Shariati: Ideologue of Iranian Revolution." In *Voices of the Resurgent Islam*, Edited by John L. Esposito. New York: Oxford University Press, 1983/1991.

Schimmel, Annemarie. *Muhammed İkbal.* Translated by Senail Özkan. Ötüken Yayınları, 2012.

Shariati, Ali. *Biz ve İkbal* (We and Iqbal). Translated by Ergin Kılıçtutan. Bir Yayıncılık, 1985.

Shariati, Ali. *Kültür ve İdeoloji* (Culture and Ideology). Translated by Orhan Bekin. Bir Yayıncılık, 1986.

Shariati, Ali. *What is to Be Done.* Edited by Farhang Rajaee. Houston, TX: The Institute for Research and Islamic Studies, 1986b.

Shariati, Ali. *Ali Şiası Şafevi Şiası* (Alid Shiism and Safavid Shiism). Translated by Feyzullah Artinli. Yöneliş Yayınları, 1990.

Shariati, Ali. *Aşina Yüzlerle* (With Familiar Faces – Persian *Ba Muhatabay-i Aşina*). Translated by Davut Duman. Fecr Yayınları, 2010.

Shariati, Ali. *Kendini Devrimci Yetiştirmek* (The Education of A Revolutionary – Persian, Hûdsâzî Enqilâbî). Translated by Hicabi Kırlangıç and Derya Örs. Fecr Yayınları, 2012.

Shariati, Ali. *Çöle İniş: Hubut/Kevir.* Translated by Hicabi Kırlangıç and Derya Örs. Fecr Yayınları, 2012b.

Shariati, Ali. *Öze Dönüş* (Returning to the Roots) Translated by Ejder Okumuş. Ankara: Fecr Yayınları, 2013.

Shepard, William E. "Islam and Ideology: Towards a Typology," *International Journal of Middle East Studies*, Vol: 19 (1987).

Şimşek, Tacettin. "Mehmet Akif'in Poetikası" (The Poetics of Mehmet Akif), *Atatürk Üniversitesi Türkiyat Araştırmaları Enstitüsü Dergisi*, TAED 53, Erzurum, 2015.

Subqi, Imam. *Tabaqat al-Shafi'iyyah al-Kubra*, Vol. IV. Cairo: 1324/1906.

Vakily, Abdollah. *Ali Shariati and Mystical Tradition of Islam*, Abdollah Vakily. Unpublished M.A. Thesis. McGill University, Institute of Islamic Studies, 1991.

Watt, Montgomery. *The Faith and Practice of al-Ghazali.* London: George Allen and Unwin Ltd, 1953.

Yıldırım, Ercan. "İslamcı Hareketin Özgün Fikir Adamı: Said Halim Paşa" (The Authentic Intellectual of the Islamic Movement: Said Halim Pasha). *Umran*, December, 2013.

Zeidan, David. "Ali Şeriati: İslami Köktenci, Marksist İdeolog ve Sufi Mistik" (Ali Shariati: Islamic Fundamentalist, Marxist Ideologist and Sufi Mystic). *Bilge Adamlar*, Vol: 30, August, 2010.

CHAPTER 15

Musulman-e Marksisti: The Islamic Modernism of Ali Shariati in *Religion vs. Religion*

Bader Mousa Al-Saif

During the second half of the twentieth century, the Iranian intellectual Ali Shariati advocated an Islamic modernism based on the ideals of Shiite Islam and Marxism. While such a pairing may seem paradoxical, Shariati finds no contradiction between his Shiite faith and Marxist principles. They are two sides of the same coin for Shariati, reinforcing one another and marking an intellectual break from the pioneers of Islamic modernism of the late nineteenth and early twentieth century.

Ervand Abrahamian rightly notes that 'there is not one Shariati but three separate Shariatis: the sociologist ... the devout believer ... [and] the public speaker.'[1] Yet these three separate Shariatis blend into one when Shariati promotes his version of Islamic modernism. Shariati's *Religion vs. Religion* vividly articulates this fusion. Shariati was addressing a Husayniyah audience in 1970 when he delivered the two lectures that became the backbone of *Religion vs. Religion*.[2] Both Shiite and socialist themes saturate the lectures in support of one another, thereby advancing Shariati's theme that 'true socialism is true [Shiite] Islam and true [Shiite] Islam is true socialism.'[3] In this study, I first explain how Shariati is different from other Muslim modernists through his conceptualization of religion and his adoption of select Marxist principles. Second, I will analyze Shariati's attachment to Shi'ism by identifying and studying his eight explicit references to Shi'ism in *Religion vs. Religion*. Finally, I will argue that the main tenets of Shi'ism are not fully portrayed in Shariati's eight references to Shiite thought but, instead are portrayed through his abundant use of Marxist motifs, which mainly revolve around action, revolution, class, and the oppressed. By analyzing both Marxist/socialist and Shiite references in *Religion vs. Religion*, we shall appreciate the inescapable interconnectivity between both elements in Shariati's thought.

---

1 Ervand Abrahamian, *A History of Modern Iran*. (Cambridge: Cambridge University Press, 1982), 24.

2 Ali Shariati, *Religion vs. Religion*. Translated by Laleh Bakhtiar. Chicago: ABC International Group, 2010), 12.

3 Ibid., 6.

Just as elements of Marxism and Shiite Islam define Shariati's modernism, they set him apart from his predecessors. Early Muslim modernists shared Shariati's goal of proving Islam's compatibility with the modern world. Like Shariati, they were equally influenced by foreign, non-Muslim concepts. However, early Muslim modernists were not confronted with socialism. Thus, it was not part of their ethos or frame of reference. Instead, the Egyptian scholar, Muhammad 'Abduh, for instance, sought to prove that Islam is compatible with reason, while the South Asian modernist Ahmad Khan stressed the affinity of Islam with nature.[4] Similarly, Shariati was convinced that Islam was not only compatible with socialism, but that Islam was its true originator – through the Muslim figure of Abu Dhār: According to Ervand Abrahamian, '[Shariati's] *Abu Dhār: The God Worshipping Socialist* ... argued that Abu Dhār had been the forerunner of socialism in world history.'[5]

More importantly, Shariati was further set apart from earlier modernists through his conceptualization of religion as demonstrated by his Shiite faith. Shariati divested himself from Islamic history and its institutions, whether it was past empires, legal schools or juristic consensus and *taqlīd* (imitation).[6] Shariati's Shiite identity liberated him. To him, it is a religion of monotheism. It is a way of life and a means towards a higher truth that is based on the Qur'ān and was applied for ten years by Prophet Muhammad in Medina.[7] Ever since the death of the Prophet and the usurpation of power from his cousin Ali, the seemingly monotheistic religious communities have been practicing a second form of religion: the religion of "hidden multi-theism," which promotes injustice and oppression.[8] Therefore, Shariati did not have to accustom himself to past traditions and theories, as 'Abduh did, nor did he have to excuse himself due to a lack of knowledge of past Islamic juridical fields, as Khan did.[9] Shariati was also different from other non-Arab Muslim modernists like the Southeast Asians, who (1) perceive religious 'authority lying in the Arab world' and, (2) looked up to 'Abduh and other early Muslim modernists.[10] According to Charles Kurzman, such 'Abduh scholars include

---

4   Charles Kurzman, ed. *Modernist Islam 1840–1940: A Sourcebook*. Oxford: Oxford University Press, 2002), 50–60, 296.

5   Abrahamian, *A History*, 143.

6   Shariati, *Religion vs. Religion*, 46–47, 67.

7   Ibid., 55, 79.

8   Ibid., 41–43, 47.

9   Kurzman, *Modernist Islam*, 291, 301.

10   Peter Riddell, *Islam and the Malay-Indonesian World: Transmission and Responses*. (Hawaii: University of Hawaii Press, 2001), 209.

'Mamaqani ... Muzaffar ... and Sharara.'[11] Shariati is not only absent from this list, but also Kurzman's anthology as a whole, because it abruptly ends in 1940, prior to Shariati's arrival on the intellectual scene. If Kurzman included Shariati on such a list, he would not have been part of the Shiite modernists who were influenced by 'Abduh given Shariati's different frame of reference. Based on his *Religion vs. Religion*, Shariati was not bound by previous Islamic models, except for the model produced by Muhammad's Medina. This led him to create a freshly amalgamated Islamic modernism that was primarily composed of Shi'ism and Marxism.[12]

Some may question the role of Shi'ism in *Religion vs. Religion* when there are only eight pithy references to Shiite thought and one outright use of the word Shi'ism. After consolidating and analyzing the eight references, I have grouped them into two categories: the political and theological. In five references, Shariati condemns Muawiyah's usurpation of power from Ali and his use of religion to quell protests and elicit loyalty.[13] Here, Shariati appeals to his audience's Shi'ism by linking their understanding of history and the injustice done to the first Imam to introduce his concept of the "religion of legitimation."[14] The first set of references do not state much about Shi'ism. Rather, these references negatively define Shi'ism: they condemn the Murji'ite embrace and propagation of the concept of fate and pre-determination as much as they repudiate the abuse of power for personal gains, which comes at the expense of justice and the average person's wellbeing.[15]

On the other hand, the second set of references presents some elements of Shiite theology. In three passage, Shariati lauds Shiite resistance to 'accepting what was offered to the world in the Middle Ages as [a form of] Islamic power.' He also praises their holding steadfast to the true religion of monotheism that, for the most part, did not last beyond the Medinan phase.[16] For Shariati, Shi'ism is a fight for monotheism. It is a fight won by Muhammad who successfully confronted polytheism (*shirk*). This same war was later fought by Ali, who was eventually defeated because he faced a more arduous form

---

11   Kurzman, *Modernist Islam*, 5, 12.

12   While criticizing the religion of multi-theism that refers to both Sunni and Shiite authorities throughout the ages, there is no outright sectarian language in *Religion vs. Religion*. In a separate article, Shariati has a high regard for Sunni Muhammad Iqbal. See http://www .yanabi.com/index.php?/topic/58875-dr-muhammad-iqbal-was-a-sunni/.

13   Shariati, *Religion vs. Religion*, 33, 37, 40, 43, 53.

14   Ibid., 36.

15   Ibid., 37, 40.

16   Ibid., 46–47.

of polytheism, hidden by those who claim to be Muslims.[17] Shi'ism is not a 'mercantile religion ... it is [Ali's] religion, which is born out of liberation, love, [and] the establishment of human justice in the world,' Shariati said.[18] While the second set of references defined Shi'ism more than the first, it still did not provide much detail. This is the task that Shariati left to Marxist principles in *Religion vs. Religion.*

Shariati evoked classical Marxist ideas in (1) his repetitive call to action and, (2) his unequivocal denunciation of class-bound societies. These two Marxist ideals parallel and therefore complement Shariati's Shiite beliefs, summarized in his (1) rejection of fatalism and, (2) his call for justice. The religion of monotheism, or Shi'ism, is also the religion of revolution.[19] True monotheists are called upon to 'rebel against anything other than He [God],' especially when faced with injustice.[20] Prophets are naturally rebellious; they go against unjust values and customary social norms. Thus is the spirit of both Muhammad and Ali. However, since Ali's revolutionary attempt failed, it became incumbent upon all his followers to continue the revolution until victory.[21] Furthermore, true Islam calls for genuine equality between all members of society. Shariati relentlessly attacked what he coined polytheism for its propagation of inequality and class differentiation. Shariati's worldview was shaped by Marxism's sensitivity to class stratified societies; he stood against 'human societies [that were] divided into the noble and un-noble, master and slave, captive and free.'[22] True to his Islamic-Marxist form, Shariati traced the 'roots of [polytheistic] religion to economic [factors] ... the ownership of a minority over the abased majority ... [and] the promotion of class superiority.'[23] The few will continue to own the majority of the world's wealth and resources and as such, subjugate the majority, unless the people rise against the religion that comes from "above to below."[24] Everyone is summoned to fight for the oppressed because it is God's will: 'Abrahamic traditions reflect that ... God is the refuge for the deprived and oppressed.'[25]

Not only does Shariati demonstrate this mix of Marxism and Shiite Islam in *Religion vs. Religion*, it appears as an ongoing theme in many of his other writings. As demonstrated by Abrahamian, various religious terms were 'injected

---

17   Ibid., 62–63.
18   Ibid., 67.
19   Ibid., 35.
20   Ibid., 34.
21   Abrahamian, *A History,* 144.
22   Shariati, *Religion vs. Religion,* 37.
23   Ibid., 38–40.
24   Ibid., 54, 61.
25   Ibid., 44–45.

[by Shariati] with radical meaning: *ummah* is transformed into a dynamic society in permanent revolution; *tawḥīd* into social solidarity; *imāmate* into charismatic leadership ... *mujahid* into revolutionary fighter ... *momen* into genuine fighter.'[26] Shariati masterfully intertwined Marxist and Shiite concepts in order to illustrate his unique brand of Islamic modernism, which calls for the overthrow of the status quo in Muslim lands in general, and Iran in particular.

In conclusion, Shariati extols Ammar Uzighan, the author of *Le Meilleur Combat*, calling him 'a *Musulman-e Marksisti* [a Muslim Marxist].'[27] While Shariati ascribes this label to another person, he deserves the "Muslim Marxist" label for his lifelong commitment to reinvigorating Shiite Islam with Marxist principles. Shariati truly embraced Camus' famous statement, 'I revolt, therefore I am.'[28] This revolutionary spirit is further empowered by his understanding of Shi'ism. As Abrahamian notes, '[Shariati's] prolific works have one dominant theme: that the true essence of Shi'ism is revolution against all forms of oppression.'[29] Shariati's *Religion v. Religion* may not seem to be focused on Shi'ism when compared to his other works, such as *Red Shi'ism: The Religion of Martyrdom & Black Shi'ism: The Religion of Mourning,* or *Where Shall we Begin,* and other books. However, Shariati purposefully relied on his socially infused themes of activism and equality to complement and expand upon his eight explicit Shiite references. Thus, *Religion vs. Religion* displays a compelling marriage between Marxism and Shi'ism. Labeled "the Doctor" by his disciples, Shariati differed from earlier modernists in his whole-hearted adoption of both Shiite and Marxist values, which formed his own genre of Islamic modernism. It is Ali Shariati's vision of Islamic modernism that many believe was the intellectual inspiration, along with Imam Khomeini, behind the 1979 Islamic Revolution of Iran.

Bibliography

Abrahamian, Ervand. *A History of Modern Iran.* Cambridge: Cambridge University Press, 2008.

Abrahamian, Ervand. "'Ali Shariati: Ideologue of the Iranian Revolution." *MERIP Reports* (1982): 24–28.

Kurzman, Charles, ed. *Modernist Islam 1840–1940: A Sourcebook.* Oxford: Oxford University Press, 2002.

---

26   Abrahamian, *A History,* 144–145; Shariati, *Religion vs. Religion,* 9.

27   Abrahamian, *A History,* 144.

28   Shariati, *Humanity and Islam,* 4.

29   Abrahamian, *A History,* 144.

Riddell, Peter. *Islam and the Malay-Indonesian World: Transmission and Responses.* Hawaii: University of Hawaii Press, 2001.

Shariati, Ali. "A Manifestation of Self-Reconstruction and Reformation–Mohammad Iqbal." *tr. Ali Abbas. http://www.shariati.com/english/iqbal.html* (accessed April 25, 2016).

Shariati, Ali. "Humanity and Islam (1969)." In *Liberal Islam,* edited by Charles Kurzman. New York: Oxford University Press, 1998.

Shariati, Ali. *Religion vs. Religion.* Translated by Laleh Bakhtiar. Chicago: ABC International Group, 2010.

Shariati, Ali. "Shariati's Books." http://www.shariati.com/kotob.html (accessed April 28, 2016).

Voll, John O. "Shi'i Philosophical and Sociological Modernism: Ali Shariati." Class lecture, Georgetown University, Washington, DC, March 20, 2013.

Index